PUNISHMENT IN PARADISE

perpetual galleys?

✤ PETER M. BEATTIE ✤

PUNISHMENT IN PARADISE

RACE, SLAVERY,

HUMAN RIGHTS, AND A

NINETEENTH-CENTURY

BRAZILIAN

PENAL COLONY

DUKE UNIVERSITY PRESS   DURHAM AND LONDON   2015

Printed in the United States of America on acid-free paper ∞
Designed by Heather Hensley
Typeset in Minion Pro by Westchester Publishing Services

Library of Congress Cataloging-in-Publication Data
Beattie, Peter M., 1963–
Punishment in paradise : race, slavery, human rights, and a
nineteenth-century Brazilian penal colony / Peter M. Beattie.
pages cm
Includes bibliographical references and index.
ISBN 978-0-8223-5816-9 (hardcover : alk. paper)
ISBN 978-0-8223-5830-5 (pbk. : alk. paper)
ISBN 978-0-8223-7589-0 (e-book)
1. Prisons—Brazil—Fernando de Noronha—History—19th
century. 2. Prisoners—Brazil—Fernando de Noronha.
3. Fernando de Noronha (Brazil)—History—19th century.
I. Title.
HV9594.F47B43 2015
365'.34—dc23   2014034850

Duke University Press gratefully acknowledges the support
of Michigan State University, Department of History, which
provided funds toward the publication of this book.

Cover art: Fernando de Noronha Island, 2008. Photo by Bruno
Barbey. © Bruno Barbey / Magnum Photos.

I dedicate this book to my wife,
ERICA MELISSA WINDLER BEATTIE
And to my son,
AODHAN WINDLER BEATTIE
The two souls most responsible
for my regeneration.

The Idée Fixe

So, long live history, voluble history, which is good at anything, and, getting back to the *idée fixe*, let me say that it's what produces strong men and mad men. A mobile idea, vague or changeable, is what produces a Claudius—according to the formula of Suetonius.

A Project

The need to regenerate him [Quincas Borba], get him back to working and having respect for his person was filling my heart. I [Brás Cubas] was starting to get a comfortable feeling, one of uplift, of admiration for myself.

JOAQUIM MARIA MACHADO DE ASSIS, *THE POSTHUMOUS MEMOIRS OF BRÁS CUBAS*

CONTENTS

ACKNOWLEDGMENTS

The act of writing acknowledgments inspires a mournful trepidation of one's forgetfulness that can only be resisted with somber humility. I owe an untold debt to many individuals who go unmentioned in these acknowledgments. I apologize in advance to the unnamed friends, family, and colleagues whom I memorialize here with an imagined, prehumous tomb for heroic unknown historians, archivists, librarians, and those too clever to pursue capturing the past in prose.

I thank my wife, Erica Windler, who has put up with all my *idées fixes* during research and writing with patience, kindness, love, and encouragement, even when I did not know exactly how to accept them. This project has benefitted from her many insights as a historian of Brazil. My son Aodhan has taught me many lessons about the limits of authority and the power of letting go that have shaped my thinking about the historical agents examined between these two covers. His uncomplaining, courageous, and swift adaptation to life in Brazil and to Portuguese twice as a young boy was inspirational. As I let go of this book, I think of the many good experiences I was lucky to share with both of you while this project gestated. My *saudades* are mixed with forward-looking hopes for future good times, travels, meals, body surfing, and shared obsessions.

I lost my former advisor and friend Robert M. Levine to brain cancer some years ago. I like to think that he would see some of himself in what I have written about Brazil. Elizabeth Kuznesof became my unofficial advisor and friend even before Bob died. She has generously read, corrected, and criticized various manifestations of this manuscript, and her scholarship has informed many of my ideas. Celso Castilho also read this manuscript and saved me from numerous errors of fact and interpretation. Both Celso and Elizabeth helped me to reconceive the manuscript's organization. Although I am not sure I was able to fully capture their sage advice in my reworkings, their scholarly and collegial generosity has made this a much better book.

My compadre Professor Marcus Joaquim Maciel de Carvalho read parts of this manuscript and gave me invaluable comments about his home ground of Pernambuco. He was an amiable host to Erica and me as visiting CIES Fulbright scholars in his department at the Universidade Federal do Pernambuco (UFPE) on two different occasions. He introduced me to invaluable sources and many colleagues and students who helped me with intellectual and bureaucratic matters, Bruno Câmara in particular. Marcus and his beautiful wife, sociologist Andrea Tereza Brito Ferreira, our *comadre*, arranged Aodhan's baptism in a Catholic church in Boa Viagem. They even trusted us with their talented daughter, Sofia Brito de Carvalho, who spent a couple of months with us in our home in East Lansing in 2014. A special thanks to your family and your colleagues and students at UFPE.

I thank my mother, Regina O'Connor Beattie, who at ninety-four years embodies perseverance and love. She taught me at a young age to love reading and learning. Bonnie Messe, my mother-in-law, recently moved to the great white north. She has helped Erica and me to raise our son. My brothers, sisters, nieces, and nephews have always been supportive, and as I grew up, the youngest of nine, each of them taught me, and continues to teach me, something different.

Jeffrey Lesser read an earlier, much cruder version of this manuscript and provided guidance and insight as he has on previous occasions. Jerry Davila, and the participants in his graduate seminar at the University of Illinois, Urbana-Champagne, read the manuscript and helped me to draw out the meaning and significance of the process of "category drift" analyzed herein and to reconsider popular attitudes toward the antiflogging and anti–death penalty movement in Brazil. My Michigan State University colleague Lisa Fine also read and provided valuable feedback on an early draft of this manuscript.

Many years ago James C. Scott, while a visiting scholar in our department at Michigan State University, encouraged me to read Lewis Coser's work, which helped me to conceptualize the benefits that Brazilian authorities believed marriage had for men and women of the free and enslaved poor, even those living in penal exile. This turned out to be consequential for my analysis of gender and sexuality.

The members of Recife's Instituto Arqueológico, Histórico e Geográfico Pernambucano (IAHGP) honored me in 2006 with a corresponding membership (sócio correspondente) to their august institution (a distinction I later learned I shared with some of Fernando de Noronha's commanders). My colleagues at the IAHGP shared documents and ideas with me and helped me to feel at home in Recife. A special thanks to Reinaldo Carneiro Leão, primeiro secretário perpetuo do IAHGP, who shared so many stories of Pernambuco's past on the *paralelepípados* below the Igreja Matriz da Boa Vista on the Rua do Hospício.

Grazielle Rodrigues generously arranged for me to give a talk on my research to the residents and tour guides of Fernando de Noronha on the Day of Black Consciousness in Remédios in 2008. This was a gratifying experience that allowed me to contribute to and learn from the historical memory of this unique island community. I thank them for their warm hospitality and openness.

Numerous other colleagues and friends have been helpful to me directly and indirectly on this long walk to completion: Marta de Abreu Estevez, Marília de Azambuja Ribeiro, B. J. Barrickman, Fernanda Batista Bicalho, Dain Borges, Marcos Luiz Bretas, Suzana Cavani Rosas, Sueann Caulfield, Marcos Costa, Celso Castro, Sidney Chalhoub, Timothy Coates, Hebe Maria da Costa Mattos Gomes de Castro, John French, Tácito Galvão, Flávio Gomes, Gilberto Hochman, Marc Hertzman, Marc Jay Hoffnagel, Vitor Izecksohn, Silvana Jeha, Simone Petraglia Kropf, Michael LaRosa, Hal Langfur, Linda Lewin, Joseph Love, Mara Loveman, Ana Maria Lugão Rios, Marcelo Mac Cord, Maria Helena Pareira Toledo Machado, Beatriz Mamigonian, Bryan McCann, Frank D. McCann, Gillian McGillivray, Joan Meznar, Zach Morgan, Gizlene Neder, Jeffrey Needell, Clarissa Nunes Maia, Gláucia Pessoa, João José Reis, Rogério Rosa Rodrigues, Thomas Rogers, Martha Santos, Carlos Sebe Bom Meihy, Carlos Eugênio Líbano Soares, Nísia Trindade Lima, Barbara Weinstein, Joel Wolfe, Christine Paulette Yves Rufino Dabat, and so many others. In the end, I accept full credit for any errors herein, but I share credit for what may be useful in these pages with many collaborators.

The archivists, librarians, and staffs of the Biblioteca Nacional, the Arquivo Nacional Rio de Janeiro (especially Sátiro Nunes), the IAHGP, the Arquivo Público Estadual Jordão Emerenciano, and the Instituto Histórico Geográfico Brasileiro all collaborated generously to uncover useful documentation and secondary sources during the research process.

The editors and staff at Duke University Press have been extremely attentive and helpful from the review process to overseeing my revisions and into the production phase. Editor Gisela Fosado expressed enthusiasm and encouragement for my manuscript and made many helpful suggestions that improved it. Editorial associate Lorien Olive went beyond the call to help me with the images for the cover and those interspersed in the text.

Finally, I would like to recognize the insights and feedback I received from my many colleagues in Michigan State University's Department of History, especially Liam Brockey, Glenn Chambers, Walter Hawthorne, Vanessa Holden, Jessica Johnson, Gwendolyn Midlo Hall, Edward Murphy, Javier Pescador, David Wheat, and Erica Windler. I hope we will get our on again, off again reading group on the lusophone and hispanophone Atlantic worlds going again soon.

INTRODUCTION

Fernando de Noronha Island: Foil, Paradox, Paradise, or Inferno?

The memory does not make me fearful
Nor does crying make me feel sympathy:
I'll send you to Fernando de Noronha
I'll shove you into that depraved prison
If you grumble, you get clapped in fetters.
If you cry, you get flogged.
—SEVERINO PERIGO ("SEVERINO DANGER," C.1870–1930),
A POPULAR BLACK BRAZILIAN SINGER

Severino Perigo depicts the agricultural penal colony on the island of Fernando de Noronha as a place of suffering where prisoners were shackled, whipped, and subject to debauchery. The colony held the largest concentration of convicts from across the Brazilian Empire (1822–1889), and Perigo's imagery of it mirrors accounts of France's Devil's Island, Britain's Tasmania, Argentina's Ushaia, or Russia's Sakhalin. Other voices, however, countered this image of an Atlantic hell some two hundred miles from Brazil's northeastern shores. In 1884, the American novelist and geographer Frank de Yeaux Carpenter, a member of Brazil's Geological Commission, described the colony as an "ocean resort" for criminals who lived the Life of Riley under rustling palms, ringed by golden beaches and azure waters.[1] Carpenter echoed Brazilian mainlanders who felt that convicts there enjoyed a leisurely life that was exasperating, especially in the case of slave convicts. Similar idyllic portrayals of Tasmania, Devil's Island, Ushaia, or Sakhalin are rare.[2] What do these conflicting images tell

MAP I.1 Fernando de Noronha in relation to mainland Brazil.

us about imperial Brazil? This remote island is an illuminating foil that highlights evolving cultural values, practices, and perceptions on Brazil's mainland and across the Atlantic in relation to justice, punishment, rehabilitation, color, class, civil condition, human rights, and labor. Brazilians of all classes long used Fernando de Noronha as a reference point to define social norms and the meanings of freedom and captivity.

The conflicting portrayals of Fernando de Noronha reflect different perspectives on crime and punishment in a new nation that underwent momentous transitions. Independence brought Brazil to a crossroads where new penal practices associated with the rise of nations challenged those of the old regime. The implementation of liberal ideals of equality in a fledgling nation where a large proportion of the inhabitants were enslaved proved a paradox that induced lawmakers to establish distinct punishments for bonded criminals. For many, prison seemed a reward for slaves. As Senator Paulo de Souza put it, "Will the slave who lives bowed under the weight of his labors by any chance have a horror of being incarcerated in a prison where he can abandon himself to laziness and drunkenness, the favorite passions of a slave?"[3] With this stereotype in mind, Article 60 of Brazil's Código criminal (1830) specified that slave convicts could be flogged rather than imprisoned unless sentenced to capital punishment or *galés* (literally, forced labor in Mediterranean naval galleys; but in Brazil, it meant prison at labor in fetters). Save for the gallows, the empire banned corporal punishment for free convicts.[4]

Anxieties over appropriate criminal punishments grew more fitful after 1850 as the slave population diminished when the government effectively enforced laws that banned the transatlantic slave trade. International public opinion turned against cruel punishments and bondage, and Brazilians found themselves increasingly isolated as advances in human rights became gauges to measure a nation's progress. After 1865, Brazil became the last independent nation in the Americas to tolerate slavery, and many Brazilians expressed their embarrassment over their "national shame." Emperor Pedro II (1840–1889) personally opposed slavery and the death penalty, and he worked with allies to abolish them.[5] These profound transitions shaped life in Fernando de Noronha and mainland perceptions of it. Brazilians inherited the island from the Portuguese, who had inhabited it mostly with soldiers and convicts from Brazil. After independence, Brazilians continued to populate it with convicts and soldiers. In the 1870s, an official referred to the island as "Brazil's central depository for civilian convicts" because it held more than 1,500 inmates from the empire's twenty provinces and capital district.[6]

Fernando de Noronha provides a little-considered perspective on the interconnected struggles against flogging, the death penalty, and slavery on Brazil's mainland. Pedro II used his constitutional powers to commute many capital sentences to life imprisonment beginning in the 1850s, and many of the beneficiaries of his clemency, including slave convicts, ended up in the penal colony. Therefore, the treatment of slave and free convicts there uncovers the extent to which the state exerted itself to maintain distinctions between slave and free. As Lynn Hunt put it, in the old regime "those guilty of crime could only be controlled by external force. In the traditional view, ordinary people could not control their own passions. They had to be led, prodded to do good, and deterred from following their baser instincts."[7] Thus, the ghastly spectacle of executions near the sites of crimes freshened the hoi polloi's respect for the law. While Brazil's new laws adopted tenets of modern penology for free citizens, Brazil continued to treat slaves according to older precepts. Brazilian law maintained the legality of flogging for slaves and enlisted soldiers and sailors, but it reserved the gallows for the heinous crimes of murder, rebellion, and treason. This contrasts with Britain and the United States, where courts applied capital punishment to a far wider variety of felonies, especially for slaves.[8]

These struggles for human rights fed anxieties about whether enslaved, freed, or even common freeborn Brazilians could be disciplined without recourse to harsh punishment. As Carpenter's aside suggests, the image of impunity for Fernando de Noronha's convicts had become a part of master-class folklore, a colorful story to regale a foreign visitor. While slaveowners constructed one vision of Fernando de Noronha, less privileged men, like Severino Perigo, presented a decidedly different one. Both have elements of truth, but neither is entirely precise. This book analyzes how historical actors' views of the colony changed over time and how their experiences and political positions shaped their perceptions of it.

Beyond insights into social anxieties over crime and punishment in a society making a slow transition from slave to free labor, why is the history of an isolated penal colony of broader significance? I believe there are a number of reasons. First, Fernando de Noronha offers an unparalleled panorama of justice in imperial Brazil. The colony held the largest population of convicts from across Brazil, so its records reveal the crimes and criminals that a precarious justice system spent scarce resources to try, convict, and exile. Too often, the study of crime and criminality is limited to a study of arrests or trials, but Fernando de Noronha's documentation allows one to explore how convicts lived their sentences.[9] A collective biography of convicts and an analysis of their treatment and how they responded to it brings new insight into how contemporaries grappled with questions of justice, individual responsibility, citizenship, honor, status, family, and clemency. This case study also lends itself to comparative Atlantic history. In contrast with the United States, for example, Brazilian authorities did not expend significant resources to defend the evolving lower boundaries of "whiteness" in basic state institutions like prisons, penal colonies, and the military's enlisted ranks, but they more consistently used marriage and heterosexual conjugal living to rank, reward, and discriminate among slaves and marginal members of the free poor of all colors.

Second, Fernando de Noronha was in essence a large, if exceptionally isolated, plantation where convicts provided most of the labor. The level of record keeping there allows for an unusually detailed microhistory of interactions between many more spheres of life than is possible for mainland plantations and communities. In this sense, the colony is a somewhat exaggerated metaphor for Brazilian society as it exemplified state making on its social and geographical margins. Though sui generis, the army officers who served as colony commanders faced challenges similar to those of plantation owners who employed slaves and mainland army officers whose enlisted men were mostly summarily pressed into service.[10] This study suggests the interrelatedness of these different civil conditions. A telling sign of their connection is found in a column for "civil condition" in the colony's convict matriculation books that used the following categories: free, slave, freedman, army enlisted man, navy enlisted man, arsenal worker, Indian, and national guardsman. In part, the column indicated that military men were subject to courts martial while Indians in government-organized villages were sent to juvenile courts. However, this cannot be the rationale behind the column's creation because slaves and freed persons were subject to the same courts as free Brazilians. The column's construction made it impossible to list military enlisted men, arsenal workers, Indians, freedmen, and even relatively privileged national guardsmen as "free." The logic behind the column's construction suggests that these categories marked degrees of "unfreeness." It reveals how officials constructed ways of seeing individuals like a state and their often-frustrated attempts to fix them geographically and taxonomically.[11]

I use a shorthand of my coinage, the "intractable poor," to refer jointly to convicts, slaves, military enlisted men, Indians in government-organized villages, and free Africans (Africans liberated from ships illegally transporting slaves from 1821 to 1856 who served fourteen-year apprenticeships in Brazil).[12] The term "intractable poor" reflects how powerful social actors stereotyped these unsavory social categories as unruly, wanton, and shiftless. I am aware that referring to the enslaved as "poor" seems incongruous given their legal status, but in effect, their status made the vast majority of them poor. I do not naively suggest a social or legal equivalence among these categories, but they did share a vulnerability to coercive labor extraction and their treatment presents revealing parallels and divergences. By comparing convict workers to those in related coercive labor regimes, my approach highlights patterns that are less visible when examined separately. In a nation so dependent on bonded labor in almost every part of its economy, there was a basic contradiction between the influential British penal reformer Jeremy Bentham's belief that labor was the best method to rehabilitate convicts and the aristocratic view of Brazilian masters that manual labor was not ennobling, but a duty fit for dishonorable slaves.[13] Fernando de Noronha was a penal laboratory where compromises and clashes between modern and old regime values and practices played out.

A penal laboratory

Third, Fernando de Noronha highlights the little analyzed circulation among categories of the intractable poor that I refer to as "category drift."[14] For example, the Brazilian state mobilized hundreds of slaves (purchased with taxpayer money or "patriotically" donated) to fight as soldiers in the War of the Triple Alliance (1864–1870). In return for their service, the state granted freedmen-soldiers conditional letters of liberty if they fought at the front and completed a nine-year military contract. It also mobilized scores of convicts from Fernando de Noronha and other jails to fight the same war. In peacetime, military convicts who completed their sentences were routinely reintegrated into Fernando de Noronha's army garrison. Discharge would have been a reward because most enlisted men had been summarily pressed into service for vagrancy or suspected crimes. Unscrupulous Brazilians illegally reduced free and freed men and women of color to slavery. Enlisted men, slaves, free Africans, and Indians could be convicted of crimes that made them prison laborers in jails, arsenals, and penal colonies. Many free Africans worked alongside convicts and enlisted men in penitentiaries, forts, and arsenals. Still others were sent to live with Indians in state-organized villages in Paraná. Officials often ignored laws and contractual obligations that applied to the intractable poor with impunity. Specific examples in the chapters that follow demonstrate category drift and how members of these categories frequently interacted. Category drift on the social margins shows how these low-status civil conditions were interrelated, and in many ways, mutually reinforcing, even as they allowed for small steps up or down the lower end scales of social mobility. I argue that they are a key to understanding how Brazilian society transitioned from slave to free labor because reforms that benefitted one category of the intractable poor became more difficult to deny to other categories. As slavery declined after 1850, the status of being free began to lose its luster, and as a result even relatively privileged members of the free poor became more anxious about their vulnerability to category drift and the coercive labor extraction it could represent.[15]

Category drift among the intractable poor highlights the relationship between slaves, convicts, free Africans, Indians, and military enlisted men, but circulation extended to the lower ranks of the police, National Guard, paramilitary forces, and organized crime. Not a few former enlisted men became police, and many policemen and national guardsmen became soldiers during the War of the Triple Alliance. Authorities punished undisciplined police, guardsmen, and the soldiers of regional insurgent forces with service in the imperial army and navy. Not a few deserters from the police, National

Guard, and the military became feared criminals, insurrectionary leaders, or chiefs of maroon communities. Some later became convicts. This is not to mention bandits and *capoeiras* (practitioners of the Afro-Brazilian martial art, dance, and musical form who often formed urban gangs) who provided paramilitary security for political bosses. Thus, the criminal underworld and the foot soldiers of order and insurrection interpenetrated one another, and many moved between a number of these categories in a lifetime.[16]

Fourth, Fernando de Noronha serves as an institutional limit case because of its isolation, dangerous labor force, and multiple purposes as a site for punishment, exile, rehabilitation, colonization, and production. Out of necessity and tradition army officers developed hybrid penal practices that combined modern and traditional understandings of these multiple missions. They drew on their mainland experiences to forge the everyday practices that they felt maximized discipline while still meeting other institutional and personal objectives. The island's officers, employees, convicts, soldiers, and other residents' pursuit of personal gain often contradicted formal institutional hierarchies, missions, and rules. This makes Fernando de Noronha an ideal site to examine corruption's role in promoting cooperation and conflict among the colony's different social strata. In part, corruption emerged because the administration failed to supply convicts essential goods and infrastructure. Thus, an unplanned commerce emerged from absolute necessity. The state also had a habit of underpaying and neglecting to pay in a timely fashion many of its officials (including convict workers). This encouraged bribery and other kinds of unorthodox payment for services and goods. Both reveal problems of bureaucracy, economy, and ideals that surpassed the state's institutional capacity to deliver. These conditions inevitably induced commerce and corruption to resolve institutional shortfalls and provide incentives.

Fifth, Fernando de Noronha is also a limit case for evolving notions of color, slave, and criminal status. For many Brazilians, penal reforms were emblems of national progress, and modern penology offered a "scientific" answer to the feared decline of seignorial authority as Brazil's slave population declined after 1850. This belief in rehabilitation confronted the Italian criminologist Cesare Lombroso's idea of the born criminal in the 1870s. Despite these theoretical countercurrents, most imperial penal officials espoused a continuing belief in the reformative power of hard work, family living, and "normal" heterosexuality without reference to a convict's color, class, or civil condition. After the republic's promulgation in 1889, a new generation of criminologists more rigorously applied Lombroso's theories to

Brazil's diverse population.[17] It is still unclear, however, the extent to which these ideas influenced everyday penal practices under Brazil's republic, but conflicting ideas about how to treat slave convicts in relation to free ones troubled imperial officials. Conflicts between the Justice Ministry and the army officers who managed the colony reveal differences of opinion about segregation on the basis of civil status (slave or free), much less color, and indicate a broad Brazilian preference for integration in state institutions that incorporated the intractable poor.

Sixth, Fernando de Noronha's history lends itself to international comparisons of the sequencing and depth of institutional reforms, an approach that I describe elsewhere as "institutional fit."[18] This highlights the case study's utility as a foil not only for institutions on Brazil's mainland but also for comparative Atlantic history. Why was Brazil the last independent nation in the Americas to tolerate slavery while it was among the first to bring about a de facto (1876), soon followed by a de jure (1890), end to capital punishment? By comparing the institutional fit of reforms in Brazil to other nations, new hypotheses of conditions that favored or hindered the evolution of human rights can be pondered.

Finally, Fernando de Noronha provides unexpected insights into conceptions of gender, sexuality, and heterosexual conjugality. Authorities allowed some married convicts to be joined by their wives and dependents and permitted others to marry or to live with a heterosexual consensual lover (*amaziado*) in exile. The policies reflect the clashes and compromises between liberal ideals of individual responsibility and traditional patriarchal duties and privileges. They also highlight how assumptions about gender undergirded debates about how to make convict workers productive and moral. Imperial justice displayed a keen gender bias in that the vast majority of defendants convicted were men. However, the segregation from society that modern prisons, poor houses, asylums, barracks, and penal colonies required ran counter to critiques of inhibiting a man's heterosexual release through continence or imposed abstinence. Brazilians disagreed over the access priests, slaves, physicians, soldiers, and convicts should have to nubile women, but most shared beliefs about the male sex drive, even as they bickered over how to manage it. Conditions in the colony sometimes forced actors to articulate cultural understandings that did not arise with the same urgency and frequency on the mainland. In English, "nubile" denotes a marriageable woman, but in Portuguese, *núbil* applies to both genders. These usages suggest distinct cultural views of gender, marriage, and sexuality, and to highlight this, I use the incongruous term "male nubility" to describe men whom authorities granted heterosexual conjugal privileges within total institutions.

My approach to heterosexual penal conjugality among convicts on Fernando de Noronha and other categories of the intractable poor requires a brief digression. David Garland's appraisal of the Marxist, Durkheimian, and Foucauldian traditions in penology accents the need to combine strengths of each to create "more of a three dimensional perspective than is usually perceived." I share Garland's view, and to examine heterosexual penal conjugality, I invoke two scholars whose work is less cited in recent scholarship: Erving Goffman and Lewis Coser.[19] These sociologists offer points of departure to rethink the relationships between disciplining institutions, family, and gender to elucidate how Brazilians mediated the individualized punishment of liberal penology.

Goffman shrewdly conveys the tensions between families and total institutions (penitentiaries, mental asylums, barracks, and so forth) in his 1961 classic *Asylums*:

> Total institutions are . . . incompatible with another crucial element of our society, the family. Family life is sometimes contrasted with solitary living, but in fact the more pertinent contrast is with batch living, for those who eat and sleep at work, with a group of fellow workers, can hardly sustain a meaningful domestic existence. . . . Whether a particular total institution acts as a good or bad force in civil society, force it will have, and this will in part depend on the suppression of the whole circle of actual or potential households. Conversely, the formation of households provides a structural guarantee that total institutions will not be without resistance.

I build on this insight to explore batch and household living in Brazilian institutions that integrated the intractable poor. Goffman developed these conceptions in his study of mid-twentieth century U.S. total institutions. I use them to explore nineteenth-century Brazilian slavery, military barracks, prisons, and penal colonies, which, as the process of category drift outlined earlier suggests, were considerably more porous and less totalizing than twentieth-century U.S. asylums.[20]

Inspired by Goffman, Coser defined a related group of "greedy institutions" that sought to monopolize the primary loyalties of individuals from competing societal associations without necessarily segregating them. Greedy institutions cultivated individuals whose authority could not be preserved without the institutional leadership's support. Thus, sovereigns

(margin note: Goffman)

(margin note: Coser)

(handwritten note at bottom: greedy institutions - sought to monopolize the primary loyalties of individuals from competing societal associations without necessarily segregating them.)

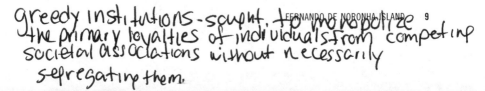

sought trusted administrators from court Jews, eunuchs, foreign mercenaries, and others. Likewise, the Catholic Church, radical organizations, and millenarian groups limit their members' abilities to develop entangling relationships with outsiders who might put their loyalty to the test. The Catholic Church, for example, requires clerical celibacy in deference to theological considerations, but also to bolster fidelity to the hierarchy and to protect institutional property from dissipation through inheritance. Coser even includes housewives and live-in servants as subject to the greedy institution of the nuclear family. Writing in the 1970s, he notes feminist critiques of gender expectations that pressured housewives to limit commitments and contacts outside of the family in deference to their roles as mothers and caretakers. While Coser stresses the family's limitations on mothers and wives, he does not address whether it limits husbands and fathers. Clearly, in the 1970s most husbands developed more commitments outside their families than their wives, but Coser's silence also reflects an era before gender became a more established analytical category.[21]

Intriguingly, many nineteenth-century Brazilian authorities (almost all men) posited that male jealousy for a wife or consensual heterosexual partner "naturally" bound him to a more orderly, productive, and moral lifestyle.[22] Somewhere between and overlapping with Coser's greedy and Goffman's total institutions, officials experimented with hybrid penal practices that combined modern and traditional elements to cultivate what I term the "jealous institution of heterosexual conjugal living." The jealous institution is a male codicil to Coser's characterization of housewives as subject to the greedy institution of the nuclear family. It describes an idealized belief in the less restrictive but still limiting "natural" influence that heterosexual conjugality and family had over male lovers, husbands, and fathers. Authorities tested the potential of heterosexual penal conjugality on Fernando de Noronha in deference to deep-seated beliefs about gender. They argued that the presence of wives and dependents would make convict men more productive and stem same-sex eroticism. This study analyzes officials' faith in the jealous institution's power and how their experiments with it fared.

In general, my study is distinct from Foucauldian studies of prisons and sexuality that tend to focus on transgressive sexual behavior and Jeremy Bentham's panopticon architecture. Instead, I privilege the nuclear heterosexual family as a reputed source of male discipline and productivity in a hybrid penal regime bounded not by walls but by ocean.[23] It has long been argued that the penitentiary evolved from medieval monastery practices that sought to modify individual behavior with cellular isolation. Other studies suggest that some colonial prisons developed from prisoner-of-war camps. I argue that the conjugal penal experiment on Fernando de Noronha evolved from a repertoire of Portuguese strategies to manage the labor, discipline, and strategic diaspora of intractable poor men and women.[24] In so doing, I seek to put the little explored subject of labor and conjugal relations on a more rigorous theoretical and comparative footing. This Brazilian case study is a precocious example of a state developing and implementing policies intended to promote heterosexual citizenship.[25]

I bring together the analytical threads laid out here within and among chapters in a layered fashion. Most chapters are thematic save for chapter 2, which provides a historical narrative to situate Fernando de Noronha's evolving place in Brazil's penal system, politics, and imaginations. In so doing, I offer a critique of the shallow southward reach of Atlantic history. This book seeks to expand this subfield geographically by "Re-Capricorning" the Atlantic to bring the south Atlantic more fully into Atlantic history's purview, and temporally to follow Atlantic history themes out of the early modern period and into the long nineteenth century.[26]

This Brazilian case study is a precarious example of a state developing and implementing policies intended to promote hetero sexual citizenship.

GETTING TO KNOW "FERNANDO"

An 1853 dispute between the "preta Izabel," the colony commander's slave, and fourteen slave and free convicts allows us to zoom in to explore the contradictions of everyday life on what penal colony residents referred to as "Fernando." The convicts declared that they had provided Izabel with produce that she sold in her store and complained that she had not paid them. This incident likely produced more paperwork than normal because a recent decree forbade commanders to sell goods, but because the commander owned Izabel, it could appear that he skirted the decree's spirit. To placate critics, he ordered an inspection of Izabel's home, where an officer found green corn, pumpkins, and food cooking on a fire. If it was a store, it was a humble venture, but the depiction suggests that Izabel prepared and sold hot food to convicts to make the money that she paid weekly to the army convict Antonio Joaquim de Alencar for her home that doubled as a store.[1] Izabel followed a tradition of many slave women in Brazil's cities who had their own residence and worked in urban markets where they sold goods. They paid their masters a weekly sum from their earnings in lieu of their labor.[2]

The complaint included the convicts' names and the produce that they supplied Izabel from their provision grounds. Commanders granted provision grounds to well-behaved convicts in a fashion that paralleled those of mainland plantation owners who granted similar privileges to trusted slaves. Since Izabel's master was the commander, the convicts likely believed that he would guarantee their payment. The list included a nearly equal number of free and slave convicts:

the slave Jerônimo supplied Izabel 14 hands of fresh corn; the slave Joaquim Mesquita, 400 pumpkins; the slave Elias, 60 pumpkins; the slave Dionisio, 50 pumpkins; and the slave Lourenço, 100 pumpkins.[3]

The complaint reveals the web of relations that extended from the commander to lowly slave convicts. In his own statement, the commander acknowledged Izabel as "a member of my family," and a number of employees wrote out declarations testifying, as the ensign Raimundo José de Souza Lobo did, that "the preta Izabel is treated by the convicts as a slave, but that because of familiarity they commonly refer to her as godmother [comadre]." The documents do not state why this point of social etiquette was in question, but it hints at confusing questions of status and the quality of relationships between the commander's slave and convicts. The dispute reveals that slave and free convicts had access to provision grounds and through them, they literally cultivated ties to the commander's household. This commerce presented contradictions that compromised formal institutional and social hierarchies. In this case, through his slave, a commander ironically became indebted to slave convicts. Historians have observed similar contradictions when mainland masters gave their slaves provision grounds, and in this case, the convicts sought to insinuate an apparently awkward ritualized kinship to the commander's family by referring to Izabel as godmother.

This brief episode exemplifies many of this book's themes: the integration of convicts of various statuses and colors; the convict's affinity and business relationships with the nonconvict slave Izabel; the parallels in the strategies army officers used to motivate convict workers with those used on the mainland; and how convicts responded to these strategies. The episode also indicates the presence and significance of family. Officers often served with their families in tow. So did civil servants, soldiers, vendors, and the so-called unattached residents. Officials even permitted some convicts the right to be joined by their wives and dependents in exile and others to marry or live in consensual heterosexual relationships. The penal regime reveals a distinctive hybridity: some methods inspired by modern penology and others linked to traditional ideals.

In many ways, the island's capital, Remédios, was Brazil's first planned city, a humble precursor of Brasília, Curitiba, and Belo Horizonte. Its national farm was in some ways a forerunner of modern collective farms. The state invested the army officers who ran Fernando de Noronha with extraordinary authority to plan the lives of convict laborers down to the schedule of their everyday work and leisure activities, housing, and diet. As the dispute between convicts and Izabel suggests, the unplanned-for initiatives of convicts and nonconvict residents shaped the colony's everyday functions. Perhaps the best way to introduce the colony's everyday routines, geography, and built environment is to imagine a convict arriving there in the 1870s, when its population reached a peak.

Some convicts destined for Fernando de Noronha spent years in jails in other provinces before arriving in Pernambuco's penitentiary, the House of Detention. Schooners could take many days to voyage from Recife to Fernando de Noronha depending on conditions. In 1819, a commander observed that ships from Recife sometimes did not return for three or four months, but by the 1850s, commercial steamships usually resupplied the colony monthly.[4] The American geologist John Branner, who would later become Stanford University's second president, made the voyage in 1876. He described a "small crew," six convicts, and a security detail for the two-and-one-half day voyage.[5] An 1885 manifest from the colony reveals that ships could transport larger cohorts: "On the night of Aug. 16 at 8:00 PM, the steamship Mandahú anchored here [Recife with] the following passengers. . . . Capitão Bacharel Baptista Pinheiro Corte-Real, his wife and eight children; Alferes Victorino Leopoldino da Silva Costa in command of a squad of 30 soldiers with 46 convicts and one sergeant and fifteen [convicts from the House of Detention] quarantined [on Fernando de Noronha] for beriberi; the pharmacist Pedro de Chastinct and twelve women and some children of the convicts and soldiers."[6] The security detachment may have segregated convicts from other passengers, but the confined space mitigated these efforts. Some prisoners travelled in irons. As a steamer captain reported in 1881, "At the last minute I received a verbal order from the Chief of Police that the cavalry soldier and criminal Antônio Carbeiro de Santa'Anna, who made the entire voyage in chains because I was informed that the soldier had committed the crime of murder."[7] The fact that the captain wrote a letter explaining why he had transported a prisoner in fetters suggests that this was not routine, and many likely made their brief middle passage to exile unshackled.

Convicts would first spy their new home's basalt peak, which towered 321 meters above the ocean. It broods over Fernando de Noronha's shore like a melancholy, sentinel erection known blandly as "pico" (peak). The name *pico* might have stuck as a homoerotic pun because it is also a slang for penis. The archipelago is a series of peaks from a mostly submerged volcanic mountain range. Fernando de Noronha, the main island, is eighteen square

MAP 1.1 Map of the Fernando de Noronha Island and surrounding islets near its main port, Santo Antonio. Jackie Hawthorne.

kilometers; it accounts for 90 percent of the archipelago's land. Twenty-one satellite islands and islets ring it; the second largest, Rat Island (Ilha Rata), was home to troublesome convicts. An exile within exile, convicts on Rat Island lived what one visitor described as a "Robinson Crusoe existence."[8]

As their steamship drew closer, the rocky cliffs that lined the island's western shore would come into view. At the feet of these cliffs lay narrow beaches whose sizes ebbed and waned with the tide. Natives referred to the western ocean as the "inside sea," whose limpid waters teemed with dolphins year round and migrating whales in August and September. Patchy green tufts of vegetation festooned seabird-infested cliff walls and rocky islets where it found precarious toeholds. As their steamer approached the archipelago's northern end, they could view Remédios, the island's capital, nestled on a gentle downhill slope above an attractive beach. Parts of the year, it was possible to disembark passengers and goods there, but more often ships disgorged their cargo at Port Santo Antonio on the isle's northern strand. Towering above Remédios was a basalt precipice where the stone battlements of Fort Remédios stood. This topography partly protected Remédios from the prevailing winds, but the founders chose the location because of its proximity to a fresh water reservoir.[9] Fort Remédios's cannons protected Remédios on one side and Port Santo Antonio on the other.

John Branner described landing at the beach below Remédios:

> [We] arrived at the anchoring-ground—for there is no wharf or pier, and no small boats are allowed on the island—I could see upon the beach about seventy-five half-naked men tugging at a huge two-storied raft, trying to get it into the water. When this was launched, a large cable was secured on shore, and the great raft was paddled slowly in our direction . . . the other end of which was finally made fast to the steamer. The personal baggage, five or six newly arrived convicts with their guards, and myself and servant, were placed on the upper story of this peculiar craft, and it was then drawn in near the shore by means of the cable. When we struck bottom I was taken on the wet, slippery, naked back of a convict, who waded ashore and deposited me on the dry beach. . . . I was escorted by a man who took me in charge, and whom I afterward found to be a convict directed by the commandant to look after all persons and all things landing, and escorted up the very steep hill, through the well-paved streets of the village, to the house of the commandant, closely followed by the newly arrived convicts under guard.[10]

Convicts and distinguished foreign scholars clumsily disembarked together.

Most convicts, however, landed at Port Santo Antonio, where a string of small islands protect it from the open ocean, but the straits they formed channel powerful currents that complicate landfall. A British ornithologist noted in 1902: "At its best this is a difficult place from which to embark without getting wet, and it was seldom that we landed there or got away without getting soaked by the waves."[11] After what was often a queasy landing, convicts surveyed the port: a low-lying spit of land without a pier. Small rafts used for fishing sometimes surrounded a small fortification and a warehouse. In good weather, it took five days for officials to complete the transfer of passengers and goods and to prepare paperwork before the steamship could return to Recife.[12] The island's treacherous reefs and primitive port discouraged most ships from landing there. A maritime historian noted another reason that few ships called: "Lacking grog shops or brothels, mariners had little more use for Fernando de Noronha other than to use it as a landmark to check their chronometers."[13] Yankee whalers, whose crews often included Portuguese immigrants to the United States, sometimes stopped to trade whale oil, used to illuminate Remédios's streets, for fresh stores.[14]

After inspections at Port Santo Antonio, convict porters transported goods and escorted new convicts over a cobblestone road to Remédios. The road was mostly uphill and, depending on the season, the vegetation was either lushly green or grey and desiccated. The Confederate navy captain Raphael Semmes, who toured the island in 1863, recalled: "The winds, the rains, and the sunshine have, in the course of ages, disintegrated enough of the surface of this rocky island, to form a rich soil, which is covered with a profusion of tropical vegetation, including forest-trees of considerable size; and a number of small farms, with neat farm-houses, add to the picturesqueness of the scene."[15] Convicts might have seen skinks and mice flit across their path while a variety of seabirds circled overhead. The lands to the road's left were high and rocky with patches of fertile earth where convicts planted bananas and pumpkins to take advantage of marginal plots.[16] The road swung like a scimitar around the base of the precipice under Fort Remédios for more than a mile.

As the convicts approached Remédios, they likely would first smell cooking fires and then view more concentrated formations of houses and provision grounds. The women and children of convicts often turned out to witness the parade of newcomers. The American geologist Orville Derby disparagingly described them in 1881: "The most of the houses are, however, mere kennels with walls of loose stone covered in thatch. In nearly all of them women and children are seen, some few of the former being criminals, the others being de jure or de facto of the convicts who until a recent period were permitted easy access to the island."[17] Foraging chickens, lounging pigs, and barking dogs welcomed newcomers in their own way. The salty winds that buffet the island mercifully dissipated the stench of human and animal waste. The road's downward slope into the town square used gravity and tropical rains to help clean its streets, and the more substantial homes of privileged convicts lined this avenue. A few of these larger homes doubled as stores. A survey of housing in 1885 counted 846 buildings: 136 were government structures, and individuals built 710. Of the 710 private structures: 31 were constructed of stone with zinc roofs; 76, stone with tile roofs; 290, stone with thatch roofs; and 313, wattle and daub with thatch roofs. Government structures included 6 of stone with zinc roofs; 40, stone with clay tile roofs; 14, stone with thatch roofs; and 76, wattle and daub with thatch roofs.[18] Derby smugly surmised Remédios: "The village is of considerable size and in the province of Minas [Gerais] would merit the honors of a city. It affords accommodations for about two thousand inhabitants among

FIG 1.1 Early twentieth-century ink drawing of the town of Remédios, Fernando de Noronha. From Virgilio Cardoso de Oliveira, *A Patria brazileira: Leitura escolar com 260 gravuras* (Brussels: Constant Gouweloos, 1903), 184.

convicts, officers, and guards and as most of the former live in their own houses, its general aspect is not essencially [*sic*] different from that of any other Brazilian town."[19]

Convicts inhabited most private structures along with some employees, vendors, and unattached inhabitants surrounding the commander's residence. The arrangement resembled the master's big house and the *senzalas* (slave barracks) and detached *mocambos* of mainland plantations.[20] Regulations did not grant individual ownership of homes, but it did give them usufruct rights and inhabitants sold these rights. In 1868, a commander suggested that the government tax home sales that sometimes involved "considerable quantities."[21] The colony had a real estate market, if mostly a humble one. New rules required convicts to pay an annual fee (*aforamento*) for the use of imperial property and those who bought a residence had to assume its payment. These rules lent legitimacy to usufruct rights and must have encouraged building because there were half as many private structures in 1869 compared to those surveyed in 1885.[22]

When the newcomers reached the main square, they would see the colony's offices on their left alongside the commander's residence. At the top of the square stood Remédios's church, a simple but elegant façade that resembled those of Brazil's interior. Below it stood the main warehouse, where convict porters unburdened themselves. Around the square and the roads surrounding it, the more stately residences of employees huddled. An American visi-

aldeia - village

tor in 1881 described them: "The government buildings, the officers' houses, and a number of those of the convicts are constructed of stone and mortar covered in thatch."[23] Below the square and off to the west was the *aldeia* (village). This was a barracks-like structure constructed in 1856 to house the colony's growing convict population. A commander griped that the aldeia's main design flaw was the location of its kitchen near the lavatory.[24] The term "aldeia" likely referenced projects to concentrate indigenous communities in villages, where they could be more easily monitored, disciplined, and catechized. It indicates how administrators borrowed from mainland practices to organize their planned community. The term suggests the interrelatedness of different categories of the intractable poor, and it echoed the term *praça de índio* (Indian soldier), used to describe all convicts regardless of ethnicity. The latter term, however, fell out of use in colony documentation by the 1850s.

The aldeia's main compartments were not cells but large common dormitory rooms that at times congregated as many as four hundred "miserable" prisoners in a space that should have comported no more than two hundred. The aldeia's doors closed at 6:00 PM and opened again at 6:00 AM. In 1876, a commander described it as "the dormitory for bachelor convicts, those who are incorrigible, and those who are incarcerated."[25] While commanders granted bachelor convicts the right to live outside the aldeia, they still associated it with bachelorhood. The British penal reformer Jeremy Bentham's ideal of cellular isolation was absent. Jail cells were limited to two lockups within the aldeia, in each of which authorities could cram up to fourteen prisoners. Women convicts were not held in the aldeia; they either lived in a superior's home where they worked or in homes that they built, rented, or bought. Most convict homes were close to the commander's residence, but others, particularly those of night watchmen, were scattered across the island.[26] While in the late 1850s, the aldeia housed a large part of the colony's convicts, by the 1870s, when their numbers exceeded 1,500, it could only house a fraction of them. Most new convicts had to make their own accommodations. In the dry months of summer, some slept on the aldeia's patio under the stars.[27]

If a convict exited the aldeia and looked up to the northeast he would see the lone, steep road leading up to Fort Remédios where the garrison billeted. In 1864, War Minister Henrique Pedro Carlos de Beaurepaire Rohan noted that only the forts of Remédios and Santo Antonio were in good repair; the other six were in ruins. He added, however, that any enemy would find a more formidable obstacle to landing in the island's reefs.[28]

After an uncomfortable first night's sleep in the aldeia, another convict's home, or under the stars, officers assigned new convicts a work company usually headed by a convict sergeant flanked by two or three convict corporals. After breakfast, a bugle called workers into formation for roll call in a fashion similar to those of slaves on large plantations and mainland army regiments.[29] After sergeants counted heads, they read the orders of the day. A reporter described the routine in 1904: "The most comfortable prisoner was an old white man, more or less educated, with a strong voice. It was he who read before his comrades in formation the orders of the day."[30] Most of the fifteen work companies performed fieldwork to cultivate manioc, sea-island cotton, maize, beans, and other crops. A company of cobblers produced boots for the army, and a company of skilled workers kept up the colony's infrastructure: carpenters, stone masons, smiths, and so forth. Questions of production influenced whom commanders assigned to convict police and night watchmen companies. In 1872, a commander reported that the "9th company performs police duties" and they are "almost all men who are ill or of advanced age who are inapt for active service, some being incapable of any service because they are entirely blind." It is difficult to imagine that this police force would intimidate younger convicts. This same commander, like others before and after him, suggested that the government would profit by removing prisoners incapable of labor because they "were a drain on the colony's resources and besides most had already served long sentences of ten, fifteen, and twenty years in this presidio and thus they have expiated the crimes they committed."[31] Convict police led patrols and night watchmen prevented theft from warehouses and fields and watched for escape attempts. There was also a company for convicts who worked as domestics.

After communicating the orders of the day, most sergeants led their men to the fields. Two companies that tended distant fields lived in the encampments of Sambaqueixaba and Sueste. Most convicts, however, lived in proximity to the commander's residence, and they headed southwest where the imperial farms occupied the most fertile plains. One visitor estimated that there was "nearly two square miles of good cultivatable land on the island."[32] If one continued south, one would reach Sambaqueixaba. If one headed southwest, one would find Sueste, where the island's orchards and coconut plantation stood.

The colony's most vital resource was the fresh water reservoir. Colonists improved this natural formation to ensure a larger water supply, but many complained of its salinity. The island also had a few fresh water springs, but they did not produce enough to quench the thirst of more than two thousand inhabitants in the dry summer. When the colony's population grew, drought could force water and food rationing, and on a number of occasions, commanders sent men out on rafts or boats to alert mainland authorities of their desperate situation. Above the reservoir on Floresta Hill stood the cemetery where convicts condemned for life could look forward to a pauper's grave. One commander lamented that rain ran off from the cemetery into the village, and recommended moving it to lower ground where winds would carry the miasmas out to sea.[33]

By the 1870s, deforestation meant that most convicts worked unshaded from the equatorial sun. By then the trees Captain Semmes described in 1863 had mostly been felled, and scrub forest and grasses dominated uncultivated areas. In 1869, a commander observed:

> It is not possible to receive and maintain securely a larger number of prisoners who at present number 1,273, since our army detachment is small, almost all lack uniforms, and they are undisciplined by habit, and the Aldeia poorly accommodates 280 men. I plead that your excellency [Governor] . . . send no more convicts seeing as there is no place to house them, they spread out from the center of the island by necessity and are outside the view of this command which is very inconvenient. . . . The presidio presently cannot support so many people, the forests are devastated, already there is a lack of fire wood, and in summer the springs are not adequate to supply the population that grows day after day. . . . If the shipments of convicts does not cease we will suffer thirst.[34]

Despite pleas, the population continued to grow. A British naturalist remarked on the environmental toll: "The great interest of the vegetation of Fernando centres in the conflict between the uninvited satellites of man and the aboriginal flora. A ruthless, truceless war is being waged, and this issue is already decided. The invaders have mastered the plain country, and are at present engaged in storming the heights and reducing the seashore. The woods have, for the most part, already fallen, partly in process of clearing for cultivation, partly for firewood, and partly by order of the authorities lest the convicts should make rafts and escape."[35] Population growth taxed forest resources, and revealed the island's limited human carrying capacity.

The island's southeast is exceedingly rocky for comfortable habitation, much less cultivation. Some convicts hid themselves in grottoes in this forbidding zone to avoid punishment before the difficulties of life there drove them back to Remédios.[36] Likewise the windswept and rocky northeast side of the island bordering the "outside sea" is less propitious for cultivation, but at low tide, its reefs form limpid tidal pools ideal for fishing and crabbing. A visitor witnessed a convict who used a poisonous plant to foul the water and harvest fish in an "unsportsman-like" but "very effectual" way.[37]

Most convicts toiled from 9:00 AM to 2:00 PM. Thereafter, those with provision grounds could tend them, and those without might fish or crab. While the imperial farms occupied prime lands, provision grounds were scattered in less favorable plots where the soil, nourished by centuries of sea-bird dung, was still fertile. A British naturalist noted: "Of cultivated plants we have enumerated over thirty species which perhaps the most important are the coconut, banana, pumpkin, papaw, cassava, maize, sweet potato, and the black bean. Others such as fruit trees and flowers need not be speci-fied; the only thing we heard of refusing to grow being the pineapple."[38] This brief list fails to capture the variety of crops cultivated. Most convicts cultivated hearty legumes (corn, manioc, pumpkin, and beans) and fruits and nuts (banana, cashew, mango, and passion fruit).[39] Tending to crops gave the convicts a healthier diet, and as the preta Izabel case demonstrates, it allowed convicts to barter.

Toward sundown, the colony's priest held a prayer vigil with a "hymn to the Blessed Virgin, and appropriate music, and is a very striking scene."[40] A final bugle call notified convicts to assemble for roll call, and the aldeia's res-idents settled in for the night. Convicts who lived outside the aldeia, how-ever, had time to socialize more freely usually until 10:00 PM. After a day of work, most retired early, but some ignored curfew and risked being arrested by convict police. Upon awaking the next morning, convicts repeated the cycle of work and socializing until a Sunday or a religious or national holi-day gave them respite from their routine. In their leisure, some may have wondered about the origins of their new community. So after zooming in to imagine how a new convict might experience the sights, sounds, and smells of his penal community, the next chapter zooms out to place Fernando de Noronha in a broader historical context.

2 "THE KEY TO THE AMERICAS"?

Until the age of exploration, Fernando de Noronha had no human inhabitants, but its reefs teemed with marine life, and birds and rodents crowded its craggy shores. The navigator Fernão de Loronha discovered it in 1502, and Amerigo Vespucci described its fauna and flora. Words, however, could never fully capture the splendorous cobalt hues that dark rock, blond sand, and the sun's rays coax from the dazzling waters that wash this island.[1] This chapter explores the Portuguese and Brazilian empires from the perspective of Fernando de Noronha. It analyzes how a slaveholding society embraced liberal penology after independence and developed institutions that render Fernando de Noronha's role in penal justice clear. It also demonstrates how these institutions were interconnected and how penal justice became politicized. New penal regimes were keys to defining national and regional identities against Portugal's old regime. Pernambuco and the army are privileged in the narrative because they played key roles in the island's history and most convicts came from Pernambuco and other northeastern provinces. Key moments in the histories of categories of the intractable poor are highlighted to illustrate their interconnection as well as the nature of category drift. Finally, the initial prohibition of women in the colony foregrounds subsequent analysis of evolving ideas of gender, sexuality, conjugality, and penology.

ORIGINS

Fernando de Noronha was a remote dot on the map of a Portuguese seaborne empire that would span from China to Brazil. In 1504, the crown awarded it as the first New World land grant to Fernão de Loronha, but neither he nor his heirs permanently inhabited it. A Portuguese religious mission stopped there in 1612 and found a man exiled from Pernambuco with his eighteen Indian slaves, which presaged the island's future function.[2]

Portugal's population, about one million in 1500, made holding a far-flung empire a challenge. The crown used much of its treasure and manpower to defend colonies and commerce from indigenous competitors and more populous European rivals.[3] This is one reason the Portuguese depended heavily on Indian and African slavery to settle and develop colonies. They also seldom sent their countrymen to the gallows because they relied on another coercive migratory labor form: penal transportation. Explorers strategically marooned Portuguese convicts on Africa's and Brazil's shores in the hopes some would be accepted into native communities and learn their languages. When caravels returned, surviving convicts could serve as cultural go-betweens. Whether coerced or not, most European migrants to Portugal's colonies were men who often coupled with Amerindian and African women. Many of their children became allies in Portuguese efforts to thwart the incursion of European rivals, though go-betweens could turn coats and challenge Portuguese interests in this middle ground where no one group dominated.[4] Convicts were the leading edge of colonization, and they continued to arrive in Portugal's colonies, including Brazil, after they were settled.[5]

Fernando de Noronha remained unoccupied until the Dutch settled it when they invaded Brazil (1630–1654). The Dutch occupation centered on the captaincy (colonial administrative unit) of Pernambuco, where they built up the city of Recife on the Capibaribe River's delta islands. Recife became Pernambuco's main port and capital and Fernando de Noronha's principal mainland link. In 1654, an alliance of Portuguese colonials, indigenous and free black militias, and maroon allies drove the Dutch from Brazil. The restoration of Portuguese rule was a point of regional pride because Pernambucans prevailed over the Dutch without the crown's aid.[6] A 1700 royal decree transferred Fernando de Noronha's administration to Pernambuco's governors, but it remained unoccupied until the French West India Company settled it.[7] An emissary of the governor wrote a letter in 1736 that described the twelve French inhabitants, their weapons, their structures, and the crops they cultivated.[8] The Portuguese returned in 1737 with an occupation force of two hundred men and removed the French, who offered no resistance.[9]

In 1741, the crown sent army architect Diogo da Silveira Veloso to build ten fortifications "to impede contraband trade with foreigners."[10] Because the crown could not attract migrants, it peopled the colony with convicts and soldiers from Brazil.[11] These exiles laid the square of the island's capital Remédios in 1770. They also cultivated crops, but they still depended on supplies from Recife for sustenance.

Officials prohibited women from visiting the island.[12] As U.S. Navy surgeon Amos E. Evans remarked when his ship bought stores there in 1812: "This Island belongs to the Portuguese and is the place where convicts are sent. There are no women on it."[13] Henry Koster, who moved to Pernambuco in 1809, was more graphic: "There is one political arrangement of this province which, above all others, cries aloud for alteration. It is a glaring, self-evident evil, it is a disgrace upon the government which suffers its existence. I speak of the small island of Fernando de Noronha. To this spot are transported, for a number of years or for life, a great number of male criminals. No females are permitted to visit the island."[14] In 1799, Bahia's captain general made explicit what Koster implied: "There are no women there which leads men to more frequently [practice] vices of human weakness contrary to nature, among individuals of the masculine sex as noted in the letter," but he added that the exiles worked as fieldhands. They became Indian soldiers (*se lhes assenta praça de Índio*) and received 20 réis a day plus a ration of manioc flour.[15]

The captain general's letter was likely a response to Recife-born cleric Bernardo Luis Ferreira Portugal's 1797 criticisms of the colony. Two years earlier, the inquisition tried Ferreira Portugal for reading Jean Jacques Rousseau, denying heaven and hell's existence, and questioning transubstantiation. It exiled him to Belém, Pará, where he penned his missive. He protested being "expatriated" from Pernambuco and, like many Brazilians, referred to his captaincy as his fatherland. One suspects that he wrote to strike back at enemies in Recife who profited from supplying the colony, but he asserted his own motive: "the considerable expense that Pernambuco's treasury makes annually to the detriment and ruin of the nation." His nation was Pernambuco, not Brazil, much less the Portuguese Empire.[16]

Ferreira Portugal exalted Fernando de Noronha as "the key to the Americas." He boasted that it was "one of the most fertile countries in the Américas, the corn, beans, manioc, and fruits grew there in quantity, quality, and size superior to any in Brazil or Africa." But rather than reap its bounty "it is manned by [army] troops from Pernambuco . . . [and] judges, military tribunals, and courts customarily remit many penal exiles who by precedent set long ago become Indian soldiers and are paid a small wage by the crown." The king "generously provided all" that convicts needed, and their idleness encouraged the "pursuit of pleasure and corruption":

On that island, the authorities do not allow women. . . . The lack of this sex gives birth to horrible crimes [such as] sodomy, bestiality, and [illegible]. . . . The corruption is so deeply rooted that with pomp and publicity marriages between persons of the same sex are celebrated, and these unfortunate ones call one another husband and wife: jealousies over attractive young men [*ganimedes*] cause frequent disorders, this vice attacks all from the commander to the last penal exile, and once habituated to it, when they leave the island, they continue to practice it and introduce it [on the mainland]. . . . These wrongs can only be corrected by . . . entirely changing the island's governance. All of the expenses that your majesty makes to sustain the troops and penal exiles . . . all the evils of idleness that exist on that island can be resolved once you begin to populate it with married men.[17]

Ferreira Portugal makes a full-throated case for the jealous institution described in the introduction. If the crown allows wives to join married soldiers and penal exiles, and finds nubiles from "poor and honest people" for bachelors, they will husband the land, export their surplus, defend the archipelago, and contribute to, instead of deplete, revenues. Women's presence would also extinguish same-sex eroticism. As with France's Bastille, criticisms of Fernando de Noronha's ancien penal regime presaged an inchoate nationalist consciousness.[18]

Why did Portuguese authorities prohibit women? Perhaps they supposed it was a site of punishment, not colonization. United States Navy captain David Porter endorsed this conjecture when he postulated in 1812 that the Portuguese banned women to "render this place of exile more horrible."[19] Whatever the case, observers agreed that the colony's morality was lamentable because of its denizens' relative idleness and their absolute gender segregation, but larger events prompted changes in this policy. Napoleon Bonaparte's invasion of Iberia led the Portuguese to relocate their court to Rio de Janeiro in 1808. To please their British allies, King João VI opened Brazil's ports to foreign trade, including Fernando de Noronha, as the accounts quoted attest.

Officials revisited Ferreira Portugal's ideas in 1819 when a commander asked the governor to send "couples or families" and suggested that "married soldiers from Recife's disbanded regiments" would be ideal. The letter does not clarify who the troops were, but they were likely cohorts of the suppressed 1817 Pernambucan Republican Revolution. The proposal may have been a response to an anonymous 1817 essay that condemned the "forced chastity" on Fernando de Noronha "reproved by all good laws." Perhaps the author was Ferreira Portugal. In any case, the essay condemned the "sins of Fernando," which the author suggested had become a mainland euphemism for "sodomy."[20] The proposal to send women signaled new attitudes about gender segregation. In 1819, the commander noted that three married convicts already lived with wives there. He gave two families extra rations because one wife cleaned the officers' clothes and another cooked for the infirmary. A third was pregnant, and her husband's lame hand limited their ability to work. He allowed the couples to live outside the convict barracks and permitted another convict to continue farming there after he completed his sentence. If it was not an ocean resort, one ex-con preferred it to his mainland prospects.[21]

The American and French Revolutions inspired the 1817 Pernambucan Republican Revolution, but the Portuguese governor's crack down on Masonic lodges, where free thinkers like Ferreira Portugal disparaged the colonial order, sparked the revolt. He acted when an officer of the free all-black Henrique Dias militia (named in honor of a black militia officer who helped drive the Dutch from Brazil) beat a Portuguese man who insulted Brazilians during the festival of Our Lady of Estança, the saint's day when Pernambucans celebrate their victory over the Dutch. When the governor ordered suspected conspirators arrested, it provoked violence. Free Brazilian-born men of all colors and slaves took the streets to attack the Portuguese-born and loot their properties. An interim junta declared a republic and trumpeted Pernambuco's second restoration from foreign rule. Ferreira Portugal, now the general vicar of Olinda, decreed that it was Church dogma that the people obey the junta.[22]

The 1817 Pernambucan Republican Revolution dramatized the province's ties to Fernando de Noronha. Rebels sent Captain José de Barros Falcão de Lacerda to the island to gather its troops, convicts, and munitions. In 1797, this captain had "neutralize[d] a tremendous rebellion" of soldiers and convicts on Fernando de Noronha, and later he returned to command the colony in 1811. The colony's inhabitants reportedly adhered to the revolution with "thunderous enthusiasm." The rebels likely enlisted convicts to fight in return for future clemency, a case of category drift seen in other conflicts. The captain returned with three hundred men, but bad weather led one of his ships to founder and the colony's colonial archive was lost. He managed to disembark his men, but loyalist forces soon captured them.[23]

The 1817 Pernambucan Republican Revolution was not Brazil's first independence conspiracy, but it was the most menacing. Rebels controlled

Recife, Brazil's third most populous city, for three months before loyalist forces prevailed. The provisional junta unsettled the colonial caste system by declaring the equality of free men of all colors, but it guaranteed private property's inviolability to assure slaveowners. Rough estimates of Brazil's population in 1818 enumerate 3,805,000: 1,040,000 whites (27.3 percent); 250,000 Indians (6.6 percent); 1,930,000 slaves (50.7 percent, black and mulatto); and 585,000 freedmen (15.4 percent, black and mulatto).[24] Republican leaders suggested that they would slowly abolish slavery with compensation, and to defend the republic, they sought to mobilize some slaves to fight. Most masters resisted these efforts, and rebels retreated from these initiatives. The compromise belied republican rhetoric of leveling and limited their ability to appeal to slaveholders and slaves. A lack of munitions, skilled military leadership, and manpower doomed the rebellion. Loyalists executed a few rebel leaders and exiled others, including Ferreira Portugal, from their beloved Pernambuco.[25]

Not long after King João VI's forces defeated Pernambuco's rebels, a liberal Portuguese military junta took power in Lisbon and called João home to preside over a constitutional congress in 1820. The king complied, but he left behind his son and heir, Pedro, and warned him that he might be forced to declare Brazil's Independence. Pedro did just that in 1822, and his forces quickly overcame loyalist resistance without the large mobilizations and years of war that characterized independence struggles in British North America and Spanish America.

BRAZILIAN INDEPENDENCE: PROVINCIAL VERSUS NATIONAL IDENTITY

Independence won, Brazilians claimed Fernando de Noronha and continued to inhabit it with homegrown convicts and soldiers. The island's ties to Recife and its mostly Brazilian-born population justified the claim. Parliament assigned the colony's oversight to the War Ministry, which provided officers to manage it, troops for security, and convict soldiers for labor. The War Ministry in Rio de Janeiro split the colony's management with the more proximate governors of Pernambuco.[26] The overlapping authority of war ministers and governors caused many disputes. Meanwhile, a new penal system emerged that carved out a niche for the colony.

In 1823, a constitutional assembly debated a new charter, but Pedro grew leery of its debates, disbanded it, and produced his own. The 1824 Constitution established a bicameral Parliament. Voters regularly elected representatives to a House of Deputies, but the emperor appointed senators to lifetime terms from a list of three candidates whom provincial electors selected. The emperor could also call for new elections in the House of Deputies and pardon or commute judicial sentences. The constitution placed the emperor at the center of power, and ambitious politicians had to garner his patronage.[27] To vote, a man had to be free, have a modest minimum income, and be Brazilian-born or naturalized. Law enfranchised most free men and freedmen, but their vote was indirect. Voters selected electors who voted directly for candidates at a second stage. Since there was no secret vote, local political bosses could monitor their clients' ballots. Among an array of reprisals for men who voted incorrectly was summary military impressment. This corrupt electoral system limited political competition to rival factions of privileged men who mobilized retainers to vote. With some exceptions, the men elected to political office were members of the commercial and landholding elites or their surrogates.[28]

A supreme court stood atop the judiciary, while regional appellate courts (one in Recife) reviewed cases from lower courts. The Justice Ministry oversaw the vetting and nomination of municipal, circuit, juvenile, and high court judges. In 1827, Parliament created the locally elected post of justice of the peace to supplant the colonial *capitão mor*. At the outset, the judiciary's professionalism, particularly justices of the peace whose unremunerated position required no legal training, was precarious, but it matured over time.[29] The courts supplied the convicts who labored on Fernando de Noronha. The 1830 Penal Code and the 1832 Criminal Procedural Code further defined penal justice. The latter gave justices of the peace limited police powers: authority to order the arrest of suspects, gather evidence for prosecutions, determine what charges to make, and authorize military impressment. The justice of the peace, the parish priest, and the municipal council president composed electoral boards that counted ballots and determined who was eligible to vote. These powers inspired competition among local rivals to capture this post.[30]

The Portuguese carried out few executions in late colonial Brazil; instead they employed most convicts in public works. The British subject Henry Koster described Recife's convict workers before independence:

> The sight, of all others, the most offensive to an Englishman, is that of the criminals, who perform the menial offices of the palace, the barracks, the prisons, and other public buildings. They are chained in couples, and each couple is followed by a soldier armed with a bayonet. They are allowed to stop at the shops, to obtain any trifle which they may want to purchase, and it is disgusting to see with what unconcern the fellows bear

this most disgraceful situation, laughing and talking as they go along to each other, to their acquaintance whom they may chance to meet, and to the soldier who follows them as a guard. The prisoners are in a very bad state, little attention being paid to the situation of their inhabitants.[31]

These convict chain gangs continued to work in Brazil's streets after independence, but Fernando de Noronha offered an alternative for convicts to labor in isolation.

Provincial pride made Pernambucans bristle under Pedro's autocratic rule. Participants in the 1817 uprising, such as Ferreira Portugal, had returned home, and they took advantage of popular discontent over Pedro's promulgation of the 1824 Constitution to depose the governor whom he named to administer their province. They elected their own governor, decreed the Confederation of the Equator, and sent emissaries to other provinces and Fernando de Noronha to solicit adherence. Forces from Rio de Janeiro in alliance with local loyalists soon quelled the revolt. Military tribunals tried rebel leaders and sentenced a few to the gallows, including the movement's publicist, Father Joaquim do Amor Divino Caneca (Frei Caneca). Executioners, usually slave convicts, refused to hang the clergyman, so the state resorted to an army firing squad to execute him.[32] Pedro quelled the revolt but lost the trust of Brazilians who feared he would impose absolutist rule. Many accused him of favoring *reinóis* (the Portuguese-born) with promotions and plum posts. Nascent Brazilian national identity formed around *lusophobia* (fear of the Portuguese) that united the Brazilian-born across lines of race and class. Measures to curb the rights of reinóis peppered liberal nativist manifestos across Brazil.[33]

Pedro diminished his popularity by waging an unpopular war with Argentina from 1825 to 1828 and pressing poor free men to fight. He sidestepped Parliament's control of the purse with foreign loans to fund the war and hire European mercenaries. Irish and German troops in Rio de Janeiro rioted in 1828 in a dispute over corporal punishment, and it took days to restore order. Popular outrage forced Pedro to disband his mercenaries and end the war.[34] Amid war, Pedro signed an 1826 trade treaty with Britain in which Brazil's leaders committed to end the transatlantic slave trade without Parliament's approval. Even so, Parliament later decreed that all Africans brought to Brazil after 1831 were emancipated. Authorities dealt with the unpopular law by failing to enforce it effectively, and the number of African slaves shipped to Brazil reached historic highs in the 1830s and 1840s.[35]

Pedro's disputes with Parliament fueled street fights between nativists and Portuguese-born royalists. A radical republican, Antônio Borges da Fonseca, emerged as an influential agitator. Born in Paraíba, Borges da Fonseca completed his education at Olinda's Episcopal Seminary, where he likely knew Ferreira Portugal. In 1830, he moved to Rio de Janeiro, where he edited a newspaper that incited brawls between nativists and reinóis. The violence eventually led Pedro to abdicate in favor of his five-year-old son Pedro and return to Portugal.[36]

A regency government ruled in young Pedro's stead, but many questioned its legitimacy. The regents quelled an 1831 republican putsch in the capital that Borges da Fonseca and many army enlisted men supported. Parliament reacted by cutting the army's ranks in half, disbanding color-based colonial militias, and founding a National Guard as a counterweight to the army. Parliament gave the Justice Ministry, not the War Ministry, the power to vet nominees for National Guard officerships. The National Guard soon contributed to police work across Brazil. Parliament's 1834 Additional Act created provincial assemblies with the authority to found police forces. Before there were police, army regulars patrolled Brazil's streets at night, guarded convicts, and aided court officials. In 1836, governors began to appoint police chiefs, delegates, and enlisted cops. Local political bosses competed to secure the post of police delegate to protect their interests.[37] The roles of these institutions in penal justice is examined more fully later. Despite the regency's federalism, Parliament designated Fernando de Noronha as the site of exile for all convicted counterfeiters in 1832 to deter forgery. In 1859, politicians confirmed their belief that exile to Fernando de Noronha was a deterrent when they decided that only free convicts sentenced to prison with work, counterfeiters, and slave convicts with capital sentences commuted to perpetual galleys could be exiled there.[38] The idea that the colony was an ocean resort for convicts only emerged later.

Pedro's abdication and the regency's liberal reforms stirred unrest across Brazil, but Pernambucans experienced more volatility. In addition to the two revolts analyzed previously, there were the Cabanos Revolt (1832–1835), the Praieira Revolt (1848–1850), and the War of the Wasps (1852). This is not to mention smaller uprisings that could close Recife's commerce for days.[39] Some rebels ended up on Fernando de Noronha because loyalists wanted to isolate them.[40] Another response to instability was more frequent use of the gallows. The largest number of public executions took place from 1835 to 1850 when the state made examples of rebels and heinous criminals. While most condemned to die were slaves, courts also condemned free men, including a few privileged men such as Frei Caneca.[41]

The first major rebellion against the regency emerged in Pernambuco, but unlike its predecessors, the leaders of the Cabanos Revolt were restorationists who had enjoyed Pedro I's favor. Many were Portuguese-born.[42] When rebels failed to take Recife, the revolt morphed into a grinding rural insurgency led by Vicente Ferreira de Paula, whose life exemplified category drift. Ferreira de Paula had been a sergeant in a second order militia before he emerged as the Cabanos' leader. He blamed "irreligious" liberals for the difficulties that beset rural men because federalist policies enhanced the power of local strong men to make land grabs. This injustice, combined with inflation, military impressment, and unemployment, fed popular discontent. His soldiers were mostly poor rural free men, Indians, and runaway slaves. When Pedro I died in Portugal in 1834, the movement lost momentum, but it took another year to end hostilities. Even then, some one hundred rebels refused to surrender and followed Ferreira de Paula to Alagoas. They chose a life akin to maroons rather than risk impressment upon surrender and the prospect of transfer to a distant outpost, perhaps even Fernando de Noronha. Eventually Ferreira de Paula and his men founded a settlement, and he became a rural boss. He even made a failed bid to become a National Guard officer in 1841.[43]

Instability shaped new laws, lawlessness, and Fernando de Noronha's population. Revolts encouraged banditry and blood feuds as well as slave flight and insurrection that disrupted Brazil's fragile plantation economy and spurred a conservative reaction. Parliament elected Pernambuco's senator Pedro de Araujo Lima regent in 1838. He rescinded federalist reforms to strengthen the central government.[44] Parliament granted governors the right to nominate mayors, who assumed many of the powers justices of the peace previously exercised.[45] Many embraced Pedro II's precocious ascent to the throne in 1840 to bolster the state's legitimacy. The fifteen-year-old inherited his father's constitutional powers, and his use of them sped the growth of Fernando de Noronha's convict population.[46]

THE SECOND EMPIRE, 1840–1889

The young emperor's coronation boosted the state's legitimacy, but it took another decade to end regional revolts. Not only did Pedro II face internal instability, but also foreign powers and nongovernmental organizations pressured him to end the transatlantic slave trade. While the North Atlantic nations that Brazilians looked to as models competed to win arms races and colonial resources, they also vied to outdo one another in what one might call the "human rights race." In this game of moral one-upmanship, torture and the inhumanity of slavery came to be considered barbaric. Brazil's tolerance of slavery left it increasingly isolated. To address Brazil's poor international image, Pedro II and a coterie of intellectuals and politicians looked for alternative ways to improve its standing. These efforts, along with reforms to penal institutions, changed Fernando de Noronha's role and reflected the state's desire to legitimize its rule at home and abroad.

In the 1840s, the British pressured Brazilians to enforce their 1831 law against the transatlantic slave trade with stepped-up seizures of slave vessels. British and Brazilian seizures resulted in some eleven thousand "free Africans" being "liberated" from 1821 to 1856 (half of whom were impounded after 1850). By a British-Brazilian treaty, free Africans would be "servants or free laborers" for fourteen-year apprenticeships. The Justice Ministry distributed free Africans to state institutions and individuals. It awarded the army's patron hero, the Duke of Caxias, more than any other citizen. In 1850, the state even sent two free Africans, Luiz and Cristovão, to Fernando de Noronha to teach convicts stone masonry.[47]

Since they were not the personal property of their employers, free Africans often endured worse treatment than slaves. If they survived their apprenticeships, the government granted them a letter of emancipation, but many lived in a state of virtual bondage for decades. British pressure pushed Parliament to decree the liberation of free Africans in 1853 to enforce apprenticeship terms, but the Justice Ministry revealed its ineffectiveness by reissuing it in 1864. The last free Africans were emancipated in the 1870s; some had remained in unpaid service for thirty years. The historian Beatriz Mamigonian argues that legal efforts to secure free Africans' emancipation inspired parallel efforts to free slaves in the courts by proving they arrived in Brazil after 1831, which affirms the interrelated nature of these two categories of the intractable poor.[48] I extend this reasoning to other categories of the intractable poor because a reform that benefitted members of one category made human rights abuses more difficult to sustain for others.

Britain's incursions into Brazilian waters threatened sovereignty, and growing concern over slave revolts and outbreaks of yellow fever associated with slave vessels facilitated the decision of Brazil's leaders to enforce the ban on the trade in 1850.[49] At that time, 30 percent of Brazil's population was enslaved, but their numbers soon declined because historically the bonded population did not generally sustain itself through natural reproduction. By 1872, slaves numbered 1.5 million, or 16 percent of Brazil's inhabitants.

Brazil's 1872 census identified 38 percent of its 9,930,478 residents as white; 16 percent, black; 4 percent, indigenous; and 42 percent, brown.[50]

The transatlantic trade's termination coincided with the demise of regional revolts. Pernambuco's Praieira Rebellion reveals how penal justice became politicized. It began in 1848 when Lieutenant Governor Manoel de Souza Teixeira, Police Chief Antonio Machado Rios, and Police Commissioner Francisco Machado Rios challenged the establishment Liberal Party's (Praieiros) slate of candidates. Crisis ensued when Pernambuco's liberal governor Antonio Pinto Chichorro da Gama stepped down from his office to assume a seat as an imperial deputy. Souza Teixeira temporarily assumed the governorship and, because he sided with dissident liberals (Nova Praia), dismissed five hundred officials loyal to the Praieiros. Many of these office holders were police delegates. Souza Teixeira held office for only a week, so he could not carry out his orders, but many officials refused to recognize them. Conservatives sowed further seeds of dissension when they hired bandits from Alagoas to attack towns dominated by liberals.[51]

In response, Pedro called on Pernambuco's former Regent Pedro de Araujo Lima to form a new cabinet, which called new elections that brought conservatives back to power. Pernambuco's new governor assured the opposition he would not dismiss liberal office holders, but days later, his nominees appeared in interior towns with police and army escorts to replace them. In many ways, the question of who would hold local police posts sparked the revolt.[52]

Captain Pedro Ivo Veloso da Silveira, Deputy Joaquim Nunes Machado, Antônio Borges da Fonseca, and other liberals led the rebellion. On January 1, 1849, Borges da Fonseca published a manifesto that called for universal male suffrage for free men; work as a guarantee of livelihood for Brazilian citizens; retail commerce limited to Brazilian citizens; the abolition of the emperor's moderating powers and his right to grant titles of nobility; the reform of the judiciary; and the abolition of military impressment. The demands echoed those of other liberal uprisings, but conservatives claimed Borges da Fonseca's participation proved the movement's radicalism. Insurgent forces failed to take Recife in 1849 but continued a rural guerrilla war. As in other revolts, insurgent troops were loath to surrender because they feared they would be pressed into the military. In 1850, rebel leaders agreed to surrender when offered amnesty. Despite promises, authorities pressed some rebel soldiers, and convicted ten rebel leaders, including Borges da Fonseca, to life in exile on Fernando de Noronha.[53] Loyalist and rebel leaders had both tried to recruit the leader of the Cabanos Revolt, Ferreira de

Paula. Instead, Ferreira de Paula took advantage of the chaos to pillage Pernambucan farms. Loyalists captured him after they promised him amnesty and the title of "the Commander of All the Forests."[54] They summarily exiled Ferreira de Paula to Fernando de Noronha, a dramatic undertow in an extraordinary life of category drift.

After the Praiera, an era of conservative and liberal cooperation took shape, but uprisings still challenged central authority. In 1852, citizens rose up across the northeast against efforts to implement a civil registry of births and deaths in the War of the Wasps. Sociologist Mara Loveman stressed that this revolt was "most intense in a handful of settlements in the sugar-producing regions of Pernambuco." Rioters charged that the registry would be used to enslave free men and women, and others feared they could not baptize their infants without a state certificate. These rumors reflected the free poor's apprehensions about the threat of category drift and the sanctity of marriage. Pernambuco's governor sent army units to the town of Pau d'Alho to quell unrest, called up one thousand guardsmen, and enlisted Capuchin monks to restore peace. Parliament soon rescinded the law, and protests faded.[55]

Provinces had formed militarized police forces in the 1830s to prevent this type of unrest, but the beat cop's poor pay and military discipline, often including batch-living in barracks, only attracted men of humble means. Underemployed men were abundant, but police ranks failed to fill to budgeted levels. In 1871, Pernambuco's legislature budgeted for 800 policemen but only mustered 672.[56] Of these, 83 were trainees ready for duty; one had been granted leave, 34 were ill, 15 were jailed awaiting trial, 16 had been convicted of crimes and jailed, 409 were assigned to posts, 100 worked in diverse government offices, and 14 were on special assignments. The number of police available for duty was closer to 600. In 1872, Brazil's first census counted 541,539 Pernambucan residents, about 805 for each policeman. Poor pay and training limited the quality of police work. Pernambuco's governor griped in 1871: "Among us the prevention of crimes, the special mission of the police, is almost null and the pursuit of criminals is ineffective. . . . Police authorities, especially in the interior, either do not show signs of life in the exercise of their jobs or they convert themselves into forces of oppression for political ends."[57] The potential to use police authority to extort bribes or work as muscle for bosses attracted men who did not reflect well on the institution.

As police forces emerged, army personnel continued to work as police auxiliaries. While enlisted police volunteered, officials summarily pressed most army regulars for vagrancy, suspected criminal activity, abandoning their wives, or seducing young women with marriage promises. For many offenses, officials were more likely to press poor free men than prosecute them. Thus, lawbreakers became law enforcers. Married men's legal exemption from impressment indicated the power legislators believed the jealous institution had for public order. Impressment made an example of some poor married men who shirked their patriarchal duties, and protected dutiful husbands who provided for and protected their wives, dependents, and themselves from the sexual aggressions of other men. Pressing a responsible married man would be immoral because it removed the natural protector from the home and exposed his dependents to dishonor. Ideally, impressment targeted men outside the jealous institution's gravitation pull: orphans, seducers, vagabonds, criminals, prodigal husbands, "sodomites," and those who "disrespect families." Batch-living barracks, like brothels, stood at the opposite end of an imagined spectrum of values represented by the honorable family home.[58]

João Ignacio Marques's case shows how police relied on impressment. The police chief, in response to queries from Marques's mother, asked the delegate of the Recife borough of Beberibe about Marques's whereabouts. The delegate responded that he had pressed Marques into the army "because he had encountered him and others on a number of occasions in a house that served as a place for extravagant pastimes (heavy drinking, sambas [singing, drumming, and dancing], and [unspecified] immoralities)." The police captured Marques and a number of other young men, including a "number of slaves whose masters reclaimed them." They did not press slaves because they were owned by men of means, but for the free men: "In view of their comportment, João and his companions who besides being vagrants are insubordinate and incorrigible and for this reason, I remitted them to serve in the army where they will be corrected."[59] Poor men who ended up in a recruit depository could be freed if a wealthy patron paid for a pecuniary exemption. The law also exempted men who held a National Guard post or who actively plied a variety of skilled trades. Most Brazilians regarded guardsmen as part of the "protected" poor, while those vulnerable to impressment were "unprotected." Bosses sought out guard officerships to name clients to its ranks to protect them from impressment. Even so, many poor guardsmen found their duties oppressive and groused that wealthier peers avoided onerous duties, like escorting convicts, that they could not evade.[60]

Floggings, roll calls, mobility restrictions, batch living, low pay, and public displays of subordination made army enlisted life too close to slave status to attract most poor free men. Soldiering's status was so low that most attempts to use a color bar to exclude or segregate men in army ranks were abandoned after the 1830s. Like convicts, most soldiers were of mixed race, and they served with minorities of whites, blacks, ex-slaves, and indigenous men. Whiteness provided no exemption from impressment, but the disproportionately low number of white troops indicates that they were more likely to be part of the protected poor.[61]

Pernambuco's army troops doubled the number of police, and army detachments commonly performed police duties in rural towns. In 1881, the governor carped that his army garrisons were depleted because detachments served in Victória (1 officer, 30 troops), Tacaratu (2 officers, 38 troops), and Alagoas (4 officers, 92 troops). The distribution of units shifted according to conditions, but like the police, army units had fewer men than budgets anticipated. In 1875, Pernambuco had 1,046 army troops, but regiments were short 705 men.[62]

The lack of police led Pernambucan officials to grudgingly rely on the army and National Guard. The House of Detention's director carped in 1875 that the army soldiers who served as prison guards abandoned their posts to fight one another and openly drank alcohol. He added, "The indiscipline that has contaminated our army corps is notorious."[63] Police chiefs griped that they could not spare police or find army or guard escorts to take defendants to juries seated in rural towns.[64] Brazil's largest military mobilization tested the capacity and, to an unprecedented degree, merged the multiple institutions employed in penal justice.

THE WAR OF THE TRIPLE ALLIANCE (1864–1870) AND THE EMPIRE'S FINAL DECADES

Army engineer Henrique Pedro Carlos de Beaurepaire Rohan became war minister in 1864 just before war broke out. In 1865, he published a report on Fernando de Noronha with its first regulations. Beaurepaire Rohan's assignment to reform Brazil's largest penal colony before assuming his War Ministry portfolio was far from the only connection between the island and the distant war effort. Wartime mobilization catalyzed category drift on the home front, and as such, it threatened to blur distinctions between the protected and unprotected free poor. In its desperation to mobilize men to the front, the state resorted to recruiting slaves and convicts as soldiers. The War of the Triple Alliance began when Brazilian machinations in Uruguay unseated a political faction with strong ties to Paraguay. Paraguay's dictator Francisco Solano Lopez feared this threatened the river routes that gave his landlocked nation access to oceanic trade. Lopez ordered his armies to invade Brazil, and in the process violated Argentine territory. This led Brazil and Argentina, traditional rivals, to ally with the pro-Brazilian Uruguayan government. Brazilians bore the brunt of the campaign, however, because internal political turmoil limited its allies' abilities to mobilize men to a distant front.[65]

While the Brazilian army's officers came largely from middle-income families, its enlisted ranks came from what most considered the dregs of society. Wartime manpower needs and political disputes between local and national leaders led those charged with recruitment to ignore treasured thresholds of status that normally protected poor men from coercive recruitment.[66] The need for manpower was so great that in the war's second year Parliament approved the manumission of slaves who served as frontline soldiers. The state encouraged patriots to donate bondsmen, and bought slaves at market prices.[67] It also granted pardons to convicts who had served the balance of their sentences on the condition that they fight as soldiers at the front. On Fernando de Noronha, military convict Costódio José de Azevedo volunteered. The commander wrote that Azevedo had exhibited exemplary behavior, demonstrated enthusiasm to return to the army, and was a "young man and robust."[68] In 1867, a commander reported that 203 convicts had been granted pardons to fight, which forced him to reorganize his work companies.[69] Perhaps no other policy demonstrates the state's desperation for manpower.[70] The government also called up national guardsmen and police for army service. Even though many did not present themselves for duty, more than thirty thousand guardsmen and five thousand policemen became army soldiers.

War mobilization aggravated divisions at home as imperial agents pressed men whom local bosses usually protected from impressment. Popular discontent peaked in 1868 when Pedro dissolved his liberal Council of State to name a conservative cabinet. The Duke of Caxias, who commanded Brazil's troops in Paraguay and was also a conservative senator, demanded that Pedro dissolve the liberal government because their intrigues hampered his conduct of the war. He threatened to resign. Fearing Caxias's departure could break the morale for an unpopular war, Pedro acceded. Conservatives used their control of the Council of State to manipulate elections and bring their cronies to power in Rio de Janeiro and the provinces. Part of the election strategy involved the use and threat of impressment to cow voters. Conservative and liberal incumbents both used impressment to their political advantage, but the relative dominance of conservative governments made liberals more regular, if hypocritical, critics of it.[71] Liberals answered conservative victories with sweeping reform proposals such as slavery's gradual abolition. Radical liberals formed the Republican Party in 1870, and their platform pointedly decried violations of "individual freedom" when men are "subjected to arrest, to impressment, to the national guard" and are thus "deprived the right of habeas corpus." War mobilization intensified postwar partisanship and demonstrated the links between electoral politics, military recruitment, and the institutions responsible for penal justice.[72]

War's end did not bring Brazilians closer together even though men from every province joined one another to fight a common foreign foe. Parliament, despite partisanship, embarked on a spate of reformism. Pedro delivered on his cabinet's 1866 promise to French intellectuals when Parliament passed the 1871 Free Womb Law, which freed children born to slave women, although children would continue to serve their mother's owner until they reached adulthood.[73]

Parliament then passed the 1874 Recruitment Law to replace military impressment with a limited conscription lottery. In many provinces, angry crowds attacked military enrollment boards and destroyed their lists. In Pernambuco, the 1874 Recruitment Law's passage contributed to the 1874 Quebra Quilos (Kilo-Breaking) Revolt, which protested Parliament's imposition of metric weights and measures. Locals accused Jesuit clergy of stirring up hillbillies to protest state reforms because of the Religious Question (1872–1875), a dispute between the Vatican and the emperor over the conviction of bishops who excommunicated members of Masonic lodges. For numerous reasons large groups invaded rural towns where they smashed scales and destroyed public records. Police, National Guard, and imperial army troops coordinated to restore order. The courts tried a few leaders of the revolt and punished others with impressment.[74]

In 1875, a police delegate in rural Buique, Pernambuco, commented that the 1874 Recruitment Law outraged Quebra Quilo rioters. On July 1, 1875, Buique officials posted edicts convoking men to enroll for the draft. Three days later "an individual named Ponciano Antunes Gomes, armed with a knife and a shotgun, went to the Church . . . with the intent of destroying the draft enrollment edict, but because he was illiterate, he destroyed the wrong ones." The delegate wrote that Ponciano had led the local Quebra Quilos disturbances of December 19, 1874, but he enjoyed the protection of "judicial authorities," who used writs of habeas corpus to free him. He added that the "protection Ponciano enjoys . . . [is] because he supposedly is an influential individual among diverse relatives of the common people when all he is really is a proletarian and a sot." Meanwhile, the local opposition boss, "Colonel Thomaz d'Aquino Cavalcante, received on his farm whoever sought him out . . . he harbors thieves, criminals, and kilo breaking rebels."[75] Like the 1852 revolt against the civil registry, protestors worried lists would be used to enslave free men, the last step in category drift. Whether this belief was literal or figurative, the state repeatedly failed to enroll enough men, which rendered the Recruitment Law a dead letter.

The same police delegate noted another factor that "provoked" rumors: "News via telegram arrived that the House of Deputies debated a law to require civil marriage, a fact that would have gone unnoticed . . . if it were not for malicious individuals [who used this information] to stir up the ignorant hillbillies that unfortunately constitute the majority of this jurisdiction."[76] Fears that civil marriage threatened the legitimacy of Church-sanctioned nuptials marked other regional revolts and reveal marriage's significance as a marker of status. A legitimate marriage had exempted men from military impressment, but the Recruitment Law no longer recognized this exemption. This threatened formerly protected men with a new vulnerability to category drift. Rumors also suggested that civil marriage put the legitimacy of Church nuptials in question along with the honor of wives, the legitimacy of children, and their standing with inheritance law.[77]

A separate reform hampered efforts to respond to the Quebra Quilos Revolt: the 1873 National Guard reform. This measure largely decommissioned the guard from police work, and it evoked a worried editorial in Recife that it would encourage crime and disorder.[78] As National Guard duty required less of its members, it became a more popular haven for those seeking to avoid peacetime impressment. National Guard units were called up in emergencies such as the Quebra Quilos Revolt and the Great Drought 1877–1879, but their effectiveness was diminished. In 1871, Pernambuco had 30,809 active guardsmen and 5,419 in the reserve,[79] but most of their battalions became paper tigers after 1873. Olinda's National Guard regiment donated its war material to the army and closed its deposit in 1874.[80] Vila Bela's public prosecutor reported:

> I would like your Excellency to know the poor state in which this jurisdiction finds itself after the National Guard detachment, the only force that more or less guaranteed the security and tranquility of, not only the authorities, but of the inhabitants, was disbanded. . . . After its dissolution a great confluence of criminals have appeared that number forty or more and the local authorities can do nothing because they do not have

a force they can trust. . . . The small force available is composed of four policemen that guard the jail and they cannot simultaneously pursue and capture criminals.[81]

The National Guard's reform prompted provincial legislators to reorganize Pernambuco's police. They reduced the militarized police's budgeted force from eight hundred to five hundred, and created the local guard in the interior and the civic guard in Recife with a combined budgeted force of nine hundred men. Like the army and the militarized police, the local and civic guard's ranks never filled to budgeted levels and they quickly earned a bad reputation.[82] A delegate in Panelas, Pernambuco, quipped: "not to speak of the infamous local guard where this village's best thieves nest."[83] Another delegate from Itambé complained that local guard soldiers refused to obey orders: "The men of the local guard ordinarily are men of the lowest social class who take on the job to gain a meager salary they would not otherwise earn. This rule has few exceptions." He suggested that discipline might improve if officials punished disobedient local guards with military impressment.[84] The police chief reported the next month that two men had been expelled from the local guard in Itambé and Nazareth and pressed into the army.[85] While Recife's civic guard survived until 1889, the province abrogated the discredited local guard in 1878.[86]

The National Guard's retreat from police work and the local guard's abrogation made Pernambuco's police turn to the army. A familiar refrain comes from 1876: "For the convenience of police service and to guarantee individual security and the protection of private property in the first and second districts of São José, (Recife) I ask your Excellency to order six army soldiers to serve each police subdelegate every day at 6:00 PM for patrol work until midnight."[87] The use of army troops for police work became so common in the northeast that the War Ministry complained that it was detrimental to troops' training and discipline.[88]

Police, national guardsmen, local guards, and army regulars sometimes fomented the disorder they were to prevent. In 1878, a delegate reported that seventeen army soldiers escorting ten convicts to Recife refused to obey commands to board a train because their superiors refused to pay for the tickets of their wives and consensual lovers (*amazias*) who accompanied them. The soldiers then went on a drunk and fired their weapons in the air threatening "anyone and everyone." Later they calmed down and order was restored. The troops rioted to defend their patriarchal right to travel with their wives and lovers. Officers often paid for their men's partners to travel with them on detachments and campaigns where they were camp followers. In this instance, their refusal to do so led their men to mutiny.[89]

Authorities triangulated between the National Guard, police, and army, and there were many tugs-of-war over their deployment. These institutions cooperated, but at times, they saw one another as competitors, or worse, as their rival's mercenaries. A captain who led an army detachment to hunt bandits near Águas Belas reported in 1878: "I have engaged in continual patrols to capture criminals but I have not been able to succeed because of the protection that favors the following criminals: João de Barros, Antonio de Barros, Amancio de Barros, José Pesqueira, and others who enjoy the protection of the local police subdelegate Luiz Gonzaga and other members of the Liberal Party." Gonzaga insulted the captain, "saying that all of them had been bought to persecute and arrest the Barros family . . . otherwise they would not be working so hard to catch the Barros brothers."[90] The press too commonly reported the politicization of penal justice. In 1877, a liberal newspaper explained that in the rural town of Cabrobó, "a group of thieves captained by Manoel Severino, known as Manoel Preto [black Manoel], have plagued the farms of Liberals with the protection of the Conservative police of the locale."[91]

When prosecutors charged defendants, the partisan wheels of justice moved slowly. An 1872 cartoon showed tables with the names of different courts. Stacks of papers labeled trial records are piled on the tables with a rock on each, and behind the table petitions are tacked to the wall. A poem interpreted the cartoon: "In the tribunals of the city; very little justice makes progress; On each table a trial; on each trial a rock. As the sad court documents; rest days, months, years; crushed by the rocks; that the tyrants put on them. The poor ones who tire; their legs walking back and forth; but the judges out of laziness; do not dispatch their cases; while the defendants are put in difficult circumstances; in jail among misfortune."[92] The poem captured popular frustrations with inefficient and unjust courts.

Repeated crises swamped Pernambuco's judiciary, police, and prisons. The Great Drought exacerbated crime as thousands of refugees from the desiccated backlands fled to Pernambuco's humid coasts, where the state clustered relief efforts. The drought also afflicted Fernando de Noronha, where scarcity led many convicts to send their wives and family to the mainland. Rampant banditry accompanied drought, and police found it difficult to arrest so many wrongdoers. In Águas Belas in 1878: "Criminals publicly roam this entire district without the least scruples, boasting of their deeds, to the point that some audaciously live in this town. . . . The protection [that these criminals enjoy] is as scandalous as one can imagine. Robberies continue at a large scale under the protection of both political parties, if you arrest thieves of the Liberal Party they are freed by local authorities, if you jail thieves linked to the Conservative Party they are freed by the District Judge, and thus I can do nothing."[93] Brazil's northeast became synonymous with banditry as police, soldiers, and civilian volunteers chased bandits whose leaders included Antônio Grande (Big Tony), Adolfo Rosa Meia Noite (Midnight Adolfo Rosa), and Cezário. Some gangs were so large that officials relied on posses to chase them. In 1878, Gameleira's subdelegate reported an unusually large posse of 252 civilians who "sought to chase down the criminals who had congregated nearby."[94]

Despite the poor reputations of police, National Guard, and army troops, they sometimes did get their men. In 1875, officials from Águas Belas reported that eight army soldiers captured Cezário and escorted him to the House of Detention. A year earlier, São Bento's delegate reported that Cezário had plagued his district with his band of sixty assassins who continually "deflowered" young women, murdered, and robbed.[95] Some bandits ended up on Fernando de Noronha.

Once arrested, authorities struggled to find space to hold defendants and convicts. Law required provinces to construct penitentiaries to better segregate convicts from society. Instead of performing public works in fetters, the new sentence of prison at labor would ideally be carried out within penitentiaries. Four provinces (São Paulo, Bahia, Rio Grande do Sul, and Pernambuco) and the capital district built new penitentiaries conforming in some respects to the British penal reformer Jeremy Bentham's panopticon design. Pernambuco's House of Detention was inaugurated in 1855 and its construction concluded in 1867. None of these penitentiaries, however, consistently provided work for inmates or other basic tenets of modern penology such as segregation by gender, age, and severity of crime. The large size of Brazil's nonwhite population and lack of prison capacity made segregation on the basis of civil condition, color, and even gender difficult.[96]

Most municipal jails warehoused prisoners in converted residences. In 1881, Pernambuco's police chief noted that Recife's House of Detention and Brejo's jail were the only prisons that "more or less provided security and a healthy environment."[97] Brejo's jail had only three cells: one for men, another for women, and a third for military recruits and deserters.[98] Others were much more precarious. The police in Barreiros reported: "The house that serves as a prison offers no security because of its poor condition . . . [and because] there are only five policemen to serve . . . at night only

one can serve as a prison guard; the others rest from the toil of their onerous duties. . . . The prisoners can easily escape because one sentinel cannot
contain so many prisoners."[99] Pau d'Alho's police observed that only a rope
separated male and female prisoners, and the lack of slop jars and a busted
drainpipe made it so fetid that the guards refrained from entering it.[100]

Given municipal jails' lack of security, officials sent most convicts and
those awaiting trial to Recife's House of Detention. The coordination of escorts for defendants brought from Recife was cumbersome because most
towns only sat juries for two weeks each year. Pernambuco's governors used
Fernando de Noronha as an escape valve for their penitentiary. Though
much smaller than French and British penal colonies, the island's convict
numbers exceeded the intended capacity of all of Brazil's new penitentiaries
combined by 1870.[101] Though Pernambuco's jails were underfunded and un-
sanitary, there continued to be interest in prison reform. The *Diário de Pernambuco*, for example, translated a lengthy series on European prisons.[102]
This interest, however, did not translate into real reform.

One way to gauge police work is official data. Police likely manipulated
data, but even so, it provides insight into enforcement (see appendix, table A1).
Homicide, attempted homicide, and physical assaults account for nearly
three-fifths of reported crime from 1870 to 1875, whereas petty theft, grand
larceny, and attempted robbery represent about one-fifth. Offenses against
public morality constituted almost 8 percent of crimes, followed by bank-
ruptcy, prison breaks, resisting arrest, illegal weapon possession, and infanticide. All other crimes were less than 1 percent. Clearly, violent crime
preoccupied the police and courts more than other offenses. A rare 1874
table recorded crimes and arrests in Pernambuco (see table A2). The politicized nature of policing meant that many crimes went unreported, but
the table suggests that police had a better than 50 percent apprehension
rate. Almost all arrests, however, were of criminals caught in the act; 178
of 441 criminals remained at large, and police only captured thirty-three
suspects after their crime's commission. If the police did not catch a subject
red handed, they were unlikely to be arrested. The highest arrest rate was for
petty theft, which suggests that it only turned up in the record when police
apprehended someone for it.

Uprisings, drought, and banditry clogged Pernambuco's jails in the 1870s.
An 1875 report acknowledged: "In the House of Detention, there are not
only the criminals of Recife and those awaiting trial in our populous capital,
but those from all parts of the province, and even the empire, that await
to be sent to Fernando de Noronha. This brings a great agglomeration of

prisoners that are held in cells in much larger numbers than they should comport."[103] The colony's population reached its apex in the 1870s because of limited mainland prison capacity and Pedro's commutations of capital sentences. The emperor began to fully exercise his powers in the 1850s, and his clemency benefitted mostly convict bondsmen. As a result, more slave convicts appeared in Fernando de Noronha. Pedro also opposed slavery, but slavery's abolition required Parliament to act, and it had far too many representatives who supported bondage.[104] In 1876, the last convict legally executed went to the gallows; thereafter, Pedro commuted all death sentences. It was in this context that Pedro's critics propagated the image of Fernando de Noronha as ocean resort for convicts.[105] In 1877, Parliament transferred the colony's administration to the Justice Ministry in what one minister referred to as a "laconic disposition that was only explicit in decreeing the transfer."[106] Since civil courts sentenced more than four in five convicts in the colony, its prisoners more closely fit the Justice Ministry's jurisdiction.[107]

During the 1880s, the abolitionist movement's popularity grew. In 1884, the provinces of Ceará and Amazonas abolished slavery. Then in 1885 Parliament passed the Sexagenarian Law that freed some eighteen thousand elderly slaves. Later the same year, Parliament banned public authorities from flogging slaves. Ultimately, reforms, abolitionist agitation, and the actions of slaves themselves undermined plantation labor discipline to such an extent that it led some of slavery's staunchest supporters to call for abolition. On May 13, 1888, Parliament passed the Golden Law that abolished slavery and Princess Isabel signed it in her father's stead. Fernando de Noronha's officials greeted the news of abolition with patriotic elocutions praising the fatherland and its enlightened monarch.[108]

The Golden Law alienated the last pillar of support for Brazil's constitutional monarchy: slaveowners. The Religious Question had distanced elements of the Catholic Church. Many army officers turned to republicanism because of their disappointment with efforts to modernize the military. An emergent urban middle class criticized the lack of public services and blamed the dominance of rural political bosses in Parliament. This estrangement left the monarchy vulnerable.[109]

THE EARLY FIRST REPUBLIC

Influential army officers in Rio de Janeiro led the bloodless republican coup on November 15, 1889, that sent Pedro into exile after a half-century of rule.[110] The coup caught many by surprise, but the lack of opposition to it indicates how hollow support for the monarchy had grown. Even on isolated Fernando de Noronha the new government was hailed. The republican junta dispatched a new officer to command the colony within a month of the coup. Given the distances and difficulties of transportation, the speed with which the regime sent a trusted official to secure the colony indicates their sense of its strategic importance. The new government soon promulgated a federalist 1890 Constitution that established classic liberal reforms like the separation of Church and state, a civil registry, and civil marriage. The 1890 Penal Code abrogated the death penalty and the use of corporal punishments against convicts, and established more uniform sentences for crimes, with a limit of thirty years imprisonment for the most heinous crimes. Those convicts who had been sentenced to life imprisonment or lengthy temporary sentences petitioned for their release, if they had served the requisite number of years according to new sentencing guidelines. Many won their freedom, which demonstrates that most convicts did not see the island as paradise.

Republicans temporarily reshaped Fernando de Noronha's population when they exiled more than one hundred *capoeiras* (Afro-Brazilian martial artists) from Rio de Janeiro. Some capoeira ruffians had provided paramilitary services for the Conservative Party, and had disrupted Republican Party rallies. The new government was determined to break them. This policy indicates that the republic's leaders believed that Fernando de Noronha remained a place to intimidate individuals who were a danger to the new regime.[111] Abolition had swept aside the controversy over slaves escaping the death penalty, and the previous generation's depictions of Fernando de Noronha as an ocean resort for criminals faded.

In 1894, Parliament ordered the island's closure as a national prison. By 1897, Pernambuco's governor reported that only fifty civil convicts from other states remained in the colony, but it would not be possible to remove the 210 civil convicts from Pernambuco and 112 military convicts because of the House of Detention's overcrowdedness.[112] In 1898, a naval mission returned the last convicts from other states to their respective jurisdictions.[113] Pernambuco's governor observed in 1899, "A new chapter [opened] in the colony, and it is destined to receive, after regularly tried and sentenced, individuals convicted of vagabondage and capoeira." In 1900, four hundred convicts, sentenced in Pernambucan courts, lived in the colony guarded by thirty army soldiers and two officers.[114]

Brazil's politicians established a modern penal justice system to signal a break with the colonial order and to lend legitimacy to its central government at home and abroad. They hoped that a modern penal justice system would contribute to a national consensus that would win over those who, like Ferreira Portugal, favored provincial loyalties. In practice, the interconnected mainland institutions of penal justice were highly politicized and poorly funded, and often employed men whom many considered criminal. Partisans employed these institutions for political ends that demonstrate the links between elections, policing, military impressment, and prisons. These institutions engendered little faith from most Brazilians, especially those who suffered the abuses of corrupt agents of law enforcement. This chapter zoomed out to consider Fernando de Noronha's role in broader Brazilian history and penal justice, a necessary narrative frame that often took us far from the island's environs. The next, however, returns to a tight focus on the penal colony to examine significant aspects of everyday life there.

3 FERNANDO DE NORONHA'S "DARK TWINS"
Licit and Illicit Commerce

In *Seeing Like a State*, James Scott analyzes modern projects and institutions that planned communities for generic citizens that could only function because of unplanned-for "dark twins." Thus, the planned city of Brasília only functions because of its unplanned-for satellite cities where most of the laborers essential for its upkeep live. I argue that contraband and licit commerce are the unplanned-for dark twins of prisons and penal colonies. Even though this unplanned commerce was sometimes prohibited, it proved essential to the planned penal colony's everyday functions. Fernando de Noronha is a case study of how and why contraband and other commerce are natural parts of the simplified ecologies of penal colonies and prisons.[1]

As the controversy over the slave Izabel's business dealings with convicts in chapter 1 demonstrates, even rather innocent licit commerce could create entanglements that could embarrass the colony commander. Army officers laid out the city of Remédios, its fortifications, and the imperial farm's fields. They erected structures similar to those used to discipline soldiers: first a barracks, and in 1856, a larger batch-living facility: the *aldeia*. Planners, however, did not anticipate the convict population's growth. Only some four hundred convicts could uncomfortably squeeze into the aldeia, but when convict numbers reached 1,500, officials let more than two-thirds of the convicts live in private homes. Officers frequently expressed their frustration about this unplanned real estate market and other commerce.

A long-term goal of the officers who planned the colony was to *arranchar* all convicts, or to house them in batch-living barracks and feed them from common mess halls. War Minister Beaurepaire Rohan set forth this goal in his 1865 regulations and explicitly called for the closing of all commerce once these barracks and mess kitchens were built. Until then, commerce would have to be tolerated because convicts and other residents relied on it to supplement their meager rations. Why were officers, who had extraordinary authority to plan convicts' lives, unable to arranchar convicts? Most immediately, Parliament never allocated funds to build the infrastructure. It was much cheaper to rely on the convicts' initiatives to house and feed themselves. The practice paralleled those of large plantations where masters allowed privileged slaves to live in unattached homes and to farm provision grounds. Similarly, army officers allowed trusted enlisted men to *desarranchar*, or to live in private homes. Instead of eating in a mess hall, these soldiers received a stipend to buy and prepare their own food. Officers who allowed some trusted convicts to live outside the aldeia built on mainland precedents to discipline mostly male laborers.

Because of these living arrangements, Brazilian and foreign visitors to Fernando de Noronha bemoaned that all inhabitants lived in a corrosive moral environment. As a Justice Ministry official reported, "There [Fernando de Noronha] military and civilian convicts, free men and slaves, men sentenced to life imprisonment and men condemned to five, two, and even one year of simple imprisonment, live in complete promiscuity."[2] Similarly, the American geologist Orville Derby deplored, "The indiscriminate and unrestrained association of criminals of every degree with each other, with the undisciplined and insubordinate soldiery with abandoned women and with innocent children makes the penal station of Fernando de Noronha a disgrace not alone to the Brazilian nation but to the world."[3] Modern penology rebuked such integration: penitentiaries should segregate prisoners by age, gender, severity of crime, and other factors, not to mention wall off criminals from society. The island's geography obviated the need for walls for all but disorderly convicts, but its size meant that all lived cheek by jowl. Work, leisure, and special occasions brought convicts (civil and military, slave and free), civil servants, officers, soldiers, vendors, unattached residents, and their families together, despite sporadic efforts to segregate them. The colony reflected a Brazilian preference for the integration of individuals of various statuses and colors in institutions that incorporated the intractable poor.

The colony also had a variety of missions that could undercut one another. Was it a center for punishment, exile, production, rehabilitation, and colonization or a place to isolate victims of epidemic diseases? Authorities disputed the priority of these missions. One way to view the colony is as a large state-owned company that employed a collage of coercive and free labor forms. The imperial farm's organization resembles those of mainland plantations and workshops, but most of its workers were convicts and its managers were not farmers, merchants, or wardens, but army officers and civil servants. Some officers and civil servants had experience with agriculture, but these were not their primary professions.

Convicts far outnumbered the colony's garrison, so security remained the highest priority. Even so, commanders professed belief in rehabilitation. As one wrote in 1884: "It is generally accepted by the most serious [penologists] that the moral regeneration of the condemned must be the first penal condition, the most plausible interpretation of the law."[4] Staff and other inhabitants, however, often pursued their own interests to the detriment of the colony's missions, and competition over licit and contraband commerce could pit networks of patronage emanating from the staff to convicts against one another. The dark twins promoted both cooperation and conflict. Even though security was paramount, production remained at the heart of the colony's reason for being, and work shaped most inhabitants' lives. This chapter explores the colony's everyday life through interrelated questions: What did the colony produce? How did labor shape social life and relationships? What combinations of incentives and sanctions did officials use to motivate and discipline convict workers? What strategies did convicts pursue to improve their conditions?

THE WORKING LIVES OF CONVICT LABORERS

Convict laborers worked in army-style companies mostly directed by convict sergeants.[5] The commanders' power to nominate and dismiss convicts from privileged posts was a means to instill loyalty and obtain cooperation from them. Like mainland political bosses who used patronage to attract and mobilize free poor clients, commanders used similar strategies with convicts. The organization of labor and the incentives that officials offered to convicts uncover key dimensions of the colony's social hierarchies.

The number of convict labor companies varied over time, but by the 1860s, commanders settled on fifteen. In 1879, the 14th Company was the largest, with 160 convicts, and the smallest was the 15th, with 89, but most had a little over one hundred. Convicts who worked in agriculture numbered 808; 105 worked in manufacturing and construction; 59, office work; 189, domestic service; 16 were musicians; and 238 were night watchmen and police. An inspector estimated that 209 convicts had been relieved from work because they suffered from poor health or because they were "protected."[6] A foreign visitor affirmed this protection market in 1881: "The most refractory of the convicts are confined en masse in a large building for the purpose [the aldeia], but for the most part they have the liberty of the island with the obligation of responding to roll call and of working a part of each day if they have not the ability of escaping by favors [empenhos] from this last requirement."[7] The term "favors" and "protected" hints that corruption influenced the allotment of some labor exemptions.

Most convict fieldworkers performed tasks on a gang labor basis. They tended to fields dedicated to manioc, cotton, tobacco, and corn, and a few other crops. Work increased during planting and harvest seasons, but accounts suggest that convict workers spent far less time in the fields than mainland workers. Conversely, convict cobblers followed a task-based system and could end their workday after completing a quota. Documentation reveals little about the everyday tasks that convict laborers performed. For officials, the wielding of hoes and machetes to plant, weed, and harvest must have seemed too banal for words. An 1885 report listed the convicts who served in different companies and their salaries. Nine slave convicts worked in the night watchmen company, and six others served in the skilled workers company. Three slaves were stonemasons, and three others were carpenters. An explanatory note revealed that slave convicts did not receive the extra salary for performing skilled labor that free convicts did, but they did earn the same basic salary of plebeian convict workers.[8] In this rather small but significant way, officials discriminated against skilled slave convicts. If slave convicts had skills, commanders took advantage of them, and they even trusted some to serve in security capacities. Better yet, their skilled labor came at no additional cost to colony ledgers.

Periodic reorganizations of work companies occurred when convict populations fluctuated. In 1870, the convict population was reduced to 1,141 because scores went to fight in Paraguay. The commander observed that companies one through five cultivated exclusively corn and manioc whose production "principally benefitted the colony's employees and commercial houses rather than the nation." He admitted that corruption siphoned off imperial farm produce, but he did not explain how. He estimated that only 691 of the 1,141 convicts, a little more than 60 percent, labored and the rest were "consumers of the state's largess," an echo of Ferreira Portugal's 1797 critique.[9] Convict companies seven through ten included 505 men (nearly half of the convicts) who were "invalids and less capable of heavy labor due to physical impediments, advanced age, and the weakness of their

FIG 3.1 Contemporary photograph of Fernando de Noronha's central plains, where the fields of the imperial farm were once situated. Photograph by Celso Kuwajima, 2010.

complexion." The latter phrase reflected the belief that white workers were unsuited for heavy labor in the tropics. This is the only case I found where a commander explicitly suggested that color influenced convict work designations. Matriculation records do not specify a convict's work company, so it is not possible to verify the extent to which color influenced work assignments. I encountered this phrase before in a 1904 courts martial defense of a private who deserted an Amazon telegraph posthole crew. He protested that his superiors beat him when he did not complete his quota, which was impossible for him to fulfill in a torrid climate due to his weakness of complexion. On the one hand, the phrase averred racial hierarchy because it sustained that men of color were "naturally" suited for tropical labor, but on the other, it portrayed whiteness as a disability that defied social Darwinist ideas of European superiority.[10]

Another commander addressed color and inequality in 1871 when he groused about forgery convicts' privileges: "Justice and universal reason loudly proclaim the principle that the law should be equal for all. A principle literally consecrated in our Constitution and the code by which the rich and the poor, the man of the king's court and the provincial, the white and the black find themselves leveled by law."[11] Since most forgers were European, they presumably suffered from weakness of complexion. Despite complaints, counterfeiters dominated privileged posts. As an inspector observed in 1880, "They [counterfeiters] are employed as scriveners in diverse administrative offices and earn more than a regular convict. They are preferred for positions of confidence, such as sergeants, corporals, and nurses . . . none of the counterfeiters did fieldwork when I visited the presidio."[12] This practice mirrored army promotions where literate privates became noncommissioned officers because they could do paperwork and read written orders.[13] These and other comments show that one's color and education influenced work assignments. References to convicts themselves using racial slurs are also rare. An exception occurred in 1850 during a "prison riot" in which a convict who stabbed a cellmate proclaimed to witnesses, "I fixed the nigger!" (*Está arranjado o negro!*)[14] These cases suggest that convicts and officials remained conscious of color, nationality, and slave status despite the flowery language of equality that perfumed some correspondence.

Many convicts desired to work as domestics, an ambition of many field slaves. As a domestic, many tasks were carried out indoors shielded from the blazing sun, blustering winds, and stinging rains. In addition, domestic work gave convicts a chance to develop a relationship with influential officials who could protect them. Administrators selected their domestics from convicts who had specific skills that they desired: cooks, fishermen, launderers, and so on. Since many officers and employees lived with their families, they also considered the convict's trustworthiness. Convict domestics did not receive additional salaries, but officials expected their employers to clothe and feed their charges. Again the desirability of this work could change if one worked under an abusive boss, and the privacy of domestics who worked and sometimes lived in their employers' homes was diminished.[15] For many, however, the benefits of domestic work outweighed the risks. Since not all convicts could be encompassed in privileged networks, some developed parallel networks in gangs to promote their interests and protect themselves.

A benefit that convicts derived from close relationships with commanders was a recommendation for a pardon or commutation. One supported convict sergeant Attilio Francisco Simonelli's 1885 petition: "The supplicant has an excellent record of conduct in the colony. He has performed well in a number of posts adequate to his position and during the recent seditious movements he was always on the side of the authorities, helping the police imprison insurrectionaries."[16] A convict's loyal service could be an avenue to freedom, even for those, like Simonelli, condemned to perpetual galleys. Similarly, Commander Francisco Joaquim Pereira Lobo recommended convict Vicente d'Assis Tavares's petition. Assis allegedly led the 1885 seditious plot Simonelli helped to suppress, but in 1882, the commander extolled Assis and related his history of category drift. A jury in Itambé, Pernambuco, sentenced the police corporal Assis to a temporary sentence on December 13, 1881, because he gravely wounded the thief Manoel Antônio Diniz, whom he had been ordered to arrest. An outbreak of beri beri in Recife's House of Detention led to Assis's transfer to Fernando de Noronha. Beri beri results from malnutrition, and it indicates the House of Detention's wretched health conditions. After Assis recovered, Pereira Lobo employed Assis in his offices, where "he has demonstrated excellence in the fulfillment of his duties." To support his petition, Pereira Lobo claimed that a number of witnesses from Itambé who "merit faith" attested that Diniz had recovered from the injuries Assis inflicted.[17] Neither Assis nor Simonelli received commutations, but some others did. The histories of these two exceptional convict sergeants reemerge in subsequent chapters.

The salaries of employees and convicts provide another way to explore hierarchy. An 1869 salary list showed that the commander earned 137 times the common convict's pay, whereas privileged convicts could earn up to five times that of most inmates (see appendix, tables A3 and A4). The nominal daily wage for an unskilled free laborer in Pernambuco in 1886 was $500 réis compared to the $140 réis daily wage of most convicts.[18] Table A4 represents an 1886 negotiation between Pernambuco's treasurer and a colony commander over wages for 194 different convict workers who earned higher pay, a little more than 15 percent of convicts at the time. The commander presented a more compact wage scale that benefitted more convicts. The biggest differentials were between the lower salaries he recommended for company sergeants and the higher wages for the night school teacher, master craftsmen, scriveners, and barbers. Free civilians earned more than four times that of a convict doing the same job.

Sergeants and other privileged convicts served at the commander's pleasure. As one wrote in 1872, the sergeant post is "conferred to convicts who comport themselves well as a concession so that sergeants will continue to behave well to conserve the fruits of this favor." Sergeants enjoyed the services of two convict domestics because they are "busy during the day and do not have time to perform tasks like the preparation of meals." He added "the employment of convicts as domestics for other convicts has been common practice in the colony for a long time."[19] The number of domestics assigned to convict sergeants varied over time, but commanders permitted civil servants and officers with families four or even more convict domestics. Regulations also stipulated that convicts who performed extra labor for officers, employees, unattached residents, or other convicts during their leisure time had to be compensated. This allowed convicts to improve their incomes, and according to one commander, he had received "no complaints about the lack of payment of these extra wages."[20] Of course, convicts might have been reluctant to complain about the abuses of more powerful figures in the colony.

The frequent rotation of commanders threatened privileged prisoners. New commanders could dismiss convicts and order those excused from labor to work. In 1879, convict Antônio Maria Teixeira de Mello lodged a complaint when a new commander assigned him to a night-watchman post when he had been exempted from work. The commander dismissed the gripe because "almost the only service this post requires is to reside in a small house where one watches a beach to prevent other convicts from escaping." He admitted that presidio doctors had declared Mello unfit for fieldwork, so, he assigned him a job that did not require it. He explained that Mello was a "quarrelsome personality whose bad conduct in Rio's House of Corrections resulted in his transfer to this presidio."[21] The comment indicates why commanders exempted some convicts from work and how mainland officials selected convicts for exile. What goes unstated is that Mello likely had to move to a home distant from Remédios for his job, which may have been the reason for his complaint.

Administrative reforms could cost nonconvict employees their jobs. In 1880, the nonconvict sergeant Quirino Joaquim Madeira petitioned the governor to reinstate him as a company sergeant. To bolster his petition, Madeira mentioned that he had volunteered to "risk his life" during the Great Drought of 1877 to pilot a sailboat to Recife to get relief supplies. Madeira first volunteered for a similar mission in 1856 when a commander identified him as someone who had come to the presidio to "conduct business." He piloted the boat because he was an experienced seaman (*homem marítimo*).[22] By 1880, Madeira had lived at least some twenty-four years on the island and became one of the few nonconvict company sergeants. The commander supported Madeira's 1880 request noting that he had long served as a sergeant, but his position had been eliminated when the Justice Ministry reorganized work companies. He believed that Madeira would make a good "auxiliary" because he is "a man dedicated to work, knows something about farming, and is a faithful fulfiller of his superiors' orders." That Madeira knew "something about farming" hardly seems a ringing endorsement, but that he was dedicated to work and faithfully fulfilled his superiors' orders mattered. Loyalty and obedience trumped productivity. The commander suggested that if the governor desired, a new work company could be created for Madeira to sergeant because there were an average of 117 convicts per company, a "number quite large for one sergeant to inspect and provide the necessary vigilance."[23] The penciled-in response requested that the provincial treasurer be informed, which illustrates the degree to which the governor's office concerned itself with the minutia of the colony's affairs.

Some reputed Madeira to be the colony's *éminense grise*.[24] The newspaper *O Liberal* singled out Madeira in 1871 as the colony's "potentate" during an investigation of corruption and excessive flogging: "Here it is illustrative to cite testimony about the aforementioned sailor [Madeira], when a new commander, a government commission, or other officials [visited the island] he [Madeira] said: 'They have nothing on me, I will know how to manage them and the next day they will be in my pocket!' And this has come to pass." The testimony implies that Madeira bribed officials to keep his post. The reporter claimed that the testimony made Madeira's influence salient, and he questioned why he had not been brought to Recife to testify.[25] For critics, the employment of a nonconvict sergeant alone was suspicious because he earned a wage equivalent to that of four convict sergeants and one convict corporal. One must take these accusations with a grain of salt, however, because the opposition had an ax to grind against incumbent leaders. The depiction of a nonconvict sergeant as the island's potentate exaggerated his influence. Indeed, if he was so powerful, how did he find himself without a post?

The article went out of its way to describe Madeira as a sailor, which held derogatory connotations. Most of the imperial navy's enlisted ranks were brown and black men pressed into service. Thus, the journalist may have sought to evoke the image of a black or brown former imperial sailor as the colony's boss to shock the sensibilities of his mostly white readers. "Sailor" was also derogatory slang for Portuguese immigrants, and lusophobia was an element of Brazilian nationalism that the Liberal Party consistently invoked. They also referred to Madeira as an *ilheo*, or islander, a term used to describe natives of the Atlantic islands off Portugal's coast. They may have used the term because Madeira was a long-time island resident, but he was not born there. In any case, "sailor" carried negative racial, ethnic, and class connotations. Sailor described Madeira's skills, but the repeated use of this loaded term instead of his name was calculated. Despite the investigation and negative press, Madeira continued to live and work as a sergeant in the colony until the Justice Ministry reorganized him out of a job.

While investigations shed a negative light on colony staff, the word of convicts who testified against them was often discounted. As a Justice Ministry inspector wrote: "I believe that there have been some abuses, some immoderate punishments, but pitiful narrations that the newspapers sometimes publish and that the government receives in the form of denunciations are exaggerated or mendacious; written by convicts themselves, victims of some punishment that they darken to portray as bad as possible, forgetting the horrific facts that frequently spill blood on the island's soil."[26] Exaggerated or not, denunciations could lead to investigations that held authorities accountable.

Not only did convicts and nonconvicts petition for jobs and complain when reassigned, some challenged their commanders. In 1879, a commander wrote that army convict Antônio Joaquim da Costa Cunha conspired with other convicts of poor conduct to disrespect his orders to abolish commerce. They had forged the commander's signature to a letter that requested his resignation. He asked the governor to ignore this "criminal plan" and observed that convicts had hatched similar ploys in the past. More pointedly, he noted that these same conspirators spread rumors that he was the principal reason that debts the administration owed to vendors had not yet been repaid. He concluded: "Similar plots germinated in such perverted and passionate intelligences have found in my administration a strong shield from their acts of disrespect. . . . [They are] convinced that things will not return to the old regime as long as I am commander and they seek by whatever means to force me from my post."[27]

Power relationships between convicts and administrators were asymmetrical, but wily prisoners could pressure and embarrass superiors. Traditionally, officials considered convict storeowners as elements of order because they had been given the commander's permission to do business. But, when Justice Ministry reforms threatened their businesses in 1879, they used their nettlesome influence to undermine officials. As an inspector observed, commanders were wary of powerful convict factions and tolerated irregularities for fear of alienating them: "There were convicts who proclaimed themselves 'enemies' of the penal colony commander or the major da praça, and others declared their loyalty to the administration. Both tried to recruit adherents to their side and were referred to as political parties [partidos] on the island."[28] Here the inspector indicated that some factions identified themselves with the commander and others the major da praça. As subsequent chapters illustrate, tensions between these two officials were common and could divide patronage networks of officers, soldiers, and convicts.

Outsiders were not the only ones who used political metaphors to describe relationships in the colony. In 1885, Commander Pereira Lobo complained about how an investigative committee treated him: "The way things are going in this presidio . . . they hope to introduce the extreme spirit of political parties on this island."[29] Most Brazilians understood mainland law enforcement as a function of partisan politics; so too did colony residents. Commanders wanted trusted convicts in key posts, but unlike most plantation masters and overseers, they served brief tours. In contrast, civilian employees, like Madeira, could serve many years and develop different relationships with convicts and nonconvicts. They could use these relationships to resist the efforts of commanders to change practices that contradicted their interests.

Given the colony's limited incentive system, how productive were the imperial fields and workshops? In 1883, the annual harvest was 7:900 kilos of cotton, 48:374 kilos of corn; 26:800 kilos of corn went to Pernambuco's treasury to be sold, along with 81.5 kilos of tobacco.[30] This data did not indicate the quality of the crops or the prices they fetched, but some of the colony's exports were high in quality. In 1869, a commander bragged about the silver medal he received from the Jury of the National Exposition of Paris for the colony's sea-island cotton. He displayed the prize in his office so that it could be "seen by all the presidio's inhabitants where it will serve as an incentive to those who dedicate themselves to agricultural labor."[31] Beyond crops, the colony also exported boots. In 1876, Pernambuco's governor reported that one hundred convict cobblers had produced 15,434 pairs of boots in a year, enough to shod the entire Brazilian army. Brazilian soldiers, however, often carped about the quality of their footwear.[32] In good years, the colony exported goods, but their value was relatively small compared to the colony's budget. It thus failed to live up to Herbert Spencer's maxim: "If a criminal does not live from his work, he indirectly commits a new crime."[33] A report to Parliament in 1885 clarified that the colony's budget was 108:635$037 réis, and that the value of its exports was 11:037$003 réis. In a good year, production covered about 10 percent of expenditures, but in bad years, it could be much less. An 1877 report noted that the value of the island's production had been only 1:789$306 réis compared to a budget of 107:012$606 réis. Drought limited the colony's harvest in 1877, but exports offset a small fraction of costs.[34] A Brazilian delegate to the American penologist Enoch Wines's 1872 international convention on prisons related Fernando de Noronha's high costs.[35]

One drag on colony production was the cumbersome distribution of rations: tobacco, soap, sugar, and coffee on the fifth and twentieth and dried meat and manioc flour on the fifth, fifteenth, and twenty-fifth of each month. Convicts began to line up for rations at 6:00 AM and the process was not completed until 6:00 PM. One reason Beaurepaire Rohan wanted to build common mess halls was to avoid these four days of lost labor each month. He further noted that the distribution of rations was a security risk because it concentrated the entire convict population in Remédios. Furthermore, he described the warehouse where authorities stored the colony's harvest and dry goods from Recife as "filthy" and lamented that rats and other pests spoiled a large part of the rations.[36]

Why was the colony so unproductive? Some blamed convict laborers. Commander Pereira Lobo, who served five tours of command there, reported in 1885 that he "never observed such repugnance and even acts of insubordination as in this era because the convicts do not want to work in the fields; principally after the idea appeared here among convicts that they should have three days of rest per week! If we add these days to religious and secular holidays, how would we ever complete the work necessary for the good of the different branches of public service and the national treasury?"[37] Convict demands paralleled those the historian Walter Fraga observed in Bahia's Recôncavo in the 1880s and 1890s among freedmen who stayed on the plantations where they had been slaves. Former slaves demanded three days a week or more free from obligations to work for the plantation owner, so they could cultivate their own gardens. Perhaps new mainland labor arrangements influenced ideas of an appropriate convict work week.[38] It would be flip, however, to blame convict fieldworkers for the imperial farms' poor productivity. These workers had little incentive to make the collective farm profitable. It also ignores many other factors that made its upkeep exorbitant: high transportation costs to markets; the lack of agricultural, artisan, and managerial expertise; the island's humidity and pests that complicated the storage of harvests; and the corruption and theft that syphoned off surplus.

The assignment of privileged posts to a minority of trusted convicts gave commanders needed leverage. They promoted some convicts because of their competence, but they considered loyalty and obedience to be of the highest premium. Some trusted convicts partnered with officers and employees to sell contraband and mount other illicit schemes. These enterprises could be facilitated by yet another privilege commanders could grant convicts: the right to open a store.

TROUBLESOME COMMERCE

When the colony was founded, there were few restrictions on commerce. Permission to run a store was a carrot that commanders awarded to a few trusted convicts and other inhabitants, but this commerce could undercut formal lines of institutional hierarchy. To counteract the entangling relationships between merchants, soldiers, convicts, and other residents, restrictions on who could operate stores and what could be sold emerged in the mid-nineteenth century.

In 1819, Captain Joaquim de Souza Murelles reported that a drunken Lieutenant José Vicente de Vargas had publicly insulted his "post and his person" when he referred to the captain as a "tavern keeper" because he brought with him "some items that I ordered to be sold by a clerk, just like all who have come before to govern and command troops on this island." The practice of bringing items to sell on Fernando de Noronha was venerable, and the chance to profit from convict consumers was one of the post's attractions. The lieutenant's retort of "tavern keeper" suggests that the main product the commander sold was alcohol, a practice that presaged the infamous rum corps of Britain's Australian penal colony. The lieutenant's insult implied that it was unseemly for a commander to sell liquor to convicts and soldiers. Or, did he resent competition from the commander for his own grog sales? Commercial competition could create tensions among the colony's inhabitants up and down the social scale.[39]

To diminish such tensions, new regulations emerged to regulate commerce. An 1849 decree prohibited the colony's commander and the major da praça (garrison commander) from selling goods, and a slow process of curbing trade ensued. Still, lower ranking officers, employees, unattached residents, and convicts could operate stores, and thereafter commanders became harsh critics of vendors. An 1850 list of storeowners included the civilian warehouse manager Joaquim Pedro de Lima, the scrivener Antônio Manoel Estevão, the retired lieutenant Manoel Bezerra do Vale, and the retired ensign in charge of construction, Raimundo José de Sousa Lobo. It divulged that storeowners had a convict liberated from fieldwork to labor as their clerk, another plum posting that a commander could bestow on convicts.[40] A second group of vendors were convicts and their family members, and a third were unattached residents who came to the island, as the sailor Madeira did, to do business. An 1858 report catalogued the value of fourteen vendors' stock and identified their associates (see table A5). The goods stocked by the wealthiest storeowners were equivalent to the average price for four young adult slaves in 1858.[41]

A number of convicts' wives ran stores, a fact that confirms that married convicts received favored treatment, and not a few of their husbands were convict sergeants. A number of capitalist convicts were Europeans, which mirrored the dominance of Portuguese retailers on the mainland, and a few amassed small fortunes charging steep prices for goods on credit at usurous interest rates. As an inspector observed in 1879: "There are, finally, the so-called 'capitalists' that conduct transactions with the presidio's administration, to whom they loan money to pay expenses for administrators, employees, and their comrades."[42] The dark-twin businesses of convicts and other residents became linked to the administration and opened the door to corruption. To this day, making change on Fernando de Noronha can be difficult and in the nineteenth century, officials often lacked the appropriate notes and coins to pay convicts, soldiers, and employees. Administrators relied on vendors to help them in these and other instances.

The collection of convict debts created conflicts. In 1867, Commander José Lucas Soares Raposo groaned: "The payment of convicts is made in a highly inconvenient way turning my office into a house of commerce because the vendors who have sold goods to convicts on credit gather at the exit to collect what each one owes them and many times disputes arise when convicts deny the validity of their debts; and when there is a lack of money in the presidio to pay convicts their salaries, which happens often, none of the vendors want to sell goods on credit without guarantees." Because convict pay was often delayed, storeowners demanded and received guarantees that debts would be honored. To avoid the commotion, Raposo ordered sergeants to pay convicts in the vendors' stores, which indicates how they served as commercial go-betweens and directed the business of their men to specific stores. Convict sergeant Simonelli, whose petition for a commutation was analyzed above, climbed to the top of the convict social hierarchy to become a convict sergeant and storeowner. He and others sold goods on credit at 20 percent interest per month.[43] If convicts did not pay, sergeants could use their authority over their men to make their lives miserable. As an inspector revealed: "Vendors abused their positions as sergeants to guarantee their subordinates would become their customers."[44] Commander Raposo lamented that he did not have the means to build a convict mess hall, as Article 35 of Beaurepaire Rohan's regulations mandated, to lessen convicts' dependence on vendors.[45]

Commanders and other consumers also railed about price gouging. In 1852, a commander asked that the governor decree that vendors could make no more than a 50 percent profit on sales and urged him to build dwellings to house vendors to prevent them from building and selling their own homes. The discomfiture with capitalism went beyond whether civilians and convicts had a right to real estate and extended to the relationships that trade developed. Garrison troops and convicts bought goods on credit, and sometimes stole or were falsely accused of stealing from vendors.[46] The consuming desires of convicts and soldiers created an underground economy fed by theft. The relationship between convicts and vendors resembled illicit trade that slaves conducted with country storeowners. The historian Stanley Stein observed that some slaves stole coffee to sell to nearby storeowners in exchange for food, cane brandy, and tobacco.[47]

The social and commercial relationships between vendors and soldiers troubled commanders who urged Pernambuco's commander of arms to replace troops every six months. On the one hand, officers worried that if troops became too familiar with the convicts it could make it difficult for them to carry out their orders to punish them; and on the other hand, they feared that conflicts between soldiers and convicts could spawn disorder. As one explained: "The Ministry of Justice advised on Oct. 19, 1881, that the presidio's army garrison be changed every three months, and it would be very efficacious if this was followed faithfully because it is undeniable that soldiers in this presidio are corrupted by the relationships that they develop with convicts, who are mostly men of bad character, grifters [*velhacos*], and assassins, and moreover the garrison serves to maintain public tranquility and to repress convicts when they need to be punished."[48] These social pollutions between garrison soldiers and convicts were everyday events despite the fact that troops bivouacked in Fort Remédios.[49] On the mainland too, soldiers had conflicts with merchants who sold or refused to sell them goods on credit, a problem exacerbated by chronic delays in the payment of salaries.[50] The rotation of garrison troops was never as regular as desired. In 1873, Commander Sebastião José Basílio Pyrrho pleaded, "There is a great disadvantage to the excessive delay in replacing the army troops stationed here because the soldiers become familiar with the convicts and vendors with whom they live in entire comradeship and this has grave consequences for the discipline and good order that should always reign in a military presidio."[51] An inspector complained about the conviviality of officers and convicts: "Indiscipline is rife among soldiers and even officers. Some that I came to know, including the commissary, went to a birthday party for a *galés* and had dinner in his house, and another I had the displeasure to see in a state of inebriation."[52] Soldiers, officers, and convicts shared food and drink and celebrated together. The chummy relationship between a galés and the commissary officer raised suspicions of corruption.

Like commerce, restrictions on alcohol began at midcentury. In 1850, the commander pleaded with the governor to prohibit all alcohol, even for employees, because disorders and crimes resulted from inebriation. He despaired that convicts did without nutrition to obtain alcohol that ruined their health and made them unfit for work.[53] An 1851 letter reported that inhabitants consumed more than forty *pipas* (420 liter barrels) of cane brandy annually. If one divides this among the 657 inhabitants of the colony in 1852 (including women and children) it averages to 25.5 liters of cane brandy per inhabitant (not to mention other spirited beverages). Contemporary Americans consume an average of 9.4 liters of alcohol per anum; the English, 15.5; and Russians, 27.[54] In 1851, however, Pernambuco's governor ordered all *cachaça* (cane brandy) found in the colony's stores confiscated, and the commander reported: "I made all the vendors aware that from this day forward the sale of aguardiente was prohibited."[55]

Despite prohibitions, alcohol continued to flow into the presidio. In 1852, a commander pontificated: "Since gluttony and libertine behavior [*crápulas*] are the dominant vices among the growing number of soldiers and convicts of the presidio, spirited beverages are the articles most sold and from which vendors take a 900% profit. . . . A bottle of aguardiente costs 100 réis in Pernambuco but vendors ordinarily sell it for 1,000 réis here." He reported that wine sold at a 400 percent profit, but it continued to be sold legally because the colony physician insisted that it was good for one's health. When wine went on legal sale, however, binge drinking left a number of convicts so ill they had to be carried to the infirmary.[56] In 1853, the chaplain accused merchants of using stores as fronts for contraband sales: "Aguardente is the basis of their business that they disembark secretly to sell at more than 2$000 réis a bottle." [57] The same chaplain moaned that even licit goods like dried beef sold at 400 réis a pound in presidio stores, five times its price in Recife.[58] In 1855, a commander issued price controls to "avoid the abuse of excessive prices." Following his predecessor's suggestion, he limited the markup on goods to 50 percent, which would "guarantee a reasonable profit of twenty percent or more," and he shared a list of adjusted prices with Pernambuco's governor.[59]

Antônio Borges da Fonseca, an exiled leader of the Praieira Revolt, became a convict storeowner. One commander complained in 1851 that despite the governor's ban of the sale of cane brandy, Borges da Fonseca "tried everything" to procure it to sell. He then irritated the commander with a letter demanding explanations for the ban referring to "unspecified rights."[60] Vendors often irked commanders. As one complained in 1871: "This vendor [Claudino José Correa] constantly involves himself with everyone in the presidio murmuring and criticizing the acts of this command, and with other inhabitants he provokes and foments discord between employees, officers, and convicts." Further, the vendor considered himself a colony employee because his wife was the teacher of the girls' school, and therefore, he believed the convicts were his subordinates. When they failed to take off their hats in his presence (as convicts were required to do with employees) "he abuse[d] them with insults and threats."[61]

When the Justice Ministry ordered all colony stores shuttered in 1879, Commander Pereira Lobo dismissed the convict police company's sergeant and storeowner João Ignácio Martins Maise because he did not trust him to enforce orders contrary to his interests.[62] A further exploration of this dismissal in a subsequent chapter indicates that it also sprang from a conflict among members of the commander's family. The attempt to ban commerce, however, was never complete. Some individuals lost their positions and their stores as a result of the ban, but others soon took their place.

The colony's 1865 regulations banned all spirited drink, but it also specified that a ration of cane brandy be distributed to convicts on "certain occasions." Beaurepaire Rohan did not specify what these occasions might be, but Commander Pereira Lobo suggested that fieldworkers received a dram on cold days to inure them to the chill. He griped that mainland officials conspired to deny this same "aid to employees to facilitate in the digestion of the weak diet that almost always is consumed in this presidio." He was disgruntled because the governor had not approved his personal order of alcohol: eight bottles of cachaça and an *ancoreta* (small barrel) of wine for the "daily alimentation of my numerous family" of nineteen individuals. He observed that the previous governor had approved similar requests and suggested that some of the governor's appointees abused this privilege: "Without a doubt they feared that I would order the sale of some of these goods as some of your employees do here with great scandal."[63] The Pernambucana Steamship Company's crews lived among convicts during the five days they spent in Remédios each month, and Pereira Lobo claimed that they "almost always" smuggled alcohol. Crew members "come ashore and find shelter wherever they please, and then they begin their negotiations without the least attention to this command's orders."[64]

In 1871, Pernambuco's commander of arms ordered Captain Trajano Alípio de Carvalho Mendonça's arrest for selling alcohol to convicts. The drunken convict Francisco Joanes de Souza revealed the captain's role after he walked about Remédios insulting others carrying bottles of alcohol. De Souza claimed that he bought the alcohol from Captain Mendonça as on other occasions. Further inquiries led the commander to interrogate a female storeowner who testified that Captain Mendonça pressured her to sell his alcohol, and when she refused, he threatened her. The commander investigated others linked to this network, but apparently word got out. When the steamship arrived on October 20, 1871, the commander became suspicious of the nonconvict Sergeant Querino Joaquim Madeira (the Sailor Madeira): "I consented, with no objections, to allow Madeira to withdraw from his duties of unloading the ship's cargo where for many years he has been employed. . . . This led me to believe that Madeira had been privy on other occasions to alcohol disembarked from the steamships."[65] This report implicates Madeira in the contraband alcohol trade in collusion with an army officer.

While nonconvict employees, like Madeira, profited from contraband trade, an anonymous 1884 letter alleged that a few ex-convicts made small fortunes from it. The letter accused ex-con Antonio da Silva Campos and his business, "Almeida, Campos, etc. and company," of smuggling alcohol to the colony. Campos had served a seven-year sentence in the colony for killing his girlfriend's father. By the time he had completed his sentence, he had amassed some tens of *contos de réis* with which he allegedly bought a billiards hall on fashionable Imperial Street in Recife. As an ex-con, he continued to supply alcohol. When a new governor denied him permission to travel to or do business on the island, Campos got around the restrictions by sending goods through the firm of Guimaraes, Fonseca, and Gomes Maia.

The same letter fingered Campos's partner Manoel de Souza Almeida, who had served a seven-year sentence for robbery. Almeida did not have a cent to his name when he finished his sentence, but he began to profit from contraband when he returned to the mainland and accumulated twenty contos de réis (equivalent to the average price of more than thirty-three young adult slaves in 1884). The letter affirmed that Almeida was presently on the island where he owned two stores. As the letter writer pointed out, so much for the Justice Ministry's ban on commerce. One of Campos's stores was run by his consensual lover, the convict Idalina Cordeiro da Silva, and the other by a partner, convict Manoel Henrique de Villa Real. The letter alleged that Almeida had shipped three contos de réis worth of goods. The informant detailed the ingenious packaging used to smuggle alcohol in boxes of sugar and cans of gas.[66] There are a number of reports of alcohol apprehended, but colony correspondence makes no mention of whether Almeida was detained. He must have had friends in high places in the colony and Pernambuco. In 1884, Almeida was listed as a nonconvict employee who had permission to receive a large order for alcohol. This ex-convict had returned to become a nonconvict company sergeant and storeowner.[67]

The following year, the interim Commander José Ignacio Ribeiro Roma reported that he had found *aguardente* disguised in twenty cans. From "letters enclosed" they deduced that the cans had been sent by the ex-con Almeida through the firm Ferreira, Silva, and Company to elude detection and "make condemnable profits."[68]

Justice Ministry inspectors indicated that Almeida and Campos were not unique. One mentioned that two Portuguese convicts had made fortunes in exile. One had been a coach driver in a provincial capital when a jury condemned him for murder: "But instead of suffering the horrors of punishment, these two individuals benefitted from it, and perhaps blessed the day they became criminals."[69] There likely was some exaggeration in these convict rags to riches stories, but contraband trade was lucrative.

Convicts who could not afford contraband alcohol could make intoxicants from fermented fruit. An 1894 list of punishments is illustrative: "Ambrosio Benedicto de Vargas was imprisoned on Oct. 17 and released on Oct. 25 because he was found making alcohol from fermented cashew fruit [*garapão de cajus*] that he sold or gave to his companions to the point that they became inebriated." The commander punished de Vargas with eight days in an aldeia jail cell on a diet of bread and water, and thereafter, he had to dwell in the aldeia's domitory for an unspecified period.[70] This case is also notable because Republican officials eschewed flogging in favor of alternative nonviolent punishments unlike their imperial forebears; but even under the republic, convicts continued to be flogged for serious infractions.

While some convicts and soldiers made their own rot gut, commercial alcohol never dried up. The colony's argot for cane brandy affirmed its accessibility: "white line" (*linha branca*), "little Annie" (*Aninha*), and "twine" (*retrós*).[71] Fernando de Noronha was not the only place army officers peddled alcohol to convicts. The political prisoner Cypriano José Barata de Almeida criticized officers who sold booze at usurious prices to convicts they guarded who constructed Rio de Janeiro's dikes by day and who were held in fetid ship hulks at night.[72] Fernando de Noronha's dark twins mirrored commerce officers conducted on the mainland, and convict demand for alcohol made it too lucrative for many to resist selling it. Disputes between officers and employees often included accusations and counter-accusations of involvement in contraband trade. Only a few convicts, ex-cons, and non-convicts, however, achieved the apogee of social mobility: to become a company sergeant and a storeowner. Commanders depended on a more widely available privilege to garner support from a broader swath of convicts.

PROVISION GROUNDS

Commanders had long granted some convicts permission to work a provision ground. Among the colony's earliest records, a commander observed that he had allowed some the right to cultivate their own plots in their leisure.[73] This was a privilege that, like others, commanders could revoke if a convict misbehaved.

By the 1850s, convict provision grounds had become commonplace, especially for married convicts living with wives and dependents. As a commander wrote in 1858:

> For many years, convicts have been granted permission to farm provision grounds in their leisure time on Sundays and saint's days, and being that the number of those granted provision grounds is more than 400 and that they harvest 4, 6, 8, or more alqueires [a measure that varied between 13 and 22 liters] of vegetables, the surplus abounds which they can use as they wish . . . to buy clothes to cover their nudity and purchase what is necessary for their wives and children, but if they do not sell their legumes (beans and corn) it is all reduced to spoiled dust by the insects that attack quickly here and oblige farmers to sell their harvest quickly.[74]

In 1858, there were 663 convicts in the colony, so a little more than 60 percent of them had a provision ground. This probably included all convicts permitted to live outside the aldeia at the time. By 1869, the spread of provision grounds led to deforestation. To stem it, one commander suggested that individuals limit their production to crops such as corn, beans (*feijão de corda*), and fruit trees in accordance with Article 16 of the colony's regulations, whereas the production of manioc, cotton, brown beans, and *carapata* seeds would be exclusive to imperial fields. This would make it harder to steal crops grown on the imperial farm because they would be distinct from those grown privately. In addition, he argued that "a single piece of land be designated for planting the food stuffs to be divided among officers and employees," and that the same should be done for the sergeants and corporals who headed work companies. This would mean that these plots would be tended by the domestics of "employees, officers, sergeants, and corporals" to ensure that there would not be excessive planting "without occupying a large number of convicts from the different companies that work in the [imperial] fields in favor of this or that individual." As for convicts, the commander suggested that they too have a piece of land divided equally among them and urged that "the inveterate practice . . . of locating provision grounds in different places be eliminated to prevent those individuals who benefit from them from cutting down forest at their whim." The commander ended by bemoaning deforestation and suggested that tree varieties more appropriate for construction be planted.[75] These reforms, however, were never put into practice. The commander blithely ignored regulations that forbade staff provision grounds and the right to exploit convict labor to tend their private fields.

In 1871, an investigative commission documented how company sergeants exploited convict workers:

> Finally, the commission verified that in the Fernando de Noronha presidio there were two men raised to the rank of sergeant of the aldeia, Joaquim Querino Madeira and José Prudencio de Bittencourt, who both owned stores and who used their authority to oblige convicts to purchase goods from their stores and they have large plantations even though Colonel Moraes Rego has prohibited employees from having them. They also have convicts at their service that go about mounted on good horses and even more surprisingly they punish fellow convicts with beatings as if they had the authority to do so.[76]

José Prudencio de Betancourt appears in table A5 as a convict whose wife ran a store in 1858 with stock valued at 800$000 réis. The other sergeant was the infamous sailor Madeira. They both added "plantations" to their other ventures and employed unpaid convicts to work their farms.

Despite regulations that prohibited staff from farming, they continued to do so. An 1891 Justice Ministry report observed: "The employees have their own plantations where they employ some two hundred convicts without paying them any salary." Commanders also allowed a "great number" of convicts to open stores and negotiate imported and locally produced goods in violation of regulations.[77] Attempts to prohibit commerce failed miserably in part because the administration could not supply for many of the convicts' needs. While incentives provided commanders with some influence over convicts, they also employed sanctions that went beyond the suspension of privileges.

PUNISHMENT

The punishment of convicts for disciplinary infractions and crimes reveals the tension that existed between efforts to implement modern penal rehabilitation and traditional ideas of discipline. Whatever limited social mobility available to convicts was fragile, and there were relatively few privileged positions. Time and again, commanders argued that corporal punishment was essential to maintain order among desperate men, but they also had other sanctions at their disposal.

One nonviolent punishment was exile on Rat Island. As a commander observed in 1850: "This place serves as a place of correction for some of the most recalcitrant convicts principally those that give themselves over to alcoholic drink."[78] Rat Island's high rocky shores made the disembarkation of humans and goods complicated. Its lone water supply came from a single saline spring that made quenching one's thirst an unpleasant chore. Convicts dreaded exile there.

Convicts and commanders considered certain posts hardships, and one's work company determined where one resided. An 1879 conflict between the army convict Braselino Rufino Gomes and the slave convict José Elenterio illustrates the relationship between work, residence, and behavior. The commander ordered Elenterio to move out of the work company stationed in the village of Sueste because Gomes constantly harassed him. On one occasion Elenterio injured Gomes when he insulted and assaulted him. The commander clarified that Gomes had "irregular conduct" and had recently spent six months in the aldeia's jail because he had injured convict Victorio dos Santos with a knife. Elenterio, conversely, had good behavior.[79] This case illustrates a variety of sanctions. First, Gomes had spent six months in one of the aldeia's jail cells for injuring a fellow convict. Temporary imprisonment was limited, however, because the two small cells available could hold about fourteen men each.[80] This confinement could be combined with shackles and dietary restrictions. Those so confined could be held during the workday or forced to work under guard, usually cleaning Fort Remédios. Limited space and the desire to make convicts work meant that commanders usually resorted to imprisonment only when a convict committed a serious crime. When the commander released Gomes, he further punished him by ordering him to live and work in Sueste. As an inspector observed: "The convicts do not like to live there because of the isolation."[81] Convict life in Remédios offered more amenities and possibilities for sociability. Many convicts sent to Sueste were there to be disciplined, but not all; Elenterio had had a record of good behavior after all. The episode illuminates the latitude that commanders had in enforcing the law. Gomes had injured a comrade with a knife, and although the extent of the injuries are not detailed, this was a crime for which he could have been tried. This, however, would be costly and burdensome because it involved sending the accused and other convict witnesses to Recife for trial. Commanders often punished convicts with their own summary justice and exercised considerable latitude when deciding which crimes merited court proceedings.[82]

A list of "occurrences" from 1894 gives a glimpse of how commanders doled out punishment for infractions and less serious crimes. The commander jailed Tortuliano José de Lima for eight days because he was found playing cards, presumably gambling; Manoel Dias Barboza, an accessory to the murder of a burro, six days of jail with a diet of bread and water; Manoel Martins de Souza stole goat skins from one comrade and sold them to another, eight days in the lock up with a diet of bread and water; José Antonio Francisco, known as "Cobbler," received the same punishment for buying said goat skins; Roberto Alves de Souza, known as "Monster Cat," fought with his comrade and then procured him for "immoral acts," three days in jail and afterward a transfer to Sueste; Antonio Hermino da Cunha injured his comrade de Souza with a knife and for his "immoral precedents" he spent ten days in jail with a diet of bread and water and afterward would live in the aldeia for an unspecified period; Francisco Pereira Lima, armed with a knife, entered the home of his comrade, where he tried to "offend his comrade's wife," four days in jail; Aprigio José Ribeiro for once again selling the clothes of his superiors, eight days in jail, transfer to Sueste, and prohibition from serving as a domestic in future; and Felisbeiro José dos Santos stole food from the commander's residence where he was a domestic, four days in prison and transfer to Sambaqueixaba.[83] As the Santos case shows, Sambaqueixaba was also a hardship post.

Commanders sometimes combined exile with other punishments. In 1885, the commander explained why he punished convicts Manoel Rodopiam Barbosa da Santa Barbara and Antonio Maria Teixeira de Mello. Santa Barbara allegedly conspired to kill another convict while he slept, so the commander ordered him fettered and sent to work in Sambaqueixaba. Mello had an altercation with Sergeant Assis in Remédios's streets at 10:00 PM. Sergeant Assis ordered Mello to submit to arrest, but Mello armed himself with an ax that he used to resist arrest. The commander had Mello clapped in irons and sent him to work in Sambaqueixaba. Days later, Mello simulated an illness and returned for treatment in Remédios's infirmary. Pereira Lobo ordered the shackles removed, but Mello behaved in an "insubordinate and disrespectful" manner toward the commander, so he ordered him shackled again to maintain discipline at the "desired and necessary level."[84] In 1883, Commander Pereira Lobo wrote that Mello had been sent to Recife as a witness to the civil convict Pedro Antonio Vital's murder of the slave convict Matheus. He clarified that Mello made false accusations that included a claim that Commander Pereira Lobo had slain a convict. The commander insisted that Mello "had suffered all the punishments permissible in this establishment and has not been rehabilitated but to the contrary has only become a more audacious slanderer." He asked that Mello not be returned because "the presence of this convict in this presidio is too pernicious to good order."[85] While officials often fingered mainland convicts for exile to the colony because of their unruliness, it could also be a rationale to remove them.

Fettered convicts had to labor, but diminished productivity was one reason that authorities did not enforce the sentence of galés, which required a convict to be fettered. In 1850, the commander noted that Article 44 of the Penal Code demanded that prisoners condemned to galés have their feet fettered, but he lacked the shackles to enforce the sentence. He requested 125 pairs of chains for all the convicts sentenced to galés. Mainland authorities could have resolved the situation, but they never did. Fetters were usually only employed when a convict committed a new crime.[86]

Beyond exile within exile, incarceration, irons, and formal prosecution, commanders relied heavily on flogging. A British naturalist gave a favorable depiction of flogging and convict discipline in general in 1887:

> One prisoner was flogged while we were on the island, the offense being a violent assault. It was a solitary case, and we never saw any of the officials carrying weapon whatever. The discipline of the place requires that no convict shall wear his hat in the great square, nor remain on horseback when he meets the Director, otherwise there are but few restrictions. . . . These negroes, Indians, and half-breeds are mostly there for murder, but that only means that where an Englishman might use his fists, they have used a knife. The forgers are a very quiet set, and often rise to posts of trust. Altogether the convicts with whom we talked were far from being degraded or ruffianly—in fact, in many cases they were quite the reverse. Just complaints may always be made before the Director and we often heard little favors granted. The system, in fact, in his able kindly hands, works excellently, as we had every opportunity of seeing.[87]

This depiction of orderliness is belied by colony correspondence, but to this outsider, the island seemed relatively nonviolent. The American geologist John Branner, however, gave a much bleaker assessment of flogging and convict discipline:

> But, while some of the convicts were indulged, others were treated with unnecessary severity, which merged into cruelty. This unequal justice, or

rather the disproportionate punishment meted out to offenders, and over which the officers in charge had full jurisdiction, was, in itself, demoralizing to the convicts. . . . No effort was made to fit the punishment to the crime. Flogging was the one remedy for everything, and, as it always took place in the presence of the assembled prisoners, this became a new element of degradation to the entire community. A convict having stolen a pig, was sent for and flogged. The very next morning the commandant was called to the front door, and there on the veranda stood a man horribly mangled by an assassin. "What does all this mean?" said the commandant. "John Doe has killed me," said the convict. "Away with you to the hospital"; and, turning to an officer, he continued, "and bring Fulano here to me." And Fulano was brought and flogged. The influence of such a system of treatment upon the less depraved classes of criminals may readily be imagined.[88]

Commanders ordered offenders to be flogged in public before fellow convicts as a general deterrent, a practice common in Brazil's military. Similar floggings of urban slaves at public whipping posts on the mainland began to disappear in the 1830s, but authorities continued to flog slaves behind prison walls, an indication of growing unease with public corporal punishment.

Commanders considered flogging even more essential for serious offenses. On March 10, 1850, around 8:00 PM the convicts prayed the rosary, and when they implored, "O Merciful Lord," the corporal of the aldeia, Francisco Rodrigues de Moraes, observed that the convict Francisco Caracioles de Lira Bastos was sitting, and he ordered Bastos to kneel, but he refused. The sergeant of the aldeia, Manoel da Rosa Araujo, then arrived and ordered Bastos's arrest. Bastos assassinated his arrestor and injured another convict who attempted to intervene. As punishment, the commander ordered that Bastos be placed in fetters and flogged five hundred times, although he observed that regulations only allowed him to be punished with a maximum of 320 lashes.[89]

Convicts combatted corporal punishment in a climate where mainland public opposition to cruel punishments was mounting. Commander Antônio de Campos Mello discovered this in 1871 when the opposition newspaper *O Liberal* named the convicts who had been flogged: José Francisco da Silva, Eustaquio Pereira da Silva, the slave convict Anton, Manoel Francisco dos Santos, William Bell, the slave convict Luis, and Afonso Ribeiro de Lima. The commander admitted that these convicts had been flogged but insisted that the newspaper exaggerated the number of lashes. *O Liberal* alleged that between July 11 and August 2, 1871, convicts had been flogged for "frivolous" reasons. Manoel Francisco da Silva received 160 lashes because the "islander Sailor Madeira," claimed "he had shown disrespect for his authority!" Further, the slave convict Antonio received 150 lashes for showing up an hour late for his duties. Manoel Francisco dos Santos received 220 lashes for fighting with a comrade in the presence of sergeant Madeira. Lambe, an Italian, and William Bell, an American, were flogged 220 times for boarding a Prussian ship in port without permission and spending the night on board. The slave Luiz received 150 lashes for stealing corn from the imperial fields. Finally, Afonso Pereira de Lima was flogged twice (150 and 140 times for inattention in the presence of Sergeant Madeira). In his defense the commander insisted that the number of lashes applied varied between thirty and fifty. The exception was the convict Afonso Ribeiro de Lima, who received one hundred lashes for injuring an unnamed "woman."[90]

The commander explained that he did not like flogging, but he believed it was essential:

> Colonel Luis José Monteiro sought to discipline the convicts by way of persuasion and fasts, and the result was that he learned of a convict rebellion only fifteen minutes before it was to break out. . . . Then he had to employ corporal punishment with rigor and thereafter he governed the island for two years without incident. Flogging is of the utmost importance in the presidio, it is the guarantee of the employees' lives and the honor of families; and that was how my predecessor . . . the dead Conselheiro Marquez de Paraná put it in . . . 1850: "only one who does not know Fernando de Noronha, the number of convicts, the small army garrison, and only one sixth of the prisoners sleep inside a prison because it has insufficient space. . . . There are convicts here that will not hesitate to repeat their crimes . . . to govern 1,300 perverse criminals that do not recognize law or religion, as the crimes they are serving time for prove, it is not possible to prohibit corporal punishment, unless one wants to see the inhabitants of this island sacrificed."[91]

The reference to family honor indicates the fear that convicts would rape the wives and daughters of families without the intimidation of flogging. For commanders, old-regime flogging was the only way to keep convicts in check. Many masters expressed similar views of slaves, and officers vilified their enlisted men with similar tropes. While commanders admitted that they flogged convicts, they evinced increasing embarrassment about it as the century wore. The Justice Ministry temporarily banned flogging convicts in 1879, and it became part of a larger national debate over the efficacy and propriety of corporal punishment that I examine in greater detail in chapter 9.

This case study demonstrates that contemporary prison corruption in Brazil or elsewhere should be an expected dark twin of the planned penal environment. Prisons and penal colonies create captive consumers in restricted economies who will pay high prices for goods and services, especially prohibited ones. The risks that purveyors of illicit goods take are outweighed by the potential for hefty profits. While these unplanned and repressed markets can create conflicts that subvert the planned penal environment's order, they also provided incentives for convicts to cooperate with authorities for their mutual benefit. In 1891, Justice Minister Manoel Ferraz de Campos Salles, who would be elected Brazil's president in 1898, gave a perspicacious assessment of why efforts to ban the colony's commerce failed: "To control these criminals, in numbers much greater than the garrison troops, commanders rely on the power some exercise over others and this is the source of a series of abuses many times repressed and many times renewed. For good or bad motives such as security, order, insufficiently organized public work, and the most damaging of all, complete idleness, the concessions granted to these convicts, the sergeants, gradually increase to the point that they are permitted to establish their own industry where they put tens of their companions to work and open a store."[92] The massive prison uprisings of twenty-first-century Brazil began when authorities denied convict gang leaders privileges that they had come to consider rights, such as conjugal visits, and cracked down on the circulation of banned goods, like cell phones and drugs.[93] Campos Salles's analysis seems as applicable today as it was in 1891.

On Fernando de Noronha the imperial state never exercised the kind of total institutional control that advocates of prisons and penal colonies imagined possible. Indeed, the prohibitive costs of appropriate facilities and trained personnel led the state to rely on convict initiatives to subsidize the colony's expenses. Besides, Beaurepaire Rohan's impulse to arranchar all convicts in batch-living facilities contradicted another initiative in his regulations: to expand the numbers of families whose convict patriarchs needed to live in unattached homes to care for and protect their dependents. These two projects were at cross purposes. The convicts' participation in licit and illicit commerce made it possible to supply and distribute many of the necessities and luxuries that the population demanded. Without it, the colony could not function well, and this explains why attempts to ban commerce failed miserably.

4 "BROTHERS OF THE PEAK"
Prosopography of a Penal Community

A phrase in common use among the inhabitants of that island expresses better than anything else could the general feeling of the prisoners in regard to their isolation . . . from all that is interesting and attractive to them on earth. For them . . . the earth is divided into two parts, one of which—that inhabited by themselves—is known as "Fernando," the other part is known and usually spoken of as "the world." This term was in constant use, and I frequently heard among them such expressions as these: "When I was in the world," "This came from the world."
—JOHN C. BRANNER, "THE CONVICT ISLAND OF BRAZIL"

Convicts spoke of themselves as exiles from "the world," and the daily parade of ships that used the island to check their headings heightened their sense of exile. The peak also marked an important social distinction. Those sentenced to life there were "brothers of the peak," but when the republic did away with life sentences, even nonconvict residents used the term to describe themselves as venerable residents.[1] The term indicates how penal tenure shaped the ways convicts perceived one another. While some returned to the world, others awaited a pauper's funeral in Remédios's cemetery. Perhaps they adopted the term to mock their fate and mainland lay brotherhoods who provided their members a decent burial. Instead of "Brothers of the Rosary," they were "Brothers of the Peak," which carried a sacrilegious innuendo of same-sex eroticism.[2]

This chapter surveys the traits of individuals whom officials expended limited public resources to prosecute and exile. It also

FIG 4.1 An 1878 engraving of the Hill of the Peak (Morro do Pico) of Fernando de Noronha Island. From Sir C. Wyville Thomson, *The Voyage of the "Challenger": The Atlantic* (New York: Harper, 1878), 2:108.

conducts a qualitative interrogation of the categories devised to map convict identities.[3] Records reveal their makers' worldviews, and the "ideological assumptions and political concerns" that authorities "brought to bear in enumerating, classifying, and ordering" a convict population.[4] Public officials' efforts to classify convicts and citizens illuminate the phenomena of category drift and how convicts often interpreted and used categories differently from officials. A final section explores the identities of the colony's nonconvict residents.

BROTHERS AND SISTERS OF THE PEAK

Because army officers managed Fernando de Noronha, colony records bear a family resemblance to the army's. Ideally, when prisoners disembarked, their escorts would deliver their *guias*, a document that identified prisoners, their crimes, and their sentences. The term *guia* also denoted documents masters gave their slaves to show they had their permission to be out and about on their own reconnaissance, a usage that suggests again the connections between categories of the intractable poor.[5] Matriculation books for the 1830s and 1850s recopied guias, but 1865 regulations stipulated categories. Thereafter, scriveners fit data from guias and other sources into preconceived columns.[6]

Most guia and matriculation records preserve a wealth of data, but some list only a name, a crime, and a sentence. In an age before cheap photography, a convict's description could be used to track them down if they escaped.[7] Records could also include information subsequent to a convict's arrival such as when they completed a sentence, received a commutation, died, or were punished. Most data provides a snapshot of a convict when he or she was sentenced or arrived on the island, but new data could be added. Here is a typical guia entry: "José Gonçalves do Nascimento entered the prison of this capital [Recife] on Jan. 9, 1845, age 27, son of José Gonçalves and Damana Maria, single, light brown, missing his left eye, medium height, kinky black hair, patchy beard, accused of the crime of murder."[8] Since courts in different towns produced guias, the data they convey is less consistent. For this reason, the uniform categories of matriculation books will be the focus of analysis. What columns include and exclude reveals how bureaucrats created ways of seeing like a state.[9]

The first column in matriculation books enumerated entries, and the second listed names. Army officers did not assign convicts a number for identification even though this was common for soldiers. This is surprising given that many convicts had the same or similar names. Instead, scriveners made cumbersome designations: John Doe second, John Doe third, and so on. Some convicts tried to exploit misidentification. In 1880, the slave convict Domingos matriculated without his guia. He claimed his name was Domingos, slave of Tidoncio de Macedo, but inquiries revealed that he had been the slave of Vicente Pereira Pinto. He knew Domingos, slave of Macedo, because both did time in São Paulo's penitentiary until the latter was pardoned in 1874. Officials surmised that Domingos's ploy was to win his freedom through mistaken identity.[10] Where Domingos failed, others succeeded. An inspector warned that it was unsafe for convicts to work as scriveners for the secretary because a galés who had held this post altered his record and escaped a life sentence.[11]

Scriveners included convict nicknames in the name column prefaced with the phrase "known as." Nicknames varied widely: Gato (Cat), Sabetudo (Know It All), Verga de Aço (Steel Penis), Pajeu (Indian Chief), Chico Damnado (Chico the Damned), and Manoel Viado (Passive Homosexual). A foreign visitor remarked on convict nicknames: "Sometimes there was a ghastly sort of humor about the names. One, who had murdered a priest, was called 'o Padre' the priest; another who had murdered a man for his money and had found but half a pataca upon him, was called half a pataca (meia pataca) about sixteen cents; another, for a similar reason was called 'quatro vintens,' four cents."[12] The racy nature of nicknames indicate that convicts devised them, but their use was so handy that they became part of a convict's formal bureaucratic identity.

Names also reveal status. For example, most slave convicts had no surname, but entries included the term "slave" as if it were a surname.[13] Few convict names had titles. Exceptions were a former police chief who had the temerity to attack a judge and Dr. Felipe Lopes Neto, a political prisoner.[14] Similarly, no female convict had the honorific title "dona," which connoted the respectability of a propertied, well-married woman. The lack of titles indicates that courts seldom prosecuted persons of rank and exiled them.[15] The director of Recife's House of Detention observed that the wealthy and their clients avoided prosecution by paying a *fiança* (bond), which sprang them from jail to await trial. Courts first prosecuted defendants held in jail and, because their numbers usually exceeded the courts' capacity to try them, they granted those free on bond virtual impunity.[16] Judge Eusébio de Queiroz orchestrated a crackdown on this practice in Rio de Janeiro when he held a special jury session in 1838 dedicated to try only defendants who had paid fianças "[to] convince those out on bail and their bondsmen that putting up bail is not the same as being pardoned."[17] Apparently, few of his peers followed his lead.

Convict names reveal gender in every case, so records did not have a column for it. This omission likely reflects the presumption that convicts were male. Female convicts comprise less than two percent of the entries (21/1091) in my survey, although their numbers grew after 1850. In 1846, there were only three women convicts, but they increased to more than thirty in the 1870s.[18] The American convict William Bell informed a visitor in 1876 that most women prisoners had been convicted of poisoning their husbands.[19] This insight reveals a gender division, as men used violent means to murder that were more likely to have witnesses and facilitated their prosecution.

A convict's name was followed by five columns: age, birthplace, marital status, civil condition, and profession. Convicts' ages spanned from fourteen to seventy years; the average was 31.4 years. Most convicts came to the colony in their prime, but officials exiled some older convicts, which suggests that, in many cases, they paid little heed to the island's need for younger, robust laborers to make the imperial farm more productive.

More than one-third (366/960) of convicts surveyed hailed from Pernambuco, and another third (362) from other northeastern provinces (see appendix, table A6). This confirms that governors of Pernambuco used their access to the colony to allay their overcrowded jails. As a Justice Ministry

official moaned in 1880: "Those condemned by juries in the interior are usually sent to the House of Detention in Recife and because this establishment did not have the capacity to hold the many prisoners that arrive there
daily, they resort to the expedient of sending excess prisoners to Fernando
de Noronha."[20] The logistics and costs of shipping convicts from distant regions limited their numbers.[21]

Marital status signaled an important threshold of convict respectability.
Out of 969 entries with marital status, 537 convicts (55 percent) were single;
345 (36 percent), married; and 87 (9 percent), widowed. The high percent-
ages of married and widowed convicts counter stereotypes that young unattached men were more likely to commit crime. This resembles Eric Van
Young's finding that men convicted of banditry in central Mexico tended to
be older, married men who had some status rather than single, low-status
youths.[22]

The column for a convict's civil condition, as noted in the introduction,
included seven categories: free, slave, Indian, imperial soldier, freedman
(*liberto*), military arsenal worker (*artifice*), imperial sailor, and National
Guard (see table A7). Courts martial condemned nearly one in five convicts,
and army convicts surpassed those of the navy by almost ten to one. Records
stripped enlisted convicts of their ranks but maintained their identification as enlisted men. Indeed, military convicts earned slightly better wages
than their civilian counterparts. A large-scale example of category drift occurred in 1855 when the army pardoned fifty army convicts in the colony.
Pernambuco's commander of arms suggested that they all be integrated into
the colony's garrison, transforming convicts into warders overnight. To diminish the potential for unrest, the commander of arms suggested that the
new guards could perform their duties unarmed. The commander objected
because some of the pardoned soldiers had been close to prisoners who had
sown rebellion in 1854.[23] While this episode was extraordinary, the reinte-
gration of army ex-cons into the garrison on a smaller scale was common.
As a commander wrote in 1877: "Military convicts who complete their sentences are reassigned to the [colony's] army detachment."[24]

More than seventy occupations were listed for convicts surveyed in matriculation books (see table A8). Given Brazil's largely rural population, it is
not surprising that more than one-quarter worked in agriculture, but almost
as many lacked information or were listed as without a skill or position (*sem
oficio*). Most free convicts farmed plots that they owned or sharecropped,
but courts convicted many artisans, especially cobblers. Shoemakers were not
more prone to crime, but the colony designated one company to manufacture

boots. Mainland officials sent cobbler convicts to the colony, while others learned the trade in exile. The other most common skilled occupations were in the construction trades, but others such as cowboys, tailors, and seamen are well represented. A smattering of convicts held skilled white-collar professions such as businessman, book binder, lithographer, goldsmith, sculptor, apothecary, and portrait artist. Juries condemned most of them for counterfeiting or homicide. Scriveners recorded gender-appropriate occupations for women convicts. Most performed domestic work, with the exception of a midwife and a pair of seamstresses. Other convicts had skilled manual jobs such as master sugar processor, welder, caulker, gardener, canoe pilot, butcher, and cigar maker.

The category *sem ofício* (without a skilled occupation) described nearly one in four convicts. Sem ofício does not directly translate as "unemployed," though it held that connotation. More than two-thirds of army convicts (100/144) with job data and nearly four of five sailors (8/11) are sem ofício even though they had worked for the military before their convictions: a bureaucratic slight to their status and the skills acquired in national service.[25] By comparison, one-quarter of free civil convicts were sem ofício, but only 14 percent of slave convicts were so classed. Many slave convicts were agricultural workers, but others had skilled occupations: cobblers, coopers, cowboys, distillers, cooks, sailors, muleteers, and so on. Forty-nine percent of slave convicts (99/193) performed common agricultural labor compared to 39 percent (291/475) of their free counterparts.

Why were slave convicts more likely to be identified as agricultural laborers than their free civilian and military peers? Sem ofício was the subject of a classifying gaze. Records for enlisted men rarely listed agricultural work as an ofício. In a sample from 1896 four of five army enlisted men were sem ofício.[26] This reflected the fact that the army pressed most of its men, and coercive recruitment targeted unemployed, patronless men, many of whom were rural migrants. This explains why so many were sem ofício because it was transcribed from a military record. Only a few are listed as day laborers who performed whatever work they could find, but it is likely that many men described as sem ofício could be so classed. When the agricultural cycle or economy slowed, many became indistinguishable from more dedicated vagabonds.

Slave convicts described as sem ofício were not unemployed but unskilled. Even so, sem ofício implied vagrancy, as the expression *sem ofício nem benefício* (roughly, "no occupation, no benefits") reveals. An 1848 book of Brazilian sayings defines the phrase as *sem modo de vida* (without a means to make a living).[27] It appears in Manoel Antônio de Almeida's 1855 novel, *Memórias de um sargento de milícias* (*Memoirs of a Militia Sergeant*), set when João VI ruled from Rio de Janeiro (1808–1822). The unemployed young protagonist Leonardo is upbraided by his godmother: "You are a burden, you wander around like a vagabond, penniless, without a means of earning a living [sem ofício nem benefício]." After evading Rio's police chief, Leonardo's nemesis finally captures him and presses him into an army battalion that did urban police work, in this humorous coming-of-age novel.[28] The term *sem ofício* coincided with the stratification military impressment defined between the protected and the unprotected poor. Officials found it difficult to depict slave convicts as sem ofício because they assumed that their lot in life was endless toil. Job entries contradict stereotypes of slaves as shiftless and portray them as more skilled and harder working than their free counterparts.

Job data confirms that most convicts were the salt of the earth, and the column for personal traits fills out their portrait.[29] The descriptions are similar to those found in army enlisted men's records and runaway slave descriptions in the press.[30] Entries could include parentage, stature, color, build, head shape, face, hair (color and texture), eye (color and shape), eyebrows, lip size, nose (size and shape), forehead, teeth, ears, hands, feet, facial hair, scars, tattoos, literacy, and debilitating injuries and illnesses. Few entries included all of this data, and some, none at all. In the 770 entries that included parental names (*afiliação*), most convicts (652) named their father, a few (36) named only their mother, and some inmates (75) could not name either parent. While many of the latter were African-born slaves, there were some free convicts who could not identify their parents. Matriculation books did not record legitimacy, but afiliação is a proxy for it.

Records classify inmates' color in 1,004 instances using twenty-one categories, although only three are used frequently (white, black, and brown). Table A9 organizes these categories into six groupings that are approximations, as were the classifying gazes that assigned them in the first place. The category *crioulo*, for example, does not refer to color, but to a Brazilian-born slave. I classified convicts labeled crioulo as black based on the assumption that their slave status would likely make them black. Obviously, the evaluation of one's color is in the eye of the beholder, and in this case, either prison scribes or court officials made judgments. Still, authorities applied them with an eye to accuracy, since they would be used to identify escapees. Assessments of color in colony documents constitute a summary evaluation influenced by perceptions of an individual's other traits: manners, dress, education, birth place, and so forth. Color attributions could be lightened if traits indicated that one was privileged, and Brazilian documents such as the census more commonly used the term "color" rather than "race."[31]

Those classified as white are underrepresented in the penal population, whereas nonwhites are overrepresented. Whiteness, however, did not preclude prosecution and exile. An 1890 survey confirms that inmate's color classifications remained stable for the period under study. It classified 20 percent as white, 44 percent dark brown, 4 percent light brown, 6 percent indigenous, and 25 percent black. A consistent correlation of some features to color appears in the data. Those described as flat nosed are much more likely to be black (154) or dark brown (73) than white (3), whereas those with aquiline noses were much more likely to be white (63) or dark brown (69) than black (16). Scriveners recorded twelve classifications for hair with gradations from kinky to flowing. No convict of indigenous color and only two white ones had kinky hair compared to 194 black and 72 dark brown. Few black (2) and dark brown (27) convicts had flowing hair as opposed to 21 indigenous and 49 white counterparts. The least commonly described feature, invoked in 92 entries, was lips, which was overwhelmingly used to describe black (57) and dark brown (17) convicts as wide lipped, whereas entries depict only one white and one indigenous inmate thusly. The traits most strongly identified with blackness were kinky hair followed by wide lips and a flat nose, and with whiteness, flowing hair followed by aquiline nose and thin lips.[32]

While records give us a handle on convict appearances, they are silent on other traits that could influence color classifications: speech, dress, and manners.[33] Literacy serves as an imperfect proxy for them. The overall convict literacy rate of 23 percent was higher than the mainland's, which in 1872 hovered at 15 percent for men. Documents do not reveal how authorities accessed literacy, but a comparison of color and literacy reveals the advantages of whiteness (see table A10). Light and dark brown convicts' literacy rates are nearly the same. Those described as indigenous do slightly better than their brown compatriots, while those classified as black had significantly less education, but it could be that literacy lightened an individual's color ascription.

Sometimes scriveners included details about a prisoner's scars, tattoos, disabilities, and illnesses under personal characteristics. The most commonly observed were chicken pox scars, but others were stuttering, blindness, bullet scars, hernias, moles, missing fingers, and so forth. Honório dos Santos Baptista was easy to identify because of his wooden leg. A number of entries describe convict tattoos. Most were on the inmates' forearms in blue ink, and many were on military convicts. Nineteenth-century armies, navies, and convicts cultivated the tattoo. Crosses, hearts, initials, and stars of Solomon were the most common designs. The American prisoner William Bell had a cross and a human figure on both forearms. Clemente José do Nascimento had blue ink tattoos of the star of Salomon and a heart, while Martinho Travata had three snakes on his left forearm. Damasco Mucena and Agostinho Manjolla bore facial scars of their African ethnicities.

After personal characteristics, matriculation books logged the site of a convict's trial. Unlike birthplace, which only specified a province, this entry specifies a town or city. Some 270 sites are represented: most were rural communities like Passagem Franca, Ceará; Pedras do Fogo, Paraíba; Mar de Hespanha, Minas Gerais; Cascavel, Paraná; Bananal, São Paulo; and Brejo da Madre de Deus (the Swamp of the Mother of God), Pernambuco. Only 133 of 1,058 cases originated in urban centers, and more than half (72) were from Recife. Brazil's capital, Rio de Janeiro, with some 200,000 inhabitants in 1872, placed a distant second with 13. Many rural towns contributed only one convict, but a few towns in Pernambuco's interior produced large numbers: Pão d'Alho, 30; Bonito, 20; Limoeiro, 19; Goiana, 15; Victoria, 15; and Escada,14

Among convict crimes, homicide (741/918) constituted more than 80 percent in matriculation records: 174 entries do not identify a crime, but many record a lengthy sentence that suggests a homicide conviction (table A11). Thus, the percentage of homicide convicts may have been closer to 90 percent. A survey of mainland prisons in the early twentieth century indicates that some 70 percent of inmates there were homicide convicts.[34] Homicide convicts were more likely to be true brothers of the peak and considered themselves a noble caste. The American geologist John Branner observed:

Society was as varied among these men as in other parts of the world. There were all classes . . . though, they all met on the common level of crime. Social distinctions among them were based upon money first, and second, other things being equal, upon the nature of the crime committed, certain crimes being regarded as indicative of courageous manhood. While about my work one day, my attention was attracted by a young man who was posing nearby disdainfully watching me. He was not more than twenty years of age, good looking, and well dressed. A fine felt hat sat jauntily upon the side of his head, and he wore a blue cloak, the bright red lining of which he displayed to good advantage by tossing it back over his shoulder. I saw that he was a type, drew him into conversation, and finally asked him for what he was sent to Fernando. Bridling up and throwing back his shoulders, he struck his left breast with his right hand closed, as if upon a dagger, and exclaimed proudly, "Mor-r-rte!" (murder).[35]

This geologist from New Market, Tennessee, did not mention color as a factor of stratification but noted how one's crime shaped one's status. A journalist confirmed the high opinion homicide convicts had of themselves. When a female convict approached to petition for a commutation, the commander inquired what her crime had been. Other convicts answered derisively for her: "She killed her child when it was born." She left unable to articulate a defense. The rest of the men petitioning were homicide convicts; some professed their innocence, others acknowledge their guilt. They cast aspersions on a woman who committed infanticide but viewed their own crimes as courageous.[36]

Branner related an anecdote from his days working for Brazil's geological commission that he claimed typified common Brazilian attitudes about crime:

I had the misfortune at one time to wound a Brazilian laborer—in his dignity. He thereupon threatened to take my life. . . . As the carrying out of such a determination upon his part would have caused me much inconvenience, I called upon him in person, with the purpose, if possible, of dissuading him. I found that he did not look upon the condition of a criminal with dread at all. He told me frankly that, if he should succeed in carrying out his designs, he knew perfectly well what his career would be. "At present," said he, "I am obliged to work for a living; if I am sent to jail, my living will be furnished to me, and I shall have nothing to do. If you are dead, there will be no one to appear against me in the courts as my accuser, and in the course of a year or less I shall be set free, well rested, and with the reputation in the community of being a man of courage."[37]

While this laborer likely exaggerated his lack of concern with incarceration, many humble men desired to be considered a man of courage, which led some to overblown demonstrations of truculence. The vast majority of colony residents were homicide convicts, and their crimes confirmed their manly bona fides. By contrast, most convicts regarded horse thieves with contempt and referred to them as *pitubas* (cowards) or "forty-eight": their crime's number in the criminal code.[38]

The predominance of homicide convicts confirms that the police and courts focused their efforts on prosecuting violent crime.[39] By comparison, a little more than 8 percent of convicts committed crimes against property. Despite Parliament's resolve to exile counterfeiters, their numbers were few (2.6 percent). The only other crime of dimension was military desertion. Other crimes like resistance to arrest, seduction of a young woman with false marriage promises, insubordination, and allowing a prisoner to escape account for less than 1 percent of all crimes surveyed.

A convict's sentence reflected his crime's gravity (see table A12). More than half (562/1092) were brothers of the peak condemned for life. Only one in ten convicts had been condemned to "prison at labor." Perhaps the inability of penitentiaries to offer work limited this sentence's appeal. Almost one-third were sentenced to simple imprisonment, a sentence more common for political prisoners, women, and minors, but many free men and a few adult male slaves were so sentenced. This sentence did not require labor, but on Fernando de Noronha, commanders obligated all convicts to work unless they excused them. Justice Ministry officials believed it unjust to force convicts condemned to simple imprisonment to labor, but commanders felt that idle prisoners sowed disorder.[40]

A convict's civil condition and color influenced the type and length of sentence (see table A13). Courts sentenced almost all slaves to perpetual galleys or death, but they also sentenced many free convicts of all colors to perpetual galleys (224/645). Free persons were much more likely to be sentenced to simple imprisonment than other civil categories. Those convicted of murder condemned to a temporary sentence averaged 13.5 years. The presence of 67 convicts (6 percent) sentenced to the gallows indicates that officials expected the emperor to commute these sentences.

Most slave convicts were black or brown, but many black and brown convicts were free men. The influence of slave status is clear: juries condemned 92 percent of slave convicts to perpetual galleys or death. This pattern is in part due to law and the fact that all slave convicts had been convicted of murder. If one isolates those condemned to perpetual galleys for murder in relation to color, one finds that courts convicted nearly 60 percent (132/222) of blacks to perpetual galleys compared to 36 percent (106/292) of browns and 30 percent (42/138) of whites. Juries were much more likely to condemn slave convicts to die because of the June 10, 1835, law. When one considers capital punishment for homicide in relation to color, 15 percent (33/222) were black, 7 percent (13/192) were brown, and 4 percent (6/138) were white. Lighter-skinned convicts received lighter sentences for similar crimes.

Records reveal intriguing patterns in the convict population's growth after 1850 (see table A16). In 1869 the convict population temporarily dipped after scores of convicts had been freed to fight in Paraguay. Growth picked up again in the mid-1870s coinciding with the Quebra Quilos Revolt of 1874–1875. After the Justice Ministry assumed the colony's administration in 1877 the convict population slowly diminished.

If one used the most common descriptors in records to construct a composite of the typical convict, it would be as follows. The name would be Manoel da Silva. He would be thirty-one years old, single, free, and a native farmer of Pernambuco. He would be skinny and of average stature with a dark brown complexion. His black eyes would glint under a broad forehead with large eyebrows. His face would be long and his hair black and kinky. His nose would be flat over a regular sized mouth with broad lips and good teeth. His face would be framed by a sparse black beard that partly hid chicken pox scars. His jury convicted him for murder and sentenced him to perpetual galleys. Of course, this is a composite that does not capture convict diversity, to which we now turn.

CONVICT ARISTOCRATS AND PLEBEIANS

As the previous chapter demonstrated, a convict's work assignment shaped stratification in the colony. The most ambitious convicts strove to become company sergeants and storeowners. Convicts, however, had their own ideas of stratification that did not necessarily conform to those sanctioned by staff.

In 1888, a British naturalist described convict stratification on Fernando de Noronha with reference to a system of three prisoner classes based on behavior:

> Great distinctions of privilege exist among the prisoners. The first class have in many cases official posts carrying small salaries, others live by trade, and etc., all their time being their own. Our friend Marçal had earned his first class by going to the mainland for help during a mutiny of soldiers two years ago. Good behavior brings a very substantial reward, even in admission to the second class. These are allowed to live in different parts of the island. They cultivate small patches of ground, or are picketed in huts round the coast, where they can see if any of their mates contemplate launching a raft for escape. The rest are variously employed; four to six hours a day is Government time, when they make roads, do odd jobs, fish, clean up the place, catch rats, or otherwise make themselves useful. Clothes are served out twice a year, but the climate is too perfect to require much care in dress, and rations are drawn at the market

about every ten days, dried beef, beans, manioc flour, and tobacco being issues. The classes are distinguished in dress, but one is not prevented from buying anything extra he cares to wear, nor from going about in the remains of an old sack if it pleases him. Wives and children may join their husbands if they like to, and a school is provided, and the boys are drafted into the army when they reach a sufficient age.[41]

Those who had money bought clothes that externalized their status even though the Justice Ministry attempted to require all convicts to wear a uniform that revealed their first- second-, or third-class ranking. Since the colony never reliably supplied clothing for convicts, contrary to the naturalist's suggestion, this sartorial policy soon lapsed. Other visitors rejected the naturalist's idyllic depiction of colony life. The American geologist John Branner directly criticized it: "The Proceedings of the Royal Geographical Society . . . contains an article upon Fernando by a gentleman who visited . . . in 1887. The convict system is there spoken of as 'almost unique in its excellence,' and a convict of seventeen years standing is called 'our dear old guide.' The great number of verbal errors in the article lead one to conclude that its author knows little or nothing of the Portuguese language, without the easy command of which he could get no clear insight into the working of the convict system."[42] Branner had a darker view of convict life.

The identities of company sergeants and other convict aristocrats reveal who commanders placed in positions of trust. Many privileged convicts were married men who lived with their wives and dependents in exile. Officials believed that convicts with family had a stake in maintaining order to protect their loved ones and that they needed additional salary to support their dependents. One commander described this preference when he recommended the civilian convict João Antônio Gonçalves for a pardon: "He brought with him a numerous family composed of wife and children. . . . This convict has always had excellent conduct and he lives honestly giving proof that he is a good father of family and for these reasons I nominated him sergeant of the company of invalid convicts where he has carried out his duties satisfactorily."[43] Convicts with family did not automatically receive extra rations, so commanders more readily assigned them to better paying posts, gave them quick access to provision grounds, and let them live outside the aldeia. Beaurepaire Rohan's regulations supported this policy: "The convicts generally spend the night in prison [the aldeia], where they will retire at dusk after roll call. The Presidio's Commander can, however, exempt from this obligation domestic servants, heads of family, and those with brief sentences, the old and sick incapable of disorder, and those that, due to their good conduct, demonstrate themselves worthy of trust."[44]

Justice Ministry inspectors, however, expressed shock that many convict sergeants were sentenced to perpetual galleys: "The organization of the companies is completely arbitrary; when a convict lands in the presidio, he is assigned to a work company, and neither his crime nor his sentence weighs in this designation. For this reason, convicts serve in the same work companies whether they are military or civilian, condemned to perpetual galleys, prison at hard labor, or simple imprisonment. Individuals of good and bad character [are lumped together] regardless of their sex, age, or any other considerations that guide the organization of prisoners where the penitentiary problem is known and studied."[45] Experience helped some convicts develop networks to climb the presidio's employment hierarchy. In the convict imaginary, after all, murderers were a noble caste and convict sergeants and corporals had to command respect from dangerous men. So it is not surprising that some men condemned to perpetual galleys, a sentence reserved for heinous murders, became sergeants.

Another privileged group were skilled craftsmen. In 1851, a commander extolled convict Thomé de Souza's skills as an "able" stonemason and smith who had completed his sentence. He asked the governor to allow Souza to return to labor in the colony's workshops, and noted the "absolute necessity" of a having a good smith to repair farm and shop equipment as well as weapons, shackles, and jail bars. He wrote, "There was no hope to find another convict here capable of replacing him."[46] In 1884, a commander delayed an order to remit convict Mathias Antônio de Oliveira to Recife when he had completed his sentence because "he is in charge of the service of the national farms and his absence at this time would be prejudicial to public coffers."[47] Sometimes garrison soldiers took up workshop positions. When lance corporal João Qualberto da Mota asked to return to the capital to collect an inheritance, his commander gave him a backhanded compliment: "I chose him as master carpenter not because of his abilities as an artisan but only because he has been well behaved which made him dignified to lead the workers of that workshop, he being very young and married."[48] This confirms that production was subordinated to the calculations commanders made about how to maintain order. Mota's behavior and his duties as a married man were more important than his carpentry skills.

A few nonconvicts served as sergeants, but most of their identities remain obscure. Nonconvicts earned higher wages than their convict counterparts and for this reason commanders usually preferred the latter. As one reported in 1886, "It is highly convenient for the Presidio's order and discipline, besides savings result for public coffers when convicts with exemplary conduct head work companies." He added that "all of his predecessors" sanctioned it.[49] Some nonconvict sergeants were fired for "the good of public service." The one nonconvict sergeant who left a paper trail appeared in the previous chapter: Quirino Joaquim Madeira or the "Sailor Madeira."[50]

Two American geologists and colleagues, Orville Derby and John Branner, visited Fernando de Noronha on separate occasions. Both described an unnamed Italian convict sergeant in revealing ways. Derby expressed revulsion for this "overseer":

> Many of the guards and most of the overseers are convicts and as in the latter considerable intelligence is required, some of the worst criminals are often selected for this duty which is a much coveted one since an overseer has easy work, is allowed a horse, and has four convicts detained as servants in his house. One of these overseers is an Italian convicted of the murder of an entire family of eleven persons. This man is of such a villainous appearance that one of the officers of the ship knowing the circumstances, but never having seen the man picked him out at once from among a group of nearly one hundred, his identification being afterwards confirmed from his own mouth, when the impudent scoundrel honored us with a visit on board. It was positively sickening to see this man lording it over men who, whatever their crimes may have been, were innocence itself as compared to him.[51]

Branner gave a more favorable depiction of the same convict:

> Among the convicts thus specially privileged about the [commander's] house was a tall, handsome Italian, apparently a man of education. He spoke, besides his native language, Spanish, German, some English, and Portuguese almost perfectly. I asked his story of the son of the commandant, who also told me the personal history of many of these men, and learned that he had killed five persons in less than five minutes, including the young lady to whom he was betrothed, because she had followed the advice of her father and mother, and had broken off the match upon the morning of the day on which they were to be married. As the narrator ended the story, which was told in all its dreadful details, he remarked, "And so you see he was almost justified."[52]

Branner's and Derby's accounts differed in the number of victims, but they almost certainly described the same man. I suspect that they described

Sergeant Attilio Francisco Simonelli, an Italian sentenced to perpetual galleys.[53] Simonelli appeared in the last chapter when a commander recommended his petition for a commutation and noted he had helped the staff suppress a convict insurrection. He was a convict sergeant and a storeowner who frequented the commander's household. While their depictions diverge, both Branner and Derby concur that commanders relied on wily, hard men to be company sergeants.

Commanders usually assigned nonconvict sergeants to head companies linked to security. In 1885, fifteen sergeants headed work companies, four of whom were nonconvicts. Forty-four corporals assisted sergeants, but only one was a nonconvict. Over the years the number of nonconvict sergeants varied from two to five. In 1885, nonconvict sergeants filled key posts: the company of skilled workers; another, the company in charge of cattle; another, the 2nd Company of convict police and the 10th Company of field workers; and another, the 1st Company of night watchmen.[54]

Political prisoners constituted another privileged caste. They expected to be treated differently from most prisoners, and they usually were. They were also enemies of incumbent politicians, and commanders were often suspicious of them. If they stirred up trouble, they could receive rigorous treatment.[55] Among the prominent political prisoners who did time in the colony was the leader of Pernambuco's Cabanos Revolt (1832–1835), Vicente de Paula Ferreira. So too did key figures from Pará's Cabanagem Rebellion (1835–1840): Pedro Vinagre and Eduardo Angelim; they were later joined by ten leaders of the Praieira Rebellion in 1850. The emperor pardoned many amnestied political prisoners, who often returned to privileged lives. Henrique Pereira do Lucena's son became Pernambuco's governor in the 1870s.[56] Conversely, ex-major Antônio Feitosa de Melo was later convicted of counterfeiting in the 1870s and returned to the colony as a convict.[57]

While political prisoners were usually excused from fieldwork, ordinary plebeian prisoners worked for paltry wages and rations. The dregs of plebeian convict society lived in the aldeia's cramped quarters.[58] Commanders expressed ambivalent opinions about plebeian convicts. The 1852 remarks of a commander about most convicts was typical: "Escape attempts, petty theft, and libertine behavior [*crapulas*] are the vices that dominate [among convicts]. . . . [Most convicts] are docile, obedient, and hard working." The comment reveals a dose of compassion and pity mixed with contempt. He empathized with convicts who suffered from the vendors' "usury," and deplored the fact that there were "women from the 'world' who brought with them children of both sexes . . . who cause scandals that offend family morality. They incite the perpetration of theft, increase the scarcity of food stuffs, and disturb the presidio's tranquility." In this portrayal, women from the world encouraged convicts to steal to provide them with necessities and luxuries, which contradicted the idea that women's presence would moralize the colony. The commander emphasized, however, that these were unattached women, not the wives of convict laborers.[59] Maintaining order amid the webs of relationships between officers, enlisted men, convicts, vendors, and unattached women was an arduous task. The next section explores the identities of nonconvict brothers and sisters of the peak.

THE OTHER BROTHERS AND SISTERS OF THE PEAK

While information about most convicts is plentiful, it is often sparse for nonconvicts. Commanders left a document trail, but most of their subordinate officers, civil servants, nonconvict vendors, and the "unattached" are obscure. Like convicts, many nonmilitary and nonconvict residents (referred to as *paisanos*, military slang for civilians) lived with families. Beaurepaire Rohan characterized most of this population as transient: "The presidio does not have appropriately speaking a fixed population, with the exception of those condemned to exile and perpetual galleys."[60] His statement was inaccurate, however, because some nonconvict residents lived there for many years.

Though there were shifts in the number and variety of army personnel over time, the commander was the executive and his second, the major da praça, commanded the garrison. Other officers assisted their superiors, and a handful of sergeants and corporals commanded a few scores of privates. Most subordinate officers came from Pernambuco's garrisons. After 1845, the War Ministry named the colony's commander, but Pernambuco's governor named the major da praça and civil employees. Thus, the major da praça represented the interests of the governor while commanders represented those of the War Ministry and, after 1877, the Justice Ministry in Rio de Janeiro.[61] Consequently, there were often disputes between commanders and their seconds.

One might suspect that the army would assign less prominent officers to command a penal presidio, but the evidence indicates otherwise. Most commanders from 1820 to 1890 held the army rank of major, lieutenant colonel, or colonel, though a few were generals or captains. Officers from the army's corps of engineers and artillery battalions predominated, but men from other branches also served. A few commanders served as adjutants and later returned as commanders. While most served a one-year stint, five served more than one command: Antônio Gomes Leal and Sebastião Antônio de Rego Barros served three tours, and Francisco Joaquim Pereira Lobo, five.[62]

Commanders' careers demonstrate the interconnection of institutions responsible for mainland police work: the police, National Guard, disbanded colonial militias, and the army. They also suggest links between prison administration, military impressment, and electoral politics as many commanders experienced a kind of category drift in their careers that paralleled those of the intractable poor. This uncovers yet another layer of the politicization of penal justice. For example, two cousins served as colony commanders, José Ignácio Ribeiro Roma and João Ignácio Ribeiro Roma, both descendants of Padre Roma (Father José Ignácio Ribeiro de Abreu e Lima), a martyred leader of the 1817 Pernambucan Republican Revolution. An 1886 parliamentary election inquiry described the cousins: "João Ignácio Ribeiro Roma is the principal, the most prestigious active chief of the Conservative Party in the Poço parish [Pernambuco]. . . . His cousin . . . José Ignácio Ribeiro Roma . . . was recently named Adjutant to Fernando de Noronha's commander."[63] The Ribeiro Romas mixed military and political careers.

The men who enforced penal justice were as politicized as the system they served. Colonel Alexandre de Barros e Albuquerque was a police major who volunteered to fight in Paraguay. After the war, he continued his army career and served two stints as colony commander.[64] Many who headed the presidio had combat experience quelling regional rebellions. Brigadeiro Hygino José Coelho pacified protestors in Pernambuco during the 1852 War of the Wasps.[65] Brigadeiro Francisco Sergio de Oliveira began as an officer in Paraíba's white militia regiment. He transferred to the army after Parliament disbanded colonial militias, and fought to quell a series of regional rebellions: Pernambuco's Confederation of the Equator, Pará's Cabanagem, and Maranhão's Balaiada. He became a brigadeiro just before assuming command of Fernando de Noronha in 1846 and later served as Pernambuco's commander of arms. Pernambuco's governor, chief of police, and commander of arms coordinated policing, military recruitment, and the deployment of troops, including those who served on Fernando de Noronha.[66]

Commander Pereira Lobo was a well-connected partisan of the Conservative Party who celebrated electoral victories with relish. A correspondent on Fernando de Noronha in 1885 reported: "The good news of the Conservative Party's recent electoral victory was a cause of general contentment among us but there were no acts of celebration such as illuminations, marching bands, etc. that under identical circumstances have been permitted before in the presidio, but because of recent incidents, the Excellent Senhor General Pereira Lobo, even though he is affiliated with the Conservatives, counseled his subordinates to do nothing, and he was privately congratulated by all the employees and officers."[67] Through these celebrations, convicts remained connected to mainland politics and knew their administrators' politics. Pereira Lobo became an honorary army brigadier for his service repressing the Praieira Revolt as commander of Olinda's National Guard.[68] His career confirms the links between institutions responsible for policing, military impressment, electoral politics, and prisons. In 1882, he summarized his career:

> I have served the military for 57 years, 11 months, and 26 days at different posts with important responsibilities, I commanded and organized six battalions, commanded two legions, and was Chief of the National Guard's high command, I served on a number of important and honorable high government commissions, commanded this presidio since Mar. 28, 1881, directed military recruitment in Recife and Olinda and also the entire province of Alagoas [during the War of the Triple Alliance]. I commanded the 14th Brigade during the Paraguayan Campaign, I reorganized Recife's Army Hospital which I directed for 11 years, and I even served as interim Commander of Arms for Pernambuco. . . . In all of these posts my superiors honored my service with praise and various decorations because I faithfully fulfilled their orders and because of this I am poor.[69]

The commander emphasized his poverty as proof of the relatively modest pay army officers received and to suggest that he had not used his office to enrich himself. One senses that the commander protested his innocence too much. The American geologist Branner described Pereira Lobo: "The commandant I found to be a very aged man, an officer in the regular Brazilian army. His thin grey hair was cut close to his angular head, and his mustache was white with age and yellow with tobacco smoke. He received me indifferently. . . . I afterward found that this was due to a suspicion that I had been sent here by the government on some secret mission."[70] The brigadeiro's behavior indicated he was suspicious that he was under investigation, and as subsequent chapters will show, he had reason to be.[71]

Travelers' accounts provide unique portraits of some commanders. In 1888, a British naturalist gave a favorable impression of Lieutenant Colonel Agripino Furtado de Mendonça: "At the head of the whole is the Director, a Brazilian officer who has earned distinction in the Paraguayan War and in subsequent service under Government, and has received the Order of the Rose and another decoration."[72] In 1863, Confederate captain Raphael Semmes of the css *Alabama* gave a wry depiction of Major Sebastião José Basílio Pyrrho as a "thin, spare man, rather under medium height, and of sprightly manners and conversation."[73] Semmes also noted that Pyrrho was the "shade of tanned shoe leather," but this was not the case for the former Prussian officer João Bloem. This Tueto-Brazilian commanded the colony from 1825 to 1827, and he went on to lead reform projects in Recife and the army's iron works in Ipanema, São Paulo.[74] While historians and other scholars have argued that the management of plantation slave labor contributed to the development of industrial capitalist labor practices, here is a case where the management of convict plantation labor likely contributed to Bloem's reorganization of the Ipanema iron works, which the historian Jaime Rodrigues described as one of Brazil's primordial industrial establishments.[75] A number of presidio commanders joined elite cultural institutions in Recife. Pereira Lobo and Antonio Gomes Leal were members of the Instituto Arqueológico e Geográphico Pernambucano (today the Instituto Arqueológico, Histórico e Geográfico Pernambucano), the most venerable organization in Brazil's Northeast dedicated to the study and preservation of history, geography, and archeology.

The connections of Fernando de Noronha's commanders to policing, electoral politics, and military impressment on the mainland indicate that this was a sensitive post. As subsequent chapters show, the opposition frequently used events in the presidio to criticize incumbents. The island was not nearly as isolated as it appeared on a map, and convicts could become political agents of no small consequence.

The second in command, the major da praça, led the garrison troops and usually lodged in Fort Remédios. Most majors da praça held a junior officer rank of lieutenant or captain. One visitor gave a brief description of the commander's subordinates: "Under him [the commander] is the ajudante do presidio and the chief accountant and the medical officers. The military are quite distinct; they have their quarters in the Fort, which, though antiquated, is quite strong enough for all practical purposes, and their duties are mainly sentry duty and ordinary drill."[76] This passage highlights how officials tried to keep troops and convicts segregated. While some, like José Ignácio Riberio Roma, served as junior officers before becoming commander, many young officers, served there briefly and never returned.

Beyond the major da praça and the medical officers there is little information about subordinate officers. In 1885, a commander wrote that Ensign Theophilo de Mattos of the 14th Infantry Battalion died of tuberculosis. He paid the Ensign's wife 100$000 réis according to regulations for his burial and "other indispensable expenses because they are a poor and large family." The ensign lived with three children, two unmarried sisters, and a brother who was a minor. The low pay of junior officers made the temptation of supplementing one's income through graft hard to resist.

Pernambuco's commander of arms assigned the presidio's enlisted men from local battalions. Most troops were illiterate men of all colors, although most were men of mixed race who hailed from Pernambuco. Their ages varied widely from the teens to late fifties.[77] This reflected patterns found in the larger army, where officers could not be too choosy about the men they led. Commanders commonly maligned their troops. The pithy comment of João Bloem in 1827 about a soldier was typical: "João dos Anjos, 33 years old, married, conduct: good when he is not drunk."[78] Another wrote in 1852 that his soldiers were ordinarily those whom mainland officers sought to discard, and after they disembark, they become more undisciplined through their contact with convicts. "Therefore," he blithely mused, "one cannot place one's entire confidence in all of them." One commander claimed that he had curbed unruliness among the troops by paying part of their salary in goods rather than cash. He did this because the soldiers misspent their money on drink and other trifles that contributed to the vendors' "exaggerated profits." Then, money spent, they complained of hunger. Hunger led some troops to commit petty thefts, and at other times, vendors falsely attributed thefts to soldiers. For this reason, the commander urged that new uniforms be distributed in a timely fashion, and that rations be delivered promptly every two months because the humid climate did not permit the storage of food-stuffs for more than eight weeks.[79]

Colony troops were similar to the army convicts they guarded, and not a few were former convicts. For Pernambuco's commander at arms, reintegrating convict soldiers who completed their sentences into the presidio's garrison cut transport costs and provided a piecemeal solution to perennial troop shortfalls there. From the commander's perspective, however, it threatened security. The case of the convict soldier Antônio Francisco das Chagas is illustrative. Chagas arrived without his guia (the document that identified convicts and their sentences), but he immediately petitioned for a commutation of his capital sentence. For some reason, Chagas, who been assigned to live in the aldeia, was integrated into the garrison with rights to wages and uniforms. Five months later, his guia arrived and confirmed his sentence. The commander discharged him and ordered him to return to the aldeia.[80] The line between convicts and enlisted warders was flimsy, and officers worried about preserving order among their troops as much as their convicts.

While many former army convicts became garrison soldiers overnight, convict Serafim Manoel dos Anjos proved that even serial killers could experience repeated bouts of category drift. In 1879, the commander reported that Anjos had assassinated Maria Francisca da Conceição, a nonconvict in the late stages of pregnancy. This was Anjos's third and possibly his fourth murder. A jury acquitted him for the murder of a woman with whom he lived in a consensual union in Ceará, but authorities pressed him into army service at the Paraguayan front. In Paraguay, he allegedly killed another woman he lived with, and he subsequently deserted. He was captured and tried for wartime desertion, not homicide, and ended up on Fernando de Noronha. Army officials pardoned him in 1871 and reintegrated him into a Rio de Janeiro regiment. Like other pardoned soldiers, Anjos had to serve out a new six-year contract. In Rio, a jury condemned Anjos for the murder of another woman and sentenced him to fourteen years of incarceration. Subsequently, he returned to Fernando de Noronha, where he stood accused of killing Conceição.[81]

Documentation reveals more about the identity of soldiers and convicts like Serafim than it does for the presidio's civil servants. Details about their identities come through in fragments, usually when a conflict emerged. Most had ties to Pernambuco, since they were designated by its governor. Since their positions required literacy and some accounting, they usually came from the educated middle-class strata, and they often served longer stints in the presidio than commanders. Their numbers varied over time, and their positions included warehouse manager, secretary, scrivener, assistant secretary, chaplain, schoolteacher, doctor, pharmacist, and company sergeants and corporals.

Commanders often complained about their civilian subordinates and called their dedication into question. In 1827, Captain João Bloem asked the governor to send him a copy of the constitution because his warehouse manager, Caetano Xavier da Almeida, was constantly showing him legislation to argue that he did not have to fulfill his duties.[82] Another commander fired his "lazy" scrivener Antônio Manuel Estevão and launched an investigation of his bookkeeping in 1852. He found that Estevão had altered records that had pages missing and other irregularities. The commander was also angry that his scrivener had sold for 120$000 réis a house that was no more than a "hut" with a straw roof where he had maintained a store. Some employees like Estevão supplemented their wages with commerce that distracted them from their duties and led to entangling relationships with convicts and soldiers.[83] Civilian employees lived in intimate contact with convicts because they depended on their gratuitous services for cleaning, cooking, tending gardens, washing clothes, fishing, providing child care, and so forth. The children of employees and convicts attended the same schools, one for boys and the other for girls.

Alongside civil servants and army officers were clergy. Finding clergymen to fill the two posts called for in regulations was difficult. Many times, there was only one priest in residence. Henry Koster observed that the priest sent to Fernando de Noronha had to be forced into service in a process akin to military impressment.[84] On the island, many priests became closely associated with the commander's household. Captain Semmes breakfasted at the commander's residence with the chaplain, a trusted convict, and the convict's daughter in 1863: "The chaplain of the penal colony . . . a portly and dignified priest, was also at the breakfast table, and my paymaster and myself spent a very pleasant half-hour around this social board, at which were represented so many of the types of mankind, and so different moral elements."[85] Most priests were Brazilian-born, but a few were foreigners. As one commander observed in 1871: "I cannot comment on the capabilities of Father Ruibert because he does not speak Portuguese." Father Ruibert refused to give final rights to convicts who had not recently received the sacrament of confession, even if their death was precipitous.[86] The services provided by clergy mirrored those carried out on the mainland. One visitor observed: "The Church is served by a priest, and there is high Mass every Sunday at 8:00 AM, and occasional services at other times, such as festivals etc., besides the regular daily Mass."[87]

Vivandeiros (unattached nonconvict storeowners) were another class of residents. As noted earlier, officers, employees, and convicts also ran stores, but vivandeiros were civilians who had permission to conduct business. Beaurepaire Rohan depicted them as parasitic carpetbaggers: "There is another even more fluctuating element that is composed by a type of pilferer that comes here to traffic, or better, extract, by way of commerce full of fraud, the money that the government contributes to the presidio's expenses. This class of commercial agent should be banned from an establishment of this order, and the supply of the population made by other means."[88] No wonder Beaurepaire Rohan desired to house all convicts in barracks and feed them from mess halls.

The identities of unattached residents are little known. Governors permitted these men and women to live in the colony, and some commanders were more tolerant of them than others. An 1852 dispatch from Commander Francisco Feliz de Macedo e Vasconcelos, three days after he assumed his post, revealed: "I found the presidio reduced to an asylum. . . . For whoever wants to seek refuge [*asilar-se*] on the island it is enough to obtain from the governor's office a business license and present it to the ship captain that supplies the colony, others come even without this license." Vasconcelos asked families to show him their authorizations, but they claimed that their permits remained with the ship captains who brought them. He evicted a number of them and wrote that if the governor approved, he would remove more because they complicated his efforts to keep the colony "well policed." He investigated their backgrounds to verify whether there might be among them men wanted by the police or recruitable men (*recrutáveis*) who had fled from Recife. In 1852, Brazil was at war with Argentina and needed men to fight on its southern frontier.[89] The commander believed that some came to the penal colony to escape criminal prosecution and military impressment, which shows he believed them to be contemptuous rabble.

A few nonconvict slaves accompanied staff and convicts. An 1851 steamship manifest listed "the former Chaplain Vicente Ferreira do Rego, 22 enlisted men from the 4th Battalion of Artillery, the civilians Manoel Thomas dos Santos and his son Francisco Xavier dos Santos, Francisca Rosa Lima and her slave Laurinda, and the brown slave of the convict Dr. Felipe Lopes Neto."[90] Lopes Neto was a political prisoner, but officials did not bar him from bringing a slave with him into exile. Nor was he unique. In 1858, a presidio census recorded nine slaves: seven belonged to officers and two to convicts.[91] The fact that prisoners could bring slaves with them is another example of how Brazilians mitigated the individualized and leveling punishment implicit in liberal penology. The presence of slaves meant that the touchstone of free status remained a relevant distinction there, but their numbers were too few to cause concern. Beaurepaire Rohan observed: "The slaves who are on the island, and those that accompany their owners there, are so few in number that no inconvenience results."[92]

THE FAMILIES OF THE PEAK

Some members of every major social category lived with family even though bachelors predominated in the population. Exile separated many married convicts from their wives and family, and there were no small number of widowers as some had been convicted of killing their wives. Some bachelors formed alternative families by living in consensual unions with other men, and others courted the few available women: female convicts and the daughters of other convicts and garrison soldiers.

An unusually detailed 1890 census shows that most civil servants and all officers lived with their families (see table A14). Almost 16 percent of nonconvict soldiers and 10 percent of convict men lived with their wives and dependents. Almost 4 percent of convict men lived in a consensual union with a woman. Almost 40 percent of women married to convicts were white or "semi-white," nearly 50 percent were brown, and those classed as indigenous and black were roughly 6 percent each. All convict wives were Brazilian, save for a Portuguese and a German. Illegitimacy rates among convict children were under 13 percent, lower than on the mainland (see table A15).

The survey did not record similar information about the race, nationality, and legitimacy of officers, employees, or garrison soldiers' wives and children. Most officers and employees brought their immediate family with them, but family could also include a variety of extended family members. Given that uprisings and violence among convicts arose with some regularity, officers and employees must have felt guarded about bringing their families, but not to the extent that they chose to live apart from them. The number of family members of employees and officers remained consistent after 1850. Staff wives mostly occupied themselves with maintaining their households and rearing children.[93]

The wives of convicts and soldiers could earn extra income by washing clothes for soldiers and administrators or by preparing food to sell to men returning from their duties. Many also cared for young children until they were old enough to attend the colony's grammar school. A few ran stores and most tended to family provision grounds while their convict husbands toiled in the imperial fields.

Table A16 relates the community's growth after 1850. Earlier reports did not systematically record inhabitants, but Captain Bloem related in 1827: "I have only 53 men capable of work, the rest are old, lame, or sick in the hospital." He griped that officers and the chaplain had "old or lame" convicts that worked as domestics, but if he assigned them each another convict to work their provision gardens, he would not have enough men to advance the imperial farm's agriculture.[94] The population grew from some 500 inhabitants in 1847 to some 2,300 in the mid-1870s. Much of the colony's growth came after Beaurepaire Rohan's regulations formalized convicts' right to petition for their wives and dependents to join them in exile. Convict family members grew from 78 in 1854 to 500 in 1886. It is likely that vendors were lumped into the "unattached" category in the 1850s, but in the 1860s and 1870s they were counted separately. When commerce was banned in 1879, they disappeared as a category.

The sisters of the peak were a distinct minority. Wives, daughters, and female dependents, convicts, and unattached residents constituted some 20 percent of the population in the 1870s. Most were children. While most female convicts were not well known, there was a notorious exception: Carlota Lucia de Brito. Brito fled drought in the backlands in 1845 and migrated to Areia, Paraíba, where she became the lover of the Liberal Party boss, Joaquim José dos Santos Leal. When one of her lover's conservative rivals, Trajano Chacon, publicly insulted Brito in a church, she hired a dependent living on Santos Leal's lands to assassinate Chacon on the day that he defeated Santos Leal in an election for federal deputy in 1849. This occurred during the Praieira Revolt, which, though centered in Pernambuco, had repercussions in neighboring Paraíba. Santos Leal himself had publicly declared his support for the rebels. While the emperor pardoned Praieira rebels in May 1851, conservatives focused their ire over the rebellion on Brito and her lover as suspicion for the murder immediately fell on them. The couple fled, but police tracked them down. The jury sentenced the humble assassin to the gallows, and Brito and Santos Leal to life in prison. Santos Leal soon died after arriving in Fernando de Noronha, but Brito survived until the republican regime's new sentencing laws freed her in the early 1890s. She then settled in Recife, where she ran a boarding house for male students from the interior.[95]

Most of the colony's prisoners were not as privileged as Brito. They had worked in agriculture, and if they lived in a city, they earned their living through manual labor. Their collective biography reflected the hierarchies of color and class in Brazilian society, where the penal justice system focused its scarce resources on prosecuting and imprisoning men who committed violent crimes, homicide in particular. Brito's exile, however, contributed to the growing numbers of women in the colony. In part, more regular and safer steamship transportation made it more affordable and convenient for families to accompany loved ones to the presidio, but this change also reflected evolving ideas of penal justice in terms of family, gender, sexuality, and patriarchal responsibilities and rights.

5 THE JEALOUS INSTITUTION AND BRAZILIAN PENOLOGY

Conselheiro Martim Francisco Riberio de Andrada, a leader of São Paulo's Liberal Party, a law professor, minister of justice (1866–1868), and president of the House of Deputies in 1882, proposed a tax for bachelors in 1879 to encourage marriage. The Italo-Brazilian illustrator Angelo Agostini lampooned his proposal and highlighted its potential unintended consequences. While humorists roasted this parliamentarian's proposal, his preoccupation with the relationship between marriage, prosperity, public order, national defense, and population growth were far from singular. As Michel Foucault and others have observed, state builders across the world shared a preoccupation with the management and growth of their populations. In France, long a cultural model for educated Brazilians, leaders fretted over their nation's slow population growth in the mid-nineteenth century and its implications for public morality and national security.[1] Nations as diverse as Argentina, Turkey, England, Italy, Germany, France, and many U.S. states debated or enacted bachelor taxes in the nineteenth and twentieth centuries.[2]

Imperial Brazilian debates over marriage sprang from historic roots over how best to develop and defend Portuguese America's vast territory. Conselheiro Martim Francisco and others felt the state should take more assertive steps to encourage and strengthen marriage. In the 1880s, the most compelling law to incentivize free poor Brazilian bachelors to marry was military impressment because it exempted married men if they provided for and protected their wives

FIG 5.1 "Marriage should be happy, an eternal idyll, in which one conjugates the verb love in all its tenses. . . . But for the marriage [*hymeneo*, a reference to the hymen and a bride's virginity] to be beautiful it is necessary to have a lot of this [illustration of money]. . . . The tax collector demanding 50$ réis from bachelors will rob them of their savings, the true basis of a happy marriage, or leave them without the means to contract a marriage that suits them [illustration of a couple hung by a rope labeled *hymeneo*]. Repeating the words of Christ, the Conselheiro Martim Francisco said: 'Be fruitful and multiply.' [But] Raise children in poverty? Multiply the miserable? [cartoon of women and children begging]. [Martim Francisco's lament] 'God knows that what I wanted was to populate my fatherland . . . but for now, they rejected my amendment to tax bachelors. All there is left for me is to cry over the ruins of this future Brazilian desert.'" *Revista Ilustrada* 161 (May 17, 1879): 8.

and dependents. Not a few men rushed to the altar to escape the clutches of recruiters. In 1874, Senator Rio Branco opposed exempting married men from the conscription lottery, arguing: "If this condition [marriage] forcibly exempts one from recruitment then it will be necessary to adopt a disposition prohibiting soldiers to marry."[3] His amendment, however, did not become part of the 1874 Recruitment Law, which in any case proved to be a dead letter.

The Religious Question (1873–1875) brought the issue of civil marriage to the fore as some clerics refused the sacrament to Freemasons. Indeed, the controversy continued even after Pedro II and the Vatican came to terms in 1875. The Recife newspaper *A Província*, associated with the Liberal Party, reported in 1877: "Yet another marriage has taken place in this city without the solemnities of the sainted mother Church, thanks to the 'tolerance' of the diocesan priest who rejected the mason from the Catholic Church's breast making him the equivalent of a heretic."[4] A similar dispute in 1885 over the marriage of a devout positivist who refused confession sparked heated reaction in the *Diário de Pernambuco*, which tended to align itself with Conservatives.[5] As noted in chapter 1, when Brazil's Parliament debated civil marriage in 1874 it stoked popular animosities that boiled over in the Quebra Quilos Revolt (1874–1875). In short, marriage was a political and social issue that preoccupied politicians, Freemasons, priests, judges, riotous plebeians, slaves, and even penal colony administrators.[6]

One of Fernando de Noronha's missions was to occupy an island, and as such, it was part and parcel of larger Brazilian efforts to inhabit national frontiers. On the mainland, this usually involved founding frontier settlements with sustainable populations, but until the independence era, authorities had banned women from Fernando de Noronha. State institutions like penitentiaries, military compounds, asylums, poor houses, orphanages, boarding schools, and so on, usually sought to segregate their wards on the basis of gender among other factors. Senator Rio Branco's amendment to the 1874 Recruitment Law echoed concerns that had long preoccupied officials who grappled with discipline in institutions that segregated men to varying degrees from women. Does intimate contact with women improve discipline?[7] If so, how should it be regulated? By examining how Brazilians tackled these questions, this chapter examines notions of gender and sexuality and their perceived relationship to discipline, health, reproduction, rehabilitation, and justice. Sexual behavior was central to social reproduction and it preoccupied leaders of a vast and thinly populated nation undergoing a slow but largely peaceful transition from slave to free labor. Marriage served as a marker of status among the intractable poor, and in a larger sense it was a bellwether of a just public and private order that actors great and small contested vigorously.[8]

The segregation that modern disciplining institutions required ran counter to critiques of inhibiting a man's heterosexual release through continence or imposed abstinence. In this context, I include slavery as a total institution even though it did not figure in Irving Goffman's original work on batch-living institutions. I do this because the conditions under which slaves lived, especially on large plantations, approximated those of convicts, enlisted military, free Africans, and Indians in government villages.

To explore male nubility I return to Irving Goffman's and Lewis Coser's insights glossed in the introduction to elucidate tensions between individuals, families, and segregating total and greedy institutions. Their insights frame more fully the jealous institution of heterosexual conjugality that members of Brazil's clergy, military, judiciary, and others believed shaped the behavior of male members of the intractable poor, or at least a large portion of them, in positive ways. The chapter then examines nineteenth-century criticisms of gender-segregating institutions and the imposition of male heterosexual abstinence. This context permits a fruitful exploration of the 1865 regulations that encouraged bachelor convicts to marry and permitted married ones to petition for their wives and dependents to join them in exile. It also compares conjugal penal policy to other institutions that included male members of the intractable poor: slaves and soldiers in particular. Authorities tested the potential of heterosexual penal conjugality on Fernando de Noronha, but to contextualize this experiment, a brief archeology of criticisms of male segregation and imposed sexual abstinence is required.

MALE CELIBACY AND GENDER SEGREGATION

Goffman argued that family ties existed in tension with institutions that required degrees of gender segregation and batch living, but for many Brazilians, sexual abstinence debilitated a man's health. Therefore, prisons, penal colonies, barracks, boarding schools, monasteries, and *senzalas* (gender-segregated slave barracks) were common sites of "perversion." As an 1898 Brazilian medical thesis on same-sex eroticism observes: "Religious communities, ocean going vessels, the navy, the army, boarding schools, and seminaries were in truth perfect habitats for the type of forbidden love we study."[9] Authorities blamed masturbation, bestiality, and same-sex liaisons in these institutions on women's relative absence much like Ferreira Portugal, who criticized the absolute gender segregation of Fernando de Noronha in 1797.

Critics of segregating men from women borrowed from Enlightenment attacks on the Catholic Church. For many, a man needed regular, but not excessive, heterosexual intercourse to maintain his physical and mental health. Ideally, this health treatment would come through regular coitus with a man's wife, but for some, female prostitutes were inferior proxies because they let single men satisfy their urges and reduced the threat of seduction or rape for honest women of families. Another practice army officers had long tolerated among their enlisted men and convicts was to permit a portion of them to live in heterosexual consensual unions that were respected as long as the couple lived in a dignified manner. If deprived of "natural" copulation with women, a man's insatiable sex drive would presumably find release in "unnatural" desires such as "sodomy," bestiality, and masturbation.[10]

Eighteenth-century reformers applied aspects of this logic to criticize Brazil's monasteries, nunneries, and missions that they felt impeded Portuguese America's economic and demographic growth. Specifically, they ended the segregation of Indians in Jesuit-administered mission villages and predicted that Indian women would then marry Portuguese men, who would be a "civilizing" influence on their wives. Pombaline reformers' economic and sexual critiques buttressed attacks on Jesuit authority that ultimately facilitated their expulsion from Brazil in 1763.[11]

When there were not enough Indian women, Portuguese officials sent females from settled areas to frontiers to form families to stabilize rough-and-tumble outposts and discourage men forced to migrate there from deserting. This reasoning influenced colonial officials who dragooned "disreputable" women from São Paulo to send to Iguatemi, a frontier military settlement near the current Paraguayan border during the Seven Years War. In some ways, these policies paralleled the crown's practice of granting dowries to orphaned Portuguese girls whom they sent to colonial outposts to wed. While many of these examples apply to Portugal's colonial frontiers, where this logic held particular appeal, a similar reasoning applied in core plantation and urban areas.[12]

As earlier chapters show, Brazilians shared these assumptions. The 1797 missive from the Recife-born cleric Ferreira Portugal censured crown policies that left Fernando de Noronha bereft of women, which he felt encouraged same-sex intimacy and even same-sex marriages.[13] Brazilian reformers continued to criticize male celibacy requirements after independence. The most notable of them was Regent Padre Diogo Antônio Feijó (1835–1837), who favored abolishing clerical celibacy for Brazil's priests. Feijó held that obligatory celibacy went against "natural" rights and laws, and that the "propensity toward marriage was innate in the species." He added, "This is why it is so rare to find a celibate priest who is not perverse." One might mistakenly infer that Feijó implicated himself, but it was well known that he had a mistress with whom he fathered five children. Some disagreed with Feijó and argued that sexual abstinence had no negative consequences, but the belief that it did continued to shape perceptions, policies, and practices. This view contrasted with North Atlantic Victorians who believed sexual continence was a sign of virility rather than an unmanly debilitating health hazard.[14]

Brazilian abolitionists and slavocrats employed a similar sexualized logic to attack the batch living common in senzalas. Masters stereotyped slaves as "vice ridden" because they were not "of family," and though the logic was circular, this justified their enslavement and gender segregation. Even Brazilian abolitionists, like Joaquim Nabuco, often used this same caricature to condemn slavery: "He [the slave] does not possess his honor because of his infamous birth and because his women are the inheritance of his master's lust. . . . Outside of the family, which he [a young male slave] does not have, there are . . . all the vices of servility—fear, cowardice, indignity, adulation, lies, and cynicism—which deposit themselves in fertile soil that is destined to burst forth in his youth." Nabuco depicted senzalas as dens of promiscuity where young women were victims of unfettered male lust:

> An adolescent female slave of fifteen to sixteen years of age, sometimes younger . . . is delivered already violated to the slave barracks. A female slave was born virtually without honor. Within reach of the first violence, without protection, without a tribunal, without a family, without law to which she can appeal, what can she do against such perfidy? There is no example for her except corruption, and thus a young woman of fifteen soon becomes a public woman in the senzala. Some masters present themselves as arrangers of summary marriages: this is a sacrilege and impudence. Thrown from one to the other in the everyday bacchanalia, plaything of the most brutal instincts, she lives between giving birth and tortures.

New research shows that slaves formally wed at higher rates than previously thought, but the idea that they were "without family" remained ensconced in free Brazilians' imaginations.[15]

For abolitionists, the senzala's batch living sullied not only slaves' character, but also their owners', their owners' families, and the nation's collective masculinity. As Nabuco put it, "Nor is there a social agent which has the same deep and wide-ranging psychological effect as slavery when it becomes an integral part of the family. This influence can be characterized by observing that slavery enveloped our entire populated space . . . in an environment destructive to all the manly, generous, and progressive qualities of our species." For Nabuco, this contagion extended to priests, especially batch-living, cloistered ones: "Many priests own slave women, and clerical celibacy does not prohibit it. That contact, more accurately—contagion—of slavery lent our religion its materialist tendencies, destroyed its spiritual quality, and denied it any hope of performing the role of an upright force in the nation's social life."[16] Here a critique of male celibacy is powerfully combined with anticlerical and antislavery rhetoric.

Abolitionists and slavocratic critiques proceed from the assumption that bondage corrupted a slave's moral character because it allegedly denied him or her a family life, but they disputed whether that degradation extended to the families and the state that slaveowners headed. The critiques of Fernando de Noronha, the senzala, barracks, and clerical celibacy reveal broadly shared assumptions about male sexual needs.

"WITHOUT WOMEN IT IS IMPOSSIBLE TO GOVERN FERNANDO"

For many Brazilian leaders penal science offered an answer to the demise of masters' authority as the slave population declined after 1850. In the 1870s, however, this belief in rehabilitation confronted the Italian criminologist Cesare Lombroso's idea of the born criminal and social Darwinian apologies for European imperialism.[17] Even so, most imperial penal authorities, even those familiar with Lombroso, affirmed the potential reformative power of hard work, family living, and "normal" sexuality regardless of a convict's color, class, or civil condition. An 1876 Recife newspaper editorial argued that criminal activity in Brazil stemmed from the idleness of what it estimated to be half of the population and suggested a solution: an obligatory work law that would force all men to labor.[18] The concept of the nuclear family as a foundation for societal order and labor discipline was not a new ideal of North Atlantic capitalism, as some have posited, but capitalism did influence how the family was conceptualized in relation to charity and new institutions.[19]

Fernando de Noronha's commanders not only had to win the support of many convicts; they also had to motivate them to work. Since the colony's commanders were army officers, they drew on their experience managing unruly soldiers. Most also had familiarity with Brazil's frontiers and slavery.[20] Henrique Pedro Carlos de Beaurepaire Rohan, who authored the colony's 1865 regulations, had such experience. As an army engineer, he built roads in São Paulo's interior, oversaw urban reforms in Rio de Janeiro, and had years of experience working with soldiers of all colors along with slave laborers. The army itself owned slaves and employed free Africans in various enterprises such as its iron works in Ipanema, São Paulo, which a former commander of Fernando de Noronha, Captain João Bloem, reformed in the 1830s.[21]

Beaurepaire Rohan became a liberal politician and served three stints as a provincial governor and one as war minister. A noted cartographer, he published reflections on his travels in Brazil's interior that include a polemic against Francisco Adolfo de Varnhagen's condemnation of Indians. In this 1854 essay, Beaurepaire Rohan argues that Indians could contribute to imperial society if properly assimilated, but he belittled the state's use of Capuchin monks (*barbadinhos*, "little beards") to civilize frontier Indians: "The barbadinho's understanding that he is thoroughly fulfilling his mission by preaching fasting and chastity to these people!" In Beaurepaire Rohan's 1865 report on Fernando de Noronha he explains why he favored the formation of frontier penal colonies where convicts would live with their families over urban penitentiaries: first, Brazil should increase its population and occupy its frontiers; second, the family's presence deters escapes; and third, "why should one condemn these men to immoral celibacy?" Beaurepaire Rohan like many of his contemporaries followed Argentine Juan Alberdi's aphorism: "To govern is to populate." But unlike Alberdi, he did not feel this population had to be European to civilize the frontier; in Brazil, it should include multiracial convicts and Indians.[22] His 1865 regulations reflected this view as they formally allowed married convicts to apply to have their wives and dependents join them in exile. He encouraged well-behaved bachelor convicts to marry, though the pool of available women in the colony was limited.[23] Yet, this policy contradicted his other goal to *arranchar* all convicts in batch-living barracks and to feed them from a mess hall that would not allow for convict family life.

As argued in chapter 3, Beaurepaire Rohan's convict marriage policy bore a resemblance to strategies used to discipline and motivate soldiers by giving a privileged minority access to heterosexual conjugality. Beyond flogging and drills, officers rewarded dutiful soldiers with the right to *desarranchar*: to live off base and receive a per diem for meals. Commanders could also grant these soldiers the right to marry or to live with a consensual lover. If they became disobedient or failed to act as responsible household heads, officers could order them to arranchar: return to live and dine in the barracks' *rancho* (mess hall). Officers even managed the sexuality of batch-living soldiers. A 1906 medical thesis reported that "sodomy" had been common in the army during the empire, but by tolerating feminine prostitution near bases, enlightened republican officials had nearly eliminated same-sex eroticism in the barracks.[24]

Officers' strategies paralleled those of slaveowners who faced the challenge of disciplining and motivating workers whom they typified as intractable. Masters on large plantations and mines often housed slaves in gender-segregated senzalas, but new studies find that formal slave marriage rates in southeastern Brazil were as high as 25 to 40 percent, although fewer slaves married in the northeast. Revisionists observe that slaves with access to provision grounds and a private abode were more likely to be married or form consensual unions. Of course, there were limits on slave husbands' rights. Legal opinions clarified that they could exercise *pátrio poder* only to the extent a master allowed, but Catholicism supported a slave's right to the sacraments, including marriage, unlike Protestantism.[25] Anglophone masters opposed formal slave marriage because it implicitly ceded freedom of contract and patriarchal power to slaves, which raised the specter of competing systems of authority. They also argued that slave marriage sullied the institution because slaves had no honor (which bears a creepy resemblance to the rhetoric of contemporary opponents of gay marriage). Moreover, Anglophone laws often barred interracial marriage between free persons, unlike more flexible practices in colonial Cuba and even more so in Brazil, where no law banned it. Indeed, Brazil's elite embraced miscegenation as a means to "whiten" its diverse population. Divergent religious and cultural sensibilities about slave and interracial marriage, in addition to different conceptions of male sexuality, shaped these cultural contrasts.[26]

Why did Brazilian masters allow slaves to marry? Robert Slenes cites a daughter's recollection of her slaveowning father's statement: "It is necessary to marry this slave and give him a piece of land so that he learns judgment [*tomar juízo*]." Slenes argues that by allowing some slaves to leave the senzala barracks, wed, and work a provision ground, masters hoped to stem desertion and promote productivity, discipline, and morality in a fashion similar to soldiers permitted to desarranchar. Slenes's data comes largely from core plantation zones, but these practices were not limited to rural or frontier areas for slaves or soldiers. As the French artist Jean-Baptiste Debret noted: "In the houses of Brazil's wealthy, they marry their female slaves without contradicting too much their predilections in the choice of a husband; this custom springs from the hope of better tying them to the house."[27] Even Parliament began to recognize the sanctity of slave marriage: in 1866, it mandated that the wives of married slaves mobilized to fight at the Paraguayan front also be manumitted, and in 1869, it forbade masters from separating married slaves from spouses and their slave children under the age of fifteen through sale.[28] The timing of these laws and the 1865 regulations that allowed convicts to petition to have their wives join them in exile suggests the interconnection of the categories of the intractable poor and supports the hypothesis that a reform in one category could lead to similar ones for members of other categories.

The army officers who ran Fernando de Noronha applied similar marriage and batch-living strategies to convict laborers because the ideal of cellular isolation was impracticable given the lack of prison space. As noted earlier, while commanders granted many bachelor convicts the right to live outside the aldeia, they continued to associate it with bachelors.[29] An American journalist who visited the colony in 1876 confirmed that married convicts were privileged: "As a rule, the convicts spend half of their exile in prison [the aldeia]. If well-behaved, they may afterward live outside, build their own hut and cultivate their own garden, Government giving all, whether in prison [the aldeia] or out of it, a certain allowance of food. If specially well-behaved, particularly if married, they may sooner live outside, a boon granted by the Governor on application. A married convict can insist on having his wife and children beside him; and, though free, they often come from the Brazils [sic] to share a husband's or father's exile."[30] This depiction was not entirely accurate. Only a few men in the aldeia were "incarcerated" in jail cells, others slept in its large dormitory rooms for disciplinary infractions, but some "miserable" convicts lived there for lack of other options. The aldeia resembled the batch living of barracks and senzalas. Justice Ministry inspector Bandeira Filho even referred to it as a "type of barracks" (especie de quartel).[31] By the 1860s when the convict population surpassed 1,500, it was impossible for convicts to spend half their sentences in the aldeia given its capacity. As Bandeira Filho reported: "The recently arrived accommodate themselves as they can, making their residences where they can," but if they became incorrigible, they could be ordered to reside in the aldeia.[32]

Bandeira Filho found the aldeia's ambience appalling:

This house is always packed; in its two large dormitories almost 400 individuals sleep, and the capacity of the jail cells is exceeded. According to the nature of their infraction, a prisoner retires to the large rooms or the jail cells, and, they stay there with their comrades and pass their time in complete idleness. . . . I visited the Aldeia on a number of occasions to evaluate if the incorrigible individuals held there suffer, and I returned horrified by the inadmissible proposals, threats, and malicious jokes. They play, converse, and sing, but no one works, and they do not even appear discomforted by their punishment which relieves them from labor.[33]

In these passages, Bandeira Filho gives the false impression that staff did not require aldeia residents to work. Even those held in the aldeia's jail cells were often required to perform daytime cleaning duties under guard.

Beaurepaire Rohan deplored the fact that most convicts were not *arranchados* (required to live in barracks and dine in a common mess hall) and despaired that even the garrison troops were not arranchados: "I noticed that enlisted soldiers were not arranchados, a lamentable condition on this island more than anywhere else because of the exorbitant prices for all the goods sold by houses of commerce."[34] After explaining the high costs of food and convicts' low salaries, he suggested that "it would be better if all [convicts] were arranchados, which would be a great savings, not only in terms of combustibles but equally of eatable goods, besides it would diminish considerably . . . the immense number of individual fires made daily." He admitted that there existed no buildings to house a communal kitchen of adequate scale, but he felt that constructing such facilities should be a priority. He warned that if this was not undertaken, the wood used for individual cooking fires would lead to the island's complete deforestation.[35]

In 1880, Justice Ministry inspector Andre Augusto de Padua Fleury made similar recommendations: "The 600 convicts that stay in Remédios where besides the free population, there are now about 1,500 agglomerated, will be housed in the Aldeia, the Santa Anna barracks and another common building, these prisons will transform from dormitories to common cafeterias during the day and to schools in the afternoon. . . . The new villages should begin with vast mess halls [ranchos], where the convict workers will recite daily prayers and where they will receive, along with their daily meals, primary education as obligatory as their labor as a means of rehabilitation." Bandeira Filho also favored this idea, but this reform never came to fruition because the necessary infrastructure was never built.[36]

In the meantime, married convicts with family did sooner establish an unattached private home and a provision garden. But even with a provision ground, most married convicts lived miserably because they earned the same meager wages and rations as bachelors.[37] Data from a uniquely detailed 1891 report enumerated 383 married convicts and 112 convict wives. Almost one-third of married convicts were joined by wives in penal exile, but the actual percentage was lower because some convicts wed after arriving in the colony. Nearly one in ten inmates lived with a wife, and less than half that many (forty-four) lived with a consensual heterosexual lover.[38]

Despite social and institutional pressures to wed, many free Brazilians chose not to. Many preferred to live as consensual partners and practiced

TABLE 5.1 Fernando de Noronha: Convict Marital Status by Color and Condition

	Single	Married	Widowed	Total
Color				
Black	167 (75.6%)	46 (20.8%)	8 (3.6%)	221
Brown	148 (51.6%)	109 (38%)	30 (10.4%)	287
White	47 (34.3%)	71 (51.8%)	19 (13.9%)	137
Legal Status				
1—Slave	164 (82.8%)	31 (15.7%)	3 (1.5%)	198
2—Free	213 (36.5%)	291 (49.8%)	80 (13.7%)	584
3—Soldier	147 (87%)	18 (10.7%)	4 (2.3%)	169

Source: Livro da matricula . . . , Feb. 11, 1865; Livro da matricula . . . , Jan. 10, 1885.

serial monogamy. In the interior, clergy was scarce and many lived together on the basis of a marriage promise. Consensual conjugality was common among the free poor, and if a couple lived respectfully together, most viewed it as a union worthy of repute, though it did not confer the legal protections, privileges, and responsibilities of marriage. There are no surveys of marriage rates in imperial Brazil, but other data offer proxy measures. Based on the 1870 household census of Rio's São Cristóvão neighborhood, Elizabeth Kuznesof estimates that as many as 85 percent of children lived in a two-parent household, but she could not distinguish between those in formal and informal unions.[39] Silvia Maria Jardim Brügger finds that rates of legitimacy in the 1850s for adult free-born women in São João del Rei, Minas Gerais, were 67.73 percent, 40 percent for manumitted women, and 14.29 percent for slave women. Another imperfect gauge of rising marriage rates are the legitimate birth rates in the 1890 census, where they totaled 81 percent.[40]

Table 5.1 breaks down prisoners' marital status, legal condition, and color. The data indicate that marital status paralleled mainland social and color hierarchies where whites and free citizens were more likely to marry than nonwhites, slaves, and soldiers. In the sample, brown Brazilians were almost twice as likely to marry as blacks, though more slave than soldier convicts married. The high percentage of betrothed convicts indicates that marriage had not acted as an efficient brake on crime. Indeed, the percentage of married convicts even among slaves was likely overrepresented when compared to the general population. Since most were homicide convicts, it is possible that marriage encouraged violence in defense of marital honor, but the evidence here is little more than suggestive. An 1854 notice in Recife's *Diário de*

Pernambuco gives anecdotal evidence to support this hypothesis in the form of black humor. A correspondent from Rio Grande do Norte narrated the crimes of two different men who murdered unfaithful wives and concluded: "So you see . . . how dangerous the sainted state of matrimony is, because beyond the displeasures of infidelity, a poor devil launches himself into the heinous career of crime."[41]

Barracks, senzalas, and the aldeia segregated mostly unmarried men into batch-living quarters. The right to live in private quarters and to marry or live with a heterosexual consensual lover was a bargaining chip that masters and officers used to reward collaboration and raise the stakes for unruliness, sloth, or desertion. Commanders often referred to married convicts as elements of order. Convicts permitted to marry on the island often had army officers and their wives serve as their witnesses, which suggests a kind of godfatherly relationship between married convicts and officials.[42] For powerful actors, these privileges were incentives for good behavior. Slaves, enlisted men, and convicts, however, came to see as a right what superiors considered a privilege.

The faith that many officials had in the nuclear family as a bastion of social order went to the extreme that they felt they faced a dilemma when sentencing married men. Ideally, a male patriarch would provide for and protect his wife, dependents, and himself from other men's sexual aggressions. By jailing husbands, authorities removed the natural male protector from the home, and they feared that this would force a convict's wife and daughters into prostitution. The same fear led officials to exempt married men from military impressment. Authorities worried that convicts' wives and children could thus unjustly be punished for the crimes of their household head, creating new social burdens and immoralities. As Beaurepaire Rohan put it, "While their women, abandoned on the mainland, procure, for themselves and their children, resources in prostitution [*devassidão*], their husbands, isolated in the presidio, deliver themselves over to the most degrading perversions [*desvios*], from which originate the only illnesses [venereal diseases] known on this blessed island."[43] Beaurepaire Rohan and other officials ignored the fact that many poor single women headed households and lived without a husband or male lover to protect them. Most of them supported themselves and cared for their dependents without turning to prostitution or mendicancy.[44] Even so, the idea of unprotected women's vulnerability remained a powerful trope that complemented interpretations of men's relentless sexual drives. The administrator of Recife's House of Detention, for instance, bragged that when he organized paid work for prisoners, "many inmates could provide some support to their wives and daughters [on the outside] who were ready to throw themselves into prostitution's abyss."[45]

Beaurepaire Rohan's 1865 regulations provided a piecemeal solution to spousal separation and the unrelenting male sex drive. While some convict wives had been present on the island before 1865, Beaurepaire Rohan's rules facilitated conjugal penal living, and the number of convict families increased.[46] His solution made sense to other commanders. As Commander José Angelo de Morais Rego wrote in 1870:

> The union of the sexes being a law of necessity created and imposed by nature, it is manifest that . . . women . . . constitute an element of order and morality on this island . . . because when each convict finds in his partner the satisfaction of this imperious necessity, they will cease to scheme to conquer the wives of other men which has caused disturbances in the past. An element of morality because the presence of women naturally causes the abominable sin of sodomy to disappear; it is unfortunate and embarrassing but sodomy is a widespread practice here. Beyond this, experience has shown in this presidio that a woman has the great advantage of awakening . . . the love of work [in men] because of the need to duplicate his exertions to support his partner . . . transforming imbecilic and lazy men into hard-working, intelligent, and dedicated laborers.

Morais Rego then cited his predecessor's aphorism: "Without women it is impossible to govern Fernando de Noronha."[47] Morais Rego would be dismissed from his post after an investigation of his administration led by officers who had previously commanded the presidio. It appears Morais Rego had links to Pernambuco's Liberal Party as paid announcements in the conservative *Diário de Pernambuco* dueled with those published in *O Liberal*. An anonymous detractor used Morais Rego's enthusiasm for the moralizing influence of the jealous institution against him: "He arrived at the point of officially proposing the entrance of the largest possible number of women to serve as concubines for the convicts and other inhabitants of Fernando to avoid the feuds, disorders, and jealousies women had provoked given that there were too few women there."[48]

While the conservative press pilloried Morais Rego for his views on penal conjugality, other officials had acted on this same logic. Beaurepaire Rohan reported that Pernambuco's police chief sent thirty "girls" to marry bachelor convicts to "moralize" the island. So when Beaurepaire Rohan approved the practice of allowing married convicts to apply to bring wives and dependents into exile, he likely felt he was building on precedent. In addition, eighty marriages occurred between convicts and single women on the island from 1865 to 1879.[49] Among those married were the free homicide convicts Miguel Angelo de Lucena and Senhorinha Maria de Jesus, who both wed for a second time in 1876 as unimpeded widower and widow.[50]

Despite the Lombrosian theory of the born criminal, few criticized Beaurepaire Rohan's policy that allowed convicts to reproduce in exile. An exception was the administrator of Recife's penitentiary Rufino Augusto de Almeida, who, in 1874, referenced Lombroso to censure those who had sent women to the colony:

> Is it right to send to that presidio a great number of women recruited from brothels to unite them there, not by the ties of the heart, but by sensuality, with beings as depraved, if not more so, than they are? I say "recruited" from brothels because I do not believe that one will find in our society even the most miserable women willing to marry convicts. . . . If vice ridden men, inheritors of base instincts, procreate with women of sound health and spirit, they produce children that inherit all their father's physical and moral defects, what should one expect from a marriage in which both partners are equally infirm?[51]

The use of the term "recruited" was loaded because it was a euphemism for military impressment and suggests these women had been coerced. It also implies that conceptually bordellos and barracks were institutions that segregated dishonorable male and female loners from the homes of honorable families. Even more exceptionally, Almeida added: "I do not agree with the opinion of those who judge conjugal life necessary for a prisoner's physical and moral health. . . . This question is no longer discussed among the men of penitentiary science. Society is not obligated to sustain a criminal's family."[52] Here, Almeida backs an individualistic, liberal view of punishment and he observes that European prisons did not allow conjugal penal living or visits.[53] Indeed, liberal penal codes had repealed dishonoring, ancien-regime punishments of a convict's family, but Brazilian authorities' preoccupation with the impact of married men's incarceration on their wives seems exceptional. British debtors' prisons had allowed families to visit and sometimes live with jailed patriarchs in private jails, whose owners charged prisoners rent and sold them food and drink. When Charles Dickens was twelve his father was sent to a debtor's prison and many of his family members resided with the father there, but these jails were banned in 1869. Other British convicts, however, were not allowed conjugal penal living or visits.[54]

While Almeida felt that philanthropic societies should help convict families, he spurned arguments that men required conjugal life and heterosexual sex for their health. Despite these critiques, Almeida admits that conjugal living could aid rehabilitation if the government built a prison with eight hundred individual cells to isolate men: "[Through] his good conduct and love of work, he can reside outside the prison in the company of his family which will produce beneficial effects and bring him to a sincere atonement that will result in moral regeneration." Any scandal or infractions would require him to return to cellular isolation. Almeida had found a logical way to square Beaurepaire Rohan's convict marriage policies and the goal to arranchar convicts. War and Justice Ministry reports echoed Almeida's call for the construction of such a prison, but Parliament never heeded their pleas.[55] Bandeira Filho made similar criticisms of the colony's administration of conjugal penal living, but he too felt it could be effective if well regulated: "The concession of family could bring advantages if there was a distinction made among prisoners based on their conduct, permitting the entrance of women, or of marriage for those with exemplary comportment; that way, it would serve to stimulate discipline. The actual state [of the presidio] is an embarrassing anomaly for the nation because many foreign ships frequently visit there."[56] Like Almeida, Bandeira Filho argued that better regulation of conjugal privileges could produce desirable results, but as it stood, Fernando de Noronha's immorality remained a national embarrassment, particularly because foreigners published stories about their impressions of it.

In the end even penal authorities, who challenged articles of faith in the jealous institution, felt that it could work. This would change in the 1890s under republican government when a new generation of criminologists, like Raimundo Nina Rodrigues, championed Lombroso's idea of the born criminal. In the twentieth century, Brazilian penologists used eugenic "science" to argue against permitting conjugal penal living and conjugal visits to convicts in mainland penitentiaries. Criminals would beget criminals.[57] Even so, some twentieth-century penal experiments that combined heterosexual conjugality with imprisonment took place along with the inauguration of conjugal visits in Brazil's penitentiaries.

REASSESSMENTS OF BEAUREPAIRE ROHAN'S POLICIES

Since independence, Fernando de Noronha had been part of the War Ministry's portfolio, but Parliament transferred it to the Justice Ministry in 1877. The Justice Ministry sent inspectors Conselheiro Fleury and Bandeira Filho in 1879 to study the colony. Fleury would later be named director of São

Paulo's law school in 1883 and elected as an imperial deputy for his home province of Mato Grosso in 1885. Bandeira Filho was born in Recife and worked as a lawyer, diplomat, and essayist. Both Fleury and Bandeira Filho had traveled to Europe to study prisons. The Justice Ministry charged these well-educated men to propose reforms to Beaurepaire Rohan's regulations.[58] Fleury and Bandeira Filho were determined to put a civilian stamp on the colony. To these outsiders, life there was a *bagaceira*: the loose moral environment allegedly characteristic of plantation sugar mills. Consciously or not, they echoed Ferreira Portugal's 1797 prognostications when they attributed much of the colony's lax discipline and dissolution to excessive leisure because most convicts only worked from 9:00 AM to 2:00 PM daily. To the inspectors' horror, even slave convicts had time on their hands.[59]

The inspectors questioned the wisdom of women and children's presence in the colony. Fleury was horrified that "prostitution had assumed frightening proportions. There are girls of eight and nine years of age who are already perverted and depraved with the knowledge and approval of their parents. Convicts often seek to marry for ignoble ends, to the point that husbands encourage their wife's infidelity to profit from it."[60] In these instances, inmate husbands subverted the "natural" powers of marriage to make them into avid protectors of their wives' fidelity and their daughters' virginity.

Bandeira Filho called for the removal of female convicts and argued against the logic that more women benefitted morality: "Experience proves the contrary; when one allows, without discrimination, convicts to live with women, morality will not be possible and one can expect the augmentation of vice on the island."[61] He condemned the "independent women" who lived there and recommended that only women connected to convicts who had proven their good behavior be allowed to stay. His colleague Fleury opined that with a few exceptions there were "no honest women in that place," and like the director of the House of Detention, he decried officials who had sent women to Fernando de Noronha from the "dregs of society, already corrupted by vice." Bandeira Filho observed that "even high ranking employees are many times guilty of lamentable weaknesses that diminish their moral force as I had occasion to witness."[62] Some officers and civil servants engaged in illicit sexual relations with the colony's women.

Bandeira Filho blamed women's presence for "causing constant disturbances and atrocious crimes," and there was evidence to support this assertion in colony records. For instance, on September 9, 1876, the convict soldier Afonso Ribeiro de Lima stabbed the nonconvict Maria Agostinha da Conceição to death. The commander wrote that his motive was "without a doubt because of his miserable unrequited sexual passion for her." He added that the killer was age twenty-five, but that he had already committed two murders after his original homicide conviction.[63] This was one of many crimes attributed to heterosexual desire.

Given such incidents, Bandeira Filho ironically cited Commander Morais Rego's assertion that a greater gender balance would bring greater morality among convicts. The inspectors seemed preoccupied with women's immorality and less interested in same-sex eroticism. Like others of their era, they may have ascribed to the view that once a woman had been sexually "tainted," she would corrupt "honest" women with whom she came into contact. Bandeira Filho worried about the exposure of convict, vendor, soldier, and employee families to the island's bagaceira, which contradicted Fleury's assertion that there were almost "no honest women" there.[64] Convict women's "liberty" vexed inspectors. Most worked in the infirmary's laundry, but these duties were not onerous, and many allegedly occupied their free hours prostituting themselves, a fact that Bandeira Filho wryly noted was the "only way they fulfilled their sentences." If women were necessary to govern Fernando de Noronha, the inspectors believed that they had to have their liberty curtailed.[65] They recommended removing women convicts and some nine hundred male convicts whose sentences by statute did not qualify them for admission to Fernando de Noronha, but their proposal was impractical because there was not enough mainland prison capacity to hold so many convicts.[66]

POLICING FAMILY HONOR IN A PENAL COLONY

Justice Ministry inspectors did not recognize the efforts of commanders to police family honor. Commanders wrote wistfully of the "honest" wives of convicts and soldiers who deserved respect and of good husbands and fathers of family. Fleury's perception that there were almost no honest women may have reflected the different experiences of elite law school graduates versus military officers who worked daily with the intractable poor. Where inspectors saw an undifferentiated group of dishonored men and women, officers may have seen status distinctions where marriage and conjugal living were important markers of difference.[67] This section explores their efforts to police family honor and how convicts and their dependents responded to them.

The growing number of women had consequences that Beaurepaire Rohan failed to anticipate. In 1866, a commander protested that convict widows and children could not pay for their passage to the mainland, and that they became "subject to prostitution and misery" when their husbands completed their sentences and were returned to the mainland.[68] This problem was never fully resolved. In 1888, a commander justified paying the passages of a convict's wife, daughter, and son to "prevent a crime." He explained that the convict husband had returned to the mainland but his dependents remained. If they stayed, however, the women would have to "give themselves over to prostitution [to survive]," and then he would have to pay "to send them back to Recife for incorrigible behavior."[69] Similarly, another commander returned a convict wife to the mainland months after her convict husband abandoned her. He had not sent her away earlier because "she had always behaved well," but he changed his mind when he learned that her husband allegedly decided to "market" or prostitute her.[70]

Commanders used methods similar to those employed on the mainland to defend family propriety. When a convict seduced the fourteen-year-old daughter of another inmate, her father put her on deposit in the house of an inmate sergeant, "a married man that lives his life honestly." The commander ordered the offender jailed and found that he had seduced the girl with "frivolous promises." The parents opposed their daughter's marriage to a man of "bad character and insolence." Meanwhile, another inmate offered to marry her and repair her honor. The parents and the girl accepted, and after the priest confirmed that there were no impediments, the couple wed.[71]

Convict wives were not the only ones who caused scandal. As a commander griped in 1884:

Article 70 of the Regulations . . . authorizes me to expel any woman who behaves scandalously. But the inmates and soldiers that are sent to fulfill their sentences and soldiers who serve in the garrison bring their families composed many times of wife, children, mother, and siblings besides others who obtain permission from the governor to bring along their lovers. These women after sometime in residence in this presidio unfortunately throw themselves into the life of prostitution [and] have obliged me . . . to expel them . . . at government expense to avoid disorders and crimes that have occurred in the past.[72]

In other cases, the commander expelled wives whom he suspected had inflamed jealousies. In 1888, a commander wrote: "Today I sent the free civilian Rita Maria da Conceição to the Chief of Pernambuco's police to accommodate her as there are no appropriate prisons for women in the presidio. This woman is married to convict Juvencio Bispo Machado who murdered Joaquim Gaspar de Freitas, and I believe that she was the primary cause of this homicide."[73] Most mainland observers recognized that jealousy was a volatile emotion that could trigger crimes of passion, yet apparently these cases never shook the overall faith officials placed in the jealous institution's powers to promote order and productivity. Indeed, commanders showed clemency toward married men whose jealousy got the better of them. One convict wounded his wife with a knife, but the commander reported: "I did not bring charges against Domingos Martins Nogueira, who injured his wife in a domestic quarrel on April 9, 1877, because the injuries were slight and the life of his home as a married man is more important. Even so, I punished him . . . [due to the] the necessity of [sustaining] good order in this prison."[74] The unnamed punishment was likely a public flogging.

To support petitions for clemency, commanders often noted whether a convict had been a good worker and family man. In 1886, to support Manoel José Maria's petition for pardon the commander wrote that he had always demonstrated good conduct and through his hard work had been made the convict police company's sergeant. He added that Maria lived with his family, whom he "treated with great care."[75] Similarly, convict Joaquim Jose Felix Espada petitioned for pardon in 1887, after forty-two years of incarceration. To recommend Espada's appeal the commander observed that during "this long period of time . . . he has always been well-behaved as a prisoner, has proven himself to be a good father of family, and for this reason he is among the first class of convicts [those who were well behaved]."[76]

Many convicts sought to wed for love, companionship, status, and labor for the house and garden. Married convicts more often garnered better-paying jobs, and trusted bachelor inmates were more likely to be permitted to marry. Bandeira Filho incorrectly suggested: "When any prisoner intends to marry he asks the commander's permission, and he agrees if the Church's precepts are satisfied."[77] However, evidence shows that they did not allow just anyone to wed, though there were intriguing exceptions. The infamous former convict sergeant Vicente d'Assis Tavares petitioned a new commander for release from an aldeia jail cell where he was held in irons in 1889. His letter admitted that he had mistakenly joined in the turmoil that roiled the colony in 1885. He and fifty-seven other convicts allegedly led by Assis were shipped to Recife for trial for plotting insurrection. As proof that he had mended his ways, Assis mentions that he had wed months earlier, but his detention kept him from living with his "unfortunate" wife. Here Assis manipulates ideals of husbandly duty in a bid to win release. While the commander expressed sympathy for Assis's "disgrace," he rejected his request because he had not changed his ways: "Vicente, Cosme José do O and [the slave convict] Sebastião . . . plotted crimes and terrorized other convicts."[78] Why had a former commander let such an infamous convict wed? Perhaps, like the slaveowner cited earlier, he hoped nuptials would cause Assis to "learn judgement," or maybe Assis had impregnated his lover and she desired to wed to repair her honor. It is also possible that the commander sought to coopt a convict gang leader. Whatever the case, Assis's petition shows that marriage alone did not qualify a convict for privileges; it needed to be combined with hard work, submission, and respectable family living.

Commanders sometimes intervened in the family lives of convicts. In 1868, the commander reported to the governor about a convict who returned to the mainland because he had completed his sentence:

> The civil convict Maximiano Lopes de Araujo . . . presented me with three boys of his that live in his company so that they could be given passage to travel with him to the mainland. I sent the boys with their father to Recife, but I stipulated that they present themselves to your excellency because this convict is completely useless and to me he seems to be an idiot. I believe that his sons would be better off if they were sent to the Army arsenal to be educated. The older one is fifteen and because of my orders he worked in the Presidio's arsenal learning leatherwork and he has demonstrated some progress. He is well behaved and respectful. The two minors one six the other seven attend primary school.[79]

While authorities often praised convict family men, they sometimes separated children from parents. For boys of convict families, the common remedy was to send them to Recife's army apprentice school, where they would learn a trade. If they demonstrated skill, they might become artisans employed in the arsenal. If not, they served as regular army enlisted men when they reached the age of majority. This was a type of intergenerational category drift that once again illustrates how categories of the intractable poor were linked.

The belief that women would curb same-sex eroticism went unfulfilled, and colony records affirm that authorities knew this. For instance, in 1870: "The minor Raymundo Francisco Lopes . . . despite his own father's efforts to correct him . . . is constantly running away and hiding in the houses of convicts who use him for their libidinous ends . . . [and jealousies over the boy] have led to fights. Therefore, I sent him to . . . a military Arsenal, where as an apprentice he will learn a trade and may still become useful to himself and his country."[80] Military apprentice schools themselves were renowned for same-sex eroticism, but the commander believed that Lopes would have a better chance to lead a productive life there. Similarly, in 1875, a commander suggested that the boys on the island be sent to the army's apprentice school to be "educated in the precepts of morality and learn to hate crime."[81] This issue continued to bedevil officials. In 1889, the commander sent a number of boys to military apprentice schools because their "parents did not give them the correct education and they were being raised in a vice-ridden and corrupt environment." He added that the boys made money by fishing, but "their pay was insufficient and they resorted to begging or to acts that morality repudiates." Some boys turned to prostitution to better their conditions.[82]

Commanders often linked same-sex eroticism to violence. When a murder occurred among the aldeia's "recluses" in 1873, the commander reported that it was motivated by the "nefarious vice of sodomy."[83] Similarly, in 1876, the slave convicts Ignacio and José murdered convict Henrique Pereira Cardoso. The commander stated that their motive had been robbery, but he went out of his way to relate that the assailants were lovers "continually habituated [useiros e vezeiros] in the practice of reprehensible acts and of irreconcilable conduct in this presidio against which all repressive discipline is useless." He blamed the actions of these "bocaes" (boçais, a derogatory term for African-born slaves who did not speak Portuguese well and implied savagery) on their ignorance and "perverse instincts."[84]

It is difficult to assess the extent to which convicts believed in or cynically manipulated prescriptive ideas of marital honor and masculinity. Some allegedly cajoled, consented, tolerated, or expressed frustration about wives, daughters, and sons who turned to prostitution. Others at least partially rejected prescriptive norms and formed alternative households with men whom they lived with as consensual lovers. Commanders, however, were not the only ones who censured indecent behavior. Convict José Antônio de Oliveira requested that his wife be sent to the mainland because of her immoral behavior, a petition the commander obliged.[85]

For inspectors, the experiment with conjugal penal living had not succeeded because many convicts did not behave like proper patriarchs. They questioned the wisdom of allowing women and children to live in the colony without stricter regulation. As Bandeira Filho concluded, "I am forced to say that the hopes deposited in the influence of women over the presidio's morality have faltered."[86] He recognized some of the difficulties faced by convict families, and he criticized the fact that they had to abandon plots they had made productive when convicts finished their sentences, unlike married exiles in Australia and New Caledonia. Despite the inspectors' recommendations, most convict wives and dependents continued to live with inmate husbands until the colony reverted to Pernambuco's dominion, but thereafter, Pernambucan authorities continued to allow some convicts to live with their wives and dependents in exile.[87] Inspectors did not concede, however, that material conditions, insecurity, and gender imbalance impelled some men, women, and children to at least partially reject prescriptive ideas of honor to cope with conditions.[88]

6 "A STENCH IN THE NOSTRILS OF GOD"?
The Material and Social Life of Exile

When the American geologist John Branner visited Fernando de Noronha, he interviewed the colony's priest:

> The only priest of the island, after years of labor, went through his sacred duties in a perfunctory manner, for, as he gave me to understand, he had long since come to realize that the seed he sowed fell into the fire. Speaking to him one day regarding the peculiar charm of the place, he replied: "Ah me! I can't see these things now, for though it is, externally, all that you see and say of it, this quiet, this seclusion, this beautiful and bountiful nature are turned by man into a stifling, suffocating hole—a stench in the nostrils of God."[1]

Branner's Protestant faith likely shaped his dismissive depiction of the priest, but Brazilian staff and inspectors gave similar evaluations of presidio life. Beaurepaire Rohan declared, "As to the customs of the population generally, they present a horrible picture of the presidio."[2] Even Branner described the island as "lofty, beautiful, and sin-cursed."[3] The trope proved hard to escape. Despite these dismal depictions, colony life was not all degradation and despair. Even marginal convicts had time for respite. Not all were flogged and shackled, and those who were, were not abused continually. A refreshing swim on a beautiful beach was a luxury most rural Brazilians did not know, and though few knew how to swim, coral reefs formed limpid tidal pools where even a fretful bather could bask in calm seawater. After all, Brazilian physicians recommended sea baths as a treatment for numerous ailments.[4]

None of Fernando de Noronha's convicts lived the "Life of Riley," but if reasonably well behaved, they did have leisure to socialize. As recent labor history has shown, while work was important in defining laborers' sense of themselves, their leisure played a powerful role in shaping networks of collaboration and rivalry.[5] This is no less true of convict laborers. An exploration of colony social, material, and spiritual life illuminates hierarchies of color, ethnicity, class, and education that exemplify the Brazilian preference for integration that never forsook prejudices. Colony documentation and especially travelers' accounts preserve fragments of the colony's social fabric.

ELITE SOCIAL LIFE IN THE COLONY

The commander's residence was the hub of the presidio's elite social life where the colony's head received and often housed foreign visitors. Some visitors recorded aspects of social life there, whereas colony documentation is reticent in comparison. This may be because traveler narratives reveal that commanders integrated privileged convicts into their social circle.

The confederacy's Captain Raphael Semmes of the css *Alabama* provides the most vivid account of a commander's household when he spent two weeks off the colony's shores in 1863 while his crew transferred coal from Yankee prizes. As in classical comedy, his narrative humorously plays on the confusion of status. He first indicates his amusement when an English-speaking German boarded his ship to negotiate the sale of stores. When the negotiator revealed that he was a convict, Semmes's steward, "who felt the honors and dignity of my station much more than I did myself," hastily recorked a second bottle of champagne he had opened to honor the "ambassador." The incident illustrates how polyglot European forgers worked as go-betweens for commanders when foreigners called and indicates a prodigious level of trust in them. Semmes and his paymaster accepted an invitation to visit Commander Sebastião José Basílio Pyrrho. After a horseback ride from the port, the landing party found the commander at breakfast with family and guests. Their host insisted that the Confederates join them for "a variety of roast meats as well as fruits and vegetables." Pyrrho's larder was well provisioned.[6]

Semmes evokes his American readership's consciousness of racial, ethnic, and class hierarchies when he observes that, "like most Brazilians,"

Pyrrho, whom he called the "governor," was the color of "tanned leather," an unsubtle reference to the African and indigenous ancestry that most Brazilians, even some of rank, shared. He then described the commander's wife:

> I discovered that her ladyship the governess, was a very sprightly and not uncomely mulatto, and that her two little children, who were brought to me with all due ceremony, to be praised, and have their heads patted, had rather kinky, or should I say curly, hair. But I was a man of the world, and was not at all dismayed by this discovery; especially when I observed that my vis-a-vis—one of the guests—was a beautiful blond, of sweet seventeen, with a complexion like a lily tinted with the bit of rose, and with eyes so melting and lovely, that they looked as though they might have belonged to one of the houris, of whom that old reprobate Mahomet [sic] used to dream. . . . She was a German, and was seated next to her father, a man of about sixty, who, as the Governor afterward informed me, was one of his chief criminals.[7]

Here Semmes distances himself from his readership to insist that he was not "dismayed by this discovery" of race mixture among Brazilians in authority because he was a "man of the world," not an insular Southern landlubber.

In Semmes's narrative, his tolerance and charm dissuaded the commander from protesting his violation of Brazil's neutrality in the U.S. Civil War, which he sets up with his titillating depictions of the commander's wife and the German daughter. This "man of the world" depicted himself as a lady's man with savoir-faire and an open mind to feminine beauty. The counterpoint he makes between the complexions of the "governess" and the German girl highlights a sort of orientalism in reverse, as he imagines "that old reprobate Mahomet" dreaming of this chaste voluptuous white woman.[8] Does his reference to Muhammad betray a concern over the presence of an attractive white virgin amid so many dangerous men of color? Does Semmes use "governess" to allude to colored "mammies" who cared for their master's children in his confederacy? Did he use the term "ladyship" with a sense of irony given her color? His juxtaposition of the German convict's daughter and the commander's wife suggests a waggish and salacious tongue-in-cheek wink to his American readers. Brazilians unabashedly subverted the Southerner's expected hierarchies of race and honor.[9]

Semmes's countenance betrayed him when he learned that the German girl was the daughter of the commander's chief convict: "The Governor seeing me start a little as he gave me this information, made haste to explain, that his guest [the German] was not of the canaille, or common class of rogues, but a gentleman, who, in a moment of weakness, had signed another gentleman's name to a check for a considerable amount, which he had been clever enough to have cashed. 'He is only a forger, then!' said I to the Governor. 'That is all' replied he; 'he is a very clever old gentleman, and, as you see, he has a pretty young daughter.' "[10] Semmes divulges his incredulousness at the array of dishonored scoundrels breaking bread with the commander. While this seemed remarkable to Semmes, it was not for the commander and his guests. A more self-conscious commander might have dismissed convicts from his home during a foreigner's visit, but Pyrrho apparently felt no need for such pretensions.

Semmes mines this ironic vein further when Pyrrho held a reception in his honor:

> The paymaster and myself were personally presented to most of these distinguished gentlemen—some military men, some civilians. Among others, was present the ambassador of the day previous. . . . The Governor had evidently been select in his society, for most of these gentlemen were not only well dressed, but well-mannered, and some of them distinguished in appearance. They were mostly homicides and forgers, and seemed rather to pride themselves upon the distinction which they had attained in their professions. There was one young fellow present, upon whom all seemed to look with admiration. He was a dashing young German, who had evidently driven fast horses, and kept the best company. He wore an elaborately embroidered shirt-bosom, on which glittered a diamond brooch of great brilliance, and there were chains hung about his neck and signet and other rings on his fingers.[11]

Semmes narrated how this young man demonstrated his skill at forging signatures. The bystanders applauded his skill and informed Semmes that he had cheated the Bank of Rio de Janeiro out of a large sum. Semmes further observed: "Wine and cigars were brought in, and as we chatted and smoked with these fellows, the paymaster and I were highly amused—amused at our own situation, and by the variety of characters by whom we were surrounded."[12] Semmes stresses his amusement, not his concern, at sharing the company of so many distinguished convicts, but his remarks reveal how privileged convicts shared in the routines and extraordinary events of the commander's household. These convicts had the resources to dress well, which made them easy to distinguish from most convicts. Indeed, the young convict with a diamond pin stood out from his counterparts, even the commander's nonconvict entourage. These convicts had income well beyond salaries paid to convicts with privileged posts.

After the reception, the commander took Semmes on a tour of his "dominions," and when it rained, "its only effect was, to induce the Governor to call a temporary halt, at a manioc factory, in which he was interested and whistled up a boy, who brought each of us a very small glass filled with the villainous aguardiente of the country. The Governor tossed off at a single gulp and not to be discourteous, we made wry faces and disposed of as much of ours as we could." Semmes emphasizes that he and his paymaster hid their distaste for Pyrrho's drink. Even though regulations banned alcohol, it was openly served to inmates invited to the commander's house. It was even available at a manioc roasting station to warm a body chilled by the rain. Plantation overseers and army officers commonly distributed rations of cane brandy on cold days to enure workers to the cold.[13]

While Semmes expresses a bemused and indulgent disdain for the Brazilians he met, convict and nonconvict alike, his narrative is careful to emphasize that he did not let it show:

> The paymaster and I pulled on board at 5:00 PM without having suffered any inconvenience, either from the rains or the Governor's aguardiente; nor did our morals suffer materially from what we had seen and heard in the island of Fernando de Noronha. The next morning the governor's wife sent me a fat turkey for dinner, accompanied by the most charming of bouquets. This was evidently my reward for patting the little curly heads of her children. My diplomacy from this time onward was all right. I did not hear a word from the Governor, or any one in authority about neutral rights, or the violation of neutral jurisdictions. Brazil had, I knew, followed the lead of the European powers, in excluding prizes from her ports, and I had fully expected to receive some remonstrance . . . but Madame was too strong for the Governor, and . . . I received fat turkeys and bouquets instead of remonstrances.[14]

Semmes affirms that his diplomacy and charm won the affections of Pyrrho's wife, who was "too powerful" for Pyrrho, whose uxoriousness put his manhood in question. Semmes indicates his ultimate disdain for Pyrrho's hospitality, but it favorably highlights his own wiles. After he had sacked the Yankee whalers, Semmes ordered them burned and bargained with a Brazilian schooner to take his 110 Yankee prisoners to Pernambuco.[15]

Union diplomats steamed over the plunder of Yankee vessels in Brazilian waters. As a result, the War Ministry removed Pyrrho and replaced him with Coronel Antonio Gomes Leal, who had strict orders to enforce neutrality.[16] Documentation does not reveal why Pyrrho allowed Semmes to violate Brazil's neutrality without complaint, but he lacked a vessel capable of coercing or intimidating Semmes into respecting Brazilian neutrality. Fort Remédios's cannon were in ill repair, and the soldiery was not trained to fire them. Semmes's purchase of provisions did present a rare boon to the commander and others to profit from the sale of stores, but it seems hard to believe that Pyrrho could imagine the incident would go unnoticed given that Yankee prisoners would end up marooned in Pernambuco. Did Pyrrho harbor Confederate sympathies? Did he simply want to meet the famous Civil War blockade-running captain?[17] It is difficult to know what motivated Pyrrho, but his actions cost him his post, and Fernando de Noronha became the center of an international diplomatic dispute. Despite this incident, Pyrrho returned to command the colony again, so it apparently did not stunt his career.

Pyrrho was not unusual in hosting trusted convicts. John Branner depicted the convivial life of Commander Pereira Lobo's residence in 1876:

> He [the commander] gave me a room in the official residence, the seat of honor at his bountifully served table, and a motley crew of convicts for servants, while the slender resources of the island were in reality placed at my disposal. At the house of the commandant certain ones of the convicts were admitted freely and treated with more or less indulgence. The chief amusement of the officers of the garrison and their wives was to assemble during the evening around the big table in the reception-room in the official residence, and there to play kino. On such occasions (and this game was played every evening of my [six-week] stay save two) there were from one to five privileged convicts standing about the room as lookers-on, and some of them were even invited to take, and did take, part in the game. At meal time they frequently dropped into the dining room, and gently encouraged the old governor to scold them while at his meal. Some of them, being ready conversationalists, were permitted to talk freely, and were even asked, before the meal was over, to take places at the great dining table; and, before the meal was over, though they always sat below the wine, were generally given some sweetmeats or a cup of coffee at the end of the meal.[18]

The admittance of privileged convicts to the commander's social circle was more restrained under Pereira Lobo in that he did not share spirited beverages with convicts (at least not in the presence of visitors), but they did share in the repast of the commander's well-served table, which, given the simple diet of most convicts, was welcomed. They even shared in what must have been some low-stakes gambling at kino even though regulations forbade it.

Why did commanders include privileged convicts in their social circle? These educated convicts were able secretaries, scriveners, translators, and go-betweens. Commanders sought to keep these "clever" prisoners close and to garner their favor as they could become dangerous if they opposed the administration. These educated convicts provided company for commanders who had few alternatives other than that of fellow officers and employees.[19] For their part, privileged convicts gained access to the commander's ear, tasty fresh food, parlor games, and conversation. The commander's residence was limited, however, to a select few convicts who enjoyed his favor and indulgence, a privilege most prisoners did not enjoy. These privileged convicts became part of the island's elite cultural circle and illustrate how the commander's patronage extended beyond job assignments to include the social life of his household. The extravagant dress of some convicts suggests that they may have shared in profits through licit and contraband trade. Many of the convicts who enjoyed the commander's hospitality were European, although some were Brazilian-born. Again, color, ethnicity, and education demonstrate the prejudices that separated privileged convicts from their plebeian peers. Another group of educated prisoners who did not always enjoy similar privileges were political prisoners.

POLITICAL PRISONERS

Commanders feared political prisoners because some tried to subvert other convicts. Antônio Borges da Fonseca was known for using the Lancastrian system, where more-advanced students teach less-advanced ones literacy, to raise inmates' political consciousness. Commanders also knew that some garrison soldiers, officers, convicts, unattached residents, and employees were sympathetic to rebel causes. Just as penal justice was politicized on the mainland, so it was in the penal colony. Commanders were wary of political prisoners because of their potential to foment convict uprisings. Even so, political prisoners were usually excused from rehabilitative labor, which reflected the educated class's prejudice toward manual labor, but they could be treated rigorously if they engaged in subversion.

When Borges da Fonseca arrived in the colony in 1850, it was the hey-day of political prisoners. He and nine other leaders of the Praieira Re-volt had been sentenced to life imprisonment on Fernando de Noronha. Commander Cypriano José de Almeida accused Borges da Fonseca of joining forces with Pedro Vinagre, a leader of Pará's Cabanagem Revolt (1835–1840), who had resided in the colony for years. Almeida reported that the two political prisoners planned to take the ship that supplied the colony to escape: "The conduct . . . of the political prisoners had been what one would expect. . . . They demonstrate their faith in the triumph of their cause . . . and have not abandoned deftly promoting their ideas among the prisoners. They [the prisoners] have sought the aid of Borges da Fon-seca and Vinagre to execute their plans to take the [ship] Priampama dur-ing the convict's mass when their numbers are many, the convicts would assault the garrison troops and take their arms. The arrival of the navy Brig Caliope frustrated their plans." To foil this plot, Almeida ordered his troops to remain behind the convicts at mass. At this point, the com-mander resolved to exile Borges da Fonseca and Vinagre to Rat Island and prohibited correspondence with the islet. He forwarded a letter signed by "the liberals" that implicated the commander himself in an escape plot. It alleged that Almeida would forge an order from the governor decree-ing their freedom, but he assured the governor that "he was not capable of such treason."[20] Almeida took extra precautions because of rumors that their mainland comrades would rescue them from Rat Island. He described them as "desperate because they could not consummate their plans, [even so] they continue to employ 'seduction' to find among the convicts those who have no fear to agitate the judgment of men sentenced to life in prison and others sentenced to prison at hard labor." He forwarded four letters penned by Borges da Fonseca that he claimed "proved his irrepressible perversion that, even in exile on Rat Island, he occupies himself writing criminal correspondence."[21]

The same day the commander wrote about the escape plot, he reported that the nonconvict Manoel Pereira do Nascimento had forged an order with the commander's signature so that he could leave the colony. The com-mander speculated that this may have been a test to see if this ploy could be used for more deadly ends. He described Nascimento as unmarried, robust, and without exemptions for military service and suggested that the gover-nor punish Nascimento with category drift and press him into the army. No wonder the commander doubted the loyalty of his troops; some may have been former soldiers in the Praieira's forces pressed into service.[22]

Correspondence also reveals how the commander used spies to monitor political prisoners. Almeida reported that the convict navy corporal José de Melo was assigned "to guard and monitor Borges da Fonseca" on Rat Island, but he had finished his fourteen-year sentence. He suggested that convict Miguel Pereira de Carvalho replace him because he had good conduct and a brief sentence.[23] Commanders believed that prisoners who were about to finish their sentences or who had short ones were more trustworthy because they would not jeopardize their imminent release. Beaurepaire Rohan affirmed this belief in 1865: "Besides, it is convenient to make known that not all convicts inspire fear in the administration. If those who have to serve a perpetual or long sentence will involve themselves in insurrections that would facilitate their escape, this is not true of those whose sentences are relatively brief. The latter are tacitly part of the police force and will ally themselves with the authorities in the case of a rebellion."[24] In this instance, the authorities expressed faith in the integration of convicts to enhance security, not on the basis of color or condition, but by the tenure of their sentences. While authorities preferred to use convicts with short sentences for some jobs, one should recall that inspectors in 1879 complained that ten of fifteen company sergeants were sentenced to perpetual galleys, so this logic did not always guide their decisions.

In April 1850, Borges da Fonseca respectfully petitioned Pernambuco's governor to be freed from Rat Island and requested that his family join him in exile. The commander remarked that he had exiled Borges da Fonseca to Rat Island because he was "incompatible with the tranquility and discipline that should reign in the presidio." He argued that it was "inadmissible" that his family join Borges da Fonseca on Rat Island because "the lack of water and other reasons" made it impossible to maintain a large number of convicts there.[25] Borges de Fonseca wrote that "the revolution is extinct" and that he would not "escape to wander as a fugitive, I who have a family." He emphasized: "These are such reasonable requests that no matter how great the hate that your excellency has for me as a man, you should grant these requests as Governor in recognition of my rights."[26] Here a privileged political prisoner used the rhetoric of the jealous institution to assure authorities that his family's presence would deter him from an escape attempt and asserted that his duties as a head of household were a kind of natural right.

A few days later, Almeida reported that he found a note in Borges da Fonseca's hand carried by a soldier detached with a squad to supply Rat Island. The note read: "The one who carries this note is ours, like Maurício." Almeida had the soldier flogged with one hundred lashes.[27] It seems there were Praieira sympathizers in the garrison. The next month, Almeida received orders to free Vinagre and Borges da Fonseca from Rat Island to a "closed prison" on Fernando de Noronha, but he resisted because there were no secure prisons on the island. He called a meeting of his officers, and they unanimously recommended to remove all nonpolitical prisoners from Rat Island but to keep the political prisoners there and redouble their guards.[28]

Despite the officers' trepidations, the governor insisted that Borges da Fonseca be returned to Fernando de Noronha on the condition that he would remain confined to Fort Remédios's grounds. Soon thereafter, the commander reported that Borges da Fonseca had made unwanted advances toward the major da praça's wife, who also resided in the fort. Borges da Fonseca's desire to get this officer's goat may have been heightened by the fact that he had commanded troops who defeated Praieira forces in the battles of Pau Amarelo and in the town of Areia, Paraíba.[29] Borges da Fonseca's antics led the commander to take further precautions. He ordered that the fourth-class ensign Lourenço José Romão be removed from the colony because he was a "detriment to military discipline and good order." Almeida requested that the governor not allow the ensign to return because of his intimacy with the prisoner sentenced to perpetual prison, Borges da Fonseca. He further noted that the ensign had been removed on two previous occasions, but he managed to later return. He explained: "This officer is always animated by anarchist ideas of disgraceful days gone by."[30]

Eventually, a new officer took command of the colony, and Borges da Fonseca's large family joined him. At this point, he became less of a bother and more of an asset to the administration. The new commander engaged him to help with tasks such as inspecting dried beef to determine whether it was spoiled. In May 1851, Pedro II pardoned Borges da Fonseca and the other Praieira prisoners. Political prisoners were privileged, but because they posed a wider threat to the imperial order they sometimes received harsh treatment. The lives of these privileged prisoners were quite different from those of common convicts, and their special treatment again indicates how class, color, and education influenced one's treatment in exile.

PLEBEIAN CONVICT LIFE ON THE IMPERIAL FARM

The social world of most convicts did not appear in the nervous reports officers wrote about political prisoners or anecdotes about life in the commander's residence. The life of common convicts was diverse and ranged from quiet domestic evenings spent with family to bachelor *bachanalias*. Convicts and nonconvicts developed their own practices, organizations, and institutions alongside those the state and the Church controlled. Some were licit, such as a theater, bands, and Carnival groups. Friends engaged one another in conversation and pastimes such as fishing, gardening, cooking, singing, sewing, cock fighting, storytelling, and dancing. Others were illicit: gambling, drinking, prostitution, fighting, and disorderly conduct.

Brief glimpses of convict social activities arise when disorder prompted an official to write a report. Convict Carnival groups, for instance, go largely unmentioned in correspondence, but in 1882, Commander Pereira Lobo, who had an ongoing dispute with his second in command, the Major da Praça Captain Justino Rodrigues da Silveira, became concerned about what he saw as menacing behavior during Carnival. When there were feuds between high-ranking members of the colony's staff, even innocent actions could be interpreted as threatening.

The convicts formed two "nations" or *maracatu* groups named Porto Rico (Rich Port) and Cambinda Velha (Old Cambinda Woman; Cambinda refers to an Angolan ethnicity). *Maracatu da nação* is a musical and dance form native to Recife that derives from colonial *congadas* where a slave man and woman were named the king and queen of the Congo and the members of their court danced and sang in celebration. Porto Rico and Cambinda Velha are among Pernambuco's oldest maracatu nations organized for annual Carnival celebrations that combined elements of European Catholicism with African and indigenous traditions. Since a large minority of convicts were from Pernambuco, its Carnival traditions predominated there.

What is clear from the letters of the commander and the major da praça is that the two dancing groups came together outside their residences and members of the rival "nations" began to yell at one another. The major da praça, knowing the commander was ill, took the initiative to order the groups to disperse. Cambinda Velha left while members of Porto Rico remained. Then, according to the commander, Porto Rico's revelers shouted out "vivas" or long life to the Major da Praça Silveira and the colony's secretary. The commander took the vivas to be slights to his person and authority. In response to the commander's report, Silveira wrote his own. From his perspective, the vivas were the innocent "fruit of the misunderstood enthusiasm of these unhappy ones." Silveira noted that Porto Rico had shouted out vivas in his name, but he ordered them to cease and they peacefully dispersed. He also added that he had heard a second viva for the commander and not the colony's secretary. Finally, Silveira discredited the commander's account when he noted that his poor health prevented him from fully exercising his duties. Pereira Lobo suffered from chronic bronchitis that likely resulted from smoking as John Branner had described his tobacco-stained whiskers.[31] Why the traditional convict celebration of Carnival caused such alarm will be explored more fully in the following chapter. Here it is enough to note that convicts voluntarily associated themselves with different maracatu groups. These nations in turn reflected divisions among convicts that were linked to rival patronage networks among staff and convicts. This shows how convict leisure organizations could become politicized and shaped their sense of rival identities. It also shows how convicts brought their culture with them in exile and that officials tolerated these practices to a degree.

Some commanders worked to enliven the leisure of residents. In 1857, a commander reported that "it was necessary to have in the presidio some distraction to entertain the inhabitants so that they do not pass all their time in monotony, I decided to order the organization of a small martial musical band . . . to enliven the soldiers who will march to service with more gusto." He ordered the fabrication of a Brazilian flag for martial parades to celebrate national and religious holidays. He described the celebration he organized for November 28, 1857, for the "patron saint of this island," *Nossa Senhora de Remédios* (Our Lady of Remédios). The priest blessed the new flag on this sacred occasion. He clarified that all these arrangements had been made at no cost to public coffers and shared a copy of the speech he made:[32]

> Comrades. Before you is the symbol of happiness! It is the most sacred collateral that the fatherland can place in your hands. This is the flag that is your emblem. With its support your name will travel to the most remote regions if someone provokes your honor and tries to eclipse your valor. Comrades. Military honor demands from you a religious respect for this insignia of glory that today exists amid these ranks that have sworn to die for the Constitution, for the monarch, for the fatherland, and for religion. Give voice therefore from your lips this articulation of patriotic enthusiasm that you warm in your breast. Long live religion! Long live the Constitution! Long live his Majesty and Emperor Senhor Dom Pedro II![33]

Narratives of similar patriotic religious celebrations are rare in records whose prose was mostly dedicated to the mundane business of the comings and goings of convicts, personnel, and goods. While the commander addressed his speech to his soldiers, many convicts undoubtedly witnessed the event. It is difficult to know if soldiers and convicts received these words with enthusiasm or derision, but they were part of presidio culture.

While the commanders' correspondence revealed glimpses of convict social life, visitors too recorded some of their leisure activities. The American geologist John Branner reported in 1876: "The amusements of the inhabitants were cock-fighting and kino. I suggested to the commandant that cock-fighting was a degrading pastime for his proteges (I did not mention kino, because that was the favorite amusement in his own house). His reply was: 'I know it isn't good; but then.'"[34] The monotony of convict life was brightened by the drama of cock fights and the gambling that traditionally accompanied them. Even though the commander did not exactly approve of it, he did not repress it. In 1871, a commander reported that gambling was a passion that led some desperate convicts to sell their manioc flour ration to storeowners. He warned that any storeowner caught buying a convict's rations would be jailed, and their store closed.[35] In 1897, the commander wrote that there had been two murders in less than three days that had shaken discipline. He claimed that the disorder sprang from rumors spread by "some employees" that corporal punishment would again be abolished in the presidio. To return the presidio to order, he stepped up efforts to repress gambling (specifically card playing and cock fighting), the sale of cane brandy, and the excessive number of convicts who worked as domestics.[36] Periods of relative tolerance for card playing, cock fighting, drinking, and gambling were followed by crackdowns, but creative entrepreneurs found creative ways to circumvent bans to satisfy the demand for drink and games of chance.

Another diversion residents of Remédios cultivated was a theater that brought together convicts and nonconvicts. An inspector mentioned that he had attended a production of *The Miracles of Saint Anthony* "whose performance exceeded his expectations." He then noted that the audience "applauded with warmth," and that "perverted and demoralized individuals condemned to galés, slaves liberated by the nature of their punishment, criminals who should be trembling in jails as a punishment for the horrendous crimes they perpetrate were here playing happily, praying that no one would remember to remove them from this pleasant retreat. It is not surprising that after fulfilling their sentences on Fernando de Noronha, they commit another crime with the intention of returning." He lamented that convicts could attend two regular theater productions a month, a privilege most law-abiding mainlanders did not enjoy.[37] Bandeira Filho's depiction presages the American novelist Frank Carpenter's "ocean resort" trope. While he emphasizes his disgust at the convicts' happiness, he does not comment on the fact that they performed a religious play. Had they selected this play to impress visiting authorities?

There is little mention of the theater in colony correspondence until a conflict took place during an 8:30 PM performance of "Twenty Nine or Honor and Glory." José Romano authored this 1856 dramatic comedy of military customs to honor King Pedro V of Portugal's coronation. Brazilians frequently reprised it, and it became something of a cultural reference point.[38] Given the setting, the play's selection is interesting as it lionizes military heroism. A conflict began in the theater when military convict Joaquim Pedro dos Santo conducted a military maneuver on stage and unexpectedly violently struck the nonconvict private Manoel de Franca de Oliveira. When fighting broke out, soldiers outside the theater learned of it and stormed the theater to join the fray. Commander Pereira Lobo ordered the bugler to play reveille, but since he was ill, the major da praça led the troops that quelled the disorder. Pereira Lobo reported that only two prisoners and one soldier sustained injuries, but he ordered new security measures. First, he closed the theater. He demanded that all prisoners retire to their residences by 8:00 PM (an oft-ignored curfew regulation), and all soldiers were restricted to barracks after 6:00 PM unless they had a superior's written permission. He established new procedures for all soldiers and staff to gather at his residence when they heard reveille.[39] The inspector's depiction of the theater crowd stressed the harmonious conviviality of slave, free, military convicts, and garrison soldiers in attendance, but as this 1882 brawl indicates, tensions among them simmered.

In addition to theater, a convict band gave regular concerts that residents could look forward to. Convict musicians were privileged: "The musicians are dispensed from all other work requirements, their only obligation being to play a few days during the week in front of the commander's residence and during mass, or when the administration requests them." An inspector observed that there was a convict dance society that likely took advantage of the band's concerts.[40]

Many convicts spent some free time writing or dictating letters to loved ones on the mainland and anxiously awaiting replies. As an inspector observed: "The law of silence was unknown; there was complete liberty to communicate within and outside the island, the convicts writing letters and constantly receiving them through the intermediary of the post office created here."[41] Because embarrassing stories about the colony occasionally appeared in the mainland press, the Justice Ministry ordered the colony's staff to read all convict letters before posting them. In 1884, Pereira Lobo complained that the new procedure was onerous and ineffective. Beside the post office pouch, the steamship company carried its own private one that served as an alternative letter-carrying service that the administration had no authority to read. The steamship crew and other passengers could also deliver oral and written messages for convicts. Finally, employees, officers, and visitors could post letters for prisoners.[42] Convicts found creative ways to circumvent attempts to monitor their communications.

Not unlike the convicts who enjoyed the society of the commander's residence, many plebeian convicts enjoyed talking about crime. As the geologist Branner observed:

> These are simply instances of how the minds of these people dwelt constantly upon crime, how they admired crime, and consequently gravitated toward it. About their work in shop or field, the daily bread of their minds was to think and talk of crime in every shape that diseased minds and perverted natures can conjure it up. One would entertain his companions by detailing to them the story of some crime committed by himself, or of which he had knowledge, while every one listened attentively, like so many experts. The story ended, criticism began, and each one would indicate what he considered the weak points in the plan and its execution, and would suggest improvements here and there. One story always led to another, and, as might be expected, minds accustomed to this highly seasoned food soon rejected all other.[43]

This vignette affirms the cliché that prisons are schools for crime and that convicts enjoyed vying with one another to plot the perfect caper.

Beyond imaginative scheming, convicts enjoyed storytelling. Journalist Mario Carneiro do Rego Melo preserved convict legends in the early twentieth century. One relates to the spirit of a beautiful French woman who haunted the island's peak as a wandering light who sometimes took human form. One convict sighted the French woman, who appeared as a mermaid while he fished alone at twilight. He fled, and she yelled "miserable one" because he did not want to unearth the treasure she would show him. She was doomed to haunt the peak as a fatuous light until she gave the treasure she guarded to someone. Another tale was of a gypsy woman who had resided on the island and planted a cashew tree near her humble home. She prostituted herself, and after she died the place where she planted the tree became haunted. It was said that the Dutch had left a treasure buried somewhere near the tree. One night a convict saw near the cashew tree a general, his attendant, and a chaplain on horseback. He then fell to the ground in "ecstasy" and only woke the following morning.[44] These tales of Dutch treasure hidden on the island date back at least to the nineteenth century.[45] A British naturalist who visited the island in 1887 reported : "We returned laden with treasure—not the hordes of Dutch pirates that the convicts to a man thought we were in search of, but with new species."[46] Searching for buried pirate treasure may have been a hobby for some, but the real treasure was in the legends themselves. Tales of beautiful women and treasures reflected the desire of many convicts to strike it rich and live a life of ease: the "Life of Riley" that, like the Dutch treasure, most never found on Fernando de Noronha. To get a better sense of what life was like for most convicts, the next section explores their material and social conditions.

THE QUALITY OF LIFE IN THE COLONY

Scholars have used a number of indicators to compare the quality of life of different populations in history.[47] Nothing so ambitious will be undertaken here, but a brief examination of some elements of colony life invite comparisons. This section examines nutrition, wages, clothing, housing, education, spiritual life, and health care. The presidio paid most convict laborers a pittance for their labor and provided the elements of their basic nutrition, but what exactly could convicts consume? How might they improve their lives there?

Fernando de Noronha's convicts had luxuries that most of their mainland counterparts did not. One was access to health care from trained medical professionals. Given the quality of nineteenth-century Western medical care, one might question the value of this benefit, but most mainlanders had no access to trained physicians. Even in urban areas, most poor Brazilians relied on *curandeiros* (faith healers), barbers, and midwives for medical needs. For instance, Pernambuco's medical authorities felt compelled to allow the black slave curandeiro Pai Manoel (known as Dr. Manoel da Costa) to openly treat victims of cholera in Recife's naval hospital in 1856. The ineffectiveness of authorized physicians in preventing the disease's spread eroded public faith in scientific medicine.[48] The colony employed, in addition to physicians, convict barbers who not only cut hair but who also provided medical services like blood letting. In addition, at least one slave convict woman provided the services of a midwife, work considered too intimate for male physicians to perform.[49] As on the mainland modern and traditional medical practitioners complemented one another. Commanders repeatedly referred to the island as a healthful place free of disease, save for sexually transmitted ones. This is why it was a favored site to quarantine victims of epidemic disease.

A list of 308 treatments provided by the colony's infirmary in 1850 indicates the kind of ailments convict patients suffered: "14 for pains from venereal disease; 47 for injuries from floggings; one for gonorrhea; 10 for 'freckles' [*sardas*, perhaps skin cancer], seven for venereal ulcers; three for urinary infections; and six for inflammation of the scrotum."[50] Convict men who mistakenly used the leaves of the local *leite de burra* plant to clean themselves after defecating endured painful swelling of their scrotums that could leave them bedridden for days. While inexperience led some convicts to self-inflicted injuries, intentionally inflicted ones were far more common. The infirmary gave forty-seven convicts treatments for flogging. If these treatments were for forty-seven different men, this would mean that nearly one in six convicts had been flogged that year. This rather liberal use of flogging debilitated convict workers for a time and depleted the infirmary's scarce resources—further evidence that security trumped production. The colony's medical records also indicate that sexually transmitted diseases were common. The island was famous for its sexual promiscuity and prostitution, which propagated the spread of venereal disease, but again, both were common on the mainland. As Gilberto Freyre famously observed, "Brazil would appear to have been syphilized before it was civilized."[51]

Another benefit that convicts and their children had was education. The colony provided separate daytime schools for boys and girls, and at night, a school for convicts. Convicts who taught school were among the highest paid prisoners. A woman, often the wife of an employee, officer, or unattached resident taught the girls. While the quality of this education might have been low, it was a privilege most free poor Brazilians could not afford or access.

Convicts also had ready access to the sacraments and priests who served a small number of souls compared to mainland clergy. Most mainland towns the size of Remédios had only sporadic contact with circuit priests. Beaurepaire Rohan believed the presidio needed an active ministry to rehabilitate convicts, but he criticized regulations that forced convicts to attend mass:

> Beyond the causes I have pointed out as the origin of the depravation of customs, the absolute lack of any religious culture contributes even more to this problem. There is nothing there that reflects our duties to God but a chapel where mass is celebrated on Sundays and saints days. The chapel is of such small dimensions and is only served by one priest, few convicts attend Church ceremonies. But, even if it could hold all the convicts, what influence could it have over these brutish spirits, a mass which they attend in the presence of troops that watch over them with loaded weapons? Once they have fulfilled this formality that they are obligated to attend by the commander's orders they return to their habits as faithless

as they were before. A mass in itself only has value for people educated in the sentiments of religion; but for the convicts that attend mass as part of their sentence, it is no more than a boring spectacle. It is necessary for the priest to speak to the hearts of these men, calling them to a sincere repentance of their errors, and procuring through words of hope to reconcile them to God and society. Some Capuchins in the presidio would provide relevant services that are more necessary and with better results than those who preach to the savages who inhabit our forests.[52]

As noted earlier, Beaurepaire Rohan had extensive frontier experience, and he had criticized the Capuchins' missionary work with Brazil's Indians in other publications. When it came to convicts, however, it seems he felt they might deliver better results. The advocacy of similar policies for Indians and convicts again indicates the interrelatedness of categories of the intractable poor.

The celebration of mass brought together large numbers of convicts in Remédios, and commanders, steeped in the arts of domination, feared the potential for uprisings to occur during these gatherings.[53] Therefore, those convicts required to attend Mass did so under armed guard. These were not the most propitious conditions for convincing hardened criminals to repent and seek their salvation. As described previously, one convict killed the sergeant of the aldeia after he refused orders to kneel during the saying of the rosary. Many convicts may have appreciated religious services, but others resented requirements to attend Mass. Convicts living in Sueste, Sambaqueixaba, and Rat Island joked that at least they were not obligated to go to Mass.[54]

Some convicts, however, were known devotees of religion. Vicente Ferreira de Paula, who had led the Cabanos Revolt (1832–1835), professed a devout Catholicism that criticized liberal reforms as godless. Another religious convict was Benedicto José da Costa. In 1850, a commander relayed a request from Costa that his family be sent to live with him. The commander reported that he had been jailed for "wandering about preaching a type of religion and winning over a number of followers among slaves which had made him dangerous."[55] The case of Costa is similar to that of Agostinho José Pereira, who, as the historian Marcus Carvalho demonstrates, was prosecuted for similar religious activism in Recife in 1846.[56] It is unclear whether Costa continued to propagate his unspecified religious views among the convicts, but it does show that some religious dissenters turned up in the convict population.

References to Afro-spiritist religion on Fernando de Noronha are rare. An exception was the use of a statue of an elderly black woman that likely belonged to the Cambinda Velha Carnival group. Since this observation was part of an investigation into a convict uprising, I will discuss it further ahead, but it is probable that colony documentation does not reveal Afro-spiritist practices among convicts because devotees celebrated their faith in secrecy.[57]

While not all convicts partook of spiritual life, all received basic rations. When the Justice Ministry assumed responsibility for the island's administration it established convict rations: 500 grams of dried beef, 50 grams of coffee beans, 100 grams of sugar, 10 grams of tobacco, 13,3 grams of soap, and one liter of manioc flour.[58] As noted earlier, rations were distributed every ten days in the case of food and twice a month for other staples. The meager rations are devoid of fruits and vegetables but define what officials believed were minimal nutritional and hygienic needs. The inclusion of coffee, tobacco, and sugar, demonstrates how goods once considered luxuries had become necessities.[59] These rations were much better than those provided to convicts at mid-century, when authorities distributed a liter of manioc flour. Government authorities issued similar daily rations for slaves employed in public granaries and enlisted soldiers in that era.[60] Provision grounds, animal husbandry, fishing, and crabbing allowed convicts to balance their diet with seasonal fruits, vegetables, and proteins that were a welcome addition to dry rations. That a few convicts lived to ripe old ages indicates that some managed to acquire adequate nutrition.

While consuming adequate nutrition could be a challenge for convicts, the most basic element necessary for survival was potable water. Administrators made a number of attempts to clean and extend the size of the colony reservoir to augment the water supply. It could be supplemented by a few natural springs, but they were small and could not quench the thirst of the growing population. When drought struck, the springs could be reduced to a trickle. Officials periodically warned that the island could not support more convicts due to the water supply's limitations. During the Great Drought 1877–1880 and another in 1888, circumstances on the island became so dismal that commanders allowed convicts' wives and dependents to return to the mainland to escape the misery they faced. Administrators obliged these requests in part because it meant fewer thirsts to quench. Since most of these dependents could not afford the costs of their passage, the state subsidized their exodus.[61]

Even in good years, the lives of most convicts and their dependents were ones of relative squalor. In 1868, Angelica Francisca de Lima, the wife of convict João Gomes da Silva, went to the commander and explained that she and her six children lived in a state of "indigence." She requested free transportation to the mainland for herself and her children so that she could "seek shelter from misery" with her relatives. The commander believed that the request was fair because given the paltry wage paid to convict laborers (140 réis per day) it was truly impossible to provide for such a large family. By way of comparison, in 1874 a cane cutter in Pernambuco earned a daily wage of 1,000 réis per day, more than seven times that of a common convict.[62] Beaurepaire Rohan also stressed the low pay of convicts and the high prices charged in stores for goods. He noted that military convicts earned a slightly better wage of 270 réis per day.[63] Regardless, life for most convicts and their dependents was hardly comparable to an ocean resort. In 1857, convict Leoncio Bezerra Cavalcante de Albuquerque had the commander forward a petition to the governor requesting a double ration of manioc flour so that he could feed his family. The commander thought his position just because the normal ration could not provide his "onerous family" with sufficient nutrition. He added that another convict in identical circumstances had been granted an additional ration. While authorities sometimes made exceptions and provided convicts with families more food, their hardship was palpable.[64] An inspector confirmed these difficulties: "Finally, there is the inequality of families, since all who desire to live with their families have free permission to do so and because the salaries of bachelors and married men are equal, these convict families struggle with invincible difficulties, and almost always live in misery, begging for change and creating difficulties for the administration."[65] Some convict family members turned to prostitution and mendicancy to supplement their diet.

Visitors often commented on the fashionable garb of privileged convicts, but most convicts and their families lacked adequate clothes that posed a problem for health and morality. Branner described typical convict garb when he depicted those who had helped him with his geological work: "He stood barefooted and uncovered, his warped, reddish-brown hat held in his left hand behind him, his coarse shirt of dirty cotton cloth hung, in the customary fashion, outside his coarse trousers, and these were rolled half-way up his bare, brown legs." While Brazilian slaves were forbidden to wear shoes, many poor free men also went unshod. Indeed, this convict's dirty and coarse cotton clothing and warped leather hat made him rather well dressed compared to many of his peers. Branner also described a group of convicts who bade him farewell: "There came about me seven men with rough clothing—what there was of it—rough, hard hands, and hard faces. They stood uncovered, and, without speaking a word, one after another held out to me a thick, horny right hand."[66] Most convicts did agricultural labor that soon frayed their clothes and made their hands leathery.

In 1850, the commander requested that fabric be sent so that convicts could have shirts and pants made because so many walked about in a state of nudity. While some used flour sacks to make clothes, they soon fell apart, and he complained that because of this he had to excuse many from their obligation to attend Mass.[67] In 1871, the commander noted that there was a great influx of new prisoners who disembarked in a state of nudity. For "the love of decency," he ordered the manufacture of three hundred sackcloth pants and shirts.[68] In 1872, another commander found it ironic that inmates in mainland prisons received new clothes every six months, but that on Fernando de Noronha, where convicts worked, they did not, and the convicts' meager wages meant they had no funds to purchase their own clothing.[69] Officials commonly combined the terms "nudity" and "misery" to describe convicts and their families. Of course, the nudity of some slaves on the mainland led some municipalities to issue ordinances that fined masters who failed to clothe their slaves adequately. Similarly, army officers periodically reported that northeastern army recruits arrived in Rio de Janeiro partially or entirely nude. Inadequate clothing was not uncommon for categories of the intractable poor.

The 1879 ban on commerce had the unintended consequence of turning the penal colony into a partial nudist colony. The Justice Ministry had required that prisoners be placed in three classes according to their comportment and given uniforms that identified their class. The commitment to this sartorial classification did not last long because convicts never regularly received clothing. In 1880, a commander offered nude prisoners flour sacks to cover themselves, but since he had no more sacks, he predicted that "soon prisoners would be walking about nude to work and in the streets." Months later the same commander pleaded that clothes be provided because commerce had been prohibited and prisoners had no means to acquire clothes, which for the "convicts is vexing and for me is embarrassing."[70] Many convict children lacked clothing, which prevented them from attending school. In 1878, a commander clothed these children at his own expense so they could go to classes.[71] An inspector confirmed that the convicts' complaints about clothing and the poor quality of the food they received were entirely accurate.[72]

Similarly, convict housing was mostly inadequate and insalubrious. In 1850, the commander noted that the convict barracks was too crowded for the number of prisoners that slept there, and this same building also housed the primary school and the paint shop. Married convicts and others who were well behaved would spend the night in shacks that they constructed.[73] Later in 1856, convicts constructed the more spacious aldeia building, but even this structure could not keep up with the growing number of prisoners. As a commander noted in 1869: "It is an absolute necessity to enlarge the Aldeia building because it can only accommodate 283 convicts while there are 1,233 prisoners, even if they construct, in addition to those homes already built, four new houses of stone and tile roofs and thirty one of wattle and daub for those of good conduct . . . for whom company sergeants vouch and assume responsibility, it has been necessary to assign two or more convicts to each [unattached] house which is prejudicial to the presidio's discipline because almost always housemates have disputes with one another." Prisoners could use their rations of soap to bathe themselves in the ocean to provide for their personal hygiene. While latrines existed in the aldeia, most individual homes likely collected urine and feces in slop jars that were dumped in the ocean.[74]

While the material conditions of most convicts were dismal, those of employees were not ideal. The commander's pantry was well stocked, but most employees did not enjoy so rich a diet. Beaurepaire Rohan warned that employees had to be better paid to prevent corruption:

If they go with satisfaction attracted by the information that they have about the island's healthful environment, its alimentary resources, and other comforts, that the military officers take advantage of, soon they perceive that the presidio is not what they imagined, an approximation of the earthly paradise. Then appears disgracefully the idea of taking the maximum advantage possible of the difficult and dangerous situation in which they find themselves in compensation, even though illegitimate, of the sufferings that they see themselves condemned to, far from their relatives and friends, and removed from any society that they could possibly enhance through their morality.[75]

This observation seemed a partial apology for the corruption Beaurepaire Rohan witnessed.

Beaurepaire Rohan reported that employees and officers opened stores to augment their incomes and exploited convict labor to produce goods to sell in Recife:

As the presidio is a public establishment . . . all labor should be exclusively used to benefit public coffers. This, however, does not occur. Hundreds of convicts are employed in private service, and receive no salary for their work. Each employee and each officer in the presidio has, on their own account, extensive plantations of manioc, beans, corn, and fruits that they sell in Pernambuco. Persons worthy of repute assure me that many times the ship that transports these goods to market in Recife also carries the Commander's requests from the Governor of Pernambuco for supplies because the presidio has none! How many times has the treasury purchased goods in the public market [to send to Fernando de Noronha] that have recently arrived from there?

Beaurepaire Rohan clarified that an advisory of December 15, 1859, permitted employees and officers to cultivate lands in return for a small fee paid to the government, but that the scale of these operations abused the spirit of the order.[76] Furthermore, no one bothered to collect the specified fees. For these reasons, he added provisions to the regulations that prohibit employees from participating in commerce and farming. As evidence already examined has shown, administrators did not make these rules stick.

Was the life of a convict laborer better than that of a slave? Though he wrote about Rio de Janeiro's ship hulk prisons where convict chain-gang laborers were held at night, the political prisoner Cypriano José Barata de Almeida believed that the condition of convicts was inferior: "Prisons change the nature of man so that he becomes a slave; and in consequence prisoners should not receive the barbarous treatment that they do; treatment that is one thousand times more tyrannical than that given to captive blacks that come from Africa."[77] Of course, slavery was a touchstone against which all social categories were frequently compared. To be treated like a slave was the ultimate injustice for free men and women, even free members of the intractable poor. The lives of slaves, like those of convicts, were variegated, and they cannot be easily reduced to numbers. Even if sources allowed one to compare reliably the probability that a convict or slave would be flogged, fettered, raped, married, adequately fed, treated for illness, and receive the sacraments, would this answer the question? Few would choose to be a slave or a convict not only because of the material conditions attendant to them, but also because most Brazilians, even humble ones, considered them dishonored. The most common terms used to describe convicts is telling: "unhappy ones," "disgraced ones," and "miserable ones." In a society where honor could limit opportunities and acceptance, one should not overlook convicts' pariah status. Even the most privileged slaves and convicts yearned to be free, which indicates how the categories of the intractable poor were interrelated and mutually constitutive.

While convicts on Fernando de Noronha enjoyed certain luxuries that many of their free mainland counterparts did not, there were other real drawbacks to life in the colony. Many of their peers were notoriously dangerous, and security was a concern for all. Convicts may not have characterized their community as a stench in the nostrils of God, but most convict and nonconvict wives and children were exposed to scenes of immorality and violence that, if not uncommon on the mainland, were less conspicuous there. No small number of convicts turned to crime to earn extra income to ameliorate Spartan conditions, and these activities could lead to violence. Some of this violence sprang from disputes over commerce, which in turn was often linked to disputes between members of the island community up and down the social hierarchy.

7 CRIME, CONFLICT, CORRUPTION, AND COOPERATION ON AN ATLANTIC FRONTIER

According to John Branner, the colony's staff frequently voiced concerns about security: "Often in private conversation these men would discourse to me upon the moral and social condition of their companions. . . . I frequently heard such expressions as these: 'You must look out for Fulano [so-and-so].' 'Some people have no consciences.' 'Lord deliver us from a convict!' 'These convicts are a bad set, I tell you!'"[1] Fears of convicts spawned mistrust, but conflicts also cemented cooperation as it encouraged or coerced individuals to choose one set of allegiances over others. While some convicts opposed the administration, others were its agents. Just as mainland political bosses used patronage to attract clients (some of them bandits and *capoeiras*), commanders and other officers cultivated convict clients. Conflict and cooperation shaped relationships up and down the social scale much as it did on the mainland. As Commander Pereira Lobo wrote: "The actual garrison under the command of the dignified Capt. Antonio Francisco da Costa and even the better comported convicts supply this command with the support needed for any extraordinary emergency."[2] One might think that the staff's dread of convict violence would unite them, but they often feuded. When a commander reported an 1838 conflict between two civil servants, he stated they were "fractious, like almost all the employees on the island."[3] Staff sometimes involved convicts in their disputes with one another.

The island's isolation meant there was little direct oversight, but Remédios was a small town where rumors flew and secrets were hard to keep. From time to time, the mainland press aired its dirty laundry. The colony's garrison provided security, but its small size led one officer to poetically depict them as a "dike set against a sea of a thousand passions."[4] Commanders used patronage to solidify support from inhabitants, but parallel networks of patronage often competed with one another. Much of this rivalry centered on attempts to dominate profits from the dark twins of licit and contraband commerce. This chapter explores cooperation and conflict within and among the colony's social strata through case studies of crime, disputes, rebellions, and mutinies. These case studies demonstrate how corruption could undercut formal lines of colony authority.

CRIME IN THE PRESIDIO

Many convicts took pride in their criminal skills. Some committed new crimes to better their conditions, to intimidate or take revenge upon rivals, or simply to pass the time and prove their competence. Convicts were not the only lawbreakers in the colony. Evidence reveals criminal complicity among officers, civil servants, vendors, and soldiers. Scarcity typified most convicts' lives. Salaries were low; goods for sale, dear; and the ability to earn extra income legitimately, limited. The environment nourished theft and extortion that fed an underground economy in stolen goods.

Convicts committed many petty thefts, but only ambitious capers elicited reports. Major Manoel Pereira d'Abreu reported such a case when in 1879 intruders burgled the commander's home and stole various items including 3:600$000 reis (a sum equal to the value of four young adult slaves) from a locked suitcase.[5] Who would bring such a large sum to a penal colony? The report did not comment on why the commander had so much cash, nor its provenance, but it suggests that he had found ways to profit from his post. The master carpenter, a convict, examined the scene and determined that at least two burglars had pried open the roof. The major must have suspected that the evidence of a break-in was a ruse because his investigation focused on the commander's convict domestics. He detained all four and searched their homes. In convict Antonio José dos Santos's home he found 447$000 réis and some of the commander's clothing. Santos confessed that he and his fellow domestic, the slave convict Benedicto, stole the money. Benedicto also confessed, but insisted that his share had been stolen.[6] The major suspected that the "black" slave convict Luiza, Santos's consensual lover, was involved. Weeks later, they found the rest of the money in the possession of the slave convicts Dionisio and Ismael. Santos, Benedicto, Luiza, Dionisio, and Ismael later embarked to Recife for trial.[7]

Documents do not reveal how staff selected domestics, but in this case, a commander chose two who betrayed him and tarnished his reputation. Brazilians revered the principle of the home's inviolability, and household heads had to defend it.[8] The commander griped that the conservative newspaper *O Tempo* unfairly suggested that he lacked "the prestige or moral force to govern the island" because he could not prevent his home from being burgled. He suggested that this critique was building "castles in the sky" because he had been robbed by domestics already inside his home.[9] Despite his remonstration, the robbery had embarrassed him and his enemies seized upon it. The case also reveals convict relationships. Santos lived with the slave convict Luiza, and this may have made him a trustworthy partner for the slave convict Benedicto. Despite their different statuses, Santos's and Benedicto's work brought them together, and they trusted each other enough to pull off the dangerous theft. Benedicto then gave his take to two fellow slave convicts, which suggests a bond of common identification and trust among them.

Other reports reveal how thieves laundered stolen goods. In 1885, Captain Manoel Accioly de Moura Gondim solved a case of stolen turkeys. The crime was minor, but it allowed Gondim to seize evidence to prosecute the colony's most notorious fence: convict Manuel da Rocha Wanderley. According to Gondim, there was an axiom among convicts: "As long as Wanderley is in this presidio, burglaries and robberies will not cease." The captain received a tip that the inmate José Pedro had stolen two turkeys. Pedro informed the captain that, as on other occasions, he sold his pilfered goods to Wanderley. The captain had unsuccessfully searched Wanderley's home on numerous occasions, but this time he found the stolen turkeys. Wanderley resisted arrest, and as a result, the captain admitted that he had received some blows. Wanderley's wife filed a complaint that accused the captain of applying fifty-five blows to her husband, but Gondim countered that there had been no more than a dozen.[10]

Individuals were not the only victims of theft. Commander Pereira Lobo brooded that thefts constantly depleted warehouse supplies because convict porters carried goods from the port to the warehouse without a security escort.[11] Then again, Pereira Lobo may have profited from pilfering warehouse stores, and his report provided cover for his misdeeds. Other convicts stole crops directly from the fields. Theft was common enough to support a network of stolen goods, and the goods thieves did not consume often found their way to storeowners' shelves.

The theft of goods or money could besmirch a commander's reputation, but when convicts stole their own persons, they could threaten mainland security. Convicts who conspired to escape required coordinated planning and mutual trust. Escape was risky because fugitives had to traverse more than two hundred miles of ocean and furtively gather materials: logs, an adequate piece of cloth for a sail, rope to lash the logs together, and vessels for fresh water and food. Despite the dangers, escape had a venerable tradition. One of the colony's earliest extant letters reported that prisoners had escaped on rafts in 1819.[12] Officials insisted that the rafts used by convict fishermen be too small for the open sea. To build a more seaworthy craft, convicts secured logs from large trees, but commanders regularly harvested them to deter escape. Once convicts had logs, they hid them near out-of-the way inlets where they would surreptitiously launch their craft. Commanders located night watchmen's homes in locales where they could survey secluded beaches, but the dedication of these mostly elderly convicts was not reliable.

On November 4, 1871, the convicts Lourenço Justiniano de Mendonça, Silvano Xavier de Paiva, and Luiz, the slave of Dr. Pedro Gaudiano de Rates e Silva Jr., missed morning roll call. The commander ordered a search. The next day he concluded that the three had constructed a raft after he found vestiges of their preparations. Normally he would send the "intrepid and diligent" Sergeant Querino Joaquim Madeira (the sailor Madeira) in pursuit, but he was on leave on the mainland. He did not send the navy convicts who could sail the ship out of concern that they would take the opportunity to escape themselves. Instead, he sent the convicts' descriptions to the mainland to facilitate their capture. The three fugitives were young men with lengthy or life sentences who felt that a dangerous escape was worth the risk. Records do not indicate what brought them together, but they reveal that slave and free convicts with life and temporary sentences trusted one another enough to attempt it.[13] While some escaped with their lives, others were not so lucky. An 1881 report indicated that when the colony sailboat intercepted four fugitives, only two remained alive on a battered raft.[14] Some escapees cobbled together raft materials that seemed unsuitable, which indicates their desperation and the difficulties of escape. At first light on February 21, 1884, four convicts fled on a "fragile" raft constructed from tree trunks bolstered by "banana tree trunks." The nonconvict sergeant Manoel Correia de Albuquerque pursued them, but he could not find them even though he knew that they had a blue sail.[15]

While most fugitives relied on improvised rafts, some seized the colony's sailboat. The Major da Praça Captain Trajano Alípio de Carvalho Mendonça removed the sailboat from Remédios's warehouse in 1871 to transfer a convict go-between to a visiting Prussian vessel. Instead of securing the boat in the warehouse, the captain stored it in Port Santo Antonio under the guard of two convict watchmen. The commander placed full responsibility for the escape on Mendonça's shoulders because he planned to sell chickens to the Prussians the next day. At night, a group of ten convicts armed with knives tied up the guards and escaped.[16] Mainland officials captured one escapee, convict Antonio Justiano Barbosa de Lima, and returned him to the colony in 1874. Ten years later when he appealed for a commutation the only thing the commander mentioned was that he had escaped on November 15, 1871.[17] The fates of the other escapees are unclear, but their case shows that not all escapees died at sea. The 1871 escape inspired others. In 1872, ten prisoners plotted to steal the colony sailboat. The commander found the materials they had gathered: a makeshift mast, an anchor, and stored water. He had them publicly flogged, "because this is the only effective means of repression given the limited preventive resources of the Presidio and the pitiful moral state of almost all the convicts." A foiled escape had dire consequences, but brutal floggings did not deter escapes.[18] In 1874, the colony's sailboat delivered food to Rat Island. The sergeant in charge disembarked and left two soldiers on board to guard it. Meanwhile, four convicts overpowered the guards and escaped.[19]

Convict Gustavo Augusto Cardoso Pinto made the most original escape attempt when he hid himself in a chest that belonged to his lover Maria Marcionilia Beltrão when she returned to Recife in 1878. The chest had accompanied Beltrão on a number of voyages, so no one suspected anything. The next day, however, Pinto missed roll call, and the commander deduced what had happened. The warship *Magé*, which was visiting the colony, intercepted the steamer and arrested Pinto.[20] An inspector came to know Pinto and described him as an educated young man from Pará who wrote good poetry. But "this prisoner, who could be so useful, is, to the contrary, one of the presidio's biggest headaches. Prison life, instead of promoting remorse, completely ruined his character, making him into a perverse spirit, always inclined to evil, loaded with vices, and capable of all miseries." Pinto's antics had led colony officials to jail him and clap him in irons on a few occasions. The inspector concluded that Pinto, a homicide convict, "judged himself a martyr." Despite his bad behavior, however, officials allowed his lover to visit him regularly. Someone must have paid handsomely for this favor.[21]

Like escapes, the details surrounding homicide reports provide rare glimpses of everyday colony life. For example, at 3:00 PM on Sunday, July 27, 1873, the military convict Afonso Ribeiro de Lima killed the military convict Manoel Borges after an argument. Lima used a dagger to stab his companion nine times. These two had entertained themselves with a guitar in the slave convict Antonio Pardo's home with a group of fellow convicts. There appeared to be no rigid social divisions as military convicts chose to spend their leisure in a slave convict's abode. Even so, the case illustrates the mistrust among convicts, because Lima, like many convicts, went about armed for self-defense, not with a kitchen knife, but a dagger.[22]

Homicides undermined the community's sense of security, especially when they portended collective violence. For example, the convict Cosme José d'O committed a brutal assassination of convict José Bento Pereira and his wife Josepha Maria da Conceição in 1885. He also injured their young daughter Maria Ana de Conceição. To add to the tragedy, Josepha was six months pregnant at the time.[23] Officials believed these murders precipitated an uprising among convicts a few months later that year as well as a subsequent double murder in 1886, when convict Lindolpho Rodrigues Captivo murdered both his lover, convict Marcelina Maria da Conceição, and convict Maria Josepha da Conceição (not to be confused with Josepha Maria da Conceição mentioned previously). Captivo had been sent to be tried in Recife for his role in the 1885 uprising, and he returned to the colony in 1886 when he committed the double murder with "all the premeditation and perversity he is capable of." Captivo had been confined in an aldeia jail cell but was released under guard to work on a cleaning detail. He eluded his guards, went to Marcelina and Josepha's home, and there "stole their blood like an indomitable beast." For the commander, Captivo had been one of "the most dangerous and rebellious convicts involved in the lamentable events of August 1885." Perhaps Lindolpho killed his lover for informing about his part in the uprising, but records do not divulge his motive.[24]

These cases demonstrate that residents faced real dangers, but convicts, employees, families, and children did not live in constant trepidation. The American geologist John Branner commented on his sense of security there: "It is often asked whether there was not great danger in trusting one's self with men so many of who were known to be desperate characters. . . . Whether there would be danger would depend almost entirely upon how one conducted himself. The commandant was so solicitous regarding my personal safety . . . that he wished to send an escort of soldiers with me in order to secure me against possible danger, and it was with difficulty that

I persuaded him to allow me to dispense with such cumbersome attendance."[25] Of course, Branner spoke fluent Portuguese and had worked with working-class Brazilians and slaves on geological missions. The only unpleasant incident he reports is with the American convict William Bell:

> When working in parts of the island remote from the village [Remédios] I sometimes found it necessary to pass the night in the huts of the convicts. At such times I was never treated otherwise than with respect by them, and I never had the least reason to feel disturbed about my personal security. One day, when alone in my room in the house of the commandant, a tall mulatto came to the door and handed me a begging letter, written in very poor Portuguese. In this letter he called himself my "afflicted fellow-countryman." Addressing him in English, I found that he had been an American sailor, and was here for murder. As he seemed eager to be in my service, I employed him; but, when I informed the commandant of the arrangement, he endeavored to dissuade me from having him about me, assuring me that he was the most unconscionable, incorrigible criminal in the entire settlement. In spite of these protests, I took my "fellow-countryman" with me, and for three days his services gave entire satisfaction. At the end of that time he was discharged for the only impoliteness shown me during my stay upon the island.[26]

The convicts gave Branner no concern for his security except for Bell's unspecified impoliteness. In truth, most violence was episodic and the level of anxiety about it varied over time.

Through theft, escapes, homicides, and contraband trade, many convicts foiled the efforts of staff to create the kind of order envisioned in regulations. Scarcity, boredom, rivalry, greed, fear, or a desire for freedom inspired many convicts to commit new crimes. The episodes examined here demonstrate how convicts of different civil conditions, colors, and genders came together to execute plans that required trust, secrecy, and cunning. It seems that what mattered more to bring together convicts in these prohibited activities were the relationships they formed through work and leisure. This is not to suggest that prejudice against former slaves and convicts of color did not exist, but it did not prevent them from cooperating with one another. As the next section shows, similar forms of cooperation and conflict extended to nonconvict residents.

CONFLICTS BETWEEN STAFF

Like convicts, the colony's staff had their share of feuds. To minimize them, some commanders sought to appoint relatives as subordinates. Despite their best efforts, however, commanders had limited control over who served with them. Pernambuco's governors nominated the colony's major da praça and civil servants, but bureaucrats in Rio de Janeiro named commanders. Since many commanders had ties to Pernambuco, some consultation with provincial authorities likely took place, but there were often tensions between provincial and imperial appointees. This created a kind of check and balance between authorities in Rio de Janeiro and Recife that often left the two highest-ranking officers mistrustful of one another. Commanders and majors da praça often had different networks of support on the mainland and among the colony's inhabitants. When disputes broke out, accusations of corruption flew. Allegations centered on the exploitation of convict labor for personal gain, the theft of imperial property, the sale of privileged posts, inappropriate relationships with convicts, and contraband commerce. These moments reveal practices and relationships that otherwise go unmentioned.

In 1821, Major Antonio José da Motta wrote: "I have to report . . . the lack of military character and discipline I have encountered among the majority of officers, NCOs, and soldiers that reside in this detachment among whom I have only witnessed thefts and drunkenness. It has come to my attention that in the barracks. . . . Private João José do Nascimento maintains a tavern and gambling operation for which he charges usurious prices to obtain the money of his comrades and, for this reason, I had him assigned to Fort São José do Morro."[27] São José do Morro was isolated from Remédios, and it separated Nascimento from his comrade customers. In the same letter, the major reported a case of corruption that involved an officer, soldiers, and convict fishermen: "I punished Private João Antonio of the 2nd Infantry Battalion because he was an associate of a mulatto tavern keeper and the servant of Lieutenant Joaquim de Souza Mierelles who suborned the colony's fishermen so that they would only sell him [the tavern owner] their catch. In this way, they cornered the supply of fish and charged high prices which resulted in hunger among the presidio's people."[28] The incident shows a high level of collusion between inhabitants of different statuses. These social and commercial entanglements bound together a network that undercut formal presidio hierarchy and created hardship for residents.

Sometimes accusations centered on political loyalties. In 1851, the commander feuded with Captain Fernando Antonio Rosauro. To discredit the captain, the commander suggested that he plotted with Praieira political prisoners Antônio Borges da Fonseca and Father Francisco Pio Pereira Campos. He also accused Chaplain Joaquim da Cunha Cavalcante and the surgeon João Domingos da Silva of harboring Praieira sympathies and plotting intrigues to discredit him. For this reason, he justified replacing the captain with one of his trusted lieutenants.[29] The sympathy of some clergy and military officers for the Praieira cause shows the extent to which the island remained linked to the mainland. It is difficult to access the truth of the commander's accusations, but in the rebellion's wake, mainland authorities were loath to question the actions of commanders in situ. This offered a perfect climate to purge mistrusted subordinates.

While employees and officers sometimes attacked one another, at other times, they victimized their rival's clients. An 1888 dispute between Lieutenant José Ignacio Ribeiro Roma and his commander occurred when the latter ordered the slave convict André, a domestic in the lieutenant's household, to be fettered and sent to work in Sambaqueixaba for stealing manioc. Witnesses observed that André had been left to care for Roma's house when he took leave, and he allegedly transformed it into a gambling den. When Roma returned and learned of his client's fate, he asked the commander if "he wanted to demoralize him because he would not be demoralized." Roma insulted and threatened the commander in front of troops and convicts. The lieutenant interpreted the commander's actions to discipline his domestic as an attack on his prestige because it demonstrated that he could not protect his convict client. The commander relieved Roma of his post, but Roma questioned his authority to give such an order because the governor had appointed him. Later, the governor ordered Roma to return to Recife.[30]

This clash over convict domestics was not uncommon. An 1873 investigation of Lieutenant Miguel Joaquim de Rego Barros Jr. alleged that he spoke against the commander's authority in public. The commander insisted that his "style of language" had "undermined the presidio's morality and discipline." His declarations could plant the seeds of a rebellion as he "declared himself to be an enemy of the commander and asserted that he had published articles against his administration in the mainland press." According to the commander, the lieutenant was upset that his domestic, convict Amancio da Silva, had been injured when convict police arrested him for gambling. Allegedly, the lieutenant warned those in Jeronima Maria da Conceição's tavern that if the commander reassigned and flogged his domestic, he would have all domestics reassigned. The commander added that the lieutenant had illicit relations with convict Manoel Ignacio de Limas Jr.'s wife and "many others."[31]

Given the sensitivity of their positions and their connection to mainland political figures, commanders were targets of partisan vitriol. This makes it difficult to determine the veracity of accusations, but occasionally, they led to investigations. In 1871, the newspaper *O Liberal* covered the investigation of Commander Joaquim Antônio de Moraes Rego, who was accused of conspiring with counterfeiters and other crimes. The first witness, Domingos de Souza Barros, testified that Moraes Rego built two rooms attached to his residence where the counterfeiters Manoel Oscar de Villa Maré and José de Tal, known as Menci, fabricated money. The second witness, the slave Luiz, declared that he heard from a woman named Luiza who was Moraes Rego's laundress that she had seen money in bundles and other bills drying in the commander's residence. The fourth witness, Feliz d'Araujo Lins, declared that he had heard from the convict Romero that the nonconvict sergeant Madeira, the island's "potentate," had invited him to counterfeit money on the commander's behalf and offered a number of benefits such as exemption from work details and Madeira's protection.[32]

While *O Liberal* had a political ax to grind, an investigative commission of former presidio commanders expressed astonishment that an insurrection had not broken out before Moraes Rego was relieved of his command. They determined that the price table and a tax on goods he had instituted was "truly an extortion that had no legal precedent" and recommended that those forced to pay them be reimbursed. Convicts, employees, officers, and unattached residents unleashed a torrent of accusations. They testified that Moraes Rego inflicted cruel punishments, smuggled alcohol, and lived openly with his lover, a woman from Recife. Storeowners claimed that Moraes Rego told them to sell to convicts on credit, but when convicts were paid, he said they were not obligated to pay their debts. Convicts grumbled that the commander kept them so busy that they had no time to tend their provision grounds. The commission noted that witnesses were almost unanimous in their condemnations of Moraes Rego, who was an "irascible personality with little common sense."[33]

While these disputes illuminate the tensions among staff and convicts, a more extended examination of Pereira Lobo's commands exposes deeper layers. From 1867 to 1885, Pereira Lobo commanded the colony five times, a post he must have found attractive. Why? Inspector Bandeira Filho provides a clue: "Happily, I visited the presidio in an auspicious era because I only found the traditions of scandalous facts practiced by previous administrations whose members became rich with their earnings from the establishment, at the expense of public coffers, and made fortunes from the sale of goods formally proscribed by regulations. The island's administration was held in such discredit that it was the golden dream of many army officers that aspired to make a lot of money in little time; or if respectable citizens exercised the command they became the targets of implacable criticism."[34]

The potential to make money through corruption made this post attractive to officers who competed to attain it.

In 1882 Pereira Lobo charged his major da praça, Captain Justino Rodrigues da Silveira, with corruption: "Poor as he always was, in 17 months of service on this island, [he amassed enough wealth] to buy a building in Recife and boasts of his honorable position in a place where his actions so palpably undermine the fulfillment of his duties!"[35] Silveira countered: "Brigadeiro Francisco Joaquim Pereira Lobo, his son Antonio Gracindo de Gusmão Lobo, and his son-in-law Captain João Baptista Pinheiro Corte Real have all turned against one another in a dispute over power, and trade public . . . insults with one another which men from even the lowest social classes would not tolerate." Pereira Lobo's son-in-law allegedly nominated two convict sergeants with the commander's permission for the price of 300$000 réis (a young adult slave in 1882 was 350$000 réis). To afford such a bribe, sergeants must have expected to make illicit profits from their post.[36] Silveira claimed that this upset the brigadeiro's son, who "also had clients of his nepotism." The dispute escalated on February 7, 1882, when father and son shouted insults at each other in front of the military guard. Their quarrel grew so heated that they nearly drew swords. Afterward, Gusmão Lobo went to his brother-in-law's house with a riding crop to beat him before another officer dissuaded him. Silveira insisted that these facts were known to all and requested that the governor "spare this portion of unhappy ones [convicts] from the sad examples that daily afflict their consciences and immerses them in error and crime."[37]

When Silveira took leave in Recife, Pereira Lobo made further accusations. He listed goods made by convicts under Silveira's direction: 432 dozen wooden forks, various pieces of furniture, and other finished goods that he shipped to Recife to sell. He also charged that Silveira assigned large provision fields to favored sergeants who raised crops that Silveira sold in Recife along with crops he stole from the imperial farm. Pereira Lobo asked that the governor not return Silveira to his post, but the governor retained Silveira, which demonstrates the limits of the commander's influence on the appointment of subordinates.[38] The two officers carped about each other until they were eventually reassigned. Silveira and Pereira Lobo's accusations did not spark an investigation, and both later returned to serve as commanders.[39]

Against this backdrop, one can more fruitfully return to analyze Pereira Lobo's dispute, glossed earlier, with Silveira over the *maracatu* group, Porto Rico's vivas during Carnival in 1882. The maracatu nations Cambinda Velha and Porto Rico caused a ruckus when they encountered each other near the officers' residences. After Silveira asked them to disperse, Cambinda Velha moved on, but members of Porto Rico stayed and shouted vivas to Silveira. The incident enraged Pereira Lobo who queried the governor about why convicts were permitted to celebrate Carnival. The governor replied that "better behaved convicts" could form "small" Carnival groups to dance before Ash Wednesday "because it was custom, and it reminded the convicts of imperial munificence and that they could still be useful to the Empire." Pereira Lobo griped that allowing these groups to parade was dangerous and clarified that the governor would be responsible for any violence that resulted. It is rare for commanders to take such a high-handed tone. Pereira Lobo groused that most convicts dancing were not well behaved and there was no definition of what constituted a small group of revelers. While Pereira Lobo saw sinister motives in the vivas, Silveira made light of them in his report.

Porto Rico and Cambinda Velha had existed for some time as a colony tradition. Despite decrees to regulate them, the commander suggested that large numbers of convicts participated in the dancing irrespective of their conduct. As with mainland Carnival, it would be surprising if participants did not imbibe alcohol, which could embolden them to acts of insubordination or induce conflicts between rival groups. Disputes between mainland Carnival groups sometimes led to brawls. One cannot determine if members of Porto Rico hoped to heighten tensions between the feuding officers by shouting vivas, but the commander believed they were.

Perhaps it is not surprising that governors allowed convicts to celebrate Carnival. Masters also permitted slaves to sing and dance on special occasions, but mainland authorities debated whether it was advisable to allow slaves to gather in numbers to revel.[40] Pereira Lobo wanted to ban the parades because he could not control the "vertiginous impulses of a crowd . . . [whose] brutishness shows itself on these occasions without regard for one's position, place, or any other circumstances."[41] During Carnival the poor dressed as the rich and powerful and at least symbolically subverted traditional hierarchies. In addition, revelers could use the anonymity of the crowd to lampoon and insult authorities, just as mainland revelers did [42] Pereira Lobo permitted fireworks and marching bands to celebrate Conservative Party electoral victories, so his opposition to presidio celebrations that involved convict revelers was selective.

Other evidence indicates that the maracatu nations may have corresponded to rival convict networks linked to Pereira Lobo and Silveira. In 1885, the *Diário de Pernambuco* described an object found in the house used as a "headquarters" for a subversive plot. Investigators found "a wooden figure of a black woman, a type of fetish, that was used in the convict's sambas and maracatus. This figure has on its right arm, a bracelet with a pendent of a small brass knife, a significant emblem of the good intentions of this group."[43] It seems probable that this Carnival figure (*colunga*) belonged to Cambinda Velha. Maracatu *calungas* represented ancestors in the African tradition, and Cambinda Velha was a variation on the *preta velha* (black woman elder) of Afro-spiritist religious and Carnival traditions. The preta velha is sometimes depicted with a rosary hanging from her wrist, so it is possible that what reporters interpreted to be a knife was actually a cross. This symbolized the devotion that many Afro-Brazilians had to *Nossa Senhora do Rosário* (Our Lady of the Rosary), a devotion of black lay brotherhoods across Brazil, including Recife. Other representations, however, depicted colungas bearing knives that carried special meaning in Afro-spiritist religious healing practices.[44]

If the colunga was a symbol of Cambinda Velha, it suggests that Periera Lobo had ties to its members through the convict sergeant Vicente d'Assis Tavares. As noted earlier, Pereira Lobo had promoted Assis to plum posts and supported a petition to commute his sentence. Investigators later fingered Sergeant Assis as the leader of fifty-six convicts who planned an uprising for September 7, 1885, Brazil's Independence Day. The evidence is circumstantial, but it is plausible that Porto Rico had patronage ties to Silveira and Cambinda Velha to his rival Pereira Lobo. This may explain why the vivas shouted out by members of Porto Rico incensed the commander.

Why would a commander and the major da praça hurl such ugly recriminations against each other? It is probable that they competed to dominate contraband trade. In 1884, Pereira Lobo accused another major da praça of smuggling in collusion with the steamship crews. His complaints forced the steamship company to replace the crew. Even so, alcohol continued to be uncovered, and Pereira Lobo blamed his second: "There was either entire negligence or intentional tolerance on the part of the Major da Praça Manoel Ferreira Escobar in the formal intent to create each time more difficulties for my administration." The commander learned from another officer that steamship crew members had landed several times on the Ilha do Meio, an uninhabited islet, to hide smuggled alcohol. He suggested that the governor remove his appointee Escobar and nominate someone else.[45] The governor removed Escobar and the colony's secretary, João Baptista Pinheiro Corte Real (Pereira Lobo's son-in-law), and nominated Major Guilhermino Paes Barreto and Captain Manoel Accioli de Moura Gondim to replace them.[46]

Later that month, the governor questioned requests from staff for alcohol that Pereira Lobo had approved. Pereira Lobo claimed he had approved the requests from "employees and officers" in quantities "reasonable for one's dietary needs." But in response, the governor asked which names on the list were convicts. Eleven names were so identified with blue pencil. One of the names listed was Manoel da Rocha Wanderley, the notorious fence whom Captain Gondim would later catch red-handed with stolen turkeys. Pereira Lobo later included Gondim in a list of his enemies whom the governor nominated. The amounts of alcohol Pereira Lobo permitted Wanderley for dietary needs seem excessive: one big bottle of wine, nine bottles of cane brandy, and four bottles of wine. Since supply ships came monthly, one presumes this would be a month's supply. Another name on the list was Manoel de Souza Almeida, the ex-con storeowner and nonconvict sergeant introduced in chapter 3. Almeida's order was even larger than Wanderley's: "24 bottles of port wine; 6 of orange liquor; 4 of Bordeaux wine; 6 of beer; 16 of cachaça; and three big bottles of wine."[47]

Pereira Lobo insisted that his seizures of alcohol evidenced his dedication to stifle contraband, but was he merely seizing the goods of his competitors and protecting others who shared proceeds with him? This is what Silveira argued. On February 18, 1882, Silveira, acting as the island's customs official, apprehended eleven bottles of cane brandy addressed to the convict José Fernando da Silva, a convict well known for his involvement in the sale of contraband alcohol (*useiro e verseiro neste genero de contrabando*). Silveira also reported that Silva was "scandalously patronized by the chief of the administration [Pereira Lobo]." When he learned of the confiscation, Pereira Lobo informed Silveira that the cane brandy was his and ordered it delivered to his residence. Silveira reported to the governor that it was strange for a commander to order cane brandy in a convict's name, and added that it would "betray his conscience as a customs official" if he remained silent about it.[48] One may recall that Pereira Lobo had at first treated the American geologist John Branner coldly when he arrived because he suspected he was on a "secret government mission" to spy on him.[49] Did Pereira Lobo have something to hide? He repeatedly charged that his enemies sought to undermine him. When falsified currency appeared in the colony in 1885, he expressed anger at allegations that it was produced there: "As to the falsified money I assure your excellency that our investigation will leave no stone unturned to discover any thievery of this nature. Up to now, we know it was a bill forged by vile speculators, and the denunciations that it was fabricated in this presidio (unless it happened in the distant past) but now? . . . My enemies will say anything against me for vengeance, as it would permit . . . these poisonous snakes their desire to return here, no one can deny the loyalty with which I serve the government."[50] Pereira Lobo was not the only commander to suggest that subordinates worked to discredit him, but he also suggests that enemies on the mainland did so because they hoped to return to command the colony. This suggests a heated level of competition for the post.

Who were these enemies? Some were political foes and others army rivals. Pereira Lobo was well connected to the Conservative Party. Other officers, however, had connections with the Liberal Party, and rivalries among officer cliques and within party ranks were rife. The disputes between the army's top generals Marshal Manuel Luís Osório, the Marques de Herval and a senator for the Liberal Party, and Marshal Luís Alves de Lima e Silva, the Duke of Caxias and a senator for the Conservative Party, were the subject of political cartoons. Another indicator of the importance of patronage within the army is the term *pistolão* (big pistol), army slang for a person of influence who can intercede on your behalf that became widely used in civilian circles. Tensions were also common among officers who commanded the colony. As noted previously, former commanders investigated allegations against Commander Rego Morais. One of Pereira Lobo's detractors was Commander Sebastião Antonio do Rego Barros, an officer related to a family prominent in Pernambuco's Conservative Party. Rego Barros complained that his predecessor, Pereira Lobo, failed to give him a final report: "I am convinced he did so intentionally because I myself gave him such a report on October 15, 1867, when he came to replace me as commander." He enumerated reasons why Pereira Lobo did not file a report. First, it was "entirely necessary to replace all the garrison troops, both those of the army and the National Guard, because they inspired no confidence because of their insubordination." He observed that the troops had no uniforms and that his predecessor had not corrected them. He also objected that no beans had been planted and that there was no seed corn, so he had to buy it from individuals to plant. The report decried Pereira Lobo's management, but for Rego Barros, it shielded him from accusations of corruption if the harvest was poor. The report implied that his predecessor had pilfered or had not prevented others from pilfering imperial produce.

Rego Barros also noted that "his predecessor had given some convicts dispensation from fieldwork because they owned stores." He immediately ordered these stores closed and put the owners to work in the fields.[51] He even closed stores owned by convict wives. The wives, however, complained that they had been given the governor's permission to conduct commerce. The governor forwarded a copy of a letter to Rego Barros from the commander of arms that clarified that the regulations forbade employees from selling goods but not convicts or their dependents: "It is convenient that they [convicts and their dependents] are not idle and thereby given over to vices, they should be occupied in their leisure time. . . . If they cannot do business, they will prefer idleness and as a consequence will continue in the state of nudity and misery in which they find themselves with their families."[52] Interestingly, authorities appealed to the logic of the jealous institution to defend the rights of convicts and their dependents to conduct commerce. Not all storeowners were married men, but many were, which shows that married men were more likely to be granted this favor. Rego Barros harassed the convicts that Pereira Lobo had protected, which gave him the opportunity to name his own clients to positions of privilege. His report suggested a rivalry with Pereira Lobo, but it did not prevent Pereira Lobo from returning to command the colony.

An 1885 murder confirms the close ties Pereira Lobo had to Sergeant Assis. Pereira Lobo reported that on July 29, 1885, at 9:30 PM, "a few convicts gathered in the house of the convict sentenced to temporary imprisonment Antonio Joaquim dos Santos." Santos celebrated his marriage peacefully when one of the colony's "notorious troublemakers," the slave convict Josias, appeared without invitation. The commander described Josias as "a ferocious assassin who has killed two soldiers here," and he appeared at Santos's home "without a doubt with the intent of causing disorder." When Josias arrived he asked for Assis, who had been Santos's best man. Assis put down a guitar and left to speak with Josias. While convict houses were small, some were commodious enough to host a modest party. Once outside, the "drunken" Josias, "without the least motive," tried to knife Assis. Assis deflected Josias's blows, which injured his left hand, and retreated into Santos's house declaring that he had been wounded, which created a panic. Josias ran toward Travessa Street, a place where he allegedly had enemies because of past "impudences." "At 11:30 PM more or less, I [Pereira Lobo] was notified that Josias had been mortally wounded, that he had fallen on his own knife. I ordered that he be taken to the infirmary where he later died. Even though I was suffering from bronchitis, I immediately investigated who had wounded the unhappy Josias." Pereira Lobo interrogated Santos, his guests, and others, but "it was not possible to ascertain who assassinated Josias."[53]

The report shows the freedom of movement that convicts enjoyed well after dark. Even Josias, a slave convict who had killed two soldiers in the colony, was not confined to the aldeia. He roamed Remédios after the official 8:00 PM curfew. It also shows that Pereira Lobo gave favored convicts permission to celebrate a marriage with a party and music. There is no mention of the celebrants drinking alcohol, but the commander indicated that Josias was inebriated. While alcohol was expensive, it was available, and the wedding party was likely consuming it. Assis led a powerful group of convicts who involved themselves in a variety of intrigues. By making Assis his best man, Santos solidified ties to a convict boss. Since Assis had ties to Pereira Lobo, perhaps it was no accident that the investigation failed to implicate anyone. Pereira Lobo's report does not question Assis's motives but goes out of its way to discredit Josias. He did not even dismiss the dubious claim that Josias fell on his own knife.

In Pereira Lobo's last command, conflicts abounded. In January 1885, Lieutenant José Joaquim de Aguiar reported that Dr. Francisco Jacintho Pereira da Motta, his son (a student of Recife's Law School), Motta's father-in-law (the colony's pharmacist), and the doctor's three convict domestics attacked and insulted him in the street at 10:00 AM. The group attacked him with whips and punches and hurled insults: "rogue, thief, and infamous." From afar the doctor's wife yelled: "Kill that thief, teach him to speak badly of our family." A convict scrivener rescued Aguiar and "probably saved his life." The lieutenant claimed that Dr. Motta's son had brandished a pistol and threatened him: "For you low life Lieutenant I have a whip but for your soldiers, I have a gun." After the attack, three of the lieutenant's soldiers asked to take revenge, but he ordered them to restrain themselves. Pereira Lobo demanded that the physician's son be sent to Recife, but the physician initially refused, stating that his son suffered from a colic that needed his treatment. This infuriated Aguiar, as witnesses emphasized that his insults and injuries had been made in a "highly public fashion." Aguiar demanded that the son be removed "in the name of the presidio's morality and discipline and the rights of my military rank and dignity as a man."[54] Here Aguiar invoked his sense of wounded manhood and insulted corporate honor. The son eventually returned to Recife, but the events reveal growing tensions between competing networks of patronage examined further in the next section.

In a culture where honor was esteemed, it mattered not only what one said or did, but also where it happened and who witnessed it. Officers condemned disrespectful words, deeds, and gestures made in public, especially in front of subordinates. The public nature of the offenses made them more scandalous and suggested the perpetrator's lack of concern for duty. As on the mainland, rivals often took revenge against their enemies' clients. When rivals took actions against another's client, it threatened to "demoralize" their patron. These incidents illustrate how networks of patronage could collide and bring officers and their clients into conflict. Whether the specific allegations were true or not, those who made them felt that they were believable. Some officers profited from selling privileged positions, and convicts bought them because of their potential for profits. Staff exploited the colony's labor, land, and materials for their own benefit despite regulations prohibiting it. The contraband trade led to competition and created conditions that led some convicts to hatch subversive plots and some soldiers to mutiny.

PRESIDIO INSURRECTIONS AND MUTINIES

Officers, employees, soldiers, and convicts themselves dreaded collective violence that officials described as "revolts" and sometimes "revolutions." While documents give glimpses of how and why riots occurred, it is difficult to judge the extent to which some were premeditated, much less inspired by a "revolutionary" conscience. Convicts and soldiers interrogated about their involvement were often reticent for fear of incriminating themselves or of inviting reprisals from peers. Officials too could exaggerate the threat convicts and soldiers posed to support their petitions for resources and to justify their own violence.

In 1854, a commander reported a convict plot to surprise the garrison during Mass to "immolate the officers and employees along with their innocent families." He blamed the plot on Vicente Ferreira de Paula, the former leader of the Cabanos Revolt (1832–1835). The *Diário de Pernambuco* reported that the governor himself accompanied the ship that carried troops and munitions to the colony in the conspiracy's wake.[55] When we last spoke of Ferreira he had been exiled to Fernando de Noronha during the Praieira Revolt (1848–1850).[56] The commander depicted Ferreira as a born-criminal in 1854: "Since a most tender age up to now, he is almost a septuagenarian, he has committed the most detestable crimes and even so he does not wish to end his enervating career without implanting thoughts substantially unfamiliar to the inhabitants who for a long time have completely forgotten such manipulation."[57] Unfortunately, he does not detail the ideals Ferreira advocated. Did he hold fast to his restorationist ideals? This seems unlikely given that Pedro II had assumed the throne. Had he developed sympathies for the Praieira Revolt cause through contact with Borges da Fonseca and other political prisoners? Records do not give a clear indication, although the commander implies an allegiance with the ideals that fueled the cycle of regional revolts. Unlike the more privileged Praieira Revolt leaders, pardoned in 1851, Ferreira, a humble man of the forests, was released only in 1861. He never faced trial for his alleged crimes, which again reveals how class influenced the administration of justice.

While Ferreira's motives remain obscure, the colony's staff interpreted them in a published note of thanks to the commander. They credited him for saving "their tranquility, honor, and lives" because after the subversives attacked the garrison, they planned to "go to the warehouse and divide up the money there among themselves and what is more horrible to humanity . . . they would [then] penetrate the bosom of the families, and steal from their arms . . . their most sacred objects, their dear and innocent daughters and perpetrate . . . the crime most horrible and wicked: rape!!!" The reference to families is vague. Did the letter writer refer to the families of staff, or did he include convict families? The way it is written does not suggest that the author made such a distinction. Contrary to the commander's analysis, the letter suggests the uprising was devoid of ideology and motivated by greed and lust. The "assassins" would wait for the steamship that supplied the island to escape en masse. They would land at Barra Grande and make their way to Pernambuco's forests, where "new scenes of horror would take place."[58] The plans ascribed to convicts in 1855 recurred in later uprisings, but it is hard to fathom to what extent they reflected conspirators' plans or employees' trepidations.

The letter also describes how the commander foiled the plot. He took seriously a "vague denunciation that anyone else would have naturally dismissed." This suggests that rumors of uprisings were common and that officials ignored most as chimeric weapons of the weak.[59] The commander, however, sensed something "sinister," so he had four suspects arrested and fettered. Under interrogation, which likely included torture, he learned that some eighty convicts were involved in a plot led by the "infamous, reprobate assassin: Vicente Ferreira de Paula." Despite the commander's actions, the convicts continued to conspire, as they were "conscious of the garrison's small size and their lack of munitions." The commander, "moved by the constant tears that flowed from the families," resolved to send some men by raft to inform mainland authorities of their distress. The letter praised the commander's cool headedness and expressed appreciation for how he "reassured the families with his animated conversations."[60]

As testimony about other convict revolts reveals, officers often used torture in their interrogations of insurgents. Under duress, convicts may have implicated a wide circle of acquaintances to satisfy interrogators and perhaps implicated innocent rivals as well. It is impossible to determine whether Ferreira was a scapegoat. The commander reported that convicts had made or obtained knives and clubs, but as noted earlier, convicts often carried weapons for their daily security. Other than testimony, officials offered little evidence that Ferreira led the plot.[61]

Despite the qualms commanders expressed about the growing convict population and the potential for political prisoners to lead revolts, colony security remained lax. In their defense, commanders often made requests for troops, munitions, and warships that mainland officials ignored or were slow to heed. After the uprising, security did not undergo significant change with the exception of the aldeia's construction in 1856, which gave commanders options for securing some convicts. Not surprisingly, convict plots continued to surface.

Nearly ten years after Vicente Ferreira de Paula's revolt, a commander observed that on August 2, 1864, a group of "two hundred or more military and civilian convicts attempted to assassinate the commander, his officers, and their families." The slave convict Agostinho Primeiro revealed a convict plot to capture the steamship to orchestrate a mass escape. The commander lamented that with "1,706 convicts on the island, two-thirds of whom had been sentenced for homicide, it is surprising that more disorders did not take place." He flogged the principal conspirators and had others fettered and jailed. Five rebels fled to avoid arrest, and one died resisting capture. To emphasize the colony's fragile security, the commander noted that he had only the commander of a National Guard detachment, three other officers, six subalterns (NCOs), and 169 soldiers.[62] If two hundred convicts revolted, they would outnumber security forces.[63]

Similarly, on Christmas Eve 1875, Antônio Feitosa de Mello "seduced" a group of convicts to rebel against Commander Sebastião José Basílio Pyrrho. Feitosa, a former Praieira political prisoner, returned in the 1870s condemned for the apolitical crime of forgery. His plot allegedly included convicts sentenced to capital punishment and "some garrison soldiers in Fort Remédios who would provide the rebels with rifles and munitions." The plotters would kill anyone who attempted to stop them and create panic by setting houses ablaze. The convict Bernardo Vieira da Silva, who informed Commander Pyrrho of the plot, was credited with "saving hundreds of lives." Pyrrho ordered Feitosa's arrest along with his accomplices and applied an "exemplary" punishment to them: public floggings. During the flogging, a "recruit," Braselino, cried out that there were many more conspirators.

This made the commander fear that he could not guarantee the colony's tranquility because most denied the plot for fear that their comrades would kill anyone who confessed. As evidence of their plans, the commander sent a sail they made in anticipation of the uprising. Pyrrho jailed the implicated convicts until they could be sent to Recife for trial, and requested that Silva be allowed to serve out his sentence in a mainland army fort because the informant's life was at risk in the colony.[64]

Weeks later Pyrrho complained that the press unduly criticized him. This was a nerve-wracking time because the conspiracy happened when the Kilo-Breaking Revolt convulsed Pernambuco's interior. Authorities feared they were somehow linked. Pyrrho explained that he had punished the convicts according to military law, and grumbled that his detractors referred to him as "Nero." He had flogged Feitosa, an educated member of Pernambuco's political elite, and this may have shocked class sensibilities. Pyrrho reminded the governor that Feitosa had stirred up convicts during his predecessor's command and that the plot included members of the convict police, who could not be trusted when 1,500 convicts were guarded by only 105 soldiers.[65]

While commanders disparaged the loyalty of convict police, garrison soldiers sometimes caused the very mayhem they were supposed to prevent. In 1876, enlisted men mutinied for three days. The troops refused to obey their officers, and a series of rumbles between soldiers and convicts left many injured and one convict dead. A Rio newspaper depicted armed convicts apprehending soldiers: "On Fernando de Noronha, it is no longer the soldiers who guard the prisoners, but the prisoners who maintain order disrupted by soldiers."[66] The case shows how crucial support from prisoners was for administrators.

On December 17, 1876, soldiers armed with sabers sacked convict Doca Cassiano's home. Afterward, they thrashed any convicts they came across in the street. When the commander learned of the disorder, he sent a group of soldiers to arrest them, but instead of detaining their comrades, they joined the melee in which four soldiers and six convicts were seriously injured. One soldier later died from his wounds. At this point, the soldiers retired to their quarters as darkness approached, and the commander decided to wait until morning to resolve matters.

At 2:00 AM, however, Cadet Raynero José de Almeida Pernambuco led a larger group of soldiers into Remédios to take the guardhouse, but loyal troops repulsed them. Almeida then led his men through the streets, where they beat convicts, nearly killing one. Convicts and loyal troops managed

Em Fernando de Noronha, não são mais os soldados que guardam os presos, são os presos que mantêm a ordem perturbada pelos soldados.

FIG 7.1 "On Fernando de Noronha, it is no longer the soldiers who guard the prisoners, but the prisoners who maintain order disrupted by soldiers." *Revista Ilustrada* 50 (Jan. 13, 1877): 4.

to capture Almeida, who must have been a charismatic mutineer because he convinced his comrades to free him from his cell. He and others then scaled the fort's walls and attacked convicts again. The warship *Tonelero* was visiting the island during the revolt, and its captain disembarked a marine force that captured Almeida and twenty other soldiers.[67] While newspapers identified Almeida as the mutiny's leader, he denied the charges. According to him, the revolt began because a group of soldiers refused to sell some convicts homemade alcohol (*garapão*) on credit. A conflict over contraband commerce had sparked a deadly mutiny.[68]

Soon after the mutiny, a new commander took charge, but simmering tensions remained. An anonymous 1877 letter excoriated the new commander and his predecessor: "The current commander took control of the Island, anxious to give expression to his pliable nature, much like his predecessor, that well known favorite of a certain descendant of the race of Sodom." Who wrote such a scabrous letter? Civilian employees and army officers, like Lieutenant Rego Barros Jr. in the previous section, bragged about placing stories against their enemies in the press. Convicts also could have been the authors. Whoever wrote the letter claimed that the commander conspired with convicts to skim money from residents and accused him of engaging in what army officers referred to as social pollutions by fraternizing with convict families.[69] The author alleged that the commander invented reasons to invite certain convicts as an "excuse for bringing families together for a dance which does not look good for a single man. . . . Convict families socializing with the commander!" The letter corroborates evidence that convict families enjoyed greater approximation to officials, but the commander denied the truth of the allegations of sexual and other improprieties.[70] The 1876 mutiny may have hastened Parliament's decision to transfer Fernando de Noronha's management to the Justice Ministry in 1877.

Murderous violence returned in 1885 when the convict sergeant Vicente d'Assis Tavares and fifty-six comrades allegedly planned an uprising. Sergeant Assis figured at the center of a number of killings in July and August 1885.[71] One, analyzed earlier, was of the slave convict Josias, who allegedly assaulted Assis at a convict's wedding party. The *Diário de Pernambuco* reported that the "same group of incorrigible convicts, who have been involved in numerous intrigues, assassinated the slave convict Josias." The "same group, not satisfied with that act of barbarism . . . also assassinated the convicts Miguel Barbosa and Joaquim Muniz Falcão (known as Munbêbo) and injured many others." Rumors that more violence would follow left the population with "terrifying apprehensions."[72] The press accused Assis's gang of convict Joaquim Martins Gomes's murder, and others were rumored to be marked for death.[73]

The *Diário*, whose sympathies lay with the Conservative Party, anticipated criticism of Pereira Lobo's command by reminding readers that "identical plots had occurred before . . . under the commands of Colonels Luiz José Monteiro and Alexandre de Barros e Albuquerque."[74] In response to accusations published in the *Journal do Recife* on August 26, 1885, Pereira Lobo's son, A. G. de Gusmão Lobo, published a letter in the *Diário*. He noted that recently three of the colony's most vicious convicts had been murdered. Gusmão Lobo disputed the *Journal's* suggestion that "no action had been taken against the assassin and his accomplices." He defended Assis and questioned the *Journal's* suggestion that "the families and convicts of good comportment are all under the pressure of inexpressible terror, waiting each moment to be the next victims of the wrath of the owner of the island, as they referred to the convict Assis." He explained that the commander had carried out an inquiry that cleared Assis of culpability in Josias's murder. The injured Assis had been confined to the aldeia until the inquiry had been completed. Gusmão Lobo found it exaggerated to refer to Assis as the "island's owner" because he was a convict. Despite feuding with his father a few years earlier, Gusmão Lobo offered a spirited defense of him without ever mentioning his name.[75] Gusmão Lobo's editorial was too little, too late. The next day the governor sent Lieutenant Colonel Manoel de Azevedo do Nascimento with fifty soldiers to relieve Pereira Lobo. The *Diário* reported: "The Colonel carries orders to bring to Recife the heads of the revolt that has taken place there, the convict Assis being the principal leader."[76] Up to this point there had been reports only of murders, not a revolt. On September 1, 1885, the warship *Medusa* anchored off Fernando de Noronha's coast.

Pereira Lobo claimed that he had restored calm to the colony after he jailed 103 implicated convicts. The exception was Assis, whom Pereira Lobo secretly confined in his residence, where the sergeant confessed his crimes before credible witnesses. After order had been reestablished, convict Vicente Maria Rodrigues spread a rumor that the detained convicts had escaped and would attack the guards in charge of the *Medusa*. As a result, a cadet ordered the bugler to play reveille. At that moment, Pereira Lobo was in his home in civilian clothes, and he only had time to grab his sword and put on his military cap before he ran out. As he did, he heard a soldier cry, "Here comes the man!," and soldiers aimed their guns at him. Pereira Lobo retorted, "Don't you recognize me?" Captain Antonio Francisco da Costa informed Pereira Lobo that Assis was gathering convicts to attack them, but the commander responded that that was impossible because Assis was in his quarters. They then verified that no one had escaped the aldeia. Pereira Lobo reflected, "If there was a plan to kill me, I cannot say, but what is certain is that in the middle of these perversities the families that came to my residence . . . anticipated the spilling of my blood in my home!!! It is a lot of audacity!!! And Mr. Getirana, to make things worse, invited the families to take refuge in the fort and even wanted to load the artillery!!!" Pereira Lobo conveyed the residents' panic. He saw the hands of his enemies behind events and accused them of plotting to kill him amid the chaos.[77] He also notes the urgency to protect families, both those of the employees and those of the convicts.

Pereira Lobo named his enemies: "Lieutenant Joaquim Jorge Mello Filho in collusion with . . . Captain Manoel Accioli de Moura Gondim, the inseparable creature of the warehouse scrivener Joaquim Pinto de Almeida Jr. who moved into Mr. Gondim's residence and, in combination with Lieutenant José Joaquim de Aguiar, have forged the greatest subterfuges and intrigues so that the steam from kettles did not stop accumulating until a new force arrived and my dismissal was guaranteed which these monsters (they do not deserve another title) promoted for a long time!"[78] Gondim would later arrest Pereira Lobo's convict client Wanderley, and Aguiar had been the victim of a dispute with the colony's surgeon earlier that year. The networks of patronage and lines of cleavage among staff and convicts ran deep.

Pereira Lobo protested that he had conducted an inquiry into the murder of convict Joaquim Martins Gomes and charged two convicts, but his replacement instigated a new investigation. Pereira Lobo accused his enemies of torture: "When the gunship arrived they took actions that one never would in a civilized nation and after the prisoners who went aboard the ship were beaten. They instigated a new inquiry so that the prisoners would give the responses that pleased Lieutenant Mello Filho and his satellites. . . . The barbarity practiced by Cadet Ottoni and Alferes Antonio Valerio dos Santos Neves who plucked the prisoners' beards and hair, beating them with the broadsides of their swords, giving them numerous contusions, horrified all who witnessed these acts."[79]

The Justice Ministry confirmed that Pernambuco's governor had sent Lieutenant Mello Filho to the colony to verify news of disorder and mismanagement. He reported:

> The unloading and transportation of volumes (from the steamship) was made without any inspection or accounting and with the utmost negligence because the boxes arrived open or were opened on the beach. The steamship Captain and the assistant Commander Guilhermo Paes Barreto were involved in the contraband trade in cane brandy and other alcohol which led to the latter's dismissal and he was subject to an investigation. The state of the presidio was so bad that on July 2, 300 convicts more or less directed by Vicente d'Assis Tavares, roamed the streets, night and day, beating and injuring whoever they encountered. Convict homes were broken into and sacked. . . . Convict Joaquim Muniz Falcão, armed with a dagger, broke into the home of Gervaio Raymundo and obliged him to deliver his wife. On Aug. 18 at 11:00 PM there was a great disturbance that would have taken serious proportions if it were not for the actions of Lieutenant Joaquim Jorge de Mello Filho, seeing as the assistant commander participated in the disturbance and refused to take the necessary actions to end it. At the insistence of Mello Filho, the commander sent a force of eight soldiers that found five individuals already injured in a conflict that involved more than fifty men.[80]

The report shows that Pereira Lobo had reasons to believe that someone was spying on him.

When Lieutenant Colonel Manoel de Azevedo do Nascimento arrived he went to Pereira Lobo and demanded that all of the implicated convicts, including Assis, be turned over. Pereira Lobo declared that Assis was a victim of his enemies' persecutions. Nascimento's investigations "verified that the chief author of the chaos, Assis, had not suffered any punishment and he continued to reside with the commander, shared his table, and remained a trusted employee who used and abused the commander's indulgence." The Justice Ministry reported that Pereira Lobo had been dismissed and the implicated convicts would be tried in Recife.[81]

When the *Medusa* returned to Recife, the press depicted Assis as a treasonous rebel: "Among the fifty-seven convicts that arrived yesterday from Fernando de Noronha aboard the Meduza one finds the infamous Vicente d'Assis Tavares, the chief, the tumtunqué [a derisive Brazilian Indianism for chief], of the worst species of wrongdoers in that presidio. This group, according to information we received, intended to proclaim the Independence of the Island on September 7 [Brazil's Independence Day], and they had made provisions to achieve this end when the arrival of the steamship Medusa put an end to their plans." This was the same account that reported the wooden figure of a black woman used in the convict's maracatus and sambas in the house used as the revolt's "headquarters." Beyond the wooden figure (likely Cambinda Velha's colunga), the *Diário* noted that the conspirators had made a "national flag of fabric painted in the presidio." The conspirators apparently fashioned their own flag for the new nation they intended to declare on Brazil's Independence Day.[82] The plans attributed to Assis and his fifty-six followers seem unrealistic at best, and delusional at worst. Even if their revolt succeeded, the population relied on mainland supplies, and the government would surely send a force to retake the island.

The *Diário's* sinister interpretation of the colunga as a fetish with a knife dangling from her wrist imputed the worst motives to the conspirators. The over-the-top depiction of Assis as an Indian chief and his association with Afro-Brazilian religion seemed calculated to portray him and his retinue as nonwhite barbarians. Moreover, their plot desecrated Brazil's most sacred patriotic holiday with a rebellion whose goal was to secure Fernando de Noronha's independence. These attributes placed Assis beyond the pale in social, political, and religious terms. Assis returned to the colony after his trial, but he never again would be a convict sergeant.

Pereira Lobo and his clan meddled in presidio politics even after his dismissal, revealing again the connections between Fernando de Noronha and mainland politics. The governor asked Pereira Lobo's replacement Captain Antonio Francisco da Costa (an officer Pereira Lobo once described as "dignified") to respond to a notice in the newspaper *Rio Branco* of October 30,

1885, which lamented the colony's small harvest. The article insinuated that the bad harvest was due to the commander's corruption. Da Costa clarified that the harvest had been small because the winter weather had been poor and because during the period for weeding,

> this presidio was in disorder and confusion. . . . [Because of this] the convicts, as it is known publicly . . . delivered themselves over to idleness and the fields were abandoned because there was no force to compel them to work. . . . I ordered the convicts to harvest the corn because it was the only crop that resisted the lack of care. . . . Of the corn harvested, I sent 400 sacks to Pernambuco's treasury and fifty were distributed to the officer who cares for the company sergeants' mounts who patrol, perform watch duties, and other tasks. . . . There are still twenty sacks for any emergency.

Furthermore, in the previous year, with an abundant harvest, only four hundred sacks of corn had been sent to Pernambuco's treasury. Da Costa added that the allegation had no merit because it was made in *Rio Branco*, a newspaper edited by Pereira Lobo's son. He added that Pereira Lobo resented his dismissal and would invent anything to discredit whoever succeeded him.[83]

On December 3, 1886, another conflict over commerce resulted in four homicides and eight serious injuries. The commander observed that soldiers often used their authority to extort money and goods from prisoners; this was the source of continual disputes.[84] The disorder led the commander to send the nonconvict company sergeant João Alvarez de Seabra Freire and three convicts to sail a raft to the mainland to request troops and munitions. Sergeant Freire related the conflict's origins to the press. On Friday, December 3, 1886, at 8:00 AM, the convict Antonio José Nascimento Segundo (known as Parnahyba) worked at the counter of the convict sergeant Attilio Simonelli's store when the soldier Candido "So-and-So" asked to be sold goods on credit. Parnahyba refused to do so because Candido was a "grifter" (*velhaco*), and would not pay. One half hour later, Parnahyba was in the town market when Candido provoked him and pushed him down. Parnahyba responded by clubbing Candido. At this point, Candido and four other soldiers savagely beat Parnahyba. The commander sent Parnahyba to the aldeia and ordered the five soldiers to report to their detachment commander for discipline.

The commander presumed that order had been restored, but some soldiers returned to the market and attacked convicts. The convicts resisted fiercely and killed two soldiers. The soldiers retreated. The commander ordered all the convicts in or near the market to the aldeia, where he began an inquiry, but moments later soldiers returned armed with rifles firing wildly. They fired at the commander twice but missed their mark. The attack killed two convicts and wounded others. When they ran out of bullets, the soldiers set fire to convict houses. According to Sergeant Freire, more lives would have been lost if the commander had not ordered the company sergeants to assemble their men outside of Remédios. The situation grew calmer, but the soldiers continued to make threats that left the presidio in a "state of terror."[85]

The commander reported that the mutinous soldiers "set fire to the homes of convicts, discharged their guns in the streets, threatened the lives of employees, and fomented general panic." He clarified that an "apparent peace" reigned because of measures he had taken, but he expressed concern because the mutinous garrison apparently intended to demand that the jailed convicts be flogged after the steamship departed, and this could reignite conflict. He asked that the governor delay the steamship's departure until the garrison was replaced.[86]

These scenes of chaos inspired a group of twenty-one convicts to petition the commander: "In the name of all the unhappy ones carrying out their sentences in this presidio, still unsettled by the scenes of blood they witnessed on Dec. 3 and apprehensive that these sad and painful memories might return with even more violence if the soldiers and principal leaders of this poem of blood and destruction are not immobilized. . . . [We] implore your excellency to remove what is consistent with reason and prudence to dissipate the same storm that could convulse this presidio."[87] On December 20, Major Estevão José Ferraz arrived with eighty soldiers. The commander pleaded with him to leave the eighty men under his command and to remove the rebel garrison. The major refused. He transported only the "most revolutionary" of the mutineers and left ten of his own men and two NCOS behind. In concluding his letter, the commander mentioned a petition he received from convicts who begged him to replace the garrison: "Convict families are still horrified and upset, principally because of the terrifying rumors that after the steamship leaves, the soldiers plan to take their vengeance." This comment confirms that convicts who lived with their families were employed in positions of responsibility closely linked to the administration; these were the convicts who had the most to fear from the soldiers' reprisals. The reference to family conferred honorable status on these convicts and evoked pity for their vulnerability. The commander added that the staff families were also terrified.[88] The Justice Ministry concluded that the feud between the colony's commander and the major da praça contributed "greatly" to the disorder.[89] Eventually, the garrison was replaced, but tensions meant that residents could not be completely at ease. Even so, this was the colony's last major conflagration.

Colony rebellions bear a family resemblance to mainland slave revolts and army mutinies. Like slaves and soldiers, convicts were seldom united in their oppression. Divisions of ethnicity, nationality, color, civil condition, and patronage networks posed barriers to solidarity and made it difficult to organize collective action secretly. Commanders maintained informants to apprise them of suspicious activities, and they often exposed plots before they hatched. When discovered, they usually identified a leader and a number of conspirators for investigations and trials, but they indicated that there were others involved who could not be reliably identified.[90] Investigations into crime, disputes, and uprisings reveal how at times patronage divided the colony's population into rival networks organized to profit from the dark twins of contraband and licit commerce. In turn, these disputes were often linked to mainland political struggles.

The integrationist impulse that led Brazilian authorities to permit convicts to live in exile with their wives, heterosexual consensual lovers, and dependents founded much of its logic in assumptions about gender and family. A similar but different integrationist impulse can be found in the way authorities treated slave convicts. The next chapter explores the lives of slave convicts and interprets what their treatment divulges about how state institutions managed Brazil's slow transition from slave to free labor.

8 THE TREATMENT AND CATEGORIZATION OF SLAVE CONVICTS IN A PENAL ARCHIPELAGO

Because Fernando de Noronha gathered slave, free civilian, and military convicts from across Brazil, it offers a unique perspective on the significance of civil condition and color in imperial penology. The prosecution of slave crime has received attention in regional studies, but few follow slave criminals into prisons to examine how authorities enforced their sentences.[1] In 1881, the Justice Ministry ordered the penal colony's commander to conduct a survey of slave convicts. He interviewed 264 slave convicts and recorded data that, along with other records, make it possible to sketch their collective biography and assess their place in the penal system.[2] A simultaneous qualitative interrogation of survey categories explores the assumptions that shaped how authorities depicted a slave convict population.[3] The survey itself became part of a bureaucratic struggle in the 1880s over how to punish slave convicts, which makes its construction even more revelatory of the Brazilian preference for integration.

SLAVE CONVICTS, FERNANDO DE NORONHA, AND BRAZIL'S PENAL JUSTICE SYSTEM

The punishment of slave convicts reveals the lengths that authorities went to sustain distinctions between slave and free convicts and how they changed over time.[4] Save for the gallows, law forbade courts to punish free citizens convicted of crimes with physical castigations, but they could sentence slaves to be flogged, even for murder. Regional studies indicate that flogging was the most common sentence courts awarded to slave convicts.[5] Given the horrendous conditions in Brazil's prisons, one is tempted to contemplate whether slave convicts got the better deal. For masters, flogging was preferable because, even though it damaged and could kill their property, they stood a chance to recover their slaves after they suffered the prescribed torture and paid the state for its services.[6] With medical care, a battered slave might still labor for their masters for years to come, and the state saved incarceration costs. Article 60 of the Código Criminal specified that all slave sentences that were not galés (galleys or prison at labor in fetters) or capital punishment be reduced to flogging, but this directive was not always followed.

Many Brazilians took comfort in the idea slave convicts did not escape labor, and courts sentenced the vast majority to perpetual galleys. Because Fernando de Noronha consistently required labor, Parliament designated slaves with sentences commuted from capital punishment to perpetual galleys as one of the categories of convicts that could be sent there in 1859.[7] Slave convicts also labored in military arsenals and public works, but more and more officials tried to segregate convicts from civil society.[8]

The historian João Luiz Ribeiro counted the number of capital sentences in Justice Ministry documents and then verified the number of executions that were carried out. He confirmed the execution of 199 slave convicts between 1833 and 1876, but he found another 135 condemned to hang whose executions he could not verify. Between 1833 and 1860, Brazilians executed 39 free or freed civilian convicts and 13 military enlisted men, but he could not corroborate the executions of another 30 civilian convicts condemned to die. Ribeiro systematically researched cases for São Paulo, Minas Gerais, Rio de Janeiro, and the Capital District, where more than two-thirds of slave executions took place in 1830s and 1840s. Justice Ministry inspector André Augusto de Padua Fleury confirmed in 1880 that it was in these provinces where the internal slave trade concentrated more than half of Brazil's slaves in the 1870s that slaves most commonly perpetrated heinous murders.[9]

Ribeiro acknowledges that more executions likely took place in other provinces, but he is confident that he counted the vast majority of legal executions. Perhaps more significantly, he found that 523 slaves and 120 free citizens and manumitted slaves had death sentences commuted to perpetual galleys between 1833 and 1889, far more than those executed. The slave Francisco was the last man legally executed in Brazil, on April 28, 1876, in Pilar, Alagoas; thereafter, the emperor commuted all death sentences.[10]

By 1881, it had been a long time since the Portuguese had sent convicts to row in Mediterranean naval galleys. The sentence of galés hints at the mix of traditional and modern principles in Brazilian law and its reliance on Portuguese precedent. Galés was distinct from new sentences such as "prison with work" or "simple imprisonment" because it required a convict to work in fetters, a potent manifestation of captivity in a slave society. The use of irons had an old-regime flavor more appropriate to a slave society than a leveled citizenry. As observed in chapter 4, however, juries also sentenced many free convicts to galés. Courts sentenced no less than 38 percent of free and military convicts in Fernando de Noronha in 1881 (the year of the slave survey) to galés, but Brazilians associated galés with slave status. As Fleury pithily put it, "The sentence of slaves is galés."[11]

Brazil's state confiscated slaves sentenced to death or imprisonment without compensation. Here, the law limited an owner's property rights based on de facto expectations of seignorial responsibility to discipline one's family and dependents, including slaves. One draft of the June 10, 1835, law (which required the death penalty for slaves convicted of murdering their masters, a member of their master's family, or their overseer) included a provision for the state to compensate masters when juries sentenced their slaves to galés or death, but lawmakers struck this language. In 1831, an American navy officer visiting Rio de Janeiro observed fettered convict slaves at labor in the street; he asked an Austrian friend long resident in Brazil why masters of slave convicts were not compensated. He answered, "They say it is a just punishment for not having taught the slave better." The astonished American then observed, "Taking away life is a punishment hardly known in Brazil," but after the June 10, 1835, law gruesome public hangings became more common.[12] Before 1850, there were relatively few slave convicts on Fernando de Noronha. The few there appear to have participated in uprisings. As Captain João Bloem reported in 1826: "Among the convicts on this island there are five penal exiles from the slave revolt of Alagoas sentenced to ten years of galleys whose sentences end Oct. 25, 1826, and I am sending them to Recife's prisons. . . . It is true that these five penal exiles were never castigated, worked well, and were praised by all my predecessors."[13] As we will see, many commanders lauded the comportment of slave convicts. After 1835, officials executed more slave convicts or put them to work on mainland chain gangs, but when Pedro II began to commute more capital sentences in the 1850s, their numbers in the colony grew.

Why, despite the 1835 law, were relatively few slaves executed compared to the larger number who had their capital sentences commuted to perpetual galleys? In 1890, when Brazil's new Republican government scrapped the sentences of galés and capital punishment, the deposed Pedro II carped that he was not given his due. Then in exile, he wrote that he had de facto ended capital punishment by commuting all capital sentences in the past thirty years. Pedro overstates the time frame, as the last legal execution had occurred in 1876, but he had greatly reduced executions and then brought them to a halt. In 1853, Pedro ordered procedures changed to ensure that he had the final say on all capital sentences, and he commuted most of them.[14] Slave convicts on Fernando de Noronha were living testaments to Pedro's actions. In 1881, 264 slave convicts (more than half of the 523 whose death sentences were commuted in Ribeiro's count) lived alongside 1,256 free civilian and military convicts. Slave convicts constituted almost 17 percent of the convict population; military convicts, 18 percent; and free civilian convicts, 65 percent.[15]

Many slave convicts ended up on Fernando de Noronha because authorities desired them to work, but when Pedro began to commute all capital sentences his critics questioned the colony's penal rigor. These criticisms provided the American novelist Frank Carpenter with the impression that Fernando de Noronha was an "ocean resort" for convicts. Carpenter was a geographer for Brazil's Geological Survey, which included a group of fourteen Cornell University graduate students under the direction of Professor Charles Fredrick Hartt. During his stay, Carpenter developed a good knowledge of Portuguese and Brazil. His colleague, John Branner, visited Fernando de Noronha, so he likely had secondhand impressions of it.[16] Carpenter likely learned about the island from Brazilians as well. He lived in Brazil when abolitionism began to stir deep political divisions between defenders and opponents of slavery. For many slavocrats, Fernando de Noronha became emblematic of the injustices unleashed by abolitionist reforms.

This background allows us to more fully contextualize Carpenter's 1884 novel *Round about Rio*, which narrates a Yankee family's touristic travels in Brazil. His young American narrator observes that slaves in Rio de Janeiro were aware that a slow process of abolition was afoot, and they had become "idle with impunity" because they knew that their master's instruments of torture were destined for a "museum shelf." In Brazil's interior overseers treated plantation slaves with brutality, but mistreated bondspersons sometimes murdered their overseers and in the same act bettered their lives because "capital punishment did not exist in the Brazils." Instead, "the murderer is transported to the penal colony on the island of Fernando de Noronha; but since the convict's work is lighter and his fare is better than the slave's, his last state is better than the first. In this ocean resort the slave sees a premium for crime, and, in consequence, a man might as well be a tax-gatherer in Ireland as an overseer in Brazil."[17]

Carpenter's comparative sociology of oppression inflated the dangers overseers faced in Brazil and tax collectors in Ireland, but it reveals a competitive nationalist consciousness with regard to human rights in the Atlantic. The image of impunity for slave convicts on Fernando de Noronha had become a part of Brazilian master-class folklore that an American author used to draw out dubious moral equivalencies between two empires' depraved dealings with restive subjugated populations. The United States' Civil War brought an end to slavery there, and this gave Americans more latitude to criticize similar injustices in other nations. The anecdote reveals the Brazilian master-class's fears surrounding the decline of slavery and their authority. Many masters blamed Pedro for what they depicted as a rising tide of homicidal slave violence because he had eliminated the only deterrent to it when he began to commute all capital sentences. Senator José Inácio Silveira da Mota warned in 1879, "If you do not want the violence of the death penalty, then abolish slavery.... The slave that kills his master counts on a commutation of his sentence and that he will have his provision ground to work on Fernando de Noronha." Some slaves reportedly did murder their masters and turned themselves over to authorities declaring: "I killed to serve the king! I killed to escape captivity!" In response to Pedro's clemency, some free Brazilians took justice into their own hands. A jury in Campinas, São Paulo, in 1879 denied against clear evidence that a slave had infringed the June 10, 1835, law to sentence him for a lesser crime so that he would be returned to his owner, who would render the "law of Lynch." These slave lynchings appear to have increased after the emperor brought about the death penalty's de facto moratorium. Brazilian observers mostly criticized lynchings as misguided savagery, and references to the "law of Lynch" carried unflattering comparisons to the United States, where Mark Twain once quipped that his country should be renamed "the United States of Lyncherdom."[18] The one-upmanship in the race between nations to accrue moral capital in terms of human rights in law and practice required such Atlantic comparisons and self-deprecating humor.

THE 1881 CONVICT SLAVE SURVEY

Just how true or exaggerated were the assertions of Carpenter and others about the behavior of slaves and their attitudes toward Brazilian penal justice? The 1881 slave convict survey provides a means to access them. It also permits an interpretation of what the survey categories and contents reveal about authorities' perspectives on the status of slave inmates and their place in the penal colony.

The 1881 survey began with the slave convict's name. Like slaves on the mainland, most bonded convicts had only a first name. Among those with surnames, sixteen (6 percent) indicated ethnic or geographic African origins: "Benguella, Nagó, Cabinda, Congo, Muçambique, Manjollo, and Mina."[19] Only 28 (10 percent) had second names that indicated Brazilian birth: 19 Crioulos, 7 Cabras, one "Antonio Caboclo," and one "José Cantagalo" (tried in Cantagalo, Bahia); five second names referred to color, three pardo (dark brown) and two mulatto; and one appears to refer to age (Joaquim Novo). For prison officials, these naming practices distinguished between African- and Brazilian-born slaves to the point that they obviated the need for a separate category on birthplace. The importance of African birth denoted in one's name is amplified by the fact that the names of Brazilian-born slaves did not systematically classify their place of birth. The only issue of origin treated as a survey category was the province where the slave convict had been tried. For bureaucrats, a slave's judicial origin was important, but their birthplace, if not Africa, remained a mostly unmarked category of Brazilian-born. In a different table of convicts, officials listed prisoners by status and sentence, but there they grouped African-born slaves with Brazilian-born slaves. They excluded the African-born from the tallies of free foreign-born convicts with European, Spanish American, or North American origins (see appendix, table A17). In this instance, slave status trumped foreign birth.

Perhaps the 1881 survey's most intriguing element was the expression *ex-escravo de* (ex-slave of) or *que foi escravo de* (who was a slave of), which prefaced their former owners' names. The phrase in this and other documents punctuated the state's confiscation of human property. These convicts escaped slavery without finding liberty; they traded captivity for incarceration. As the slave convict Antonio Ferreira's 1890 petition for pardon succinctly put it, "Being born under the cruel rigor of captivity, the supplicant left it unexpectedly by committing a crime."[20] The phrase "ex-slave" set them apart from freedmen and located them somewhere between the slave and the manumitted, though their convict status may have placed them beneath that of law-abiding slaves in the eyes of many Brazilians. Since some employees and even a few prisoners brought slaves with them, the distinction between slave and ex-slave (slave convicts) was not entirely eclipsed in the colony.[21]

A slave who committed a crime underwent another counterintuitive legal transformation as the respected jurist Agostinho Marques Perdigão Malheiro observed: "Under penal law the slave as a[n] . . . agent of a crime is not a thing. . . . He is a human, a man, equal by his qualities to other free men whose qualities he shares. He is therefore responsible personally and directly for the crimes he commits." According to this gendered analysis, slaves condemned to death or galés both escaped slavery and became "men," however, slave victims of crime remained "things."[22] Perdigão Malheiro ironically affirmed the dictum that men, even slave men, who committed acts of violence were manly. As Bandeira Filho reported, convicts on Fernando de Noronha informed him that "homicide convicts . . . are considered men of courage and resolution; they despise those condemned for theft."[23]

Despite escaping slavery and becoming "men," slave convicts continued to be linked to their former owners and vice versa through their legal identity: of the 264 entries for slave names, 220 included the ex-owner's name, and it was often the only way to distinguish among many slave convicts who shared the same name. Eleven owners are listed as dead or murdered (*finado*, *falecido*, or *assassinado*), and another seven, as the former property of the owner's heirs. This was not a separate survey category, but extra information crammed in the name column. Why would penal colony scriveners, who were not the most zealous public servants, include this extra information? It seems likely that they recopied it from the convict's *guia*: the paperwork that was supposed to accompany all transferred prisoners.[24] Documents in these cases went out of their way to inform the reader that these slave convicts had murdered their former owners. The survey shows that Pedro's opposition to the death penalty extended to many slave convicts who had realized the slaveowners' most dreaded fear, what one might term "mastercide."

The ex-owners' names and titles illuminate the status of the masters of convicted slaves. Only one master with a noble title appears on the list, the Visconde (Viscount) de Suassuna, although the Baronice (Baroness) de Itu is listed as the owner of a slave in a petition.[25] Twenty-three ex-owners were women, and fourteen of their names were prefaced with the honorific "dona," which suggests the respectability of marriage and membership in the propertied class. Fourteen former owners had military ranks, two were priests, one was a *doutor* (graduate of a law or a medical faculty), and one had the honorific dom. The varying statuses and occupations of ex-owners reflect the overall democratic patterns of slaveholding characteristic of Brazil, and indicate that the state confiscated the slave property of even its most prominent citizens. While Brazilian penal justice convicted few citizens of wealth and privilege, it did not spare their slaves. Only nine slave convicts

(4 percent) were literate, which indicates that few masters educated their slaves. It also suggests that even some privileged slaves took the lives of masters and overseers.

The slave convict's provincial origins reveal the preponderance of Pernambuco, which accounted for sixty-four slave convicts, nearly one-quarter of the total, but this proportion was much lower than the province's 38 percent share of free prisoners. This reflected the northeast's shrinking share of slaves nationally due to the internal trade of slaves that began after Brazilians effectively enforced laws against the transatlantic slave trade in 1850. Brazil's internal trade peaked in the 1870s, and it mostly transferred slaves from the northeast's stagnating sugar plantations to the southeast's booming coffee plantations. After Pernambuco, three southeastern provinces contributed the most slave convicts: São Paulo, Minas Gerais, and Rio de Janeiro. Perhaps somewhat more surprising is that Rio Grande do Sul, with its comparatively small slave population, contributed almost as many slave convicts to the colony's 1881 population as the former northeastern hub of the international slave trade, Bahia. Though only small numbers of slave convicts came from frontier provinces, all save two are represented: the sparsely populated and remote provinces of Goiás and Piauí (see table A18). Fernando de Noronha was in this sense more than Brazil's "central prison." The 1881 survey did not list the towns in which inmates were tried, but many matriculation records did. These records show that only thirty-eight out of 203 slave convict trials identified took place in Brazil's cities. Most slave convicts lived in or near rural municipalities like Bananal, São Paulo; Oliveira, Minas Gerais; and Codó, Maranhão, where they mostly performed agricultural labor. This pattern accords with Carpenter's depiction of field slaves escaping slavery by killing their overseers for a better life on Fernando de Noronha.

Upon establishing judicial origins, the survey turns to the slave convicts' crimes, which were invariably homicide. This uniformity makes one wonder why the administrators even bothered to include it as a category. Then again, homicide was the crime of most free convicts, but the free convict population possessed many nonhomicidal convicts such as counterfeiters, thieves, "deflowerers," and deserters. Slave convicts had to be convicted of murder to make it to Fernando de Noronha.

The convict's crime is coupled with his or her sentence. Here there was greater variation, but 252 slave convicts (95 percent) had either been sentenced to *galés perpétuas* or had had a capital sentence commuted to galés perpétuas. Only two slave convicts who had been sentenced to death had not yet received a commutation, but the fact that officials shipped them to Fernando de Noronha indicates that they fully expected them to receive a commutation. However, only one of six slave women was sentenced to perpetual galleys compared to three of twenty-five free convict women. In deference to gender, most juries sentenced slave women to *prisão perpétua* (life imprisonment). Courts condemned eleven slave males to *galés temporário*, *prisão perpétua*, or *prisão simples*. Even though the latter two sentences did not conform with the criminal code's directives, juries preferred these sentences for slave minors. In these small ways, courts made distinctions among slave criminals, but their sentences were much more homogeneous than their free counterparts (see table A17).[26]

Because the sentence of galés required work, the survey catalogued their work company, something general matriculation records did not include. Only twenty slave convicts lacked information on their work company, and officials listed sixty-six of the slave convicts as invalids; most of them were elderly or suffered from debilitating conditions, and 194 were able bodied. The census shows 191 slave convicts assigned to each of 15 work companies for an average of almost 13 each. The smallest concentration was three slave convicts, and the largest, 22. Ironically, one of the largest concentrations of slaves in a work platoon was in the *serviço de ronda*, or the convict police company, where they worked to prevent crime, disturbances, and escapes. Here former slaves were given putative authority over free convicts, but commanders named men unsuited for fieldwork to this company, so they may have been assigned to it because of their old age or physical disability. Another twenty served as lookouts who watched over buildings where valuables were stored or beaches where escapes on improvised rafts were common.

This data vividly demonstrates that authorities consciously integrated slave convicts into all work companies. Work details determined where a convict lived, so this practice also meant that slave convicts lived alongside free convicts. Administrators and free inmates likely continued to view slave convicts as inferior, but commanders often sang their praises as the best-behaved workers. Laconic sources make assessments of how free convicts viewed slave convicts difficult, but free and slave convicts shared leisure time and participated in daring escapes and crimes together. To be fair, they also indicate that some convicts and administrators continued to harbor prejudices against former slaves and free convicts of color.[27]

A central factor commanders considered when assigning convicts to work companies was their occupational skills (*ofícios*). Eighty-five slave convicts had no occupational skill listed (*sem ofício*), but officials listed 104 as agricultural workers. There were also ten masons, eight cobblers, and two cowboys. Convict slave women worked washing clothes and linens for the infirmary, an occupation "appropriate to their sex." Former slave status did not trump gender in their work assignment. Other trades with only one slave convict represented included lumberjack, baker, fisherman, leather worker, carpenter, and arsenal worker. Many slaves brought valued skills to the colony that the commander carefully enumerated.

The slaves' disciplinary record (good, regular, or bad) constituted the next column. The commander designated only seven slave convicts' comportment as "bad"; none were regular, 222 had good behavior, and 35 lacked an entry. Compare this to Justice Ministry inspectors in 1879 who reported that of 1,678 convicts only 196 had good behavior; 1,001 were "regular"; and 481 had bad behavior.[28] The commander's ranking of slave convict behavior put his work to discipline and reform prisoners in a positive light, but as will be shown, he had other motives to emphasize their good behavior.

Because a number of slave convicts were unable to work, the survey recorded their illnesses and disabilities. Slave convicts with no health problems numbered 240, but nine suffered from hernias, four from mental illness, three from blindness, three from lung disease, and three others from "various ailments." One slave was ill with beriberi, and another expired while the survey took place; his illness is listed as "dead."[29]

There was no survey category for age, an odd omission given that matriculation records included it, but the survey did record the age of slave convicts older than sixty. While life in the colony was tough, a few slave convicts lived to a ripe old age for the era. Thirty-nine former slaves were in their sixties, two had reached their seventies, and one was in his eighties. It seems age sixty had come to define what contemporary Brazilians refer to as the *terceira idade*, or the age of retirement, when prison authorities stopped requiring older slave convicts to work. This concept would be confirmed by Parliament later in the decade with the passage of the 1885 Sexagenarian Law, which provisionally freed slaves age sixty-five and older.[30] In April 1889, a commander noted that some three hundred convicts were elderly and incapable of even moderate labor. He suggested that Pedro invoke his power of clemency to pardon them, which would result in "great savings to public coffers."[31] The motivation behind some of the pardons granted to slave convicts in the 1880s may have been in part to rid the colony of unproductive mouths to feed.

The survey recorded when slave convicts had been sentenced and when they arrived in the colony. Some, especially those from Pernambuco, were sentenced and transported to the island in the same year. But many, especially those from distant provinces, spent years in traditional jails before being transferred. Lorenço José, for example, had been sentenced in Pernambuco in 1837 and arrived in the colony in 1848, making him the slave convict with the most time on the island; but Antonio Cabinda had been sentenced in São Paulo in 1834 and only arrived in 1871, making him the prisoner with the longest span of time incarcerated. On average, slave convicts spent eight years in traditional provincial jails before they were sent to the colony. This casts doubts on Carpenter's assertion that slaves who murdered their overseer could soon expect to be tending a provision ground on Fernando de Noronha.

Most slave convicts arrived on the island between 1868 and 1877. The peak year was 1876, when 41 slave convicts disembarked, followed by 1868, when 40 came ashore. Earlier guia records indicate that before the 1860s slave convicts formed a smaller minority of inmates. From 1835 to 1850, slave convicts were more often executed, but as Pedro brought a slow end to capital punishment, they began to crowd provincial jails. Minas Gerais's governor complained in 1873 that 400 prisoners overcrowded his jail. Some 100 of his inmates were sentenced to galés; many of these "were slaves who had killed their masters or overseers."[32] These complaints moved authorities to relocate more slave convicts to Fernando de Noronha through coordinated shipments. In 1871, sixteen slave convicts arrived from Minas Gerais; Rio Grande do Sul sent fourteen in 1868, and São Paulo remitted 42 slave convicts in nearly equally divided annual groups from 1871 to 1874. The liberation of scores of convicts to fight in the War of the Triple Alliance opened space for slave inmates.[33] Incomplete records make it complicated to calculate the number of slave convicts who served time on the island during the empire, as many slave convicts died or were transferred to or from the island before and after the 1881 survey. A ballpark figure of three hundred to four hundred slave convicts would be a conservative estimate.[34]

The survey's final column recorded sundry comments on slave convicts, a space used to add information to twenty-three entries. The first such entry noted that Luduvico, "the ex-slave of the assassinated Domingo Pereira de Azevedo Terra," was the "the infirmary's coffee roaster." It is unclear why this fact deserved comment other than to recognize the apparent importance of coffee for medicinal purposes, or maybe this was a charitable service Luduvico contributed. The second comment recorded that the "ex-slave Agostinho Primeiro," who had been sentenced in Sergipe in 1853, "performed the great service of denouncing a plot for rebellion by convicts in the days when Colonel Luiz José Monteiro commanded the island." Other comments noted if a convict had petitioned for a pardon or the date when a capital sentence had been commuted.

Comments on a few slave convicts, however, showed that they did not contribute to security. José, the "ex-slave of the Visconde de Suassuna," and Sebastião, the "ex-slave of Pedro Theotonio de Sá Cavalcante," both committed new murders in the presidio. In José's case, he had received a second sentence of perpetual galleys. Based on his record, it would be hard to argue that slave convicts had good disciplinary records because they feared the gallows. Indeed, Antonio Bandeira Filho believed that the courts failed to deter hardened criminals: "There are individuals on Fernando de Noronha for whom the sentence of galés has been imposed two or three times . . . [and] some condemned to perpetual galleys have been subsequently sentenced to temporary prison sentences for new crimes [homicides], and return to the colony laughing about the severity of justice having enjoyed, because of their trial, a visit to the world [mainland]." Bandeira Filho presaged Carpenter's assessment of slave punishment on Fernando de Noronha: "In the existing situation on Fernando de Noronha free men and slaves, the regime being equal for both, is worse for the former. The slave in the presidio suffers almost no unpleasant impression with their imprisonment, to the contrary, they better their state and according to the authorities, they are the prisoners with the best comportment."[35]

The commander's use of survey categories reveals much about how he perceived slave convicts, but what the survey did not record is also illuminating. For instance, color, a trait included in general matriculation records, was not recorded. Because the 1881 survey targeted only slave convicts, authorities likely felt that they could assume their color, even though some of their names referred to their "brownness" or indigenous appearance.[36] The category of color was reliably found in colony documentation from the 1830s through the early republic, unlike the court records analyzed by Hebe Mattos in Brazil's southeast, where references to the color of court witnesses began to disappear after 1850. Color remained a consistently valued descriptor in convict records because of the need to accurately describe prisoners if they escaped.[37]

Another silence is marital status, a category unswervingly found in matriculation books. Even though the 1881 survey targeted slave convicts, one wonders why officials left it out. They probably adhered to the stereotype that slaves were "not of family" or that they did not marry and maintain family ties. The Justice Ministry inspector Fleury gave voice to this stereotype in 1882 when he criticized Rio's police chief for sending street urchins to work on plantations because it would expose the boys to "pernicious contact with slavery, that is to men without family, without religion, without morals, brutalized by ignorance, violence, and the stupor [*embriaguez*] of vices."[38] Fleury would play a key role in a debate over how to punish the slave convicts.

The 1881 slave convict survey did not include marital status, but my survey of matriculation records captured this status for 198 of 205 slave convicts. Of these, thirty-one slave convicts were married, and three were widowed. Since local courts produced guia records, I assume that only convicts married in a church ceremony would be legally identified as such. Almost 17 percent of the sample had formed a family before their convictions. Since most slaves married other slaves, it is not surprising that I found no evidence that authorities permitted slave convicts to bring spouses or dependents to the island. The fact that many slave convicts had married before their conviction reflects what we now know from regional studies that show high rates of slave marriage in southeastern Brazil, though these rates were lower in the northeast. This data also indicates that marriage did not necessarily create the subservience and restraint among slaves that some masters attributed to it. Indeed, as scholars of the slave family have argued, marriage could give a slave new reasons and resources to commit a crime.[39]

As noted in chapter 5, a bondsman's rights as a married man were limited. Take the 1854 appeal of the slave Caetano condemned to hang in Rio Claro, São Paulo. Caetano had complained to his owner that his *senhor moço* (master's son) maintained amorous relations with his slave wife. When the owner asked his son about it, he denied the allegation. With that, the owner ordered another slave to bind and whip Caetano for two days. Later, Caetano took his revenge. He killed his young master and the slave who flogged him. In the opinion of one member of the emperor's judicial section, "The defendant is a slave and a slave, despite being married in the same way as a free man ... only the latter have rights [the slave exercises] pátrio poder and other rights of family that the master permits him. The law does not give the slave husband means to exercise these rights." He concluded therefore that the sentence be carried out because *abyssus abyssum invocat* (the abyss invokes the abyss). Even so, Justice Minister José Tomás Nabuco de Araujo signed an order that commuted the double murder's capital sentence to galés perpétuas.[40]

The 1881 slave convict survey is distinct from the 1835 census of Iguape, Bahia, examined by B. J. Barickman. The latter encompassed the local free and slave population who were organized by households. As Barickman noted, there were two visions of society expressed in the Iguape census: one of the individual and the other of households. The tension that exists between these two visions is not present in the 1881 slave convict survey. By default, it implies that slave convicts are without family. As Barickman observes of the Iguape census, "in no instance does a slave senzala rank as a 'fogo' (household),"[41] nor does the 1881 survey hint at the possibility that slave convicts headed households. The only evidence of family in the survey is expressed in owners' names; twelve groups of slave convicts shared a former master. The omission of marital status as a survey category accords with the logic of Brazil's patriarchal society. Being a head of household entailed privileges and responsibilities incompatible with slave status.[42]

Other documents belie the 1881 survey's silence and show that some slave convicts founded households and had children. For example, the commander forwarded an 1884 petition for pardon for "Luis, the ex-slave of Joaquim Theodoro Teixeira." Luis's matriculation record shows that he had been born in Rio de Janeiro but was sentenced in Campinas, São Paulo, in 1865 and arrived on Fernando de Noronha in 1871. Luis practiced carpentry, and this skill may have won him the commander's favorable recommendation. His color is described as *fula*, and by 1884, he was nearly fifty years old. In favor of his petition, the commander mentioned that Luis had a long record of good behavior and that he "has family and is old and poor."[43] Luis's matriculation record shows that he was a bachelor, but the commander's petition for pardon indicates that he had married or maintained a consensual union since he arrived in the colony. While the petition failed to win Luis a pardon, he was among a large group of slave convicts released on February 19, 1891. Similarly, an 1890 ship manifest that listed slave convicts who had been pardoned recorded that some were accompanied by children: "Januario Clementino ex-escravo of João Nepumuceno de Mello who brings with him 5 children" and "Benedicta, ex-escrava of Manoel Ferreira da Rocha, brings two children." The matriculation records of Benedicta and Januario show them to have been single when convicted, so they must have formed families in the colony. While a few slave convicts formed consensual heterosexual unions or married, others may have formed alternative households with same-sex partners.[44]

The 1881 survey's silence on marriage and color as well as the categories it delineated illuminates the liminal position of "ex-slave convicts." Subsequent correspondence shows the vulnerability of their position as the Justice Ministry intended to use the survey to support reforms that colony commanders opposed.

NEW ORDERS

In 1879, Justice Ministry inspectors Fleury and Bandeira Filho arrived on Fernando de Noronha determined to put a civilian stamp on the colony. Both had studied prison systems in Europe, and they considered themselves experts. As Bandeira Filho reported, "In [penal] institutions of this order, the military regime has always proven inapt; accustomed to a vigorous life of discipline, military officers have little knowledge of penitentiary studies, and content themselves with simply maintaining order. . . . Add to this the poor selection of personnel, and the sequences of brief tours of duty, because commanders are alternated almost annually, and one can comprehend the impossibility of the 1865 reforms to produce the desired results when they carried within them the original vice."[45] Fleury, whose gripes about the insidious influence of slaves were cited above, was particularly determined to reform the treatment of slave convicts. The Justice Ministry charged these educated envoys to make recommendations to transform the colony from a military presidio into a civilian penitentiary.

The inspectors perceived life in the colony to be a burlesque of mainland norms. They expressed special concern that slave convicts, like their free counterparts, worked only about five hours each day. Furthermore, slave convicts labored and rested unimpeded by the fetters mandated by the sentence of galés. The inspectors noted that numerous free convicts sentenced to galés were not shackled either, but they focused on the need to apply the rigor of galés to slaves. Bandeira Filho noted that of 15 company sergeants, 10 had been sentenced to galés, and of 30 corporals, 16 were galés, but he does not clarify whether any of these galés had been slave convicts. The interpretation of the inspectors' reports is complicated by the fact that they often use the term "galés" as a synonym for slave convicts. As Fleury wrote: "Besides establishing a harsher regimen for galés, where the condition of being a criminal slave is not superior to the condition of an innocent slave, [the colony should] provide for hygiene, apply the rule of silence, prohibit correspondence, ban the use of tobacco and alcohol, require work for 12 hours a day, and furnish religious instruction with an appropriate system of rewards for improvement and other measures to lessen the evil of impunity that these malefactors enjoy." The inspectors warned that if news of the ease of slave convicts' lives spread to the mainland, it would give slaves incentive to commit heinous crimes.[46]

The inspectors suggested that slave convicts labor for at least twelve hours per day and that, unlike free convicts, they would be subject to corporal punishments. The flogging of prisoners had been regulated in 1865 to avoid "frivolous" abuses of the *gameleira* (the tree root was used to castigate prisoners), but the rule was often broken. In 1871, for instance, Pernambuco's governor urged that flogging be applied with more moderation. According to an American who visited the island in 1875, "This lash is quite often and freely used in the square, and every convict must be present to see it administered. For laziness they get from fifty to one hundred strokes, but sometimes from 150 to 300. Very recently 1,500 were administered to a Brazilian convict for stabbing his wife." The Justice Ministry banned corporal punishment (even for slave convicts) in 1878. The inspectors approvingly reported that after five "atrocious" murders occurred in 1879, the commander had unilaterally reinstated it.[47]

Meanwhile, the Justice Ministry sent instructions for handling slave convicts that required the commander to enforce the sentence of galés. They were to be fettered and isolated from the free prisoners in two work companies in the outlying villages of Sueste and Sambaqueixaba, where they would perform the colony's most unpleasant and arduous work. Thus, the Justice Ministry hoped to discourage mastercide by making slave convict punishment more disagreeable. The Justice Ministry hoped the 1881 survey would support their plans, but the commander opposed them, and this shaped how he directed its construction. Commander Pereira Lobo wrote that "the ex-slave convicts here number 263, 21 are artisans, 57 invalids, and others are of advanced age, including three who are blind and five, insane, leaving only 185 able-bodied field workers." Thus, the survey on slave convict health and skills served the commander as an instrument to limit who would be affected by the new orders. The commander voiced objections to the new orders, but he dutifully sent the able-bodied slave convicts to work and to live in Sueste and Sambaquixaba. In 1881, he suggested that corn be planted on Rat Island and "then a great number of convict slaves could be employed in the planting."[48] Convicts and staff understood that assignment to these parts of the archipelago was a punishment. Pereira Lobo lamented, however, that "most of these prisoners [slave convicts], with rare exceptions, are those with the best discipline records, and there are many who have performed good services, including . . . Agostinho, who denounced a plot for a general uprising by prisoners in August, 1864, in time for it to be quelled." The commander echoed findings he stressed in his survey.

The commander declared, however, that he had not complied with instructions to fetter slave convicts because it impeded their productivity. He noted that his predecessors had "never" shackled the "unhappy slave" convicts, nor separated them from their "comrades in the expiation of punishment, be one sentenced to perpetual galés or temporary imprisonment." Pereira Lobo, a Conservative Party partisan, waxed on: "How could this be in our beloved nation whose destiny is guided by a government that maintains liberty, having at its head a magnanimous monarch, who combines wisdom and virtue, and the least favored class, the most tortured in its jails, where only a misfortune put them there, and just when the whole country is uniting to fight for the liberty of their brothers in captivity?" He concluded that "the absolute separation of the slave convicts from other prisoners is not proper nor is their shackling. . . . Neither would improve discipline in the presidio."[49] Here Pereira Lobo voices the idea that the segregation of slave convicts was not only morally wrong but also dangerous. Segregating slave convicts made no sense to those who maintained the colony's everyday discipline, and it violated traditions that had long regulated the archipelago's ethos.

An 1881 petition from a slave convict is a telling testament to the relatively undifferentiated treatment given to slave and free plebeian inmates before the Justice Ministry's reforms. Gregorio Pereira Leite petitioned the justice minister and the governor of São Paulo to send documentation to prove he was a freedman when he had been sentenced to galés in Areias, São Paulo, in 1861. Leite had arrived on Fernando de Noronha in 1871, so for more than ten years, he had felt no need to have his official status as a slave convict corrected. When Pereira Lobo sent slave convicts to serve in segregated work companies, however, that changed. A response confirms that his letter of liberty arrived on March 2, 1882.[50]

In 1884, a commander reiterated warnings about the dangers of segregation. First, he argued that many slave convicts were excellent skilled workers, and the new policy meant that the colony would go without their valuable skills. More pointedly, he stressed the dangers of their isolation, which "segregates and unifies them [slave convicts], like a race of vile pariahs, which awakens in them amor proprio (egotism) and resentment, even more so because this island is a presidio in which comportment was always the only distinction made among prisoners." Among convicts on Fernando de Noronha, a true penal meritocracy emerged in the commander's depiction.

Further, he argued that the policy was an injustice to slave convicts who have for "ten, twenty, or more years always maintained good comportment, demonstrating themselves to be always subordinate and true elements of order."[51] The policy did mean real hardships, as many slave convicts had to leave homes they had built in Remédios for less comfortable quarters and many lost access and the time to cultivate provision grounds. Thus, many slave convicts lost privileges earned through years of good conduct. The commander depicts the policy as backward: "The mere fact that because they were slaves they will suffer from an improvised reform, such a transience—transience of a kind that finds itself diametrically opposed to generally accepted modern principles." Here he seems to refer to the liberal principal of equality before the law, and he emphasizes the irony of such a measure in "an era [in which] the voice of emancipation raises itself up in every corner of the empire." Like his predecessor, he refused to fetter slave convicts because since "primitive times" galés were not fettered, reserving this penalty for prisoners who committed new crimes. For the commander, precedent seemed more important to maintain order than the harsh punishments prescribed by outdated laws.[52]

The views expressed by the colony commanders reflected broader political and social trends in Brazilian society in the 1880s, most notably the rise of the abolitionist cause. Abolitionism had stronger purchase in certain regions and sectors of society. Factions of the army's commissioned ranks in particular had become vocal proponents of abolition, so it is not surprising that the two commanders questioned the justice of punishing slave convicts differently from their free counterparts. Tensions between military officers and Justice Ministry employees about Fernando de Noronha may have been exacerbated by fractious civil-military relations in the 1880s that came to a head during the so-called Military Question of 1883. Some officers were arrested for publishing editorials critical of civilian politicians without obtaining approval from the war minister, who owed his portfolio to civilian politicians. Officers protested this censorship and referred disparagingly to civilian politicians as *casacas* (frock coats).[53]

The efforts to maintain slave convicts segregated from free convicts lasted for only a few years. Orders to shackle slave convicts were never implemented. For most of the empire's history, slave convicts performed comparable work and lived in similar conditions to most of their free plebeian convict counterparts. In 1878, new rules dropped requirements that indigent convicts who desired to petition for a pardon or commutation buy imperial stamps to register their missives. This made filing a petition much less expensive, and convicts petitioned with greater frequency. Justice Ministry officials implemented some policies that distinguished between the punishment of slave and free convicts in the early 1880s. By the decade's end, however, slave convicts would turn the tables, as their petitions depicted their years of bondage as an argument for commutation.[54]

In 1885, the slave convict Josepha, whose capital sentence was commuted to perpetual imprisonment in 1862, petitioned for a pardon. In her favor, the commander remarked that Josepha had a record of good conduct in the nineteen years since she arrived on the island, and in addition to her work as a laundress, she served as a midwife and earned the gratitude of the presidio's inhabitants. For these reasons and the many years she had served, the commander felt that her petition should be granted. A reply on the petition indicated that she was pardoned on February 4, 1889, but records show that she only returned to the mainland on June 17, 1889, a few months before a bloodless coup ended Brazil's constitutional monarchy.[55]

Similarly in 1885, José, ex-slave of João Matheus, petitioned for pardon. The commander noted that he had had a good disciplinary record in the presidio since 1864. Furthermore, José had applied himself to his work with much "subordination." The commander added that it was true what the slave alleged in his petition that he had murdered to defend the honor and dignity of his young mistress, who was his owner. Free husbands who murdered their wives for reputedly engaging in adulterous affairs most commonly employed the "defense of honor" plea in court, and many juries exonerated them. In this case, a slave convict exculpated his crime as a defense of his mistress's honor. If the assertion was true, as the commander believed it was, the jury who condemned him was not willing to grant a slave such leniency, but their clemency might have been hampered by the June 10, 1835, law. Perhaps his overseer had made unwanted advances toward his mistress, but the petition does not reveal these details. Nevertheless, José was pardoned, and he returned to the mainland on the same ship as Josepha.[56]

A few slave convicts received pardons before slavery's abolition on May 13, 1888. Authorities did not return these slaves to former owners, which highlights the finality of the state's confiscation of private property and the defendant's liberation upon conviction. On May 20, 1887, the commander wrote that he had "embarked Frederico Cabinda who here served a sentence of perpetual galleys . . . because he was pardoned . . . on April 10, 1887."[57] In Frederico Cabinda's case, his African birth was not an impediment to his pardon and ultimate release. But because of his African birth, he was still a foreigner who would have to be naturalized to become a Brazilian citizen.

Petitioners and the commanders who evaluated them emphasized a few key elements to support their appeals. On the one hand, they stressed their good behavior, obedience, subordination, and dedication to work; on the other hand, they stressed the many years that the petitioners had already suffered imprisonment. If possible, they mentioned whether petitioners were attentive to the needs of families, be it their own, those of their owners, or in the case of Josepha, the midwife, those of the penal community. Midwives had to be particularly discreet because they were privy to many private family secrets.

The years 1888 and 1889 saw what had been a trickle of slave convict petitions for pardon turn into a stream. Slavery's abolition encouraged many slave convicts to capitalize on bondage's demise. The promulgation of a republic also brought swift change to the colony,[58] and it influenced the petitions slave convicts had written to support their cases for pardon. Despite abolition and the promulgation of a republic, the title "ex-slave" and the names of former owners continued to accompany petitions for clemency as they remained part of their legal identity.

In 1890, a scrivener wrote the ex-slave Francisco de Assis's petition, which implored the "Imminent Chief of the Provisional Government to . . . pardon him—recognizing that 16 years of rigorous privations sufficient for his complete repentance for an act committed in a delirious state in which he found himself, due to his captivity."[59] Similarly, the slave convict Manoel de Miranda had a scrivener write in 1890, "This citizen supplicant who beyond being . . . subject to cruel captivity, finds himself condemned to serve a sentence of 17 years." These petitions and others make a parallel between time served as a slave with that served in prison to emphasize that the convict had suffered punishments that were not commensurate with his or her crime. Miranda ended by noting his good discipline record, and then in a patriotic flourish, "in the name of justice and the two most glorious dates for Brazil, the 13th of May [slavery's abolition] and the 15th of November [the Republic's promulgation], I ask for your clemency and mercy for my sufferings."[60] The petition boldly assumed the title of citizen as a sign of slavery's abolition and the dawn of a republic, and it embraces the fact that he had been subject to the cruelty of slavery and the old regime's unjust laws. A slave past had become an exculpatory factor for crime and a justification for clemency. The rhetorical positioning of the petition writers, many times fellow inmates, demonstrated an astute grasp of the changing political environment and legal terrain.

A few slave convict petitions described their crimes, like the one written for the slave convict Damião. The 1890 petition mentions that his "ex-senhor," João Beserra Chaves, esteemed Damião, who, "with the proper humility and submissiveness of his captivity of the time, performed all the duties that were demanded from him." Damião's scrivener plays on the image of the good master and his dedicated slave, and then adds the cruel overseer:

> One day the savage overseer pitilessly castigated his [Damião's] mother in front of him and beyond not listening to her son's pleas to stop brutalizing his mother . . . the barbarian overseer then attacked him with the deliberate intention of giving him the same beating meted out to his unhappy mother. It was on this occasion that destiny led the slave Damião to become a murderer and the spontaneous desperation generated by the castigations inflicted on his mother, to whom he dedicated the most extreme love of a son [amor filial] caused temporary insanity as would identical circumstances affect any child in his position.

He then noted that "his nation's old laws" and his jury had not taken into account the circumstances that had driven him to kill. He then appealed with the "greatest submission" to the "most distinguished functionary of his country and to the most celebrated citizen among his generation for his glorious deeds which will never be forgotten by succeeding centuries. Great citizen pardon the miserable ex-slave and galés, for him show clemency for your glory, your posterity, and your deeds."[61]

Damião's appeal is fascinating because it plays on so many registers. It certainly appeals to guilt over the horrors of slavery. It echoes other slave convict appeals that counted slavery as a punishment predating conviction. It also resonates with one of the main themes of abolitionist literature, what Paul Gilroy referred to as the disaggregation of the slave family.[62] This missive praises the enlightened laws of the republic and contrasts them to the empire's injustice. It couches this critique in the language of "submission" and praise of the great patron President Marshal Deodoro da Fonseca. In the past, similar petitions appealed to Pedro's wisdom and mercy. Damião seemed to be the model of the urban legend whom Carpenter described in his novel, a rural slave who killed his abusive overseer and came to live a better life in Fernando de Noronha. Damião's petition, however, indicates that life on Fernando was no substitute for freedom. He and most other slave convicts struck for their freedom as soon as the political winds shifted in their favor.

The appeals of Damião and many other slaves were ultimately successful. While some slave convicts succeeded in securing pardons through personal appeals, new republican sentencing rules freed most former slaves held in the colony. New laws set guidelines that limited most homicide convictions to sentences that varied from ten to twenty years. By 1892, most of those who had survived the decade following the 1881 survey had been returned to the Brazilian mainland as free citizens.[63]

The petitions for pardon show how quickly slave convicts and their petitioners adapted their appeals. Pedro II and Princess Isabel may have been popular in the black and brown communities of Little Africa in Rio de Janeiro because of the passage of the Golden Law of May 13, 1888, which abolished slavery, but among slave convicts on Fernando de Noronha, the republic was welcomed with patriotic appeals to the nation's new army leaders.[64] In less than a decade, being a slave convict on Fernando de Noronha had moved from being a liability to an advantageous argument for freedom.

The history of slave convicts illuminates the importance of moving beyond statistics on arrests, trials, convictions, and sentences to examine how slave and free individuals fared in prison. Unlike the colony commanders of the 1880s, I do not argue here for what one might term a "democracy of civil condition" among colony convicts, much less a "racial democracy." However, it is significant that slave convicts were not treated as differently as the law and their sentences would lead one to believe. Colony authorities balked at Justice Ministry reforms that treated slave convicts distinctively from their free counterparts. In the 1880s, abolitionism's popularity gave commanders a new rationale to defend the time-honored practice that integrated prisoners regardless of civil condition, let alone color. This integration, however, began decades earlier when practical considerations of discipline and production on a dangerous island frontier led authorities to adopt it, not abolitionist principles.

Given these findings, how accurate is the novelist Carpenter's portrayal of growing slave violence? The Justice Ministry's actions lend some credibility to his account in that its representatives felt it necessary to segregate, fetter, and make slave convicts work longer hours to deter slave crime. Still, even these efforts were only partially implemented and short-lived. Justice Ministry inspector Fleury made an even more radical recommendation: "It would be better that slaves were absolutely prohibited from admission to those islands [Fernando de Noronha]. The half liberty that they enjoy and their removal from the nation that held them in slavery and the masters whose presence no longer discomforts them; the gentleness of the regime is without a doubt less severe than slavery and other circumstances are more of an incentive than a means to repress the crimes committed by this class of unhappy ones."[65] There was never enough mainland prison capacity available to carry out such a large transfer of slave convicts.

A few slaves may have killed their overseer or master in the hopes of improving the quality of their lives on Fernando de Noronha as some newspapers claimed; however, if most slaves believed this, one would expect considerably more murders given the 1.5 million slaves in Brazil in 1872. The relatively low number of slave convicts prosecuted under the June 10, 1835, law (some 857) indicates that few slaves believed that murdering a master or an overseer would guarantee a ticket to Fernando de Noronha and a provision ground.[66] Once on the island, usually after spending years in a fetid mainland jail cell, slave convicts might congratulate themselves on their relative good fortune. As soon as the opportunity to strike for freedom arose, however, most slave convicts did not hesitate to petition for their release from their "ocean resort." The half liberty of Fernando de Noronha paled in comparison to hopes for a fuller freedom on the mainland.

The treatment of slave convicts on Fernando de Noronha does not sustain the historian Leila Mezan Algranti's assertion about urban slavery and penal justice in early nineteenth-century Rio de Janeiro: "Why reeducate a slave? . . . Integrate him into what society? He is a pariah in whatever environment he inhabits."[67] As the historian Ricardo Ferreira has argued, most slave and free convicts lived under analogous conditions in the jails of imperial São Paulo.[68] Similarly, slave convicts on Fernando de Noronha were not treated very differently from most free plebeian convicts. One colony commander even protested plans to segregate slave convicts for fear it would make them "pariahs." If the labor convicts did on Fernando de Noronha constituted rehabilitation, as many officials argued, then free and slave plebeian convicts both benefitted from reeducation.

The experiences of slave convicts reveal the contradictions that liberal ideals of penal justice presented imperial authorities. Their petitions reveal how abolitionism in the 1880s opened new possibilities for slave convicts to construct new narratives to find freedom.[69] Controversies about the treatment of slave convicts and other members of the intractable poor on Fernando de Noronha fed national debates about human rights and Brazil's international image. As the next chapter argues, mainland movements against corporal punishment, the death penalty, and slavery became bound up with one another in unique ways that can be better understood in a comparative Atlantic perspective.

9

OF CAPTIVITY AND INCARCERATION
Human Rights Reform in Atlantic Perspective

Events and policies on Fernando de Noronha shaped debates about just punishment on the mainland, but the colony's staff and convicts had much less influence over debates and policies than mainland actors. This chapter examines the sequencing and depth of reforms intended to abolish flogging, capital punishment, and slavery in relation to different categories of the intractable poor. Chapter 1 provided a sketch of the timing of reforms, but here I delve deeper into the national and international context to highlight how these three movements influenced one another. These political battles reveal divergent attitudes toward segregation, citizenship, race mixing, the law, and efforts to shape Brazil's international image. While some of this drama played out on Fernando de Noronha, most of the action took place on the mainland. This chapter strays from a tight focus on Fernando de Noronha and, at points, projects forward in time to examine some reforms that took place after slavery's abolition.

Often case studies are treated in relative isolation from the web of institutions fundamental to state building (for example, schools, orphanages, prisons, courts, militaries, police, national guards, asylums, and so forth). It is important to contextualize the sequencing of institutional reforms because a change in one institution (public or private) often has significant collateral implications for institutions that sometimes collaborate and at other times compete for limited resources, jurisdiction, and influence. Brazil's government and its citizenry, like those of other nations, had to decide which institutions to prioritize for reform because no state can reform all or even several major institutions simultaneously.[1] For instance, the lack of mainland prison capacity prevented imperial authorities from removing large numbers of convicts from Fernando de Noronha who by statute did not belong there. The republic's promulgation, however, established a new regime that released many convicts. The more federalist 1890 Constitution compelled states to assume the incarceration of their own convicts, and thus provided the institutional fit that made it possible to close the penal colony as a national prison.[2]

Some institutional reforms are easier to undertake than others, and new circumstances can make reforms that seemed less pressing become a priority. The difficulties of the War of the Triple Alliance (1864–1870) moved the state to attempt military conscription in 1874, but it succeeded only when World War I made it seem a transcendental necessity for national survival. The reform of basic institutions and the practices and values linked to them are sometimes sudden but often incremental. The latter was certainly the case with slavery in Brazil. In no other part of the Americas did slavery play a longer and more profound role. While abolition did not eliminate racial prejudice and other related social injustices, it constituted a major institutional shift in terms of who had legal authority over others. Whether or not former slaves could effectively exercise their rights as citizens was in many cases dubious, but slavery's abolition constituted a major shift in Brazil's institutional fit that becomes more salient when considered in conjunction with reforms related to other categories of the intractable poor.

CORPORAL PUNISHMENT IN BRAZIL AND ABROAD

Like the abolition of slavery, the Brazilian state's efforts to abrogate corporal punishment were gradualist for different categories of the intractable poor. Brazil's 1824 Constitution had banned physical castigations for free citizens, but most members of the intractable poor were still subject to flogging. Efforts to reform army recruitment led to a modification of these practices for soldiers. Similarly, Justice Ministry officials reconsidered the practice of flogging convicts in 1878, and the state's role in flogging slaves would come into question when the abolitionist movement gained momentum in the 1880s.

In 1874, Parliament abolished the tradition of flogging army enlisted men with the broadside of a sword (*pranchadas*). A conservative Parliament passed this reform before it introduced the 1874 Recruitment Law because they hoped to make enlisted service seem less servile and more appealing to "sons of families." Regardless, most Brazilians resisted calls to enroll for conscription, which stymied its implementation. The inability to develop adequate rolls to conduct a draft lottery also illustrates institutional fit. The transition to a republic made it possible to establish a civil registry (a project the imperial government scuttled after the 1852 War of the Wasps). In 1916, the government used the civil registry to compile lists of men to implement conscription because efforts to enroll male citizens through other means floundered.[3]

Despite the failure to institute conscription in 1874, the ban on flogging in the army remained on the books. Immediately after it took effect, authorities in Pernambuco and elsewhere complained that soldiers committed condemnable crimes. In 1876, Pernambuco's governor blamed the ban on corporal punishments for spurring "army troops to commit acts of insubordination and crimes of incredible ferocity . . . that alarmed the population of Recife, and awakened the population's apprehensions about the troops' discipline." He expressed relief that these crimes had not reoccurred and optimism that new moderate punishments would "raise the soldiery's level of morality."[4] The reform in army disciplinary methods even touched Fernando de Noronha, where the army shipped materials to build a disciplinary barracks in which refractory soldiers would be segregated and punished nonviolently. An inspector reported in 1879, however, that these materials had not been used and had deteriorated from exposure to the elements.[5] The fate of the colony's disciplinary barracks may have been emblematic of the ban on flogging soldiers, because there is ample evidence that officers continued to use corporal punishments to discipline them with impunity. Still, officers did risk prosecution for violating this law, and a few faced courts martial for abusing their authority.

Parliament did not ban flogging for enlisted sailors in 1874. Sailors, who were mostly men of darker skin than their army counterparts, continued to be flogged with nautical cord (*chibatas*). Republican reformers briefly banned flogging in the navy in 1890, but when mutinies broke out, they hastily reinstated it for sailors.[6]

A former navy officer, abolitionist, and republican, Adolpho Ferriera Caminha, called attention to this injustice in his 1896 novel *Bom Crioulo* ("Good Nigger"), which highlights connections between categories of the intractable poor. He set the novel before abolition to express his animus to slavery, monarchy, flogging, and military impressment. The novel narrates a romance between a muscle-bound black sailor—a runaway slave pressed into the navy—and a blond, blue-eyed cabin boy. The black sailor suffers a flogging to protect the cabin boy from another sailor. Thereafter, Bom Crioulo initiates an affair with the cabin boy in which the sailor plays the active, masculine role and the cabin boy, the passive, feminine role in coitus. Caminha clearly sought to shock mostly white Brazilian readers with these reversals in racial, gender, and sexual hierarchies. The author suggests that the yearlong affair weakens Bom Crioulo. He grows thin, tires more easily, and feels "twinges of weakness in his chest."[7] Their romance ends when Bom Crioulo is transferred to a battleship where the captain refuses him shore leave and flogs him. Meanwhile, the cabin boy begins a manly affair with a Portuguese woman. Bom Crioulo learns of this when his poor health lands him in the navy hospital. He escapes the hospital and kills his lover in a jealous rage. Caminha likely intended his title *Bom Crioulo* as an ironic reference to Bom Selvagem (the noble savage) and the romantic conception Brazilian indigenes inspired in European intellectuals such as Jean Jacques Rousseau who depicted them as archetypes of individual liberty. The interconnected categories of the intractable poor are invoked to condemn injustice. Caminha suggests that Bom Crioulo's slave upbringing and his subjection to flogging as a sailor contributed to his unnatural attraction to men, which ultimately undermined his exuberant physical health. The controversy over his depiction of an interracial, same-sex romance, however, drowned out his antiflogging message.[8] Still, as this chapter argues, novels like *Bom Crioulo* provide insight into changing cultural perceptions of human rights.

Despite Caminha's criticism, navy officers continued to flog their men. This culminated in the embarrassing 1910 Chibata Revolt when Brazilian sailors mutinied and commandeered dreadnoughts recently acquired from Britain. Black noncommissioned officers led the revolt, and several white officers who resisted the mutiny lost their lives. The rebels ably piloted their fleet around Guanabara Bay and threatened to bombard the capital if their demands for the abolishment of flogging and for better pay and conditions were not met. The government, unable to counter the rebel ships, conceded to their demands, only to renege after the sailors surrendered their ships. In 1923, the government adopted a new navy penal code that did not mention flogging; the chibata's formal abrogation would await elaboration in subsequent codes and regulations. As the historian Joseph Love observed, the Brazilian navy's procedure paralleled that of the British, who banned flogging in their army in 1881 (seven years after Brazil) but merely suspended its use in the navy.[9] In any case, the Chibata Revolt damaged Brazil's international image.

Pedro I had hired the former British navy officer Thomas Cochran to found the Brazilian navy. British influence may have played some role in the maintenance of flogging in Brazil's navy, but racial prejudice was also key. The navy's nearly all white officer corps resisted efforts to ban the lash for its mostly nonwhite sailors. As appendix table A21 demonstrates, most nations banned flogging in their armies before their navies. The sequencing here indicates the prejudice that classed sailors as a unique class of uprooted reprobates. Many felt that navy vessels were uniquely vulnerable to mutiny because of their extreme batch living. An anonymous American navy officer articulated this view in a tract that advocated flogging in the U.S. Navy when Congress debated its reform in the 1840s:

> They are without any but casual ties to link them to each other, or to identify their interests with the welfare of the vessel that they sail. They have neither wives nor children with them, nor have they any capital invested in their temporary home. They must work, eat, drink, dress, wash, mend, make, cook, sleep and play within limits that are known by no other class of men; and jostling each other as they do, their angry passions must be kept down by means powerful enough to quell the most reckless natures. . . . The navy will continue to be manned by the unsettled populations of the world, and all the chimerical plans for supplying it with a steady body of men, will expire on the pages on which they are written.[10]

Poor pay, onerous batch living, and the supposedly vicious character of sailors made them uniquely obdurate members of the intractable poor who required flogging to keep in check.

The armed forces were not the only state institutions that debated the necessity of corporal punishment. Brazil's Justice Ministry banned flogging convicts on February 19, 1878.[11] One would presume that the 1824 Constitution had precluded this practice for free prisoners, but the Justice Ministry would feel no need to ban a practice that was not common in Brazil's prisons. On the heels of this reform, Justice Ministry inspector André Augusto de Padua Fleury decried Fernando de Noronha's lax discipline in 1879:

> There is no penal regime. Those condemned to perpetual galleys do not have their feet fettered; those condemned to simple imprisonment and those condemned to prison at hard labor live together with their guards who they receive in their homes and act in plays together in their small theater, enjoying the pleasures of family life and at liberty to have strangers come to share their company, having free movement on the island and forming a separate society: These are the conditions of the presidio

in which instilling morality has become impossible and intimidation has completely disappeared; to the extent that relocation to Fernando de Noronha is desired to lighten one's sentence.[12]

The colony's commander felt compelled to unilaterally reinstate flogging after heinous assassinations undermined security. In the first case, a convict wife and her lover murdered her husband; and in the second, a husband injured his wife and murdered his mother-in-law. The commander observed that these crimes were the tip of the iceberg because since the flogging ban some six months earlier discipline had broken down. Convicts failed to show up for work and spent their time plotting intrigues.

After these grisly murders, the commander met with employees and officers to discuss his determination to reinstate flogging, and all unanimously agreed: "I recognized that the order of May 7, 1879 ending punishment with the *gameleira* was the root cause of the escalating disorder among the convicts serving their sentences here. Most of them do not fear the gallows or the rifle, but when confronted with the gameleira they become submissive. This punishment is the element of order in this presidio. If eliminated order and discipline disappear because in general the convicts in this presidio are beasts and not men." The commander asked the governor to approve his actions, which he believed had saved lives and "brought order and discipline that had been replaced by the knife and the dagger."[13] Similarly, Bandeira Filho asserted: "The better behaved convicts told me that, after flogging had been suspended, they did not feel secure because they feared the incorrigible ones." He then cited Herbert Spencer on the need to intimidate wrongdoers.[14] The Justice Ministry's experiment with nonviolent methods was brief, and traditional stereotypes of convicts as beasts rationalized beatings to contain their savagery.

The reinstatement of corporal punishment in the colony did not go unnoticed internationally. The American geologist John Branner took a personal interest in the treatment of convicts on Fernando de Noronha and corresponded with Brazilian officials on the subject. In 1889, Branner wrote that a recent British visitor to the island had witnessed a convict's flogging: "Flogging continues, therefore, in spite of the order of the Minister of Justice made in 1879."[15] Branner too had witnessed a flogging during his visit that he found difficult to put in words: "I undertook to witness a flogging once, but, as I did not get through it with credit to myself, the less said of that occasion the better. I was informed by one of the officers that, not long before, one convict had been so severely flogged that he had died of his injuries."[16] It is unclear whether Branner became ill at the sight of such suffering, but he suggests that he lost his composure.

The Justice Ministry's ban even benefitted slave convicts. For Fleury, this was troublesome, and he made a number of suggestions to make the treatment of slave convicts more severe. First slave convicts should be required to work at least as many hours as slaves on the mainland. Second, slaves should be returned to their owners after they completed a maximum sentence of twelve years of *galés*. Third, slave convicts should be subject to flogging because bondspersons who committed no crimes were subject to it.[17] Like the 1874 ban on flogging in the army, penal authorities complained that the suspension of corporal punishment immediately resulted in disorder. As in the army, the ban on flogging was often honored in its breach, but it revealed leaders' growing discomfort with how it shaped public perceptions of their institutions. It also indicates a waning faith in flogging's efficacy. It is significant that authorities did not punish enlisted men, sailors, or convicts with the whip, an instrument associated with slavery. So even though privileged Brazilians viewed these categories with disdain, institutions made symbolic efforts to maintain distinctions between them through their instruments of torture.

A further piecemeal abolition of corporal punishment came in 1886, when Parliament banned public authorities from flogging slaves. There had been earlier efforts to regulate the number of lashes that could be applied to slaves and other categories of the intractable poor, but the 1886 reform was distinct. A conservative Parliament passed the 1886 law after public officials flogged two slaves who later died from their injuries. The historian Jeffrey Needell argues that a conservative Parliament supported this law to hold on to their majority by burnishing what they claimed was their sympathy for slavery's abolition, even though they worked behind the scenes to derail it. Conservatives made the cynical calculation that the measure was hollow because it only banned public officials from whipping slaves; masters and overseers retained the right to use "moderate" punishments to discipline them. While the law helped the conservative incumbents win a vote of confidence, they miscalculated the law's impact on slaves themselves. After its passage, masters moaned about slave laborers' insubordination. They refused rigorous work and many ran away. The law contributed to the disorganization of rural labor from 1886 to 1888, which precipitated Parliament's abolition of slavery on May 13, 1888.[18]

The ban on public officials flogging slaves and even slavery's abolition did little to hasten a ban on flogging Brazilian sailors. While many militaries maintained corporal punishment after they abolished slavery at home and in their colonies, some abolished it before slavery's demise. The U.S. Congress limited the flogging of navy enlisted men and merchant marines in 1850 and banned it in 1861 before the Civil War (1861–1865) brought an end to slavery. This precocious abolition of flogging in the U.S. Navy may have been due to the strong association between military service, citizenship, and white privilege in the United States.[19] The United States would lag, however, in abolishing corporal punishment in other institutions, including prisons and public schools, but there is an even stronger contrast between Brazil and the United States when one considers the ultimate corporal punishment: the death penalty.

THE DEATH PENALTY

Pedro II used his constitutional powers to commute many capital sentences to perpetual galleys, and after 1876, he commuted all death sentences. This de facto abolition was soon followed by a de jure ban in 1890 under the new penal code. While Pedro II may have been integral in bringing an end to capital punishment, the fact that his Republican successors codified it indicates there existed a broad-based consensus of support for it. Why was slaveholding Brazil among the first nations to abolish the death penalty?

Brazil's precocious abolition of the death penalty stands in contradistinction to the sequencing of reforms in the United States. While some northern states abolished the death penalty before the Civil War and some others thereafter, the penal codes of the majority of American states today still sanction it. Scholarship on opposition to the death penalty and its links to campaigns against corporal punishment, slavery's abolition, and other reform movements in Brazil is in many ways analogous to the subject's standing in U.S. historiography. As the historian David Brion Davis opined: "Interest in the history of American feminism, temperance, abolitionism, and utopianism, has obscured the fact that for a generation before the Civil War the movement to abolish the death penalty was an important reform enterprise which aroused violent debate over the ultimate source of justice, the degree of human responsibility, the fallibility of the courts, the progress or decline of society, the metaphysical origins of good and evil, and the authority of the Bible."[20] Davis further observes that this omission is puzzling given the success of some northern states in limiting or completely abolishing the death penalty before 1860. While Davis compares American anti–capital punishment movements to those of Britain, France, Russia, Austria, and Italy, among others, he does not consider the more precocious abolition of the death penalty in most of Latin America. This is strange given that scholars of the death penalty describe Latin American nations as the "vanguard" in its abolition. Davis's omission, however, is symptomatic of the benign neglect of South Atlantic history, even by a prominent architect of Atlantic history.[21] The different paths toward abolition in the United States and Brazil open new vistas on the different outcomes in the sequencing and depth of institutional reforms related to these social movements.

After the U.S. Civil War, Brazil became the last independent nation in the Western Hemisphere to tolerate slavery. This made it a pariah state for international human rights advocates. Embarrassment over this "national shame" pushed Brazil's leaders and intellectuals to find alternative means to demonstrate their civilization to peers in North Atlantic nations as world opinion turned against the brutality of slavery and harsh punishments. After all, Pedro was related by blood to much of Europe's royalty, and on his trips to Europe, politicians and intellectuals urged him to bring an end to bondage in Brazil. Slavery was so ubiquitous and integral to Brazil's political economy, however, that it proved difficult to abolish. As noted previously, slavery's abolition required Parliament to act. By comparison, the emperor's constitutional powers made it relatively simple to institute a de facto end to the death penalty.[22]

It would be a mistake, however, to presume that opposition to the death penalty began with Pedro and emanated outward; it arose from many points in the empire shaped by local experiences.[23] A prominent example is that of the fourth-year law student Joaquim Aurélio Barreto Nabuco de Araújo, who stepped forward to defend the slave Thomaz in Recife's appeals court in 1869.[24] This was a bold act because Thomaz had made himself reviled through the commission of two murders and a daring prison escape that spread panic in Recife's streets. Nabuco's first experience as a trial lawyer prompted him to pen *A escravidão* (Slavery), which was never completed and only published posthumously.[25] *A escravidão* provides insight into how defending Thomaz solidified Nabuco's abhorrence of flogging, the death penalty, and slavery and how he believed they were connected.[26]

Nabuco and other politicians, including his father, José Tomás Nabuco de Araújo, frequently criticized two aspects of Brazilian law. The first was Article 60 of Brazil's Criminal Procedural Code, which required that any slave who received a sentence that did not require the death penalty or perpetual galleys be punished by flogging. The second was the Law of June 10, 1835.[27] They decried them because they transgressed liberal principles of equality before the law and divided Brazil into what Joaquim Nabuco termed "two races":

> The law of one race does not have power over another. In modern societies the violent impositions of invading races over conquered races is no longer possible. . . . The law that rules contemporary civilization is different. The sons of the same soil are citizens of the same fatherland, and as citizens, they have immutable rights. When, for example, as in Brazil—the nation stains itself as the only one that continues to tolerate slavery in the Americas—the people are divided by race, in which one confiscates all from the other—property, labor, liberty—one can say that the law that oppresses the black race is the law of the white race, but you cannot call it the law of the society.[28]

Nabuco articulates the ideal of a leveled and homogenized imagined national community where "sons of the same soil" were equal regardless of color or former slave condition.[29]

According to his court testimony, Thomaz was born the son of the slave Matheus in Olinda, where he grew up and continued to reside with his owner Anna Barbosa da Silva. While Thomaz's trial transcript did not include details about his first homicide, Nabuco provides an interpretation of it in *A escravidão*. First and foremost, Nabuco depicts Thomaz as a slave who enjoyed his owner's complete trust: "Circumspect, frugal, humble, proud, he had an excellent reputation in his neighborhood. They raised him like a free man and therefore he had acquired good instincts. No one spoke to him of slavery. He worked for his mistress and for himself with dedication and conscientiousness. In Olinda he was called—Mr. Thomaz [a rough translation of the honorific 'seu Thomaz']."[30] As Marcus J. M. de Carvalho demonstrates, many slaves who worked and lived independently in Recife and Olinda in the nineteenth century often posed as and were taken to be free men, but for Nabuco, it was the owner who raised Thomaz as if he were free.[31] According to Nabuco, even his neighbors referred to him as Mr. Thomaz, a title of respect that implied freedom. Nabuco's assertion that no one spoke to Thomaz of his slavery, however, is difficult to believe. Thomaz was conscious of his status. At trial, he gave his name as "Thomaz, o escravo" (Thomaz, the slave), not "Seu Thomaz."

Why was it important for Nabuco to emphasize that Thomaz was raised like a free man? It seems probable that this narrative was a better fit for Nabuco's criticisms of slavery and flogging. He implies that if Thomaz had not been subject to humiliating beatings and other servile humiliations, then he, unlike most slaves, would not be vice ridden. This changed, however, when an unnamed authority whipped Thomaz in public, a humiliation that turned Thomaz into a *fera* (beast).[32] Such a flogging was unusual because *pelourinhos* (public whipping posts) had been removed from public squares across Brazil in the 1830s. Slaves continued to be whipped by authorities, but this punishment was carried out behind prison walls. Even so, it is certainly possible that an official abused his authority to punish Thomaz in a fashion that would have been even more humiliating since it was no longer common.

Whatever the facts of the incident, Nabuco used it to deploy one of his favorite antislavery tropes: the association of cruel punishments and the inhumanity of slavery to the alleged preponderance of vices among slaves. As Nabuco puts it, "Profoundly debasing, this punishment only served to destroy the remaining good character [*pudor*] that a slave nature could have. And when this good character is spent, it redoubles; it turns into a passion, into an ardent and insatiable desire for vengeance, and thus . . . the law does not achieve its purpose."[33]

According to Nabuco, Thomaz's flogging led him to acquire a gun and assassinate the authority responsible for his torture. Although Nabuco does not explicitly use the term "vice" in the passage just quoted, he employs it frequently in *A escravidão*: "Slavery is like an airborne venom [*que se infiltram pelo perfume*]; it infiltrates through egotism. . . . What vices can a soul avoid that obeys and is always prostrate and humiliated that bows and scrapes before a man? . . . What vices, on the contrary, can one who is habituated to issuing orders, to punish men as if they were animals, to contemplate the fullest degradation of our nature, to satisfy brutally all their desires? . . . To one vice, the other corresponds, the extremes meet."[34] Nabuco was hardly the first to use the trope of slavery propagating vices, not only among the servile ranks but also among masters and their families. He borrowed from venerable Brazilian and international antislavery rhetoric.[35] No less than one of Brazil's founding fathers, José Bonifácio de Andrada e Silva, stated in 1825: "All, therefore, is repaid in this life, we tyrannize the slaves and reduce them to brutal animals, and they inoculate us with all their immorality and all their vices."[36] What are these vices? As I argue elsewhere, vice was a tensile term. It could mean bad habits, addiction, physical deformity, a character flaw, and in Brazil's northeast, it was slang for *geofragia* (the consumption of soil). Vices linked to slaves in law, literature, and runaway notices include among other habits, qualities, or acts: gambling, sloth, a propensity to run away, lying, lasciviousness, "sodomy," dipsomania, ingratitude, cursing, and bravado.[37] The narrative of vice provides important clues to the arguments Nabuco made to defend his client.

Thomaz's trial preserves testimony of the second homicide. After his jury in Olinda sentenced Thomaz to hang, he was held in Recife's House of Detention. Witnesses reveal that at 11:00 AM on October 21, 1868, they heard shouts. The guard of the north wing's gate said Thomaz approached him and did not respond when he asked him what he wanted. Instead, Thomaz pushed open the gate that had been unlocked to accommodate the prison's family visiting hours. The guard raised an alarm, and his comrade, Affonço Honorado Bastos, tried to thwart Thomaz's escape. Thomaz stabbed Bastos in the neck, and the guard fell to the floor "bathed in blood." Thomaz ran down the Rua de Sol where he tussled briefly with a Portuguese coachman in an unsuccessful attempt to steal a horse. He eluded authorities for hours, but the police located Thomaz after he broke open a door to a private residence. He resisted arrest and injured a policeman who tried to apprehend him. The provincial police commander arrived and ordered Thomaz to surrender, which he did after the commander assured his safety.[38]

Given the preponderance of testimony against his client, how did Nabuco defend him? Nabuco describes his defense as a referendum on slavery and the death penalty:

> There were two social crimes. There was slavery and there was the death penalty. Slavery drove Thomas to commit the first crime and the death penalty drove him to perpetrate the second. . . . Obliged by natural law to preserve a life that did not belong to society but to God, he tried to escape when they came again to take him to the gallows. Then he committed his second crime. Either through overwhelming fear or a fierce desire for vengeance, he annihilated the man who seized him in order to subject him to the penalty of law, just as he was about to begin to enjoy his freedom through flight.[39]

In this depiction of Thomaz's motives, Nabuco blamed flogging, slavery, and the death penalty as the root causes of his crimes. Rather than a perpetrator, Thomaz was a victim. His portrayal of Thomaz presages those presented in slave convict petitions for pardon in the late 1880s. Nabuco's narrative also includes flourishes that stretch the truth. There is no indication in the trial transcript that Thomaz was soon to be taken to the gallows when he escaped.

Nabuco likely wrote *A escravidão* to capitalize on the notoriety he attained defending Thomaz and to link the antiflogging, antislavery, and anti–capital punishment movements: "This paragraph is merely the narration of a true fact, that all witnessed and to which we already alluded how [the slave Thomaz's actions] protests simultaneously against slavery and [the] death [penalty], we do not doubt that by linking the two crimes, that these actions argue with the same eloquence against both injustices."[40] Nabuco's criticisms of slavery mostly deal in generalities except for Thomaz's trial. He concludes that the death penalty, slavery, and flogging led to the "reproduction of crimes and the considerable multiplication of them" rather than deter them.[41]

Nabuco's interest in the death penalty's injustice did not end with Thomaz's trial. He later authored in French a pamphlet, *The Right to Kill*, responding to Alexandre Dumas's *L'Homme-femme*, which sustained the right of a husband to kill an unfaithful wife. After penning this polemic against honor-based wife-killing, Nabuco wrote his French intellectual idol, Ernest Renan, and asked him to add his voice to critique the ideas of Dumas the younger, but Renan responded that Dumas's work was weak and did not merit a serious response.[42]

Nabuco's opposition to honor killings of women and the death penalty in relation to slavery fit hand in glove with ongoing debates across the Atlantic. His response to the trial of Thomaz emerged in conversation with broader national and international efforts to end the death penalty and slavery and to promote a positive image of Brazil abroad.[43] Nabuco was not the only literary figure who depicted corporal punishment as a causal factor for vice and illness (physical, mental, and spiritual). Adolfo Caminha's *Bom Crioulo* (1897), analyzed earlier, made nearly analogous associations between flogging, slavery, and vice among sailors.[44] But even more fundamental to the popularization of the anti–death penalty movement was José do Patrocínio's 1877 novel *Motta Coqueiro, ou a pena de morte* (Motta Coqueiro, or The Death Penalty), which attacked capital punishment while taking more subtle digs at slavery and corporal punishment. The links between these phenomena are apparent in a passage where Patrocínio describes the slave convict who served as Motta Coqueiro's executioner:

> There was, however, one man for whom the simple solemnity of the divine religious service did not cause the least impression. It was the hangman, the black monster, who played impatiently with his cape, twisting it in his hands. A rude statue of slavery, whose defects were filled with the asphalt of the slave prison [*calabouço*] mixed with the blood that the whips tore from his body, this misfortunate one perhaps found solace in

his bestial brutality. The whites made him a victim; denying him the opportunity to refine his sentiments through the exact comprehension of family, religion, and the fatherland; he must have been glad to be able to avenge himself on one of his oppressors.[45]

Like other abolitionists, Patrocínio borrowed tropes from slavocrats who argued that bondage corrupted the moral character of slaves because it allegedly denied them a family life. Hence, a bondsman's lack of exposure to the jealous institution perpetuated vices. Patrocínio drew the inspiration for his fictionalized anti–capital punishment novel from the real-life 1855 execution of the white slaveowner Motta Coqueiro, whom a jury condemned for murdering a sharecropping family on his estate. While slaves were the most common victims of the gallows in Brazil, in this rare instance, a heinous crime earned a prominent white man the death penalty. Not even Pedro felt that he could commute the capital sentence for the so-called "beast of Macabu," Minas Gerais. The case was even more compelling because years later a man on his death-bed confessed that he had been the author of the brutal homicides, not Motta Coqueiro. This injustice against a white man of means made the novel's plot an even more effective story to turn a mostly white Brazilian readership against capital punishment and, indirectly, slavery itself. This well-publicized miscarriage of justice must have weighed on the emperor's conscience, but he received *Motta Coqueiro*'s publication with enthusiasm. Patrocínio published the novel a year after the emperor decided to commute all death sentences to life imprisonment, and he welcomed this literary cover for a policy many criticized.[46] Patrocínio and Nabuco became friends and allies in the struggle against flogging, capital punishment, and slavery.

Nabuco and other intellectuals and politicians expressed their shame to be citizens of the last independent nation in the Americas to tolerate slavery. Unlike intellectuals of the U.S. South, Brazilians under the empire did not articulate a full-blown moral defense of slavery. Most rationalized it as an unpalatable but essential institution for the nation's economy.[47] Nabuco was perhaps foremost in arguing that slavery had impeded Brazil's economic progress, but slavery was so widespread in Brazil that it took decades to dismantle. Unable to demonstrate their superior civilization through the abolition of bondage, Pedro II cast about for other ways of competing in the international race among nations to outdo one another in furthering human rights to amass what Christopher Brown describes as moral capital.[48] The discomfiture of a portion of Brazil's political elite with their nation's tolerance of slavery made opposition to the death penalty a more feasible way for them to improve Brazil's international image.

In the nineteenth century, liberal ideals of equality before the law and a general rejection of torture began to change penal justice. Advances in human rights became an important touchstone of a nation's level of civilization. Take, for instance, the statement of a representative of Geneva's city council who at an international conference in 1833 praised the Louisiana statesman Edward Livingston for presenting a law code to his state legislature to abolish the death penalty: "It is easy to make the experiment [abolish the death penalty]. All the world would approve it. The glory will reflect on the whole nation, and history will certainly make honorable mention of the people which shall first renounce a practice no longer required by necessity."[49] Livingston's legislation did not become law in Louisiana or any other slaveholding state in the United States, but it was praised and circulated broadly. Livingston even corresponded with Emperor Pedro I, and his work influenced the penal codes of Brazil, Russia, and Guatemala. Senator Antônio Pereira Rebouças and other Brazilian politicians referenced Livingston's code, and it shaped the laws of northern U.S. states that abolished the death penalty before 1860.[50] Livingston's legacy demonstrates that the anti–death penalty movement was not alien to southern lawmakers (although Livingston himself was a transplanted Yankee). Voices from other southern states and slaveholding Brazil echoed his call.[51] Nevertheless, some scholars have argued that the South's history of bondage is a principal reason that former slave states continue to practice the death penalty. The fact that many U.S. states that never tolerated slavery practice capital punishment whereas Brazil was among the first nations to abolish it shows this to be a flawed hypothesis.[52] I argue that the divergence between death penalty abolitionism in Brazil and the United States lies in the paths each nation took toward slavery's abolition and their different legal, institutional, and cultural histories.

In Brazil, the movements against slavery and capital punishment experienced reversals, just when they gained momentum in many European nations and their colonies in the 1830s. Britain's reformist 1832 Parliament limited the number of crimes that could be punished with the death penalty, and in the following year it abolished slavery in its colonies.[53] Similarly, France exempted a number of crimes that had formerly been subject to the death penalty (for example, counterfeiting, arson, and receipt of stolen goods) in 1832.[54]

Like other Brazilians of his day, Nabuco made copious references to French and British intellectuals to support his arguments against slavery and the death penalty in A escravidão:

> Exaggerated penalties, instead of discouraging crime, provoke it: this was our thesis of which the example [Thomaz] appears to be sad proof. These details we know because we were the lawyers of the blackman Thomaz: to struggle hand to hand against slavery and the death penalty, to denounce them before the tribunal of citizens, to weigh their influence in the perpetuation of offenses, to determine the role of society's complicity in the crimes of individuals is an honorable mission that all can carry out. . . . After this session, we can repeat the words of Alphonse de Lamartine because we had touched the wounds of society: "Happy the day when legislation bans before the divine light these two great scandals of nineteenth century reason: slavery and the death penalty."[55]

By comparing his struggles to those of the French politician Alphonse Marie Louis de Prat de Lamartine (1790–1869), Nabuco placed himself in heady company. He also cites the French luminaries François Guizot and Victor Hugo. In 1848, they had a hand in the provisional French government's proclamations of universal male suffrage, the end of French colonial slavery, and the death penalty's abrogation. The death penalty's 1848 prohibition was short lived, however, and Mr. Guillotin's device was not retired in France until the 1970s.[56]

While France and Britain limited the death penalty in the 1830s, Brazil's Parliament passed the additional law of June 10, 1835, that mandated a death sentence for slaves who murdered their master, a member of their master's family, or overseer. As noted earlier, Brazilians had been abstemious in the death penalty's application before 1835. The state preferred to put convicts to work in chain gangs, as Jean-Baptiste Debret's illustration Negociante de tabaco depicted.[57]

It was not until Pedro II assumed the throne that the tide began to turn against slavery and the death penalty, institutions he personally opposed. After traveling to Europe in the mid-1870s, where he met with prominent French intellectuals and leaders who opposed capital punishment and slavery, including Victor Hugo and Adolphe Franck, Pedro decided that he would commute all death sentences to perpetual galleys in 1876.[58] Pedro's desire to impress European intellectuals and dignitaries cannot be underestimated.

FIG 9.1 *Negociante de tabaco* (Tobacco Merchant) depicts convict chain gang workers
who may have been slaves. Illustration by Jean-Baptiste Debret, from *Viagem pitoresca e
histórica ao Brasil*, 2 vols. (São Paulo: Livraria Martins, 1940), 1:261; 2:211.

Even before the emperor brought a de facto end to capital punishment,
Nabuco expressed pride in Brazil's imperial legislation. Like many Brazilians, he found comparisons to the United States irresistible as a way to
define a unique Brazilian national identity: "The legislation of Virginia and
Carolina were extreme in their repression of slave crime. In Virginia, there
were 71 crimes in which [the law] allowed only slaves to suffer the death penalty, and it permitted masters to kill disobedient slaves."[59] Philip J. Schwarz
shows that Virginia's courts executed slaves for crimes such as theft, assault,
arson, and rape, but the number of capital sentences for these crimes declined after 1800.[60] Even if one combines the 199 confirmed executions of
slave convicts that the historian João Luiz Ribeiro counted for Brazil with
the 135 cases he could not confirm from 1830 to 1876, Virginia still put to
death more slaves (338 versus 334) in a comparable time span.[61] This data is
even more remarkable because Virginia, unlike Brazil, compensated owners
the full price of slaves it executed based on an appraiser's assessment. This
cost encouraged Virginia authorities to commute more and more death sentences to transportation and sale out of state to recover compensation costs.

But this disincentive did not prevent Virginians from executing 338 slaves from 1820 to 1864 at taxpayer expense.

The Brazilian case contrasts those of the Anglophone and Francophone Americas. Like Brazil, most southern states in the United States afforded slaves accused of capital offenses the right to a trial, though many required the jury to be composed of slaveowners.[62] Mississippi, Alabama, South Carolina, Louisiana, Texas, Delaware, Maryland, and Kentucky offered different forms of partial compensation to owners. Similarly, slave law in the British Caribbean empowered juries to determine compensation for slaves sentenced to death or transportation. Courts compensated owners as an incentive to turn over slave suspects and to discourage them from selling slaves charged with crimes in other states or territories to avoid financial loss.[63] The French in Louisiana taxed slaves to create a fund to compensate owners whose slaves the state executed or exiled. The Spanish established the concept of compensation for slaves sentenced to death in the 1768 Black Code of the Audiencia of Santo Domingo, but in practice, Spanish colonial courts did not compensate owners for executed slaves.[64] Laws in much of the slaveholding Americas were more respectful of private property than Brazilian law.

In Brazil, law reserved the death penalty for homicide, rebellion, and treason, so Nabuco's comparison with the United States was favorable. He emphasized the cruel racial prejudice of U.S. citizens: "Many were the cruelties of this intolerant and exclusionary race [white Americans] in the treatment of their slaves: among us [Brazilians], these barbarities are not taken to such extremes in most cases, even though there are deplorable exceptions that have occurred which appear to double their number."[65] Unable to defend the morality of slavery, Nabuco portrays Brazilian slavery as less harsh than its U.S. counterpart. He observes real differences in the laws of Brazil and Virginia, but it is important to note that he cited Virginia's law in 1869, four years after slavery's abolition there. His argument was anachronistic.

The roots of what became known in the 1940s as racial democracy lay in the empire. Racial democracy or the belief that Brazilian society had been uniquely characterized by closer relations between its constituent races, including masters and slaves, gave rise to a nation allegedly less burdened by racial prejudices than others, the United States in particular. Thus, social distance and inequality in Brazil resulted more from class distinctions than color prejudice. In an 1882 letter to the British abolitionist Catherine Impey, Nabuco wrote:

> As for Brazil, my own country and home, I can only repeat here what I told you: even with slavery we make no difference as to colour. Coloured

men happen to be foremost in all careers: none is shut to them either by public antipathy or social pressure. Some of the most brilliant talents, in all kinds of intellectual superiority, come from the coloured people. Poets, musicians, orators, engineers, publicists, statesmen, show us how we should have deprived ourselves of real national forces, if we had condemned, by a law, or still worse, by a prejudice, a whole race to live in an inferior level to our own and not to aspire to the same pursuits, achievements and ambitions in life![66]

Nabuco played no small part in propagating the idea that Brazilians were uniquely open to men of color at home and abroad. While he railed against the barbarous treatment of Brazilian slaves in A escravidão, he insists it was better than slavery in the United States. He cites Harriet Beecher Stowe's depiction of white Americans' cruelty to slaves, especially slave families, and rebukes Jefferson Davis's use of the Bible to defend slavery. While the distinctions Nabuco made between Brazil and the United States may seem trivial, they were significant to Brazilians who longed for the recognition of North Atlantic peers as members of the civilized communion of nations.[67]

Nabuco used another historic atrocity to criticize his homeland and slavery: "We do not have in humanity, with the exception of the Inquisition, any crime so complex, but if the former was more tragic, it was more dignified: it proceeded in the name of fanaticism, which is less humiliating for its executioners than to proceed in the name of self-interest, and it awarded death, which is less humiliating for the victim than to be subjected to captivity."[68] Nabuco's reasoning contradicts the rationale of U.S. southern intellectuals who justified slavery as saving African war captives from death.[69] These arguments show the commitment of Nabuco, like many of his generation, to the condemnation of slavery without completely reproving Brazilian society. He also cast the slave's life as worse than that of a convict: "We, a humane and civilized nation, condemn more than a million persons, as so many others were condemned before them, to a condition alongside which imprisonment or the gallows seem better!"[70] For abolitionists, comparisons of convicts and slaves served to highlight bondage's injustice, but for slavocrats the "half liberty" of slave convicts on Fernando de Noronha was an incentive to slave crime.

Nabuco was not simply being jingoistic when he compared Brazil and the United States. In Brazil only homicide, conspiracy, and rebellion merited the gallows, whereas in antebellum Virginia a much wider variety of felonies applied to condemned slaves. From 1820 to 1865, slaves sentenced for homicide accounted for a little over half (50.6 percent) of those executed in Virginia, and for conspiracy and insurrection, slightly more than 8 percent (8.3 percent). But Virginia's courts executed slave convicts for rape (9.5 percent), attempted rape (8.3 percent), attempted homicide (6.8 percent), unspecified (5 percent), theft (3.9 percent), arson (3.9 percent), poisoning (3.6 percent), and infanticide (less than 1 percent).[71]

This difference can be even more deeply contextualized by comparing when and where slavery and the death penalty were abolished in selected Atlantic nations (see tables A22 and A23). While Americans and Europeans had inspired opposition to the death penalty, they made limited headway in abolishing it. Indeed, Britain, France, and Spain abolished the death penalty only after they had lost most of their colonial possessions. Portugal and the Netherlands were the outlier empires that joined the first wave of nations to abolish capital punishment. Why is it that so many Latin American nations succeeded in first limiting and then abolishing capital punishment earlier than most North Atlantic nations?

In Spanish America, the violent wars between rival political factions after independence spurred liberal legislators in the region to abolish capital punishment for political crimes first and for civil crimes thereafter (see table A22). Political instability also weakened the institution of slavery in these nations. The need for troops led factions to mobilize slaves as soldiers, sometimes in return for their manumission, and war provided conditions that made it easier for slaves to escape captivity. Thus warfare contributed to slavery's abolition in many continental Spanish American nations.[72] This was coupled with the fact that the slave populations in these nations did not form as large a part of the population as they did in Brazil or colonial Cuba. Venezuela, for example, had the largest nonwhite population of the emerging continental Spanish American countries,[73] and it was the first nation in the world to completely abolish the death penalty, in 1863. Venezuelan politicians had previously abolished the death penalty for political crimes in 1849. Thus, Venezuela and Brazil were the only nations to limit the death penalty before abolishing slavery (see tables A17 and A18), but Venezuela only definitively abolished capital punishment after slavery's abolition there in 1854. Similarly, other Spanish American nations first abolished the death penalty for political crimes and later for civil ones. This was the case for Argentina, Colombia, Uruguay, Mexico, Ecuador, and Costa Rica. This sequencing of a partial followed by a fuller abolition is a salient characteristic of the death penalty's abolition in these nations, just as it was for slavery and corporal punishment.[74]

Brazilians, however, avoided the breadth and depth of the political instability and warfare that characterized Spanish American nations. This may
explain why the sequencing of reform in Brazil was different. Brazil first experimented with a de facto abolition of capital punishment before slavery's
abolition in 1888. Shortly thereafter, it implemented a de jure moratorium
of the death penalty. It should be noted that some Latin American nations
(Brazil and Argentina) later briefly reestablished the death penalty's legality
under military dictatorships. Despite these bouts of temporary backsliding,
the prominence of Brazil and many Spanish American nations in the first
wave of capital punishment's abolition is a phenomenon that sets them apart
from other regions. This observation is not intended to diminish or to paper
over the fact that many individuals and state agents executed fellow citizens
extralegally, but to emphasize that formally the Brazilian state did not sanction capital punishment. The law, after all, should reflect our highest moral
aspirations and not our all-too-human shortcomings.

HISTORIES OF ANTI–CAPITAL PUNISHMENT AND ANTISLAVERY IN BRAZIL AND THE UNITED STATES

A brief but more detailed comparison of Brazilian and American histories
of capital punishment and slavery further illuminates why they took such
different legal and institutional trajectories.[75] The analysis here privileges
comparisons of political institutions, paths toward slavery's abolition, legal
traditions, and culture.

A major difference that shaped reform outcomes in both countries lay in
their political systems. Brazil's constitution vested the emperor with executive powers that allowed him to bring a de facto end to capital punishment,
but slavery's abolition required Parliament's approval. The United States' federal system made the battle over the death penalty a struggle waged within
the states. This made it possible for the anti–capital punishment movement
to claim some victories in a few northern states before 1860, but it hampered
more sweeping reform.

The nature of slavery's abolition also shaped attitudes toward the death
penalty. In the United States, the Civil War brought an incredibly violent
and abrupt end to slavery. It resulted in the Union army's occupation of
the Confederacy during Reconstruction (1865–1877), when many black men
won election to prominent political offices as Republican Party representatives. After Reconstruction, Bourbon Democrats led a campaign of terror
to take power from black Republicans and their white allies. Part of this
campaign included extralegal lynchings and legal executions. While it may

be argued that powerful planters and political bosses in Brazil did not protest the death penalty's abolition more vociferously because they could carry
out extralegal executions with little fear of prosecution, similar impunity for
offenders certainly existed in the United States. The lynching or legal executions of black men in the United States often hinged on accusations that they
had raped or attempted to seduce white women, which reflected fears of
racial miscegenation. Democratic Party operatives coined the term "miscegenation" in New York City when they produced a pamphlet that argued for
race mixture and claimed that the Republican Party favored it. It was a crass
hoax intended to scuttle Lincoln's 1864 reelection, but it reprised Stephen
Douglas's assertion that Lincoln favored race mixture in their 1858 debates.
Both incidents demonstrated that white citizens' concern about race mixture was not limited to slave states, serving to justify racial segregation of
varying degrees across the United States.[76]

By comparison, Brazil's abolition of slavery was gradual and comparatively peaceful. After 1850, when the transatlantic slave trade to Brazil ended,
the bonded population began to decline, which eroded underlying political support for slavery. After the War of the Triple Alliance, Pedro pushed
the 1871 Free Womb Law through Parliament, making good on his cabinet's 1866 response to the French antislavery movement. A desire to impress
foreign dignitaries prompted a commitment to hasten slavery's abolition.
Pedro was central to the abolition of the death penalty and slavery, but one
should remember the support of Brazilian intellectuals and politicians such
as Joaquim Nabuco, José do Patrocínio, and many others. Furthermore, the
actions of slaves themselves and common free Brazilians contributed deci-
sively to abolition's triumph.[77]

Differing legal and cultural traditions also shaped outcomes. In populous
Britain, authorities executed large numbers of convicts in the late eighteenth
century, even for relatively minor crimes, until transportation to Australia
and the construction of modern penitentiaries afforded less lethal alternatives. Executions were a vibrant part of British popular culture, as indicated
by the euphemism "Tyburn Fair" for Tyburn gallows.[78] Conversely, executions were rare enough that Brazilian schoolmasters, business owners, and
master craftsmen gave their students, clerks, and apprentices holidays during the work week to witness them.[79]

Less populous Portugal seldom executed its subjects; the state preferred
to send them as exiles to their colonies. This heritage is reflected in table
A22, which shows Portugal abolished the death penalty soon after Venezuela. Gauging popular support for the death penalty's abolition is difficult.

Even more difficult is to establish whether ordinary Brazilians, like Nabuco and Patrícinio, associate it with the abolition of slavery and corporal punishment. The actions of slaves who ran away and precipitated slavery's abolition in 1887 and 1888, or the Fortaleza stevedore strike led by the free man of color Francisco José do Nascimento in 1881, which precipitated Ceará's precocious abolition of slavery in 1884, manifested popular opposition to slavery, but similar public actions in favor of the death penalty's abrogation are not as easy to identify. One indicator that common Brazilians did not fully embrace the death penalty was the difficulty authorities had in finding men to serve as executioners. Officials sent the few willing to perform this duty (most were slave convicts) to distant locations in the communities where the felon's crime had been committed. This slowed down and increased the costs of executions, and it may account for some of the 135 death sentences where Ribeiro could not determine whether authorities ever carried them out. One slave convict claimed to have executed eighty-seven convicts across Minas Gerais and Rio de Janeiro, but he had to be held in isolation because other prisoners who found his work repugnant once stabbed him. While the case is anecdotal, it suggests a lack of popular support for the death penalty and its collaborators.[80]

The United States inherited from Britain an attachment to capital punishment, particularly in states that sought to maintain the discipline of the slave regime and subsequently to police Jim Crow laws. American citizens' attachment to lynching as part of a cultural grammar of popular justice faded after the civil rights struggles in the mid-twentieth century. In post–civil rights America, however, capital punishment's apologists deny its links to racial oppression, despite the fact that a disproportionate number of prisoners on death row are African Americans.[81] That Brazilians soon followed the Portuguese example to abolish capital punishment suggests that their cultural and legal heritage influenced their decision to do so.

There is no great nineteenth-century American novel that decries the death penalty of a stature comparable to José do Patrocínio's *Motta Coqueiro*, Victor Hugo's *The Last Day of a Condemned Man* (1829), or Charles Dickens's *Great Expectations* (1861). Perhaps the closest is Hermann Melville's *Billy Budd, Sailor*, but it was written in 1890 and only published in 1924.[82] There was Walt Whitman's obscure short story "Arrow Tip," published in 1845 and republished a year later as "The Half-Breed." When Whitman changed the title, he shifted the focus from the victim, the Indian Arrow Tip, who was unjustly executed for crimes he did not commit, to the mixed-race character of the "half-breed" who betrayed the innocent Arrow Tip. Even progressive U.S. writers could not escape what one scholar referred to as Whitman's dread of the "grotesque unnaturalness of racial amalgamation."[83] The feminist Lydia Maria Child published an anti–capital punishment story, "The Juryman," in 1849, but it too was little read.[84] There is no parallel to Harriet Beecher Stowe's antislavery *Uncle Tom's Cabin* (1852), which quickly became an international classic.

In her history of human rights, Lynn Hunt asserts: "Novels made the point that all people are fundamentally similar because of their inner feelings, and many novels showcased in particular the desire for autonomy. In this way, reading novels created a sense of equality and empathy through passionate involvement in the narrative."[85] If Hunt is correct, then I suggest that the lack of literary reflection on the death penalty's injustices hampered the imagining of such equalities for those U.S. courts condemned to die. Clearly novels do not change laws: Victor Hugo's and Charles Dickens's novels failed to speed the death penalty's abolition in France and Britain. The novel's power to spur reform, however, is exemplified by Herman Melville's *White Coat* (1850), which decried the flogging of U.S. Navy sailors and merchant marines. Those who sought to abolish flogging made sure that every U.S. senator received a copy of *White Coat*. Congress passed a law limiting the flogging of sailors in 1850, followed by its abolition in 1861. Politicians themselves recognized a novel's power to awaken social consciousness. When elected to the U.S. Congress in the late 1820s, Edward Livingston had little luck in advancing legislation to abolish capital punishment. He then wrote to both James Fenimore Cooper and Daniel Webster to implore them to take up the death penalty as the subject for a novel to popularize anti-gallows sentiment, but neither author took up his suggestion.[86]

Unlike the United States, Brazil never established legal racial segregation. As long as men of color satisfied electoral requirements they could vote and hold public office. Of course, new 1881 literacy requirements prevented many former slaves and men of color from voting. Even those who could vote, however, could not do so freely. The lack of a secret vote meant that clients who bucked a political boss's directives could face reprisals. Former slaves in Brazil did not form a voting block or color-based political parties until the 1930s. Such color-based political activism could have triggered white violence, as it did in Cuba in 1912, where a massacre brought an end to the Partido Independiente de Color (Independent Party of Color) under the tutelage of the U.S. Platt Amendment. Unlike black Republican politicians under Reconstruction, Brazilian men of color rarely won election to high public office, and when they did, they did not run as representatives of "nonwhite" or former slave constituencies. The corrupt, oligarchic, and state-based political party system of Brazil's Old Republic (1889–1930) discouraged the organization of color-based political parties. Furthermore, the lack of segregation meant that Brazilians of color did not have the parallel institutions of their counterparts in the United States, where autonomous black churches, universities, and segregated public schools and neighborhoods cultivated racial consciousness and developed leaders who identified themselves as representatives of their race. The exceptions were the Brazilian black press, Carnival organizations, and lay brotherhoods, but they did not have the same projection as African American institutions.[87]

Brazil's nonwhite majority meant that its nationalists faced a different scale of challenge from social Darwinian theories than their North American counterparts. North American leaders such as Theodore Roosevelt described the United States as an "Anglo-Saxon Republic," rhetorically negating the presence of African, indigenous, Asian, and non-Anglo-Saxon Europeans, who clouded his vision of America's homogenous racial and national destinies.

The observations of foreign visitors who decried Brazil's population as an example of the dangers of racial miscegenation concerned nationalist intellectuals. How was Brazil to escape the dustbin of history if social Darwinist theory was correct? Instead of rejecting it, they promoted whitening theory to subvert it. Government policy supported whitening by subsidizing European and Japanese (the so-called Aryans of Asia) and banning African and Chinese immigration. Whitening theory's proponents argued that most women of color sought out lighter skinned partners and believed that white genes predominated over African and indigenous ones. Rather than cultivate fears of race mixture, they embraced it as a means of accelerating whitening. It seems that privileged Brazilian white men remained secure that their dalliances with women of color would be the norm, not the inverse, so the policing of a sexual color line was not as potent a cultural anxiety as it was in the United States.[88]

The slave Thomaz's trial and Nabuco's interpretation of it demonstrate how circumstances linked the struggle against corporal punishment, the death penalty, and slavery. Nabuco did not need the emperor or others to persuade him to pen a manuscript condemning them; rather, the inspiration arose from his experience. Nabuco would become an important cultural go-between for Brazil as he communicated with major political and intellectual leaders in Europe and became Brazil's ambassador to the United States. His writing played a prominent and enduring role in shaping the memory of slavery and race relations. As Lynn Hunt argues: "I believe that social and political change—in this case, human rights—comes about because many individuals had similar experiences, not because they all inhabited the same social context but because through their interactions with each other and with their reading and viewing, they actually created a new social context."[89] Writers and politicians like Nabuco reshaped their social context, which made the abolition of slavery and the death penalty possible. These comparisons highlight the sociologist David Garland's observation: "This concern with the nature of punishment's social support and its cultural significance is a deliberate attempt to shift the sociology of punishment away from its recent tendency—engendered by Foucault and the Marxists—to view the penal system more or less exclusively as an apparatus of power and control, and to recognize that criminal laws and penal institutions usually encapsulate moral values and sensibilities that are widely shared—even if the older Durkheimian tradition overstates the extent to which this is true."[90] As this chapter shows, a less appreciated part of Nabuco's legacy was his opposition to the death penalty and flogging. This is an enduring legacy, as Brazil's 1988 Constitution prohibits the death penalty, even though it allows for exceptions during wartime.[91]

This consideration of institutional fit allows for some hypotheses. First, slavery's abolition preceded capital punishment's complete abolition. Hence, only U.S. states that never practiced slavery abolished the death penalty before the Civil War. Second, Brazil and many Spanish American nations show that a history of slavery was not an impediment to the death penalty's abolition. Two of South America's most prominent slaveholding nations, Venezuela and Brazil, led the nineteenth-century world. Cuba's status as a colony of Spain through the nineteenth century, its status as a neocolonial state of the United States in the early twentieth century, and its 1959 revolution propelled Spanish America's largest slave society down a different path. Cuba is among a minority of Latin American nations that tolerate the death penalty. Third, nations, especially those in the first wave of abolitionism, often practiced some form of limitation on the death penalty before adopting a fuller abolition. In Brazil, the emperor's de facto moratorium abrogated capital punishment more than a decade before its de jure abolition in 1890. In many Spanish American countries, the abolition of capital punishment for political crimes preceded its abrogation for civil crimes. In Portugal, the state had not bothered to execute anyone for two decades before it abolished the death penalty. These experiments gave officials and their citizenry confidence that capital punishment was not an effective deterrent.

Partial abolitions of the death penalty begot fuller ones, much as Free Womb laws preceded the full abolition of slavery in most of Latin America. Fourth, where the death penalty continued to be practiced with regularity, it tended to maintain its legitimacy. As two scholars of the death penalty's history in the United States hypothesize, a "history of frequent executions . . . serves as a kind of precedent, reassuring political actors that their own participation is neither inhumane nor immoral . . . on the grounds that, historically, executions do not violate local community morality."[92] This observation indicates that Pedro II's efforts to diminish and then eliminate the death penalty were well suited to establish a commitment to the death penalty's abolition. Finally, when one considers the abolition of flogging, the death penalty, and slavery the interrelationships between categories of the intractable poor becomes more apparent. A reform that improved the treatment and condition of one category made it less legitimate to continue for those in other categories.

Fernando de Noronha was both a symbolic and a literal part of the debate over corporal punishment, the death penalty, and slavery. Pedro's commutations for death sentences courts handed down across Brazil led his opponents to argue that slaves now had an incentive to kill to improve their lot in life. The relatively low number of slaves sentenced under the Law of June 10, 1835, indicates that few slaves actually believed they could better their lives if they murdered their masters and were exiled to Fernando de Noronha, where they would enjoy a provision ground, receive supplies of food, and enjoy the "half liberty" that the penal colony permitted. The actions of slave convicts who petitioned for fuller freedom as soon as the opportunity arose and those of other convicts who risked their lives to escape on rickety rafts demonstrate that the characterizations of Fernando de Noronha as a criminal paradise were overblown.

CONCLUSION
Punishment in Paradise Foiled Again

In the presidio [of Fernando de Noronha], the bandit [Zé Moleque]
became known as a good person, a worker. His manioc fields were always
the most productive and he was never jailed, never gave the prison administrators trouble.

—JOSÉ LINS DO REGO, *USINA*, 1936

Decades after Fernando de Noronha became a penal colony for the
state of Pernambuco in 1898, José Lins do Rego's 1936 novel *Usina*
(industrial sugar refinery) depicted it as an incongruous utopia. The
scion of a wealthy sugar plantation family, Lins do Rego narrates how
his young black protagonist Ricardo served three years on Fernando
de Noronha for his involvement in a Recife labor strike. When Ricardo returns to the mainland he is disillusioned. The modern refin-
eries and new agricultural labor regime have forced former slaves and
their descendants off the land and transformed them into landless
proletarians. He then recalls his time on Fernando de Noronha with
a mixture of nostalgia and shame, especially the tender relationship
he shared with the former black bandit Zé Moleque. Fernando de
Noronha initially seems an exotic criminal community of dishonored
and transgressive convicts, the antithesis of the mainland. But as the
plot progresses, it becomes a bucolic foil that the author uses to highlight hypocrisy, injustice, and corruption in Recife and Pernambuco's
sugarcane fields in the 1920s.

Why did Lins do Rego choose Fernando de Noronha as a foil? A
British ornithologist who visited the island in 1902 provides a clue:

While we were at the Governor's house a bugle was sounded to summon the convicts. There were about two hundred of them, all under long sentences, most of them having been convicted of murder. One man, who was told off as a guide to our party, was said to have committed seven murders. . . . After their names had been called, the convicts dispersed for the night, about fifty being locked up in the gaol [*aldeia*], and the rest going off to their own houses. Most of these men have wives and families, and, as far as we could judge, their lives were not hard. They have to work three hours a day for the State, but the rest of the day they can spend as they like, though all have to appear when the bugle is sounded in front of the governor's house.[1]

Deeply engrained patterns of organizing convict agricultural labor and their living arrangements, albeit on a smaller scale, remained intact after the central government withdrew from the colony's administration. Fernando de Noronha was a kind of imperial anachronism, which may be why it attracted Lins de Rego.

Lins do Rego's juxtaposition of Fernando de Noronha and the mainland, however, differed from earlier comparisons. Nineteenth-century critics usually highlighted or alluded to the prominence of same-sex eroticism on the island to condemn it, but Lins do Rego contrasts the companionate and mutually respectful relationship between Zé Moleque and Ricardo with exploitative mainland sexual relationships. Among others, he introduces the French Madame Jacqueline, who desires the beautiful young Brazilian prostitute Clarinda, who works in her classy Recife bordello. This becomes a love triangle when the nouveau riche refinery owner Dr. Juca leaves his wife and family in the countryside to squander his wealth in Recife's bordellos, where he too comes to covet Clarinda. Juca betrays his family in his pursuit of Clarinda's affections, and Madame Jacqueline encourages Clarinda's affair with Juca because it augments her profits. Lins do Rego's novel suggests that the same sexual transgressions long condemned on Fernando de Noronha were an integral part of mainland society, and his novel implies that modernization heightened this corruption. At least the rustic love Ricardo and Zé Moleque shared was untainted by self-interest or betrayal.

For Lins do Rego, modernity not only corrupted the patriarchal family but also made refinery owners distant and insensitive to their workers' needs. He narrates how cane workers lost access to provision grounds because mill owners now planted as much land as possible with cane to feed the industrial refinery's relentless maw. Workers, paid in script, bought overpriced goods from the refinery owner's store. Modernization eroded Lins do Rego's imagined social compact between masters and former slaves, patriarchs and clients. Even Dr. Juca's pampered wife perceives her new palatial country home as a kind of "penal exile" (*degredo*) because Dr. Juca puts bars on the kitchen door and forbids the wives of workers to visit the kitchen as they had in the past, leaving his wife bereft of companionship.[2]

Lins do Rego's account was fictional, but his depiction of life on Fernando de Noronha was not fanciful. Many convicts like Zé Moleque became trusted prison workers upon whom staff relied. *Usina* does not depict convicts living the "Life of Riley" or as the victims of unrelenting brutality. Indeed, Lins do Rego in some ways idealizes the rustic lives of these convict workers on Fernando de Noronha in the same way his more influential colleague and friend Gilberto Freyre portrayed the lives of slaves during Brazil's empire. As Freyre put it: "When the era of rural patriarchalism had come to an end . . . and with the beginning of the industrial epoch of large factories, and of plantations and even ranches, run more often by city corporations than families, even in the rural areas the opposite poles—master and slave—which once formed a single complementary economic or social unit, became opposing halves of what had once been a whole. In any case, they grew indifferent to one another's fate."[3] Both Freyre and Lins do Rego believed that the modernization of sugar production made the lives of Brazilian rural laborers worse than those of slaves. Thus, Fernando de Noronha's convict laborers proved a fruitful foil to reflect upon Brazil's slave past in an era in which modernization in the forms of labor unrest, consumerism, sexual liberation, and the dissolution of the patriarchal family, among other trends, real and imagined, seemed to threaten what Freyre and Lins do Rego perceived as traditional Brazilian mores.[4]

Lins do Rego followed a long line of authors who, for different reasons, found Fernando de Noronha a useful foil. Convict society there had long been used to comprehend and define mainland social norms and the meanings of freedom. These institutions segregated but at the same time agglomerated individuals in ways that many characterized as "unnatural" and "unhealthy." Authorities repeatedly deplored the integration of convicts sentenced for different crimes with one another because it did not conform to the dictates of modern penology. They further lamented the agglomeration of convicts of different genders, civil conditions, colors, and ages with one another. The interactions of convicts, soldiers, employees, officers, unattached residents, and their families compounded this integration. While authorities at times deplored this integration, they also expressed support for it. Commanders resisted attempts to segregate slave convicts because it reversed the colony's traditions, and they feared it would undermine security.

Integration was not a new theme. Prisons were institutions where ideas of punishment, rehabilitation, and social leveling clashed with those of hierarchy. A text attributed to Cypriano José Barata de Almeida, a hero of Brazil's Independence and a radical Republican, criticized the exploitation of convict workers who labored on Rio de Janeiro's dikes in the 1820s. These prisoners were held at night in batch-living ship hulks, and army troops served as their warders. Almeida reflects on the integration of white and black convicts there:

> It was always the custom and practice in Brazil to treat with a certain distinction black prisoners from white ones so as not to sully the color of masters, and in this way conserve the maxims of aristocracy; but today the opposite is practiced, as if by intention [*como de propósito*]; and they say that this proves the desire that exists to integrate citizens into the liberal system that establishes equality, and to discredit our Constitution, they say also that this is done intentionally to make masters and whites nostalgic for the absolute government of the past and make them want to embrace it once again, so that once again, there could be separation of whites and blacks. They affirm that this, and moreover the many torments [suffered], are the guile of the bosses: Could this be true? I cannot decide, I only say what I hear, the truth is valid in all and for all.[5]

Almeida suggests that after independence officials no longer segregated convicts by color. Was it an attempt to drive a wedge between Brazilians of different colors, as some said, or an embrace of the liberal ideal of equality, as others thought? Almeida does not venture his own opinion, but leaves it to his reader to decide.

I think it is more likely that the state's need for cheap labor for public works, its lack of prison capacity, and the expense of maintaining prisoners separated on the basis of civil condition, much less color, made segregation impracticable. While special slave prisons existed in Brazil's major cities until the 1870s, most other jails and penitentiaries held slaves alongside free black, brown, indigenous, and white Brazilians. Rio de Janeiro's main penitentiary reported in 1880 that it held 651 prisoners, 250 of whom were slaves.[6] Likewise, on Fernando de Noronha, the determination of who should be exiled there was only partially determined by law. In practice, provincial authorities exercised latitude in selecting which convicts to exile. Oftentimes conditions moved officials to select convicts to exile: the overcrowding of mainland prisons, the outbreak of epidemic diseases, or the undisciplined behavior of particular convicts played a larger role in determining who ended up on the penal archipelago.

While Brazilian prisons and penal colonies forced authorities to grapple with integration, they were far from unique. Pernambuco's governor expressed the belief that government-organized indigenous communities should be integrated into civilized society, as opposed to the segregation Jesuits had practiced in colonial aldeias and, to some degree, Capuchin monks continued under the empire. In 1857, he pontificated: "It seems to me that our plan should not be, like that of the United States, to segregate the natives from the European race, rather we should understand how they ought to be mixed, and in the future it would be more convenient to include Indians in the general system of national colonization . . . and the population will march toward the homogeneity that we should thus long for."[7] Here U.S. indigenous policies served to distinguish Brazilian values. Racial homogeneity came from interaction and mixture in contrast to American segregationist policies designed to avert miscegenation. The governor's sentiments echoed those of War Minister Beaurepaire Rohan, who criticized the construction of urban penitentiaries in favor of frontier penal colonies where convicts and their families of all colors, including Indians, would integrate. This philosophy presaged that of General Cândido Mariano Rondon (a descendant of Terena Indians), who in 1910 founded the Indian Protection Service, which promoted the peaceful integration of unassimilated indigenous communities.[8] For these Brazilians, integration facilitated the "longed-for homogenization" through biological and cultural whitening.

On Fernando de Noronha authorities preferred to integrate slaves in convict companies to bolster their control over a penal population that was prone to sedition and that was, like Brazil's population, mostly nonwhite. Commanders warned that new policies that segregated slave convicts would create a common bond among them as members of a "pariah race." These policies had parallels in Brazil's army. The Duke of Caxias oversaw the disbanding of the all-black volunteer Zuavo units from Pernambuco and Bahia at the Paraguayan front in 1867. Both the free Zuavos and freedmen soldiers bought or donated for the war effort were ultimately intentionally integrated in army units along with convicts sent from Fernando de Noronha.[9]

This preference for integration was not so much a reflection of a high-minded dedication to liberal ideals of equality, as Almeida suggested, but was understood as practical compromises that improved security in institutions that incorporated the intractable poor. To underpin their integrationist arguments, commanders reminded mainland officials that it was the slave convict Agostinho Primeiro who had informed the administration of a convict insurrectionary plot that averted the loss of many innocent lives. In the 1880s, they referenced abolitionism to justify integrating slave convicts into different convict work companies, but these integrative practices had developed long before abolition became popular.

These ideas of integration extended to gender as officials abandoned colonial rules that prohibited women from living in the colony. This policy contradicted another goal of Beaurepaire Rohan's 1865 regulations, to *arranchar* or house all convicts in common barracks and feed them in mess kitchens that would have made the penal colony more of a total institution. Instead, officials allowed the wives and dependents of married convicts to join their husbands in exile and remitted a small number of female convicts. Some convicts married in the colony and others lived in consensual heterosexual unions. The policy presumed that convict heads of household needed to live in their own homes so they could protect and provide for their wives and dependents. Authorities tested the jealous institution's capacity to make convicts more disciplined and productive workers. Despite the policy's mixed results, officials did not lose faith in the sexual and gendered assumptions that undergirded it. Even those who questioned whether officials should concern themselves with convicts' wives and dependents argued that the jealous institution could be effective if properly regulated. As Lins do Rego gushed, "A woman on Fernando had the value of diamonds."[10]

Luso-Brazilian and Anglo-American law differed in the degree to which they embraced the individualism of liberal jurisprudence. The Brazilian state's confiscation of slave property without compensation held owners partly responsible for their slaves' crimes. This reflected patriarchal cultural expectations that held a head of household responsible for the actions of dependents. It differed from the more individualistic Anglo-American policy of compensating owners for slaves sentenced to death or transportation, which to a much greater extent uncoupled master and slave culpability.

The British historian Douglas Hay remarked on the salience of medicalized discourse in Ibero-American rhetoric on criminality compared to Britain and Anglo-America. Nineteenth-century English law stressed marketwise individual accountability: "The courts would not save you from your mistakes; the population had to be educated into risk-taking, entrepreneurial individualism."[11] This case study shows that one might add family, gender, class, and sexuality to the medicalized discourses Hay singles out. Conjugal penal living contrasts with individualized North Atlantic penal practices and highlights distinct views of male sexuality. Brazilian officials accommodated some poor heads of household, even when convicted of homicide, because they feared that by jailing a husband and father, the state could victimize innocent wives and dependents. As David Garland argues: "Punishment is not wholly explicable in terms of its purposes because no social artifact can be explained in this way. Like architecture or diet or clothing or table manners, punishment has an instrumental purpose, but also a cultural style and a historical tradition and a dependence upon institutional, technical, and discursive traditions."[12] Brazilian penal authorities sought to use the jealous institution in novel ways to harness the productive and reproductive capacity of penal colony convicts.

The laws, practices, and attitudes toward corporal punishment, the death penalty, and slavery also reveal contrasting penal styles and traditions among nations and empires. Pedro II did not have to take a stance against capital punishment, which earned him the ire of many slaveowners, but the roots of Brazilians' opposition to the gallows anchored in the discomfiture of being the last nation in the Americas to abolish slavery. If Brazilians could not beat the United States or the Spanish Caribbean in a race to abolish bondage, they could be among the first to abolish the death penalty.[13]

Another contrast between Brazilians and Americans is their practices and attitudes toward gender, color, and sexuality. In the U.S. South after the Civil War, most southern states abandoned their penitentiary projects in part because they would have led to the integration of white and black convicts. Instead, they opted for convict lease systems, chain gangs, and state farms that mostly sustained racial segregation as a guiding principle.[14] The earliest experiments with conjugal visits for American convicts began in the 1920s on Mississippi's Parchman Farm, where black and white convicts lived and worked segregated from one another. The farm's wardens brought in "colored" prostitutes to reward productive black convict workers but developed no similar program for white convicts. White authorities' assumptions about the lascivious nature of black men rationalized this race-specific policy. As one Parchman sergeant stated: "Give 'em some pork, some beans, some cornbread, some greens, and some poontang every now and then and they would work for you." This policy was modified when it became a public scandal in the 1930s. New rules allowed married convicts, white and black, the right to conjugal visits with their wives if they were well-behaved and productive. The blues anthem "The Midnight Special" described the train that left Jackson on Saturdays at midnight to bring convict wives to Parchman Farm on Sundays for conjugal visits.[15]

Beyond Fernando de Noronha, conjugal penal living had only faint twentieth-century echoes. In Taubaté, São Paulo, and Neves, Minas Gerais, officials built agricultural penal colonies that let married convicts live with their wives and dependents. These institutions, however, were poorly funded and too small to harbor but a fraction of married inmates.[16] A more distant resonance is heard in late twentieth-century justifications for conjugal prison visits. Clearly, conjugal visits are distinct from conjugal penal living, but their rationalization is strikingly similar. When the director of São Paulo's 35th Police District was asked what options he had to promote order among male prisoners in 1997, he replied without hesitation: "The [conjugal] visits. Their greatest concern is that someone will prohibit the visits of their female lovers [namoradas]."[17] The management of convict sexuality remains a thorny issue, and disputes over these rights have fueled massive prison uprisings in Brazil's painfully overcrowded twenty-first-century penitentiaries that have spilled into the streets of major urban centers.[18]

While imperial officials relied on marital status to make distinctions among members of the intractable poor, category drift threatened all free poor Brazilians regardless of color or former slave status, though it disproportionately targeted nonwhites. The threat of category drift was one way the state regulated the transition to free labor as slavery slowly declined, because it could subject the free poor to coercive labor extraction and imperil their freedom. The threat of category drift made members of the free poor vulnerable to the caprice of public officials and led many to seek out patrons who could protect them. In many instances, the threat of category drift may have made the free poor less likely to protest injustices, but at other times, it spawned violent mass protests. The War of the Triple Alliance catalyzed category drift to an unprecedented degree because military mobilization swept up not only the intractable poor but also a strata of the free poor who under normal circumstances were protected from military impressment. This experience combined with the decline of slavery made the free poor more prone to resist reforms that they believed threatened their status, such as the 1874 Recruitment Law and proposals to implement civil marriage.

Category drift, however, was a double-edged sword because wartime legislation led to human rights reforms for members of the intractable poor. This occurred not only because slaves, convicts, police, Indians, and National Guardsmen became army regulars but also because mobilization stimulated collateral reforms. Parliament recognized the rights of slave families when it freed the wives of enslaved men mobilized to fight on the front in 1866; then in 1869, it forbade sales that separated married slaves from one another and their children until the latter reached the age of fifteen. These reforms closely coincided with Fernando de Noronha's 1865 regulations that formalized a process whereby married convicts could petition to have their wives and dependents join them in exile. The 1871 Free Womb Law came about in part because of the emperor's interest in improving Brazil's international image after he promised French intellectuals and politicians in 1866 that his government would act to hasten slavery's demise at war's end. Similarly, Pedro's discussions with Victor Hugo and Adolphe Frank on a visit to France led him to commute all capital sentences to life imprisonment beginning in 1876. Wartime recruitment difficulties led to the ban on corporal punishment in the army in 1874, followed by restrictions on corporal punishments for convicts in 1878, and for slaves in 1886. This latter reform had the unintended consequence of spurring slaves to run away and resist the terms of their bondage to the extent that it undermined the organization of the agroexport economy from 1886 to 1888. This chaos led some former opponents of abolition to call for slavery's end. The timing, sequencing, and depth of these reforms illustrate the importance of considering institutional fit among categories of the intractable poor nationally and internationally. When one looks across these categories it becomes clear that reforms that improved the rights for one category made it more difficult to sustain for other categories. It also indicates that the War of the Triple Alliance played a larger role in hastening Brazil's human rights reforms, including slavery's abolition, than is commonly recognized.[19]

Compared to the United States, Brazilian authorities did not expend comparable resources to defend the privileges of "whiteness" on its social margins. On Fernando de Noronha the integration of convicts of different colors and civil conditions stemmed from practical considerations as well as evolving perceptions of slave status, color, morality, and modernity. These cultural attitudes may have derived to a considerable extent from the much larger size of Brazil's nonwhite population, which made the costs of protecting poor whites' privileges through policies of segregation too costly and unmanageable. But beyond these material limitations, a Brazilian preference for integration is visible not only in state institutions that inducted the intractable poor, but also in the elite's ideology of whitening through race mixture and subsidized European immigration. At the other end of the social scale, however, when a Brazilian of color experienced upward social mobility and assumed putative whiteness, jocular and biting references to color could surface to contain or obstruct that mobility.[20] In contrast, American government, businesses, and labor unions went to considerable expense to police the evolving lower boundaries of whiteness. Authorities in the United States even preoccupied themselves with the dignity of dishonored white convicts by maintaining segregation in many southern penal institutions. Even at the federal level, white soldiers remained segregated from black troops until the Korean War (1950–1953).[21] The dispositions of Brazilian and U.S. authorities toward integration in basic institutions reveal strikingly different cultural assumptions about color.

Instead of defending the lower boundaries of whiteness, Brazilian institutions that harbored the intractable poor more often used marriage and conjugal living as a means to rank, reward, and discriminate among them. Authorities even defended the rights and responsibilities of poor married men sentenced to life imprisonment to live with their wives and dependents in penal exile. Color and civil condition influenced the chances that the members of the intractable poor had to achieve marriage and avoid category drift, but there were intriguing contradictions in Brazil's status hierarchies. For instance, marriage and bondage legally protected men from military impressment, but whiteness did not. Poor white men were underrepresented among enlisted men and convicts, but authorities did not police a firm line of segregation based on color or civil condition at these lower social margins in basic institutions. Brazilian institutions that incorporated the intractable poor more often lumped them together regardless of color or condition, but the respect for the jealous institution's power to maintain a just and moral social order was pervasive and durable at the lower end of the social scale, unlike whiteness.

Beyond Brazil's *senzalas*, barracks, and the aldeia, can the jealous institution open other comparative vistas? For example, is there a connection between Brazilian plantation owners' promotion of formal slave marriage and their preference for contracting Italian immigrant families in the 1880s and 1890s? Reid Andrews hints at this when he argues that many ex-slaves avoided work conditions similar to slavery. They sought to establish their homes far from the big house and former slave barracks. They also preferred to keep their female dependents from doing field or domestic work where they might be abused. This made ex-slaves less attractive employees for planters than immigrant families who were more willing to put their wives and children to work in the fields.[22]

Further afield, French, British, and Russian penal colonies made similar uses of the jealous institution to reward well-behaved convicts and to populate far-flung territories. In France's New Caledonia, male convicts could earn "tickets of leave, grants of land, and the right to marry or—if already married—the right to have their wives and families sent from France at state expense to live with them." French authorities encouraged marriage between well-behaved male and female convicts who lived segregated from one another in penal exile when they were single. Courtship was initiated by "the intended bridegroom [who] is always in possession of a cottage and a plot of land . . . [and] after their marriage, the convict couple become probationary free colonists." One observer noted that this was a return to a practice common before the Revolution when the crown exiled *forçats*—convicts released from the galleys on the condition that they marry a female convict and agree to transportation to Louisiana or Canada.[23]

While Anglophone masters resisted formal slave marriage, British officials encouraged convict marriage in Australia. Arthur Phillip made land grants to well-disciplined male convicts who married female convicts. In Tasmania, where single female convicts were housed in separate barracks, married convicts lived in their own private households. Since male convicts greatly outnumbered females in both colonies (five to one in Australia), authorities could be quite choosy about which convict men could be granted this privilege. Australian officials even permitted some black convicts (former soldiers) to marry white wives. In this case, it seems that officials' desire to people their possessions overcame Anglophone fears of miscegenation.[24]

On the Russian penal colony island of Sakhalin, part of the convict population dwelt in barracks-like quarters in the hard-labor prison. After convicts served the majority of their sentence, they became "reformees" and could live outside the prison, build their own home, marry, and possess money. Anton Chekhov, who visited Sakhalin in 1890, reported that 860 married convicts lived with wives and dependents and another 782 lived in consensual unions out of 5,905 convicts of both genders. Chekhov remarked incisively on the contradictions Sakhalin's multiple institutional missions posed:

> A prison is antagonistic to a colony, and their interests are in inverse ratio to each other. Life in the communal cells reduces a prisoner to a serf, and in the course of time, makes him a degenerate; the habits of the life of the herd stifle within him the instincts of a permanently settled man and domesticated householder; his health declines, he grows old and weakens morally, and the later he leaves the prison the more reasons there are to fear that he will not turn out an active, useful member of the colony, but merely a burden to it.[25]

If one exchanged "serf" for "slave," the passage could easily fit with Brazilian commentaries about batch living in senzalas, barracks, prisons, and

Fernando de Noronha's aldeia. The Russian, French, and British cases encouraged former convicts to stay on as settlers, whereas families on Fernando de Noronha had to return to the mainland when a convict completed a sentence or died. In this sense, Fernando de Noronha was definitively more of a site for punishment than settlement.

Beyond comparative penal colonization, the jealous institution's influence might be profitably applied to live-in labor. Raffaella Sarti's survey of domestic servants and marriage in Europe from the sixteenth through the nineteenth century shows that employers usually allowed trusted male live-in servants to marry after years of service, and when they did, most established a private domicile. Conversely, when female domestics married, most left their employment or their employers dismissed them. This shows the gender divide between jealous and greedy institutions.[26] Similarly, the jealous institution could be applied to the policies of company towns. Recent research on Chilean mining towns, for instance, highlights how employers privileged married miners in hiring and provided them separate homes while bachelors were housed in barracks. The employers believed married miners would stem worker turnover and be less prone to labor radicalism. The logic bears a likeness to that of Brazilian slaveowners and army officers who managed bondsmen, soldiers, and convicts.[27]

This case study has highlighted parallels in how authorities regulated the jealous institution among the intractable poor men in total institutions. As Robert Slenes and others have argued, slave marriage is a story of subordinates pushing for rights within the limited horizons of bondage, where the rights to wed, establish a private household, and work a provision ground likened their status to that of free sharecroppers, or what Sydney Mintz termed a "slave peasantry."[28] Some masters felt that marriage was compatible with bondage, but as Sandra Lauderdale Graham showed, slaves could "say no" to match-making masters. Slenes cautions that family ties provided slaves with new capacities and reasons to resist. Still, Lauderdale Graham critiques Slenes for overstating the degree to which masters allowed their slaves to wed as part of, in her words, a "deliberately formed strategy of persistent manipulation." She feels that "more mundane explanations suffice," and states that Brazilians "generally found family a useful way of ordering society, their own slaves included."[29] I agree, but only a minority achieved nuptials. Graham adds that there is no "detailed, persuasive evidence for their [masters'] intentionality" in permitting slave marriage. A dearth of sources frustrate attempts to establish masters' motives in this regard.

If one looks beyond the slave regime, however, patterns appear in how superiors regulated the jealous institution within total institutions that incorporated the intractable poor. The parallels at the very least suggest a more conscious policy of using conjugality to rank, reward, and discriminate among intractable poor laborers. This probably does not rise to Graham's idea of a "deliberately formed strategy of persistent manipulation," but she may be setting the bar too high given that, as this case study shows, the decisions made by subordinates and those who permitted them to marry or to live with a consensual heterosexual lover were not singular but multifarious.

In analyses of the Brazilian poor's stratification, marital status and kinship have received less attention than color and legal condition, but powerful actors often privileged them. B. J. Barickman hints at this in his analysis of the 1835 Iguape, Bahia, census: "Thus acknowledgement of kinship—far more so than 'quality' or color, as an indication of known African ancestry or birth—serves within the census to distinguish free residents from slaves."[30] The stereotype of slaves living wantonly outside of family reinforced discrimination against them, but marriage was also a means of discriminating among them. The exercise of kinship ties could ameliorate conditions in the aldeia, senzala, and barracks, but that does not mean that everyone sought them or could achieve them. Indeed, the concern with this distinction appears strongest in the minds of authorities responsible for managing intractable poor laborers. In the senzala, the barracks, and the aldeia, good behavior, hard work, and marriage marked respectability, but these privileges could be curtailed or abrogated if household heads or dependents became disorderly or indolent. Given the evidence presented here, it seems unlikely that these strategies really gave masters, officers, or warders greater leverage with subordinates, but that they practiced similar strategies in such varied settings reveals an enduring and widespread conviction that they were effective. In this sense, convicts foiled Brazilian authorities again and again on Fernando de Noronha because they never achieved the kind of control over inmates that they hoped to with modern penitentiary practices or conjugal penal living.

These reflections shine a light on a poorly illuminated legal corner in the on again, off again debates of Frank Tannenbaum's *Slave and Citizen* (1946). In no way do I endorse the concept of milder Ibero-American slavery, which any invocation of Tannenbaum risks, but this case study takes a different tack than most. Generally, Tannenbaum's critics show that laws protecting slaves in Ibero- and Franco-America did not shield them from the abuses of their masters or other more powerful actors. In this case study, however, the law is harsher than the actual punishment rendered in most instances, especially in terms of the death penalty and perpetual galleys. Does this mean that Brazilian slavery was milder or that masters were more compassionate than their counterparts in Protestant America? Certainly not, but it does highlight the importance of different legal and cultural traditions, linked to diverging paths toward slavery's abolition, that shaped law and practice in terms of capital punishment, segregation, color, and gender.[31]

I hope this study has demonstrated the utility of examining an isolated penal colony to illuminate broader issues in Brazilian and Atlantic history from gender, sexuality, and family to contraband, corruption, crime, and insurrection. The richness of this penal plantation's records makes it a unique yet revealing case study when compared to mainland coercive labor regimes. The comparison of reform for categories of the intractable poor uncovers patterns that bring new insight into the arts of domination, collaboration, exploitation, and resistance.[32] I believe these regional and international comparisons demonstrate the importance of integrating South Atlantic perspectives to build a more truly Atlantic-wide optic to the evolution of human rights. While Fernando de Noronha's use as a national prison for political prisoners would be briefly reprised in the twentieth century, today the archipelago's jurisdiction is divided between Pernambuco and a federal nature preserve. High-end foreign and Brazilian tourists travel there to enjoy this UNESCO Natural World Heritage Site's pristine beaches and reefs. In this sense, the American novelist Frank Carpenter's depiction of Fernando de Noronha as an "ocean resort" proved prescient, but most nineteenth-century convicts would not have recognized his flip depiction of their isle of exile. Indeed, most convicts sought their freedom from this alleged paradise as soon as an opportunity arose.

APPENDIX
Statistical Tables

TABLE A1 Crime Data from Pernambuco's Police Chief, Selected Years

Crime	1870	1871	1872	1873	1874	1875	Total	Selected Total (%)
			YEAR					
Resisting arrest	13	3	13	7	9	4	49	1.9
Prison escapes	12	3	14	34	12	1	76	2.9
Disobedience	0	9	6	0	0	1	16	*
Counterfeiting	0	0	6	8	0	0	14	*
Against an individual's liberty	0	0	1	1	0	0	2	*
Homicide	103	64	87	97	110	84	545	21.2
Attempted homicide	42	20	20	31	12	9	134	5.2
Infanticide	0	0	2	0	2	0	4	*
Abortion	1	7	11	13	0	0	32	1.2
Injury	54	28	171	278	149	159	839	32.6
Threats	2	0	6	2	0	0	10	*
Enter another's house	2	0	0	0	0	0	2	*
Rape	1	0	8	3	2	1	15	*
Kidnapping (*rapto*)	0	0	0	1	0	0	1	*
Attempted kidnapping	0	0	0	0	1	0	1	*
Defamation (*columnia*)	0	0	6	1	2	1	10	*
Petty theft (*furto*)	31	9	120	56	22	49	287	11.2
Bankruptcy (*bancarrota*)	12	28	8	7	0	18	73	2.8

(*continued*)

TABLE A1 (*continued*)

Crime	1870	1871	1872	1873	1874	1875	Total	Selected Total (%)
			YEAR					
Damages (*damno*)	1	5	2	1	0	0	9	*
Grand larceny (*roubo*)	17	4	31	31	17	14	114	4.4
Attempted robbery	63	17	2	10	0	0	92	3.6
Offences against public morality	0	0	76	129	0	0	205	7.9
Illicit gatherings	0	0	0	15	0	0	15	*
Illegal weapons	4	2	19	2	0	0	27	1.1
Total	358	199	609	727	338	341	2,572	

Source: Pernambuco, *Falla . . . desembargador Henrique Pereira de Lucena . . .* (Recife: Typ. de M. Figueiroa e F. & Filhos, 1875), 13–14.

*Less than 1%.

TABLE A2 Number of Crimes and Arrests in Pernambuco in 1874

	Crimes	Criminals	Captured Red-Handed (*em flagrante*)	At Large (*evadidos*)
Resisting arrest	9	19	10	9
Jail break	12	8	8	0
Homicide	110	119	58	61
Attempted homicide	12	13	3	10
Infanticide	2	4	4	0
Grave injuries	95	121	62	59
Light injuries	54	56	38	18
Rape	2	2	2	0
Attempted abduction	1	11	8	0
Petty theft	22	23	21	2
Defamation	2	2	0	2
Grand larceny	17	33	16	17
Total	338	411	230	178

Source: Pernambuco, *Falla . . . desembargador Henrique Pereira de Lucena . . .* (Recife: Typ. de M. Figueiroa e F. & Filhos, 1875), 13–14.

TABLE A3 Monthly Salaries of Officers, Employees, and Convicts in 1869

Commander (*comandante*)	444:000
Garrison commander (*major da praça*)	254:000
Secretary (*secretário*)	235:000
Chaplain (*capelão*)	91:000
Head chaplain (*capelão contrado*)	156:000
Surgeon (*cirugião*)	192:000
Pharmacist (*boticário*)	126:000
Warehouse manager (*almoxerife*)	99:999
Lieutenant of artillery (*tenente artilharia*)	40:000
Nonconvict sergeant (*sargento commandante das companhias*)	66:666
Assistant to the secretary (*amanuense da secretária*)	15:000
Nurse (*enfermeiro*)	9:000
Nurse's aide (*ajudante enfermeiro*)	6:000
Sacristan (*sacristão*)	6:000
Convict work company sergeant (*sargento de cia. dos condenados*)	15:000
Warehouse guard (*guarda almoxerifado*)	9:000
Work company corporals (*cabos*)	9:000
Master craftsmen (*mestre de oficinas*)	15:000
Artisan workers (*operários*)	6:000
Employee who records who is present (*apontador*)	12:000
Common convict laborer	3:220*
Nominal price of a young adult slave in 1870	1:425:000**

Sources: Tabella dos diarios para os sentenciados do Presidio de Fernando de Noronha, FN, March 20, 1869, APEJE, l. FN-14, f. 81; Folha de pagamento dos empregados do presidio de Fernando de Noronha, FN, Jan. 1, 1869, APEJE, l. FN-14, f. 18.

*This number was not represented on the table but was based on an estimation of 140 réis day wage for common convict laborer multiplied by an estimated average of twenty-three work days per month.

**Peter Eisenberg, *The Sugar Industry in Pernambuco, 1840–1910* (Berkeley: University of California Press, 1974), 153.

TABLE A4 Daily Wages for Convict and Civilian Workers Proposed by Pernambuco's Treasury and the Commander in 1886

	Proposed by the Treasury	Proposed by the Commander	Civilian Employees
15 Company sergeants (*guardas de turmas*)	1,300	800	1,600
1 Arsenal manager (*encarregado do arsenal*)	500	800	1,600
1 Cemetery manager (*dito de céméterio*)	400	800	1,600
1 Night school teacher (*professor aula nocturna*)	500	1,000	—
4 Master craftsmen (*mestres de oficinas*)	300	800	2,000
8 Scriveners (*coajuvantes de escritura*)	300	800	—
2 Barbers (*barbeiros*)	300	800	—
1 Arsenal employee (*apontador de arsenal*)	300	600	—
1 Head nurse (*enfermeiro mor*)	300	600	—
1 Telegraph operator (*encarregado de telegrapho*)	300	600	—
1 Maestro (*dito de música*)	300	400	—
4 Nurses (*enfermeiros*)	200	400	—
8 Warehouse workers (*serventes do almoxerifado*)	200	400	—
1 Pharmacy employee (*dito de farmácia*)	200	400	—
1 Sacristan (*sacristão*)	200	400	—
1 Arsenal doorman (*porteiro de arsenal*)	200	400	—
1 Infirmary worker (*dispenseiro da enfermaria*)	200	400	—
60 Artisan workers (*operários das oficinas*)	200	blank	blank
75 Company corporals (*chefes de secção*)	200	300	—
1 Telegraph assistant (*Ajudante de telegraphista*)	200	300	—
1 Sailboat pilot (*mestre de balsa de carga*)	200	300	—
2 Head cowboys (*encarregados de gado*)	0	300	—
1 Jailor (*carcereiro*)	0	800	—
1 Infirmary scrivener (*escrevente da enfermaria*)	0	400	—
1 Jailor's assistant	0	400	—

Source: MGPL ao JFCP, FN, Mar. 9, 1886, APEJE, l. FN-25, f. 115.

TABLE A5 List of Storeowners on Fernando de Noronha in 1858, the Value of the Stock, and Their Business Associates

1. Antonio Nunes de Oliveira: 6:000$000
2. Dionísio Joaquim Madeira: 3:000$000
3. José Caetano Teixeira da Silva (associate of Raimundo José de Souza Lobo): 6:000$000
4. Manoel Thomaz dos Santos: 1:500$000
5. Joaquim Rodrigues Maia de Oliveira: 2:000$000
6. Francelino José dos Santos Costa Monteiro (associate of the convict Manoel José dos Santos Leal): 2:800$000
7. Maria Fonseca da Conceição (associate of the convict Manoel Rodrigues do Nascimento): 1:200$000
8. Damiana Rosa Betancourt (wife of the convict José Prudencio Betancourt): 800$000
9. José dos Santos Neves (associate of his brother Manoel Saturnino dos Santos Neves): 600$000
10. Mariana Augusta Coelho (wife of the convict João Ignacio do Coelho): 300$000
11. Bernardina Maria de Santana (wife of the convict Manoel Rodrigues Baracho): 900$000
12. Genuino Gomes Soares Lopes: 300$000
13. Thomas José Pereira Guimaraes: 400$000
14. Graciano José de Freitas: 1:000$000

Source: Infomação das casas de comercio que existem nesta ilha, AGL ao BAMJ, FN, Jan. 1, 1858, APEJE, FN-7, no f. nos.

TABLE A6 Convict Origins (*Naturalidade*) in Matriculation Books (n. 960)

National			International	
Northeast	728	81.6%	Africa	36
North	21	2.4%	Portugal	19
Southeast	108	12.0%	Italy	5
Central West	2	0.2%	Uruguay	3
South	33	3.7%	USA	1
"Brazilian"	1	0.1%	France	1
	893	100.0%	Greece	1
			Paraguay	1
				67

Source: FNCD.

TABLE A7 Civil Condition

	Guia	Matriculation	Combined	
Free citizen	170	645	815	56.6%
Slave	16	205	221	15.4%
Índio	7	1	8	*
Soldado imperial	62	206	268	18.6%
Liberto	2	1	3	*
Artifício (Arsenal)	0	1	1	*
Marinheiro imperial	1	11	12	*
National Guard	1	0	1	*
No information	88	22	110	7.6%
Total	347	1092	1,439	100%

Source: FNCD.

*Less than 1%.

TABLE A8 Convict Professions

Farmer (*agricultor, roceiro, lavrador, vive de lavouras*)	281	25.8%
No information	267	24.5%
No occupation (*sem ofício*)	253	23.2%
Cobbler (*sapateiro*)	56	5.2%
Carpenter (*carapina, carpinteiro*)	29	2.8%
Mason (*pedreiro, canteiro*)	26	2.5%
Domestic service (*serviços domésticos*)	21	2.0%
Tailor (*alfaiate*)	16	1.6%
Cowboy (*vaqueiro, campeiro*)	15	1.5%
Seamen (*marítimo, marinheiro, embarcadiço, embarcadero*)	15	1.5%
Day worker (*jornaleiro, trabalhador*)	9	*
Fisherman (*pescador*)	8	*
Cooper (*tanoeiro*)	8	*
Businessman, clerk, peddler (*comerciante, negociante, comércio*)	7	*
Blacksmith (*ferreiro*)	6	*
Cook (*cozinheiro*)	6	*
Pottery/brick maker (*oleiro*)	5	*
Coach driver (*carreiro*)	5	*
Muleteer (*tropeiro*)	4	*
Furniture maker (*marceneiro*)	4	*
Baker (*padeiro*)	3	*
Master sugar processor (*mestre de assucar*)	2	*
Seamstress (*costureira*)	2	*
Sawyer (*serrador, serralheiro*)	2	*
Gold prospector (*garimpeiro*)	2	*
Launderer (*engomador*)	2	*
Soldier (*soldado*)	2	*
Painter (*pintor*)	2	*
Caulker (*calafate*)	2	*
Others	32	*
Total	1,092	100%

Source: FNCD

*Less than 1%.

TABLE A9 Color of Inmates Combined from 1830 to the 1880s (n. 1004)*

White		Light Brown		Dark Brown		Black		Indigenous and Black		Indigenous	
Branca	196	Parda clara	25	Cabra	13	Preta	237	Cafuz	6	Caboclo	39
		Morena	8	Parda	349	Crioulo	6	Cafuz forro	1	Indio	11
		Semi-branca	28	Parda escura	40	Fula	23			Mameluco	3
		Trigueira	1	Mulata	9	Criola fula	1			Caboclo claro	1
		Mulatto clara	5	Cabra escura	1						
				Alaranjada	1						
	196		67		413		267		7		54
	19.6%		6.7%		41%		26.6%		0.7%		5.4%

Source: FNCD.

*No information on color for 435 convicts survey in Matriculation and Guia records.

TABLE A10 Literacy and Color

	Literate	Illiterate	No Information	Literacy Rate
Color unknown	7	35	213	17%
Light brown	12	44	2	21%
Dark brown	66	244	40	21%
Indigenous	10	27	9	27%
Black	23	202	23	10%
White	64	59	15	52%
Total	182	611	302	

Source: FNCD.

TABLE A11 Convict Crimes

	Guia	Matr.	Combined	
Homicide	158	747	905	62.9%
Attempted homicide	2	16	18	1.3%
Attempted homicide against superiors (military)	25	8	33	2.3%
Physical injury	8	58	66	4.6%
Desertion	28	18	46	3.2%
Counterfeiting (*moedas falsas*)	27	10	37	2.6%
Seduction (*defloramento*)	0	5	5	0.3%
Larceny (*roubo and furto*)	42	44	86	6.0%
Resistance	0	3	3	0.2%
Insubordination (military)	0	6	6	0.3%
Revolt (*sublevação*)	5	0	5	0.3%
Aiding or allowing prisoners to escape	0	2	2	0.1%
Reduce someone to slavery (*reduzir a escravidão*)	5	0	5	0.3%
Other	7	1	8	0.7%
No information provided	40	174	214	14.9%
Total	347	1,092	1,439	100.0%

Source: FNCD

TABLE A12 Sentences Recorded in Matriculation Books

Perpetual galleys *(galés perpétuas)*	416
Temporary galleys *(galés temporárias)*	76
Prison at hard labor *(prisão com trabalho)*	123
Simple incarceration *(prisão simples)*	297
Life imprisonment *(carrinho perpétuo)*	45
Life imprisonment *(prisão perpétua)*	12
Life imprisonment at hard labor *(prisão perpétua com trabalho)*	22
Capital punishment *(pena última)*	67
No information	34
Total	1,092

Source: FNCD.

TABLE A13 Sentences According to a Prisoner's Civil Condition

CIVIL CONDITION

Sentence	Unknown	Slave	Free	Indian	Imperial Army	Freedman	Arsenal Worker	Imperial Sailor	Total
Unlisted	10	2	18		4				34
Perpetual galleys	3	147	224		36	1		5	416
Temporary galleys	2	1	48		23			2	76
Prison at labor	3		44		76				123
Simple prison	4	4	286	1	2				297
Perpetual *carrinho*					43		1	1	45
Life at labor		7	4		1				12
Life in prison		2	11		7			2	22
Capital punishment		42	10		14			1	67
Total	22	205	645	1	206	1	1	11	1,092

Source: FNCD.

TABLE A14 Population of the Island of Fernando de Noronha on Jan. 1, 1891

Category	#	Wives	CHILDREN		CREADOS		AGREGADOS		Totals
			Male	Female	Male	Female	Male	Female	
Civilian employees	13	9	19	6	0	1	1	2	51
Military officers	5	5	5	8	2	1	0	0	26
Military *praças*	69	11	7	9	0	0	0	0	96

Famílias dos sentenciados	WOMEN		CHILDREN		CREADOS		AGREGADOS		
	Casadas	Single	Male	Female	Male	Female	Male	Female	
	108	40	195	139	0	0	6	0	488

	MEN	WOMEN	
Sentenciados	1,161	25	1,186
Total population			1,847

Source: Relatorio do Director Joaquim Gusmão Coelho ao Cidadão Desembargador José Antonio Correia da Silva, Governador do Estado de Pernambuco, FN, Jan. 1, 1891, APEJE, l. FN-30, f. 2.

TABLE A15 Race, Legitimacy, Nationality, and Marital Status of Wives and Women of Convicts, Jan. 1, 1890

						Married with convicts			
Brancas	60	37%	Legitimate	141		112		*Brasileiras*	160
Semi-brancas	3	2%	Illegitimate	20	*Amasiadas* with convicts	44		*Portuguesa*	1
Caboclas	10	6%	*Exposta*	1	*Parentas* (relatives)	6		*Alemã*	1
Mameluca	1	1%							
Pardas	78	48%							
Pretas	10	6%							
Total	162	100%		162		162			162

Source: Relatorio do Director Joaquim Gusmão Coelho ao Cidadão Desembargador José Antonio Correia da Silva, Governador do Estado de Pernambuco, FN, Jan. 1, 1891, APEJE, l. FN-30, f. 2.

TABLE A16 Classifications of Fernando de Noronha's Population Selected Years

	1847	1852*	1854	1858	1869	1873	1874	1878	1885	1886	1891
Employees and officers	10	12	10	15	21	11	12	18	18	16	18
Staff family members	56	52	28	290#	43	31	26	22	51	60	59
NCOs and soldiers	78	98	155	182	199	127	126	202	160	175	69
Enlisted men's family	21	2	10	#	9	5	27	35	46	74	27
Civil convicts	227	305	369	603	991	1,183	1,441	1,355	1,201	1,216	1,186
Civil convict family members	58	87	78	#	276	324	241	311	375	500	488
Military convicts	N/a	N/a	N/a	33	242	231	234	296	286	251	N/a
Military convict family	N/a	N/a	N/a	#	N/a	N/a	N/a	N/a	N/a	N/a	N/a
Vivandeiros	N/a	N/a	N/a	#	13	12	11	N/a	0	0	N/a
Vivandeiro family members	N/a	N/a	N/a	#	7	0	7	N/a	0	0	N/a
Unattached residents	19	52	36	#	60	6	59	N/a	26	0	N/a
Unattached family	22	37	22	#	38	0	51	N/a	0	0	N/a
Others	1†	2	2	0	13‡	0	27	N/a	0	19	N/a
Others family	6	10	0	0	7	0	59	N/a	0	24	N/a
Slaves	N/a	0	0	10	12	9	11	3	2	3	0
Total	498	657	710	1,133	1,931§	1,939	2,332	2,242	2,165	2,338	1,847

Sources: Mappa estatística dos habitantes da Ilha de Fernando de Noronha, FN, Aug. 8, 1847, APEJE, l. FN-3, F. 97; Mappa estatística . . . , FN, Jan. 1, 1854, APEJE, l. FN; Mappa estatística . . . , FN, Jan. 1, 1858, APEJE, l. FN-7, f. 15, f. 10; Mappa estatística . . . , FN, Jan. 1, 1869, APEJE, l. FN-13, f. 1–17; Mappa estatística . . . , FN, Dec. 31, 1873, APEJE, l. FN-16, f. 291–330; Mappa estatística . . . , FN, Jan. 1, 1874, APEJE, l. FN-16, f. 182–198; Mappa estatística . . . , FN, June 30, 1878, APEJE, l. FN-19, f. 10; Mappa estatística . . . , FN, Jan. 1, 1883, APEJE, l. FN-22, f. 13; Mappa estatística . . . , FN, Jan. 1, 1886, APEJE, l. FN-24, f. 2; Relatorio do Director Joaquim Gusmão Coelho ao Cidadão Desembargador José Antonio Correia da Silva, Governador do Estado de Pernambuco, FN, Jan. 1, 1891, APEJE, l. FN-30, f. 2.

Note: Unfortunately, commanders did not use consistent categories to report on the presidio's population. In 1847 † — *Anistiados*, amnestied. *The 1852 chart does not distinguish between convicts or employees and their families, but it does distinguish gender and age. I lumped together those aged under twenty as children and women as children. Others—In 1852 and 1854, *presos do governo* as opposed to *sentenciados*; in 1874, *pertencente ao destacamento* (probably wives, *amásias*, and children). Grouped under family of all convicts whether military or civilian. #—In 1858, instead of families and other categories, the data designates only "free people" (*pessoas livres*): 18 men, 115 women, 87 *meninos*, 70 *meninas*, and 1 *preso do governo*. ‡ — *agregados* (nonfamily free household dependents) and *paisanos*. §—The commander's report for 1869 notes there were 1,934 souls resident on the island, but when he details and enumerates the different categories of residents it totals only 1,931. Thus, I use the latter number.

TABLE A17 Inmates on Fernando de Noronha Island Penal Colony on Nov. 16, 1881, by
Classification and Sentence

Sentence	FREE CIVILIANS		SLAVES		FOREIGNERS		Military Totals
	Male	Female	Male	Female	Male	Female	
Galés perpétuas	260	3	243	1	8	1	128	644
Prisão perpétua	8	10	3	5	0	0	0	26
Galés temporária	75	0	3	0	17	0	0	95
Prisão com trabalho	41	0	0	0	1	0	160	202
Prisão simples	486	12	5	0	2	0	0	505
Penas capitais	3	0	2	0	0	0	0	5
Sentenças ignoradas	90	0	0	0	0	0	0	90
Totals	963	25	256	6	28	1	288	1,567

Source: FJPL ao JASL, FN, Nov. 16, 1881, APEJE, l. FN-21, no f. nos.

TABLE A18 Provinces That Sentenced Slave Convicts on Fernando de Noronha, 1881

	#	Rough %		#	Rough %
Amazonas	1	0.3	Espírito Santo	1	0.3
Pará	4	1.5	Rio de Janeiro (Province)	24	9.1
Maranhão	12	4.5	Corte (Capital District)	3	1.5
Ceará	10	3.8	São Paulo	47	17.8
Piauí	0	0.0	Minas Gerais	33	12.5
RGN	3	1.1	Paraná	1	0.3
Paraíba	9	3.4	Santa Catarina	1	0.3
Pernambuco	64	24.2	RGS	17	6.4
Alagoas	2	0.7	Mato Grosso	1	0.3
Sergipe	4	1.5	Goiás	0	0.0
Bahia	19	7.2	No information	8	3.0
Total				264	

Source: Capitão Antonio Gracindo de Gusmão Lobo, "Relação nominal de escravos sentenciados," FN, Oct. 27, 1881, APEJE, l. FN-21, no f. nos.

TABLE A19 Slave Convicts on Fernando de Noronha in 1881 by Region

	#	%
North	5	1.8
Northeast	123	46.6
Southeast	108	40.9
South	19	7.2
Central West	1	0.3
No information	8	3.0
Total	264	100

Source: Capitão Antonio Gracindo de Gusmão Lobo, "Relação nominal de escravos sentenciados," FN, Oct. 27, 1881, APEJE, l. FN-21, no f. nos.

TABLE A20 Provinces That Sentenced Free Convicts on Fernando de Noronha, 1881

	#	Rough %		#	Rough %
Amazonas	0	0	Espírito Santo	2	0.2
Pará	4	0.3	Rio de Janeiro	12	1.0
Maranhão	28	2.2	Federal Capital	63	4.9
Ceará	17	1.3	São Paulo	10	0.8
Piauí	5	0.4	Minas Gerais	18	1.4
RGN	8	0.6	Paraná	3	0.2
Paraíba	6	0.5	Santa Catarina	4	0.3
Pernambuco	492	38.3	RGS	119	9.3
Alagoas	6	0.5	Mato Grosso	11	0.9
Sergipe	0	0	Goiás	0	0.0
Bahia	14	1.1	Paraguay	20	1.6
Uruguay	5	0.4	No information	439	34.1
Total				1,286	

Source: Capitão Antonio Gracindo de Gusmão Lobo, "Relação nominal de escravos sentenciados," FN, Oct. 27, 1881, APEJE, l. FN-21, no f. nos.

TABLE A21 Years That Select National Military Branches First Formally Banned Flogging

Army	Navy
Britain, 1881	Britain, 1949
Brazil, 1874	Brazil, 1923
Russia, 1874	Russia, 1904
Venezuela, 1873	USA, (1850) 1862
USA, (1812) 1861	Portugal, 1896
Colombia, (1845)	Germany, 1872
Mexico, 1824	France, 1860
Prussia, 1808	Spain, 1826
	Mexico, 1824

Note: The dates for Britain and Brazil mark when flogging was suspended but not banned. Britain's Parliament banned flogging for soldiers on home service in 1868, but it still could be used against those abroad or on campaign, although only for serious offenses. The U.S. Congress banned flogging soldiers in 1812, but it did not ban other cruel punishments for soldiers in the U.S. Army. Similarly, Congress passed a limited reform of corporal punishment for sailors in 1850 and then completely banned the practice in 1862. I thank Olga Gonzalez for sharing laws from Colombia and Venezuela with me; *Recopilacion de leyes y decretos de Venezuela*, vol. 5, 2nd ed. (Caracas: Casa Editorial de "La Opinion Nacional," 1890). In 1845, Colombia outlawed corporal punishment with "palos" or sticks, but it is unclear whether there was a complete abolition of corporal punishments for soldiers; *Recopilación Granadina, 1845*, Tratado sexto, parte 1 (Junio 10 de 1833), capitulo 7, art. 74.

TABLE A22 Selected Nations That De Jure Abolished or Limited the Death Penalty's Application in Civil Crimes by Year (Year Capital Punishment for Political Crimes Was Abolished)

1. Venezuela, 1863 (1849)	8. Norway, 1905
2. Portugal, 1867*	9. Uruguay, 1910
3. Netherlands, 1870	10. Colombia, 1910 (1886)
4. Costa Rica, 1882	11. Argentina, 1921 (1853)
5. Brazil, 1889; de facto, 1876	12. Mexico, 1931 (1917)**
6. Ecuador, 1897 (1851)	13. Britain, 1965
7. Panama, 1903 (never instated)	14. Spain, 1978
	15. France, 1981

Source: Roger Hood, *The Death Penalty: A Worldwide Perspective* (New York: Oxford University Press, 2002), 55 n. 144;

*Portugal abolished the death penalty for murder in 1867 but had not executed anyone since 1849.

**Abolition of the death penalty in most Mexican states. In Mexico, a contingent abolition of the death penalty for political crimes became part of the 1857 Constitution; Patrick Timmons, "Seed of Abolition: Experience and Culture in the Desire to End Capital Punishment in Mexico, 1841–1857," in *The Cultural Lives of Capital Punishment: Comparative Perspectives*, ed. Austin Sarat and Christian Boulanger (Stanford: Stanford University Press, 2005), 69–91.

TABLE A23 Dates for the Abolition of Slavery in Selected Nations and Colonies

1. Haiti, 1804	8. Ecuador, 1851
2. Mexico, 1829	9. Argentina, 1853
3. Bolivia, 1831	10. Venezuela, 1854
4. British Colonies, 1833	11. Peru, 1855
5. Uruguay, 1842	12. United States, 1865
6. French Colonies, 1848	13. Cuba, 1886
7. Colombia, 1851	14. Brazil, 1888

ABBREVIATIONS

EUB	Estados Unidos do Brasil
f.	folha
FN	Fernando de Noronha
FNCD	Fernando de Noronha Convict Database
IBGE	Instituto Brasileiro de Geografia e Estatística
l.	livro
OE	Oficiais do Exército
PC	Polícia Civil

ARCHIVES

AHMI	Arquivo Histórico do Museu Imperial, Petropolis
ANR	Arquivo Nacional, Rio de Janeiro
ANTT	Arquivo Nacional Torre do Tombo, Lisbon, Portugal
APEJE	Arquivo Público Estadual Jordão Emerenciano, Recife
BNSM	Biblioteca Nacional, Seção de Manuscrito, Rio de Janeiro
IAHGP	Instituto Arqueológico, Histórico, e Geográfico Pernambucano, Recife
IHGB	Instituto Histórico Geográfico Brasileiro, Rio de Janeiro

FERNANDO DE NORONHA'S COMMANDERS

ABA	Coronel Alexandre de Barros e Albuquerque
AC	Tenente Coronel Antonio de Campos
ACM	Antônio de Campos Mello
AEM	Coronel Antonio Eduardo Martins
AFC	Interino Major Antonio Francisco da Costa
AFM	Tenente Coronel Agripino Furtado de Mendonça

AGL	Coronel Antonio Gomes Leal
AJF	Captain Antonio José Ferreira
AJM	Major Antonio José da Motta
AJO	Coronel Aleixo José de Oliveira
CJA	Coronel Cypriano José de Almeida
CMAC	Capt. de Artilharia Cesário Mariano d'Albuquerque Cavalcante
DABMB	Major Domingos Alves Branco Muniz Barreto
DTR	Major Diogo Thomaz de Ruxlebem
FFM	Major Francisco Felix de Macedo
FFMV	Tenente Coronel Francisco Felix de Macedo e Vasconcelos
FJM	Coronel Francisco José Martins
FJMA	Major de Milícias Francisco José de Menezes Amorim
FJPC	Major Francisco Joaquim Pereira de Carvalho
FJPL	Brigadeiro Francisco Joaquim Pereira Lobo
FSO	Brigadeiro Francisco Sergio de Oliveira
GPL	Gonçalvez Pereira Lima
HJC	Brigadeiro Hygino José Coelho
JAFM	Joaquim Agripino Furtado de Mendonca
JAM	Capt. Joaquim Antonio de Moraes
JAMR (Joaquim)	Coronel Joaquim Antonio de Moraes Rego
JAMR (José)	Coronel José Angelo de Moraes Rego
JAP	Tenente Coronel José Antonio Pinto
JASV	Tenente Coronel de Milícias Joaquim Annunciação de Siqueira Varejão
JB	Capt. de Engenheiros João Bloem
JBS	Major José Bernardo Salgueiro
JBSM	Major José Bonefácio dos Santos Mergulhão
JCSC	Major Joaquim Caetano de Souza Cousseiro
JGC	Capt. Joaquim de Gusmão Coelho
JIRR (João)	Major João Ignacio Ribeiro Roma
JIRR (José)	Tenente José Ignacio Ribeiro Roma
JLSRC	Tenente-Coronel José Lucas Soares Raposo da Camara
JMIJVPM	Tenente Coronel José Maria Ildefonso Jocome da Veiga Pessoa e Mello
JPQ	José dos Passos Queiroz
JRS	Justino Rodrigues da Silveira
JS	José Soares
LJM	Tenente-Coronel Luiz Jose Monteiro
LMA	Tenente Coronel de Milicias Luis de Moura Accioly
LMAMH	Coronel de Milicias Luiz de Moura Accioli de Miranda da Henriques
LPHV	Luiz Paulino de Hollanda Valença

MAN	Tenente Coronel Manoel d'Azevedo Nascimento
MGPL	Manoel Gonçalves Pereira Lima
MIMMP	Coronel de Cavalaria Manoel Ignacio de Moraes de Mesquita Pimentel
MJC	Tenente Coronel Manuel José de Castro
MJM	Tenente Coronel Manoel José Martins
QCPFN	Quartel do Commando do Presidio de Fernando de Noronha
SARB	Tenente Coronel Sebastião Antonio do Rego Barros
SJBP	Tenente Coronel Sebastião José Basílio Pyrrho
TACM	Capt. Trajano Alipio de Carvalho Mendonca
TCB	Coronel Trajano Cesar Burlamaque
TFM	Tenente Coronel Thome Fernandes Madeira
THST	Capt. Tibúrcio Hilário da Silva Tavares

PERNAMBUCO'S GOVERNORS

AALF	Adelino Antonio de Lima Freire
AB	Adolpho de Barros
AEBC	Antonio Epaminondas de Barros Correia
APCG	Antônio Pinto Chicorro da Gama
ASL	Augusto de Souza Leão
BAMT	Benevenuto Augusto Magalhães Taques
BSL	Barão de Sousa Leão
BVB	Barão de Villa Bella
CB	Conde de Baependy
DVCA	Diogo Velho Cavalcanti de Albuquerque
FAA	Frederico d'Almeida e Albuquerque
FAPR	Francisco d'Assis Pereira Rocha
FAR	Francisco Antonio Riberio
FD	Franklin Doria
FPC	Francisco de Paula Cavalcante
FPSL	Francisco de Paula da Silveira Lobo
FPSM	Francisco Paula de Silveira Martins
FSP	Francisco Sodre Pereira
HHCL	Honório Hermeto Carneiro Leão
HPL	Henrique Pereira de Lucena
IJSL	Ignacio Joaquim de Souza Leão
IMAG	Innocencio Marques d'Araujo Goes
JACS	José Antonio Correia da Silva
JASL	José Antonio de Souza Lima
JBCF	José Bento da Cunha Figueredo
JFCP	José Fernandes da Costa Pereira Jr.
JISR	José Ildefonso de Souza Ramos

JJOA	Joaquim José d'Oliveira Andrade
JJOJ	João José d'Oliveira Junqueira
JLB	José Liberato Barroso
JLCP	João Lustoza da Cunha Paranaguá
JMF	José Manoel de Freitas
JPCM	João Pedro Carvalho de Moraes
JPMP	Joaquim Pires Machado Portela
JRC	João Rodrigues Chaves
LCA	Lourenço Cavalcante d'Albuquerque
LCQB	Luis Corrêa de Queiroz Barros
LRB	Luis de Rego Barretto
MAA	Manoel Alves de Araujo
MCCC	Manoel Clementino Carneiro da Cunha
MIMM	Manuel Ignácio de Moraes e Mesquita
MNMP	Manoel do Nascimento Machado Portella
PVA	Pedro Vicente de Azevedo
SBP	Sancho de Barros Pimentel
STM	Sérgio Teixeira Macedo
VO	Vitor de Oliveira

NOTES

INTRODUCTION

Epigraph: "Lambança [*sic*] não me faz medo / Nem choro não me faz dó [*sic*]: / Eu te mando pra Fernande [*sic*, de Noronha] / Te meto no xilandró. . . . / Si resmungar, leva peia! / Si chorar, leva cipó!" Leonardo Motta, *Violeiros do norte*, 86–87. I thank Linda Lewin for sharing Severino Perigo's verses. For more on Severino Perigo, see Nei Lopes, *Enciclopédia brasileira da Diáspora Africana*, 164.

1. Carpenter used the phrase "ocean resort" in his novel, but I added the expression "Life of Riley" to describe his depiction of the lives of convicts on Fernando de Noronha. Carpenter, *Round about Rio*, 328–29; "Cornell Men in Brazil," *Cornell Alumni News*, Ithaca, New York, May 9, 1906.

2. Beattie, " 'Born under the Cruel Rigor of Captivity' "; Hughes, *Fatal Shore*; Redfield, *Space in the Tropics*; Edwards, "From the Depths of Patagonia"; Chekhov, *Sakhalin Island*.

3. De Souza originally cited in Rodrigues et al., *O parlamento e a evolução nacional*, 2:345–346. Aufderheide cited and translated de Souza in "Order and Violence," 308–309; on improper sentencing, see Bandeira Filho, "Informações," 21.

4. In 1850, an imperial decision clarified that slave convicts could not benefit from Article 311 of the Penal Code, which substituted the sentence of galés for that of prison with work; see Brazil, *Código Criminal do Imperio do Brazil*, 26n23.

5. Barman, *Brazil, the Forging of a Nation*, 1798–1852; Carvalho, *A construção da ordem*, ch. 3; Chalhoub, *Visões da liberdade*; Needell, *The Party of Order*; Pereira, *Visões da monarquia*.

6. Fleury, "Parecer," 5.

7. Hunt, *Inventing Human Rights*, 92; Algranti, *O feitor ausente*, 36.

8. Linebaugh, *The London Hanged*; Beattie, *Policing and Punishment*. Some U.S. states experimented with the "milder" punishment of castration for slaves convicted

of rape; see Summerville, "Rape, Race, and Castration"; Coates, *Convicts and Orphans*; Bender, *Angola under the Portuguese.*

9. Notable exceptions are Aguirre, *The Criminals of Lima*; Salla and Adorno, *As prisões em São Paulo.*

10. The Justice Ministry changed the title of commander to director in 1877; but to avoid confusion, I refer to the colony's chief official as the commander throughout the book.

11. Livro da Matricula geral dos sentenciados com declaração de todas as circumstancias desde sua chegada a este presidio, e sua retirada, conforme determina o regulamento mandado executar pelo decreto, no. 3.403, de 11 de Fevereiro de 1865, Fernando de Noronha, ANR, Seção de Justiça, livro IIJ 7 94; the phrase "degree of unfreeness" invokes Rebecca Scott's *Degrees of Freedom*; I also borrow from James C. Scott's *Seeing Like a State.*

12. Mamigonian, "To Be a Liberated African"; Souza, *Escravidão ou morte.*

13. MacCord analyzes how free artisan laborers of color in Recife battled the "defeito mecânico," or the low esteem of manual labor; see *Artifices da cidadania*, 27–31. On labor and charity, see Fraga Filho, *Mendigos.*

14. I borrow from Cope's use of "racial drift" in *The Limits of Racial Domination.*

15. Mamigonian, "To Be a Liberated African," ch. 3; Kraay, "The Shelter of the Uniform"; Bieber, "Slavery and Social Life"; Beattie, *The Tribute of Blood*; Meznar, "The Ranks of the Poor," 336–337; Carvalho, "Os índios de Pernambuco"; Carvalho, "Quem furta"; Chalhoub, *A força*, esp. chap. 9. The struggle to abolish military impressment and slavery in the Atlantic world has historic parallels. Peter Linebaugh and Marcus Rediker in *The Many-Headed Hydra* show that members of Cromwell's New Model Army compared military impressment to slavery and called for bondage's abolition in Britain's Caribbean colonies. The French compared serfdom and slavery (Harms, *The Diligent*, 22–23); Brazilians noted the relationship between serfdom and coercive military recruitment in Russia to highlight the similar lowly status of soldiering in their own slaveholding nation (Beattie, "Measures of Manhood," 233–234).

16. Soares, *A negregada instituição*; Chandler, *The Bandit King Lampião*; Lewin, "The Oligarchical Limitations of Social Banditry"; Holloway, "A Healthy Terror"; Holloway, *Policing Rio de Janeiro.*

17. Nina Rodrigues, *As raças humanas e a responsibilidade penal no Brasil.*

18. Beattie, "Conscription versus Penal Servitude."

19. Garland, *Punishment and Modern Society*, 278.

20. Goffman, *Asylums*, 11–12.

21. Coser, *Greedy Institutions*; Scott, "Gender."

22. Some women of public authority were Pedro's daughter, Princess Isabel; his wife, the Imperatriz Leopoldina; and the imperial midwife, Madame Durocher; Barman, *Princess Isabel of Brazil*; Windler, "Madame Durocher's Performance."

23. Foucault, *Discipline and Punish*; Foucault, *The History of Sexuality*. For a critique of Foucauldian approaches in Mexico, see Piccato, "Such a Strong Need."

24. Ignatieff, *A Just Measure of Pain*, 11; Zinoman, *The Colonial Bastille*, 16–17; Coates, *Convicts and Orphans*, 21–41. My views coincide with critiques of the dichotomy between premodern and modern penology; see Czeblakow, "A Prison by any Other Name."

25. Canaday, *The Straight State*.

26. Beattie, "'ReCapricorning' the Atlantic"; Szuchman, *The Middle Period in Latin America*; Voss, *Latin America in the Middle Period*. Green and Morgan call for extending Atlantic history forward chronologically in "Introduction: The Present State of Atlantic History," esp. 21.

1. GETTING TO KNOW "FERNANDO"

1. FFMV ao FAR, FN, Jan. 10, 1853, APEJE, l. FN-5, f. 60.

2. Carvalho describes the lives of escravos de ganho in *Liberdade*, 253–274; on Quitandeiaras, see Silva, "Delindra Maria de Pinho."

3. Relação dos sentenciados que declararam terem vendido legumes a preta Izabel que faz parte da familia do illustrissimo Tenente Coronel Commandante FFMV ao FAR, FN, Jan. 14, 1853, APEJE, l. FN-5, f. 60.

4. DTR ao LRB, FN, June 22, 1819, APEJE, l. FN-1, f. 50–51.

5. Branner noted that his voyage to the island on a "small steamer" took two-and-one-half days; "The Convict Island," 34.

6. *Diário de Pernambuco*, Recife, Aug. 26, 1885.

7. Captain Joaquim Domingos de Carvalho ao FJPL, FN, Oct. 21, 1881, l. FN-21, no f. nos.

8. "Fernando Noronha," *Scribner's Monthly*, Feb. 1876, 538–539.

9. Beaurepaire Rohan, "A Ilha," esp. 25.

10. Branner, "The Convict Island," 34–35.

11. Nicoll, *Three Voyages of a Naturalist*, 13.

12. FJPL ao JMF, FN, Aug. 19, 1884, APEJE, l. FN-23, no f. nos.

13. Songini, *The Lost Fleet*, 177.

14. Warrin, *So This Day Ends*.

15. Semmes, *My Adventures Afloat*, 597.

16. Lea, "The Island," 427.

17. Derby, "Fernando de Noronha," *Rio News*, Feb. 24, 1881, 1.

18. Relatorio, FN, Jan. 1, 1885, APEJE, l. FN-24, f. 17, 85.

19. Derby, "Fernando de Noronha," *Rio News*, Feb. 24, 1881, 1.

20. Freyre compared slave quarters to jails in *The Mansions and the Shanties*, 170.

21. FJPL ao BVB, FN, April 28, 1868, APEJE, l. FN-13, f. 301.

22. In 1869, there were far fewer buildings owned by individuals: seven made of stone with clay tile roofs, 48 of stone with thatch roofs, and 284 made of taipa. Mappa de Edificações, FN, Jan. 1, 1869, APEJE, l. FN-14, f. 20.

23. Derby, "Fernando de Noronha," *Rio News*, Feb. 24, 1881, 1.

24. SARB ao STM, FN, Oct. 16, 1856, APEJE, l. FN-6, f. 449.

25. Fleury, "Parecer," 6; "Relação," Jan. 1, 1876, APEJE, l. FN-17, f. 145–179; Derby, "Fernando de Noronha," *Rio News*, Feb. 24, 1881, 1–2.

26. Bandeira Filho, "Informações," 27; Foucault, *Discipline and Punish*, 135–230.

27. SARB a JBCF, FN, Feb. 11, 1856, APEJE, l. FN-6, f. 369.

28. Beaurepaire Rohan, "A Ilha," 25.

29. Stein, *Vassouras*, 161–163; Beattie, *The Tribute of Blood*, 156.

30. Melo, *Archipélago*, 66.

31. Relatorio ACM, FN, Sept. 1, 1872, APEJE, l. FN-16, f. 1–4.

32. Lea, "The Island," 427.

33. Relatorio de FJPL, FN, Jan. 1, 1869, APEJE, l. FN-13, f. 1–17; Relatorio de FJPL, FN, Jan. 1, 1884, l. FN-23, f. 12.

34. SARB ao MNMP, FN, July 13, 1869, APEJE, FN-14, f. 141.

35. Lea, "The Island," 431.

36. Pereira da Costa, *Fernando de Noronha*, 8–9.

37. Lea, "The Island," 432.

38. Lea, "The Island," 433.

39. Pereira da Costa provides an extensive list in *Fernando de Noronha*, 13–16.

40. Lea, "The Island," 433.

2. "THE KEY TO THE AMERICAS"?

1. General J. I. de Abreu e Lima, "Apontamentos sobre a Ilha de Fernando de Noronha," IAHGP, Recife, Pernambuco, 1857, estante A, gaveta 17.

2. Diffie and Perkins, *A History of Colonial Brazil*, 53; Branner, "Notes on the Fauna of the Islands of Fernando de Noronha"; Pereira da Costa, *Fernando de Noronha*, 19–22; Borges, *Fernando de Noronha*.

3. In 1500, the Netherlands possessed some 1.5 million inhabitants; England, 3 million; Spain, 7 million; and France, 12 million; Skidmore, *Brazil: Five Centuries of Change*, 6; Boxer, *The Portuguese Seaborne Empire*.

4. Metcalf, *Go Betweens*; Coates, *Convicts and Orphans*; White, *The Middle Ground*; Brooks, *Captives and Cousins*.

5. Coates, *Convicts and Orphans*, xi–xx.

6. Mello, *Olinda restaurada*.

7. Beaurepaire Rohan, "A Ilha," 22; Abreu e Lima, "Apontamentos."

8. Anonymous, "Relação do que vi na Ilha de Fernando Noronha," Sept. 28, 1736, BNSM, II–32, 11, 4; Galvão, *Diccionario*, 198.

9. Beaurepaire Rohan, "A Ilha," 22.

10. Beaurepaire Rohan, "A Ilha," 22.

11. Governor and captain general of Bahia, Dom Fernando José de Portugal to Dom Rodrigo de Sousa Coutinho, Salvador, April 9, 1779, in the Arquivo Estadual da Bahia, published in *Revista Trimenal do Instituto Histórico e Geográphico Brazileiro* 60, part 2 (1897): 159–163; Beaurepaire Rohan, "A Ilha," 26.

12. I consulted with early modern specialists Timothy Coates and Liam Brockey, and neither knew of a similar Portuguese policy. The crown sent orphaned Por-

tuguese girls with dowries to marry colonial men to improve the colonial gender balance; Coates, *Convicts and Orphans*.

13. Evans, "Journal Kept on Board the United States Frigate 'Constitution' 1812," 471.

14. Koster, *Travels in Brazil*, 1:57.

15. Ofício do D. Fernando José de Portugal . . . , Bahia, April 9, 1799, IHGB, PL 105.14. The letter is published in *Revista Trimensal do Historia e Geographia (O Jornal do Instituto Histórico e Geographico Brazileiro)* 60, part 2 (1897): 159–163. There seems to have been a typo because the publication lists the date of the letter as 1779. Captain João Bloem [henceforth, JB] ao Sr. President Francisco de Paula Cavalcante [henceforth, FPC], Oct. 27, 1826, FN, APEJE, l. FN-1, f. 134–135. The initials for colony commanders and governors of Pernambuco are used hereafter; an alphabetized list of initials and names is in the abbreviations list. The expression *praças de Índio* referred to convicts, not to ethnicity. JB clarifies its usage: "Entre as praças de Índio que existem nesta Ilha se achão cinco degredados do levante de negros de Alagoas os quais forão sentenciados com 10 anos de galês." Pereira da Costa mentions an 1819 plan to relocate Indians from aldeias em Cimbres and Escada, Pernambuco to Fernando de Noronha. He speculated that the 102 Indians there in 1828 may have originated from this plan, but he may have misinterpreted the term praças de Índio; *Fernando de Noronha*, 27–28.

16. Processo do Padre Bernardo Luis Ferreira Portugal, June 20, 1796–Jan. 11, 1803, processo 7058, Tribunal do Santo Ofício, Inquisição de Lisboa, ANTT, PT-TT-TSO-IL-028-07058, http://digitarq.dgarq.gov.pt/details?id=2307127 (accessed Sept. 21, 2012); Bernardo Luis Ferreira Portugal ao Illmo. e Exmo; Dom Francisco de Souza Coutinho, Pará, Dec. 26, 1797, BNSM, código 07-04-041. Barman notes that Brazilians used *pátria* to refer to their captaincy; *Brazil*, 26–30.

17. Bernardo Luis Ferreira Portugal ao Illmo. e Exmo. Dom Francisco de Souza Coutinho, Pará, Dec. 26, 1797, BNSM, código 07-04-041.

18. Darnton, "The Forbidden Best-Sellers of Pre-Revolutionary France"; Lüsebrink and Reichardt, *The Bastille*.

19. "Journal of a Cruize Made to the Pacific Ocean by Captain David Porter in the United States Frigate Essex in the Years 1812, 1813, and 1814," 354.

20. Anonimo, "Revoluções, ideia geral do Pernambuco em 1817," 32–33.

21. DTR ao LRB, FN, June 22, 1819, APEJE, l. FN-01, f. 47–49; DTR ao LRB, FN, June 22, 1819, APEJE, l. FN-01, f. 57–59; Domingos Alv. Branco Monteiro Barretto ao LRB, July 1, 1819, APEJE, l. FN-1. f. 64; Beaupaire Rohan, "A Ilha," 30.

22. Mosher, *Political Struggle*, 23–40.

23. On "various occasions," Lacerda had also pacified by "means of persuasion" prisoners who revolted in Recife's jail; Um Contemporaneo, *Exposição dos serviços*, 5–6; Galvão, *Diccionario*, 241; Carta do AJF ao MIMM, FN, Nov. 1, 1817, APEJE, l. FN-1, f. 11; Beaurepaire Rohan, "A Ilha," 23; Mosher notes that rebels in Recife released all the prisoners in the city's jails, who likely swelled rebel ranks; *Political Struggle*, 24; Pereira da Costa, *Fernando de Noronha*, 27.

24. Burns, *A History of Brazil*, 114; these figures approximate those of D'Andrada e Silva in *Memoir Addressed to the General Constituent and Legislative Assembly of the Empire of Brazil on Slavery*, v. For a brief analysis of population figures, see Naro, "Antislavery and Abolitionism," esp. 144nn2–3.

25. Barman, *Brazil*, 29–30.

26. Beaurepaire Rohan, "A Ilha," 23.

27. Pang and Seckinger, "The Mandarins"; Carvalho, *A construção da ordem*.

28. Graham, *Patronage and Politics*.

29. Schwartz, *Sovereignty and Society in Colonial Brazil*; Flory, *Judge and Jury in Imperial Brazil*.

30. Carvalho, "Hegemony," 75–78; Marson, *O Império de progresso*, 207–208; Mosher, *Political Struggle*, 91–129.

31. Koster, *Travels in Brazil*, 37; Debret also described chain gangs in Rio de Janeiro in *Viagem pitoresca*, 1:251–252.

32. A number of foreigners remarked that Brazilians seldom used capital punishment. Koster, *Travels in Brazil*, 38; Ruschenberger, *Three Years in the Pacific*, 28; Karasch, *Slave Life*, 117, 328–330.

33. Mosher, *Political Struggle*, 71–77.

34. Barman, *Brazil*, 150–151.

35. Bethel, *The Abolition of the Brazilian Slave Trade*; Chalhoub, *A força*, 72–108.

36. Ribeiro, *A liberdade em construção*.

37. Carvalho, "Hegemony," 216–219; Koster did not feel that the militia were very useful in performing these duties in *Travels in Brazil*, 38.

38. On banditry and blood feuds, see Lewin, *Politics and Parentela*, 231–262, and "The Oligarchical Limitations"; Santos, *Cleansing Honor with Blood*.

39. Câmara notes there were eight anti-Portuguese riots in Recife in the 1840s; "O 'retalho' do comércio"; Mosher, *Political Struggle*, 194–205.

40. AGL ao JPMP, FN, June 29, 1857, APEJE, l. FN-6, F. 559; Mosher, *Political Struggle*, 47, 104, 243, 245.

41. Ribeiro, *No meio das galinhas*, 71–190.

42. Mosher, *Political Struggle*, 113–120; Andrade, *A guerra dos cabanos*; Lindoso, *A utopia armada*; Freitas, *Cabanos*.

43. Carvalho, "The 'Commander of All the Forests'"; Marson, *O império de progresso*, 108–119.

44. Barman, *Citizen Emperor*, 67–73.

45. Pernambuco pioneered this reform; Castro, *A milícia cidadã*, 183–184.

46. Needell, *The Party of Order*, 74–79.

47. CJA ao JISR, FN, June 29, 1850, APEJE, l. FN-4A, f. 143.

48. Carvalho, *A construção da ordem*, ch. 3; Barman, *Brazil*, 25–28; Mamigonian, "To Be a Liberated African"; personal communication with Mamigonian March 5, 2011.

49. Bethel credited British pressure for the Brazilian government's decision to end the transatlantic slave trade; *The Abolition*. Revisionists contend that epidemic

disease linked to the trade and fears of slave rebellion played a more prominent role; Chalhoub, *Visões de liberdade*, 186–198; Chalhoub, "The Politics of Disease Control"; Graden, "An Act 'Even of Public Security'"; Needell argues against the revisionists and adds to Bethel's interpretation the importance of struggles within Brazil's political leadership; "The Abolition"; Needell, *The Party of Order*, 138–168.

50. Instituto Brasileiro de Geografia e Estatística, 31–33.

51. Mosher, *Political Struggle*, 206–248.

52. Mosher, *Political Struggle*, 224–228.

53. Marson, *O Império do progresso*, 63; Mosher, *Political Struggle*, 206–248.

54. Carvalho, "The 'Commander of All the Forests.'"

55. Loveman, "Blinded Like a State"; Chalhoub, *A força*, 13–28, 262–263.

56. Vanderwood found a similar phenomenon among Mexico's federal police and argues that officers skimmed funds budgeted to pay police that were never hired; *Disorder and Progress*, 113.

57. Pernambuco, *Falla . . . Diogo Velho Cavalcanti de Albuquerque . . .*, 1871, 8.

58. Beattie, *The Tribute of Blood*, introduction.

59. Subdelegado Manoel Maria Caldas Brandão ao Chefe da Policia Antonio Francisco Correia d'Araujo, Beberibe, Recife, Dec. 11, 1875, APEJE, PC-145, f. 390.

60. The former army engineer André Rebouças records the complaints of Brazilians about onerous National Guard duties in *Agricultura nacional*, 98–99.

61. Beattie, *The Tribute of Blood*, ch. 2.

62. In 1871, the 2nd Battalion had 503 troops; the 9th, 543; the instructional deposit, 57; arsenal artisans, 47; and the recruit depository 138. The 2nd Battalion manned provincial forts: 144 served on Fernando de Noronha; 5, Fort Tamandaré; 29, Fort Brum; 16, Fort Buraco; 7, Fort Itamaracá; 4, Fort Pau Amarelo; and 7 in the forts of Gaibu and Nazareth. Pernambuco, *Falla . . . Diogo Velho Cavalcanti de Albuquerque . . .*, 1871, 10, 12. This had been a problem since colonial times. Henry Koster observed that army units that should have 2,500 men only mustered some 600; *Travels in Brazil*, 38.

63. He blamed the soldiers' poor discipline on the abolition of corporal punishments. Jefferson Mirabeau de Azevedo Soares a Chefe da Policia Antonio Francisco Correia d'Araujo, Recife, Sept. 30, 1875, APEJE, l. PC-145, f. 4.

64. In 1875, the police chief admitted that he could not deliver defendants to a number of juries that had been seated; Chefe da Polícia Antonio Francisco Correia d'Araujo ao JPCM, Recife, Sept. 30, 1875, APEJE l. PC-144, f. 499.

65. Doratioto, *Maldita guerra*; Whigham, *The Paraguayan War*.

66. Izechsohn emphasizes this conflict between Brazil's local and national leaders during the War of the Triple Alliance in *Slavery and War in the Americas*.

67. Beattie, *The Tribute of Blood*, ch. 2.

68. FJPL ao Presidente BVB, FN, Oct. 23, 1867, APEJE, l. FN-13, f. 140.

69. Relação do THST, FN, Feb. 6, 1867, APEJE, l. FN-13, f. 238.

70. Officers made lists of "recruitable" convicts in Fernando de Noronha; José Soares ao FPSM, FN, Dec. 18, 1866, APEJE, l. FN-12, no f. nos. Some convicts

petitioned for pardons in exchange for military service; José Soares ao FPSM, Dec. 10, 1866, no f. nos; Dec. 4, 1866, no f. nos; Dec. 3, 1866, no f. nos.

71. Beattie, *The Tribute of Blood*, 17–122; Meznar, "The Ranks of the Poor," 335–351.

72. Beattie, *The Tribute of Blood*, 81–98.

73. Needell, *The Party of Order*, 278–302.

74. Barman, "The Brazilian Peasantry Reexamined," 412–413, 422–424; Richardson, *Quebra-Quilos and Peasant Resistance*.

75. Delegado Francisco Casado da Cunha Lima ao Chefe Antonio Francisco Correia de Araujo, Buique, July 5, 1875, APEJE, l. PC-144, f. 82.

76. Delegado Francisco Casado da Cunha Lima ao Chefe Antonio Francisco Correia de Araujo, Buique, July 5, 1875, APEJE, l. PC-144, f. 82.

77. Antonio Conselheiro fulminated against civil marriage, the civil registry, and the separation of Church and state in the 1896 Canudos Rebellion. Rustics considered a woman who had a civil marriage a "witnessed whore" in the eyes of God; Levine, *Vale of Tears*, 64, 127, 151; Borges, *The Family in Bahia*, 132; da Cunha, *Rebellion in the Backlands*, 163–164.

78. *Provincia*, Recife, Jan. 25, 1874, 2.

79. Pernambuco, *Falla . . . Diogo Velho Cavalcanti de Albuquerque . . .* , 1871, 10–12.

80. Capitão da Guarda Nacional de Olinda Ignácio da Silva Braga ao Chefe da Policia Antonio Francisco Correia de Araujo, Olinda, Oct. 28, 1874, APEJE, l. PC-140, f. 181.

81. Promotor Publico Graciliano Agusto Cesar Mendelo ao chefe da policia Antonio Francisco Correia d'Araujo, Vila Bela, Oct. 28, 1874, APEJE, l. PC-140, f. 216.

82. Provincial Law number 1130, April 30, 1874. Relatório do Chefe da Polícia ao Presidente da Provincia HPL, Recife, Jan. 29, 1875, APEJE, l. PC-142, f. 101.

83. Delgado Francisco José de Lucena a Chefe de Policia Sigismundo Antonio Gonçalves, Panelas, Aug. 10, 1878, APEJE, l. PC-156, f. 184.

84. The subdelegate refers to articles 75–11 of the regulations. Delegado Christoreão (illegible) de Melo ao JPCM, Itambe, Oct. 26, 1875, APEJE, l. PC-145, f. 160.

85. Chefe da Policia Antonio Francisco Correia d'Araujo ao JPCM, Recife, Nov. 12, 1875, APEJE, l. PC-145, f. 221.

86. Maia, "Policiados," 74–91; Holloway, *Policing Rio de Janeiro*, 163–164; Neder, Naro, and Silva, *A polícia na Corte*, 158–165.

87. Chefe da Policia Antonio Francisco Correia d'Araujo ao JPCM, Recife, May 17, 1875, APEJE, l. PC-143, f. 229.

88. Beattie, "Conscription versus Penal Servitude," 857.

89. Delegado Francisco Odilon Tavares Lima ao Sigismundo Antonio Gonçalves, Recife, Oct. 23, 1878, APEJE, l. PC-157, f. 259–262.

90. Captain Manoel de Freitas Barboza Cordeiro ao Chefe de Policia Sigismundo Antonio Gonçalves, Aguas Belas, Sept. 22, 1878, APEJE, PC-157, f. 46.

91. *Provincia*, Recife, Sept. 4, 1877, 1; for complaints about police, see *Provincia*, Recife, Aug. 30, 1877, 1; *Provincia*, Recife, July 5, 1876, 2. The governor often asked authorities to respond to accusations made in the press; Police Chief Antonio Francisco Correia d'Araujo ao HPL, Recife, Jan. 16, 1875, APEJE, l. PC-142, f. 113.

92. *America Illustrada*, Recife, April 14, 1872, f. 8.

93. Commandante do Destacamento Manoel de Freitas Barbosa Cordeiro ao Chefe da Policia Sigismundo Antonio Gonçalves, Aguas Belas, Aug. 26, 1878, APEJE, l. PC-156, f. 442; Sept. 22, 1878, l. PC-157, f. 46.

94. Relação dos paisanos que acompanharão ao Delegado de Polícia de termo de Buique e subdelegado de Gameleira em perseguição dos criminosos agrupados naquela subdelegacia, Buique, July 25, 1878, APEJE, l. PC-156, f. 24.

95. Antonio Francisco Correia d'Araujo ao HPL, Recife, April 6, 1875, APEJE, l. PC-143, f. 38; Subdelegado Jose Francisco de Souza Leite ao Chefe da Policia Antonio Francisco Correia d'Araujo, Sao Bento, Nov. 11, 1874, APEJE, l. PC-140, f. 269; the reliance on civilian posses continued well into the twentieth century; Chandler, *The Bandit King Lampião*.

96. The administrator of Recife's House of Detention wrote, "Without the slightest help from public coffers, I set up shops and gave work to hundreds of prisoners who found distraction in work and the means for an honest life." But after four years, he could no longer afford these efforts and they ceased; Almeida, *Estado actual das prisões*, 11, 40–41. In Rio de Janeiro, the Calabouço prison held runaway slaves and slaves sent by masters to be flogged until the early 1870s; Holloway, "O Calabouço e o Aljube," 1: 253–281; Ferriera, "O tronco na enxovia," 1:179–215; Maia, "A Casa da Detenção do Recife."

97. Pernambuco, *Falla . . . Franklin Americo de Menezes Doria . . .* , 1881, 25.

98. Police Chief Antonio Francisco Correia de Araujo, "Relatorio," annexo A, 3–10, in Pernambuco, *Falla . . . João Pedro Carvalho de Moraes . . .* , 1876; for a description of a municipal jail, see Raulino, *Sentenciado 304 (Leitura para as prisões)*.

99. Commisario Gaspar Accioly Santiago Ramos a Senhor Major Manoel Honrato de Barros, Barreiros, Sept. 19, 1875, APEJE, l. PC-144, f. 430.

100. Delegado Luiz Candido do Carneiro da Cunha ao Chefe da Policia Sigismundo Antonio Gonçalves, Pau d'Alho, Sept. 11, 1878, APEJE, l. PC-156, F. 492; on the poor conditions and security of prisons, see Relatorio do Chefe da Policia Antonio Francisco Correia de Araujo, Recife, Jan. 29, 1875, APEJE, l. PC-142, f. 165–171.

101. Beattie, "Conscription."

102. *Diário de Pernambuco,* Recife, Nov. 10, 1874; Nov. 24, 1874; Nov. 26, 1874. The series continued in the *Diário de Pernambuco* through Dec. 16, 1874.

103. Pernambuco, *Falla . . . Henrique Pereira de Lucena . . .* , 1875, 39.

104. Barman, *Citizen Emperor*; Schwarcz, *As barbas do imperador*.

105. Ribeiro, *No meio*, 285–286, 292, 303–304, 308; even abolitionists felt that for slaves incarceration at labor was "an incentive to crime"; Nabuco, *Abolitionism*, 94.

106. Brazil, Ministerio da Justiça, *Relatorio . . . João Ferreira de Moura*, 140; Fleury, "Parecer," 7; Bandeira Filho, "Informações," 12, 29. The War Ministry favored the colony's transfer because most convicts were civilians; Brazil, Ministerio da Guerra, *Relatorio . . . Duque de Caxias*, 1877, 18; Brazil, Ministerio da Guerra, *Relatorio . . . Affonso Augusto Moreira Penna*, 1882, 173.

107. Or at least this is what a Justice Ministry report suggested in 1887; Brazil, Ministerio da Justiça, *Relatório . . . Samuel Wallace MacDowell*, 1887, 162.

108. Conrad, *The Destruction of Brazilian Slavery*, 210–238, 263–277; Azevedo, *Abolicionismo*, 147–162; Needell, *The Party of Order*, 233–234; Castilho, "Abolitionism Matters."

109. Da Costa, *The Brazilian Empire*, 202–232; Needell, *The Party of Order*, 284–314.

110. Celso Castro, *Os militares e a república*.

111. Soares, *A negregada instituição*; Holloway, "A Healthy Terror."

112. Pernambuco, *Mensagem . . . Joaquim Correa de Araujo . . .* , 1899, 12–13.

113. Brazil, Ministerio de Justiça, *Relatorio . . . Dr. Almaro Cavalcante*, 1898, 452–455.

114. Pernambuco, *Mensagem . . . Sigismundo Antonio Gonçalves . . .* , 1900, 15–17.

3. FERNANDO DE NORONHA'S "DARK TWINS"

1. Scott, *Seeing Like a State*; Scott borrows heavily from Holston, *The Modernist City*, for his insights on Brasilia.

2. Fleury, "Parecer," 6.

3. Derby, "Fernando de Noronha," *Rio News*, Feb. 24, 1881, 1.

4. Relatorio, FN, Jan. 1, 1884, APEJE, l. FN-23, f. 21–22.

5. When the Justice Ministry assumed the colony's management in 1877, it maintained the same basic organization but changed titles. To avoid confusion I use sergeant and corporal even though their titles changed in 1877.

6. Bandeira Filho, "Informações," 17–18.

7. Derby, "Fernando de Noronha," *Rio News*, Feb. 24, 1881, 1–2.

8. Relação nominal dos sentenciados militares e civis que servem de vigias nos pontos, FN, May 16, 1885, APEJE, l. FN-24, no f. nos.

9. Relatorio, FN, Feb. 20, 1871, APEJE, l. FN 15, f. 23; Fleury, "Parecer," 7; Beattie, *The Tribute of Blood*, ch. 8.

10. Relatorio, FN, Feb. 20, 1871, APEJE, l. FN 15, f. 23; On "weakness of complexion" in another context, see Ignácio Fabber, processo 690, ANR, Suprema Tribunal Militar, Caixa 13346, 1904, 25.

11. Ordem do Dia, JAMR, FN, Jan. 3, 1871, APEJE, l. FN-15, f. 65.

12. Bandeira Filho, "Informações," 19.

13. Beattie, *The Tribute of Blood*, 155.

14. Tenente Manoel Clandiser de Oliveira e Cruz ao CJA, FN, May 30, 1850, APEJE, l. FN-4A, f. 127.

15. Graham explores these dimensions of domestic slave and free female workers on the mainland in *House and Street*.

16. AFC ao JRC, FN, Sept. 12, 1885, APEJE, l. FN-24, no f. nos.

17. FJPL ao JLB, FN, May 19, 1882, APEJE, l. FN-22, no f. nos.

18. Eisenberg, *The Sugar Industry*, 186–187.

19. ACM ao JJOJ, FN, Feb. 3, 1872, APEJE, l. FN-15, f. 385.

20. ABA ao LCA, FN, Jan., 14, 1880, APEJE, l. FN-20, f. 106.

21. ABA ao AB, FN, Apr. 14, 1879, APEJE, l. FN-19, f. 141.

22. SARB ao JBCF, FN, May 15, 1856, APEJE, l. FN-6, f. 389–391.

23. ABA ao LCA, FN, March 16, 1880, APEJE, l. FN-20, f., 160; ABA ao LCA, FN, May 26, 1880, f. 225.

24. "Ilha de Fernando de Noronha," *O Liberal*, Recife, Sept. 28, 1871.

25. "Ilha de Fernando de Noronha," *O Liberal*, Recife, Sept. 28, 1871.

26. Bandeira Filho, "Informações," 29.

27. ABA ao AB, FN, April 15, 1879, APEJE, l. FN-19, f. 155.

28. Bandeira Filho, "Informações," 36.

29. Relatorio, FN, Jan. 1, 1885, APEJE, l. FN-24, f. 22.

30. Relatorio, FN, Jan. 1, 1884, APEJE, l. FN-23, f. 14.

31. FJPL ao CB, FN, Jan. 17, 1869, APEJE, l. FN-14, f. 29.

32. Pernambuco, *Falla . . . João Pedro Carvalho de Moraes . . .*, 1876, 29.

33. Bandeira Filho cited Spencer's aphorism in "Informações," 39.

34. Brazil, Ministerio da Justiça, *Relatorio apresentado . . . Conselheiro Joaquim Delfino Ribeiro da Luz*, 1886, 128; Brazil, Ministerio da Justiça, *Relatorio . . . Samuel Wallace MacDowell*, 1887, 165.

35. Wines, *The State of Prisons*, 554. A justice minister made detailed complaints about the lack of revenue from the penal colony's production for a three-year period in 1888. Brazil, Ministerio da Justiça, *Relatorio . . . Antonio Ferreira Vianna*, 1888, 138–141.

36. Bandeira Filho, "Informações," 14.

37. FJPL ao SBP, FN, Jan. 1, 1885, APEJE, l. FN-24, f. 7.

38. Fraga, *Encruzilhadas da liberdade*, 222.

39. Commandante do Destacamento Capitain Joaquim de Souza Murelles ao Governador de Pernambuco Luis do Rego Barreto, FN, March 4, 1821, APEJE, l. FN-1, f. 69–72.

40. CJA ao HHCL, FN, Jan. 22, 1850, APEJE, l. FN-4A, f. 27–28.

41. This was the average nominal price of adult male and female slaves age twenty to twenty-five; Eisenberg, *The Sugar Industry*, 153.

42. Fleury, "Parecer," 7–8.

43. An article on a disturbance in Fernando de Noronha mentions that the dispute began in Simonelli's store; *Diário de Pernambuco*, Recife, Dec. 21, 1886.

44. Bandeira Filho, "Informações," 32.

45. JLSRC ao FPSL, FN, Jan. 31, 1867, APEJE, l. FN-13, f. 8.

46. The commander notes that the only personnel prohibited from opening a store were the commander and the major da praça. CJA ao JISR, FN, July 2, 1850, APEJE, l. FN-4a, f. 170; FFMV-FAR, FN, July 12, 1852, APEJE, l. FN-4C, f. 128.

47. Stein, *Vassouras*, 86–87, 1/1–1/3.

48. FJPL ao SBP, FN, Jan. 1, 1885, APEJE, l. FN-24, f. 7.

49. As Castro demonstrates, army officers used the term "social pollutions" to scorn socializing between officers and enlisted men. I stretch the term to depict what officials saw as undue familiarity between convicts and soldiers; *O espírito militar*.

50. Beattie, *The Tribute of Blood*, 162–163.

51. SJBP ao HPL, FN, Dec. 31, 1873, APEJE, l. FN-16, f. 291–330.

52. Fleury, "Parecer," 8.

53. CJA ao HHCL, FN, May 25, 1850, APEJE, l. FN-4A, f. 127.

54. JMIJVPM ao VO, FN, Aug. 19, 1851, APEJE, l. FN-4b, F. 112; *Daily Mail Reporter*, Feb. 17, 2011, http://www.dailymail.co.uk/news/article-1357892/U-S-drinks-lowest-alcohol-developed-world-figures-reveal.html (accessed June 28, 2013).

55. JMISVPM ao Ajudante Raimundo José de Souza Lobo, FN, Feb. 18, 1851, APEJE, l. FN-4b, f. 15.

56. FFMV ao VO, FN, July 3, 1852, APEJE, l. FN-4C, f. 86.

57. Padre José de Oliveira Diniz (Capelão) ao JBCF, FN, Aug. 18, 1853, APEJE, l. FN-5, f. 158; JAP ao JBCF, FN, Oct. 4, 1855, APEJE, l. FN-6, f. 315.

58. Padre José de Oliveira Diniz (Capelão) ao JBCF, FN, Aug. 18, 1853, APEJE, l. FN-5, f. 158; JAP ao JBCF, FN, Oct. 4, 1855, APEJE, l. FN-6, f. 315.

59. JAP ao JBCF, FN, Oct. 3, 1855, APEJE, FN-6, f. 313.

60. JMIJVPM ao JISR, Fernando, March 24, 1851, APEJE, l. FN-4B, f. 28.

61. ACM ao JJOJ, FN, Dec. 8, 1871, APEJE, l. FN-15, f. 314.

62. FJPL, FN, Feb. 21, 1882, APEJE, l. FN-22, f. 123.

63. FJPL ao AEBC, FN, Jan. 14, 1882, APEJE, l. FN-22, f. 10–11; FJPL ao AEBC, FN, Jan. 16, 1882, APEJE, l. FN-22, f. 23.

64. FJPL ao JASL, FN, Nov. 18, 1881, APEJE, l. FN-21, no f. nos.

65. ACM ao MNMP, FN, Dec. 3, 1871, APEJE, FN-15, f. 294. Convicts came up with many schemes to smuggle alcohol. For instance, in 1854 a commander accused convict Antonio Gusmão Jr. of attempting to smuggle in two barrels of aguardente "under my name." JAP ao JBCF, FN, Aug. 1, 1854, APEJE, l. FN-6, f. 106. In 1871, the commander complained that his second in command, Major da Praça Joaquim Antonio de Morais, colluded with the scrivener Gentil Homem Rodrigues de Souza in the "contraband sale of cane brandy"; JAMR ao DVCA, FN, March 10, 1871, APEJE, l. FN-15, f. 69.

66. Carta Anonyma ao Excellismo Senhor [no name], no place, no date, APEJE, l. FN-24, no f. nos. The letter bears no date, but it is found amid colony correspondence for 1884.

67. A letter from the commander mentions the anonymous letter along with 93 liters of aguardente and other alcohol that was apprehended. FJPL ao JRC, FN, April 21, 1885, APEJE, l. FN-24, no f. nos; Relação nominal dos introductores de bebidas alcoolicas apprehendidos pela commissão revisera no desembarque do vapor Mandahú, FN, March 15, 1884, APEJE, l. FN-23, no f. nos.

68. JIRR (José) ao IJSL, FN, Sept. 21, 1886, APEJE, l. FN-25, F. 295.

69. Bandeira Filho, "Informações," 31. Similarly, a commander agreed with an 1871 article in the *Diário de Pernambuco* that called for removing ex-convicts who owned stores in the presidio. He then denied the appeals of four vendors for an extension to the time they needed to liquidate their stock and ordered them to leave; ACM ao JJOJ, FN, Dec. 8, 1871, APEJE, l. FN-15, f. 306; ACM ao JJOJ, FN, Dec. 8, 1871, APEJE, l. FN-15, f. 307.

70. Ocorrências, FN, Oct. 17, 1894, ANR, Série Justiça / Subsérie Fernando de Noronha, IIJ 7 84, fundo ND, Codes, 1894–1901.

71. Melo, *Archipélago*, 67.

72. Almeida, "Dissertação abreviada sobre o horrível masmona," 21.

73. DTR ao LRB, FN, June 22, 1819, APEJE, l. FN-1, f. 50–51.

74. AGL ao BAMT, FN, Feb. 16, 1858, APEJE, l. FN-7, f. 13.

75. Relatorio de FJPL, FN, Jan. 1, 1869, APEJE, l. FN-13, f. 1–17.

76. Comissão de Syndicancia ao DVCA, Fernando, April 22, 1871, APEJE, FN-15, f. 91–92.

77. Brazil, Ministerio da Justiça, *Relatorio . . . General Dr. Manoel Ferras de Campos Salles*, 1891, 105–106.

78. Relatorio, FN, Aug. 17, 1850, APEJE, l. FN-4A, f. 176.

79. ABA ao AB, FN, Jan. 14, 1879, APEJE, l. FN-19, f. 58.

80. In 1880, a commander indicated the limited capacity for incarcerating troublesome convicts in the aldeia's cells; ABA ao LCA, FN, Jan. 13, 1880, APEJE, l. FN-20, f. 2–7.

81. Bandeira Filho, "Informações," 27.

82. Beattie, *The Tribute of Blood*, ch. 8.

83. Ocorrências, FN, April 26, 1894, ANR, Série Justiça, Subsérie Fernando de Noronha, Fundo ND, Codes, 1894–1901. Ocorrências, FN, no date; Ocorrências, FN, no month or day listed, 1894; Ocorrências, FN, no month or day listed, 1894; Ocorrências, FN, no date; Ocorrências, FN, Dec. 24, 1894; Ocorrências, FN, Oct. 7, 1895; Oct. 5, 1895; Ocorrências, FN, Jan. 13, 1895.

84. FJPL ao FSP, FN, March 14, 1885, APEJE, l. FN-24, no f. nos.

85. FJPL ao JRC, FN, July 24, 1885, APEJE, l. FN-24, no f. nos; copy of correspondence, FJPL ao AEBC, July 23, 1883, APEJE, FN-22, no f. nos.

86. CJA ao JISR, FN, June 27, 1850, APEJE, l. FN-4A, f. 170–171.

87. Lea, "The Island," 425–435.

88. Branner, "The Convict Island," 36.

89. CJA ao HHML, FN, April 5, 1850, APEJE, l. FN-4A, f. 81–84.

90. ACM ao MNMP, FN, Oct. 23, 1871, APEJE, l. FN-15, f. 253; *O Liberal*, Recife, Sept. 28, 1871.

91. ACM ao MNMP, FN, Oct. 23, 1871, APEJE, FN-15, f. 251; *O Liberal*, Recife, Sept. 28, 1871.

92. Brazil, Ministerio da Justiça, *Relatorio . . . General Dr. Manoel Ferras de Campos Salles*, 1891, 105.

93. See Salla and Adorno, "Criminalidade organizada nas prisões."

4. "BROTHERS OF THE PEAK"

1. Melo, *Arquipélago*, 67; Lins do Rego depicts the archipelago's convicts identifying passing ships by their smokestacks in *Usina*, 16.

2. Reis, *Death Is a Festival*; MacCord, *O Rosário de D. Antônio*.

3. I used a number of sources to create the Fernando de Noronha Convict Database (henceforth FNCD) of convict identities. Two books of guias provide data

on inmates for the 1830s and 1850s. Two prisoner matriculation books provide data from the 1860s through the 1890s. Finally, a detailed survey conducted by a commander in 1891 provides another picture of the colony's population. Between these main sources, I coded information on more than 2,100 inmates. The following sources provided information that I coded into a databases. In each case, I coded every prisoner listed for the Livro de guias; however, convict entries were so numerous for the Livro da matricula geral record books that I surveyed every fifth inmate. Two record books of inmate guias provide information on inmates brought to the island in the 1830s and the 1850s, Livro de guias, 1830, ANR, Serie Justiça, Fernando de Noronha, Código do Fundo ND, livro IIJ 2 7, Seção de Guarda Codes, and Livro de guias, 1850, ANR, Serie Justiça, Fernando de Noronha, Código do Fundo ND, livro IIJ 2 7, Seção de Guarda Codes. Two matriculation books recorded information on convicts from the 1860s through the 1890s, Livro da matricula geral dos sentenciados com declaração de todas as circumstancias desde sua chegada a este presidio, e sua retirada, conforme determina o regulamento madado executar pelo decreto no. 3.403 de 11 de Fevereiro de 1865, ANR, Seção de Justiça, livro IIJ 7 94, Fernando de Noronha. Livro da Matricula geral dos sentenciados . . . pelo decreto no.9.356 de 10 de Janeiro de 1885, ANR, Seção de Justiça, Livro IIJ 7 61, Fernando de Noronha. The survey of the island's slave population and the directors survey are found in the APEJE. Relatorio do Director Joaquim de Gusmão Coelho ao Cidadão Desembargador José Antonio Correia da Silva, Governador do Estado de Pernambuco, FN, Jan. 1, 1891, APEJE, l. FN-30, f. 2.

4. Barickman, "Reading the 1835 Parish Censuses"; Loveman, "The Race to Progress."

5. Stein, *Vassouras*, 169.

6. In about one in twenty cases, guias did not accompany prisoners; QCPFN, FN, Aug. 20, 1866, APEJE, l. FN-12, no f. nos; Beaurepaire Rohan, "A Ilha," 24. Administrators usually assumed that prisoners who arrived without guias had been sentenced to perpetual galleys as the counterfeiter Antonio Romero's petitions reveal; QCPFN, FN, July 12, 1866, APEJE, l. FN-12, no f. nos; QCPFN, FN, Nov. 8, 1866, no f. nos.

7. On photography's use in establishing identity in Brazil, see Gomes, *Intenção e gesto*.

8. Carta de Guia o Reu Preso José Gonçalves do Nascimento, FN, July 21, 1847, APEJE, l. FN-13, f. 4.

9. Scott, *Seeing Like a State*.

10. ABA ao FD, FN, Sept. 27, 1880, APEJE, l. FN-20, f. 355.

11. Bandeira Filho, "Informações," 11.

12. Branner, "The Convict Island"; mainland Brazilians also creatively used nicknames; see Levine, *Vale of Tears*, 164.

13. Schwartz, *Sugar Plantations*, 401–402.

14. JMIJVPM ao JISR, FN, Feb. 20, 1851, APEJE, l. FN-4b, f. 19; Sodré, *História da imprensa no Brasil*, 153.

15. Chalhoub, *Trabalho, lar, e botequim*.

16. Almeida, *Estado actual*, 29.

17. Eusébio de Queiroz to Minister of Justice, May 17, 1838, Rio de Janeiro, Papers of Eusébio de Queiroz, ANR, códice 1004; cited in Flory, *Judge and Jury*, 124.

18. FSO ao APCG, FN, April 16, 1846, APEJE, l. FN-03, f. 27–28.

19. "Fernando Noronha," *Scribner's Monthly*, Feb. 1876, 538–539.

20. Bandeira Filho, "Informações," 20.

21. Most of Recife's law school graduates had political and judicial careers in the northeast, and their classmate relationships made it easier to call on favors; Pang, "The Mandarins"; Levine, *Pernambuco in the Brazilian Federation*; Kirkendall, *Class Mates*; Hendricks and Levine, "Pernambuco's Political Elite and the Recife Law School"; Hendricks, "Education."

22. Van Young, *The Other Rebellion*, 40–56; Vanderwood, *Disorder and Progress*, xxii–xxiii; Taylor, "Bandit Gangs"; Aguirre, "Cimarronaje"; Lewin, "Oligarchical Limitations"; Santos, *Cleansing Honor with Blood*.

23. SARB a JBCF, FN, Feb. 18, 1855, APEJE, l. FN-6, f. 88.

24. Relatorio, FN, Jan. 1, 1877, APEJE, l. FN-18, f. 300.

25. Note that some sixty-two soldier convicts had no information listed for occupation, so I removed them from the total of 206 army convicts.

26. Beattie, *The Tribute of Blood*, 154.

27. Camara, *Collecção de provérbios*, 122.

28. To marry, Vidigal permits Leonardo to transfer to a militia because at that time army regulars could not marry; Almeida, *Memórias*, 133, 183–186.

29. Almeida, *Estado actual das prisões*, 29; Flory, *Judge and Jury*, 124–125; Nabuco, *Um estadista do Império*, 1:45, 89.

30. See Schwarcz, *Retrato em preto e branco*.

31. Loveman, "Blinded Like a State," 17; on the usage of "race" or "color" in historical analysis, see Guimarães, "Race, Colour, and Skin Colour in Brazil."

32. A contemporary informant for Winddance Twine ranked the following features in their importance for color designations: "hair, nose, mouth and skin color"; *Racism in a Racial Democracy*, 90. My survey is similar except that lips seemed more important than noses. On contemporary ideas of beauty, color, and features, see Edmonds, *Pretty Modern*, 141–143; Goldstein, *Laughter Out of Place*, 121.

33. Roderick J. Barman observes that imperial Brazilian elites accepted talented men of color in their ranks if they were, in the words of the influential politician the Marquês de Olinda, "grave, intelligent, and restrained." The qualities that could attenuate color prejudice for talented nonwhite men included literacy, command of Latin and French, knowledge of European culture (especially of France), impeccable grooming and dress (a frock coat), and restrained behavior. The distinction for white elites was not so much black versus white but the "civilized" versus the "savage." Barman, "Listen for the Silences." The Marquês de Olinda's words are from a speech printed in Dodsworth, *Organizações e programas ministeriais*, 131.

34. Beattie, "Conscription versus Penal Servitude."

35. Branner, "The Convict Island," 37.

36. Melo, *Arquipélago*, 65.

37. Branner, "The Convict Island," 34.

38. Bandeira Filho, "Informações," 27.

39. Santos, *Cleansing Honor with Blood*.

40. Bandeira Filho, "Informações," 20.

41. Lea, "The Island," 433–434.

42. Branner, "The Convict Island," 37.

43. FJPL ao ASL, FN, Feb. 20, 1885, APEJE, l. FN-24, no f. nos.

44. Article 27 in Beaurepaire Rohan's "Regulamento para o presidio de Fernando de Noronha," annexo, in Brazil, Ministerio da Guerra, *Relatorio . . . Visconde de Camumú*, 1865; on slave barracks, see Stein, *Vassouras*, 134.

45. Bandeira Filho, "Informações," 18.

46. JMIJVP ao VO, FN, Dec. 22, 1851, APEJE, l. FN-4b, F. 162.

47. FJPL ao JMF, FN, April 26, 1884, APEJE, l. FN-23, no f. nos.

48. JMIJVP ao VO, FN, Jan. 7, 1852, APEJE, l. FN-4E, f. 8.

49. MGPL ao. JFCP, FN, March 15, 1886, APEJE, l. FN-25, f. 114.

50. JAFM ao PVA, FN, Nov. 23, 1886, APEJE, l. FN-25, f. 351.

51. Derby, "Fernando de Noronha," *Rio News*, Feb. 24, 1881, 1–2. I thank Jeffrey Needell for sharing this citation. See Branner's obituary for Derby, "Orville A. Derby," 209–214.

52. Branner, "The Convict Island," 35–36.

53. AFC ao JRC, FN, Sept. 12, 1885, APEJE, l. FN-24, no f. nos.

54. FJPL ao SBP, FN, Jan. 1, 1885, APEJE, l. FN-24, f. 2.

55. Mosher, *Political Struggle*.

56. Sodré, *História da imprensa*, 153.

57. SJBP ao HPL, APEJE, Fernando, FN-16, Jan. 7, 1875, f. 343.

58. Bandeira Filho, "Informações," 24, 28.

59. FFMV ao FAR, FN, July 1, 1852, APEJE, l. FN-4C, 92–94.

60. Beaurepaire Rohan, "A Ilha," 26.

61. Beaurepaire Rohan, "A Ilha," 23.

62. Galvão, *Diccionario*, 241–242. There are some errors in Galvão's list that do not match up with the presidio's correspondence.

63. *Annais da Camara dos Deputados*, part 3, 1886, 75.

64. Queiroz Duarte, *Os voluntários da pátria*, 5:156.

65. Loveman, "Blinded Like a State," 17.

66. Maciel da Silva, *Os generaes do exército brasileiro*, 1:139–148.

67. *Diário de Pernambuco*, Recife, Sept. 11, 1885.

68. Figueira de Melo, *Crônica da Rebelião Praieira*, 375.

69. FJPL ao AEBC, FN, Jan. 15, 1882, APEJE, l. FN-22, f. 5–7.

70. Branner, "The Convict Island," 34–35.

71. Hughes, *Fatal Shore*, 289–291.

72. Lea, "The Island," 433.

73. Semmes, *My Adventures Afloat*, 599.

74. On tensions and cooperation between black and brown Brazilian and immigrant artisans in Recife, see MacCord, *Artífices da cidadania*.

75. While historians have noted the relationship between the organization of plantation slave labor and industrial wage labor for some time, Blackburn makes the most recent and broad argument for this school of thought in *The Making of New World Slavery*, 355, 463. This argument has even come to influence studies of the history of industrial capitalist management; see Cooke, "The Denial of Slavery in Management Studies." Like Fernando de Noronha, Ipanema's iron works used slave, free African, and military laborers alongside free wage workers; see Rodrigues, "De escravos á operários," and Florence, "Resistência escrava em São Paulo."

76. Lea, "The Island," 433.

77. A rare chart of troops from 1847 indicates their ages: 6 were age 15 to 20; 25, 20 to 29; 28, 30 to 39; 17, 40 to 49; and 2, 50 to 59. FSO, Mappa dos habitantes da Ilha de FN, FN, Aug. 8, 1847, APEJE, l. FN-03, F. 97.

78. JB ao FPC, Mappa dos Praças de FN, March 6, 1827, FN, APEJE, l. FN-1, f. 183–186.

79. FFMV ao FAR, FN, July 1, 1852, APEJE, l. FN-4C, f. 92–94.

80. ABA ao LCA, FN, May 22, 1880, APEJE, l. FN-20, f. 211.

81. ABA ao AB, FN, April 9, 1879, APEJE, l. FN-19, f. 137.

82. JB ao FPC, FN, March 6, 1827, APEJE, l. FN-1, f. 181–182.

83. JAP ao JBCF, FN, July 20, 1853, APEJE, l. FN-5, f. 141; APEJE, l. FN-5, f. 141, Aug. 28, 1852, f. 144; FFMV ao VO, FN, March 6, 1852, APEJE, l. FN-4C, f. 59.

84. Koster, *Travels in Brazil*, 39.

85. Semmes, *My Adventures Afloat*, 599–600.

86. Relatorio do ano 1870, FN, Feb. 20, 1871, APEJE, l. FN 15, f. 23.

87. Lea, "The Island," 433.

88. Beaurepaire Rohan, "A Ilha," 26.

89. FFMV ao VO, FN, March 4, 1852, APEJE, l. FN-4C, f. 57.

90. "Mappa estatistica dos habitantes da Ilha de Fernando de Noronha," FN, Aug. 8, 1847, APEJE, l. FN 3, f. 97; "Mappa estatistica . . . ," FN, Jan. 1, 1852, APEJE, l. FN-4a, f. 1–10; "Mappa estatistica . . . , FN, Jan. 1, 1854, APEJE, l. FN-6, no f. nos; "Mappa estatistica . . . ," Jan 1, 1858, l. FN-7, f. 15; f. 10; "Mappa estatistica . . . ," FN, Jan. 1, 1869, APEJE, l. FN-13, f. 1–17; Mappa estatistica . . . ," FN, Dec. 31, 1873, APEJE, l. FN-16, f. 291–330; "Mappa estatistica . . . ," FN, Jan. 1, 1874, APEJE, l. FN-16, f. 182–198; "Mappa estatistica . . . , FN, June 30, 1878, APEJE, l. FN-19, f. 10; "Mappa estatistica . . . , FN, Jan. 1, 1885, APEJE, l. FN-22, f. 29; Mappa estatistica . . . ," FN, Jan. 1, 1886, APEJE, l. FN-24, f. 2; "Mappa estatistica . . . ," FN, Jan. 1, 1891, APEJE, l. FN-30, f. 2.

91. AGL ao BAMT, FN, Feb. 18, 1858, APEJE, l. FN-7, f. 21. A similar census from 1869 shows twelve slaves; Relatorio de FJPL, FN, Jan. 1, 1869, APEJE, l. FN-13, f. 1–17.

92. Beaurepaire Rohan, "A Ilha," 24.

93. "Mappa dos alunos que frequentem a aula de primeiras letras neste presídio até dia 20 de Dezembro pelo Mestre da Escola Daniel Roiz de Santana," FN, Dec. 20, 1852, APEJE, l. FN-5, f. 37.

94. JB ao FPC, FN, Jan. 12, 1827, APEJE, l. FN-1, f. 168.

95. Meznar, "Carlota Lucia de Brito"; Almeida, *Brejo de Areia*, 61–75.

5. THE JEALOUS INSTITUTION

1. A Pernambucan newspaper reported that France's population decreased by half a million from 1866 to 1871 to the dismay of its leaders, who blamed the "perversion of customs" in urban centers. It also noted that the populations of Prussia, England, and other nations grew in this same period. *Diário de Pernambuco*, Recife, Oct. 1, 1874, 8.

2. According to the *New York Times*, Argentina implemented such a measure; "To Tax Bachelors: The New Proposal in France—Extraordinary Law Now in Operation in Argentina—A Sliding Scale to Compel Matrimony," *New York Times*, Sept. 7, 1902; "French and English Marriage Market," *Punch Magazine*, Jan. 21, 1860; "Mr. Sharpe's Bachelor Tax," *Sydney Morning Herald*, Jan. 19, 1915.

3. The debate was reprinted in *Diário de Pernambuco*, Recife, Oct. 8, 1874, 8.

4. "Casamento Acatholico," *A Provincia*, Recife, Jan. 23, 1877, 3.

5. *Diário de Pernambuco*, Recife, Sept. 10, 1885; *Diário de Pernambuco*, Sept. 13, 1885.

6. On civil marriage, see Borges, *The Family*, 129–135; on men marrying to avoid military impressment, see Beattie, *The Tribute of Blood*, ch. 2.

7. Abbot, *A History of Celibacy*.

8. For similar theories in colonial America, see Norton, *Foundational Mothers and Fathers*; on Brazil, see Costa, *Ordem médica e norma familiar*.

9. Pinheiro, *O androphilismo*, 108. I thank Dain Borges for sharing this source.

10. Borges, *The Family*, 100–101; Guimarães Dias, *A Questão sexual nas prisões*; Heredia Sá, "Algumas reflexões sobre a cópula, onanismo, e prostituição"; Almeida Camillo, *O onanismo da mulher*, 39.

11. Algranti, *Honradas e devotas*, 62–81; Maxwell, *Conflicts and Conspiracies*, 15–16.

12. Peregalli, *Recrutamento Militar no Brasil*, 138–147; Coates compares how different empires made use of penal exiles and orphans in *Convicts and Orphans*, xv–xx, 141–162.

13. Bernardo Luis Ferreira Portugal ao Dom Francisco de Souza Coutinho, Pará, Dec. 26, 1797, Biblioteca Nacional, Seção de Manuscritos, código 07-04-041; Beaurepaire Rohan, "A Ilha"; Raimundo José de Souza Lobo, FN, July 1, 1852, APEJE, FN-4e, f. 106; Pessoa, *Cadernos de pesquisa*, 17.

14. Feijó, *Diogo Antônio Feijó*, 279–357; Serbin, *Needs of the Heart*, ch. 2; Reis observes that Padre Perereca (Luís Gonçalves dos Santos) penned a pamphlet criticizing Feijó's arguments against clerical celibacy in *Death Is a Festival*, 239; Borges, *The Family in Bahia*, 160nn27–28; on the ideal of Victorian manhood in the United States, see Bederman, *Manliness and Civilization*; Stoler, *Carnal Knowledge and Imperial Power*, 145–161.

15. Nabuco, *A escravidão*, 8–9, 30–32.

16. Nabuco, *Abolitionism*, 103, 132; Nabuco, *A escravidão*, 12–15.

17. Lombroso, *Criminal Man*.

18. *A America Illustrada*, Recife, Jan. 30, 1876, 1.

19. Klubock argues in *Contested Communities* that North American corporations introduced bourgeois family ideals to Chilean miners by privileging married workers; on new efforts to reform the poor in imperial Brazil, see Fraga Filho, *Mendigos*; Windler, "City of Children."

20. Brazil, Ministerio da Justiça, *Relatorio . . . Lafayette Rodrigues Pereira*, 93; Bandeira Filho, "Informações," 35.

21. Afonso Bandeira Florence, "Resistência Escrava em São Paulo," 7–32. In 1837, Brazil's first iron factory employed 128 slaves and forty-one free Africans; Rodrigues, "De escravos á operários.

22. Beaurepaire Rohan, "A Ilha," 30; Beaurepaire Rohan, "Considerações acerca da conquista, catechese e civilisação dos selvagens do Brasil," 191–192.

23. Beaurepaire Rohan, "A Ilha," 29.

24. Almeida, *Homosexualismo*, 76–85; Beattie, *The Tribute of Blood*, 198–201.

25. [Agostinho Marques] Perdigão Malheiro, *A escravidão no Brasil*, 1:17–75, 95, 181–183; 2:123–124.

26. See Bailey, *The Lost German Slave Girl*, 99–100; Bush, *Slave Women in Caribbean Society*, 98–103; Martinez-Alier, *Marriage, Class and Colour in Nineteenth Century Cuba*; on Brazil's whitening ideology, see Skidmore, *Black into White*.

27. Slenes, *Na senzala uma flor*, 86, 148–180, 188; Debret, *Viagem pitoresca e histórica ao Brasil*, 2:180–181; Florentino, *A Paz das senzalas*, 147–178; Mattos, *Das cores do silêncio*; Castro Faria, "Família, escrava e legitimidade"; Barickman, "A Bit of Land, Which They Call 'Roça'"; Schwartz, *Sugar Plantations*, 382–394. Karasch cautions that few slave marriages took place in Rio de Janeiro's most urban parishes, but they were more common in suburban ones; *Slave Life*, 287–291.

28. Conrad, *The Destruction of Brazilian Slavery 1850–1888*, 210–238.

29. Bandeira Filho, "Informações," 27; Foucault, *Discipline and Punish*, 135–230.

30. "Fernando Noronha: The Penal Settlement of Brazil," *Scribner's Monthly*, Feb. 1876, 538–539.

31. Bandeira Filho, "Informações," 28.

32. Bandeira Filho, "Informações," 37.

33. Bandeira Filho, "Informações," 28–29.

34. Beaurepaire Rohan, "A Ilha," 24.

35. Beaurepaire Rohan, "A Ilha," 26.

36. Fleury, "Parecer," 22; Bandeira Filho, "Informações," 41.

37. Bandeira Filho, "Informações," 33, 37, 41.

38. JGC ao JACS, FN, Jan. 1, 1891, APEJE, l. FN-30, f. 2. In 1876, one in fifteen convicts lived with wives (97 of 1,531 convicts); and 41 with "amazias"; Relação, FN, Jan. 1, 1876, APEJE, l. FN-17, f. 145–179.

39. Kuznesof also shows that the baptismal records of illegitimate births indicate that 25 percent had fathers present at the baptism; "Sexual Politics, Race, and Bastard-Bearing"; Kuznesof, "Who Were the Families of 'Natural' Born Children"; Borges, *The Family*, 46–47, 247–248; Ramos, "União consensual e a família no século XIX"; Ramos, "From Minho to Minas."

40. Silvia Maria Jardim Brügger, "Legitmidade, casamento, e relações," 48. In Minas, 85 percent of births were classed as legitimate in 1890, whereas in 1844, only 65 percent were; Minas Gerais, *Falla . . . Quintiliano José da Silva*, 124, Mappa 18. Libby and Frank note this trend may have begun in the late colonial period; "Voltando aos registros paroquiais," 395. Graham's data confirms this nineteenth-century trend in *House and Street*, 192.

41. "Natal 28 de Janeiro de 1854," *Diário do Pernambuco*, Recife, Feb. 6, 1854.

42. Costa, "Fernando e o mundo," 1:155–159.

43. Beaurepaire Rohan, "A Ilha," 29.

44. Kuznesof, "Who Were the Families"; Barickman, "Reading the 1835 Parish Censuses from Bahia"; Graham, "Honor among Slaves"; Silva, "Delindra Maria de Pinho."

45. Almeida, *Estado*, 7.

46. Costa, *O caos ressurgirá da ordem*, 159–171.

47. JAMR ao DVCA, Dec. 13, 1870, APEJE, l. FN-14, f. 339; Bandeira Filho, "Informações," 32–33.

48. *Diário de Pernambuco*, Recife, May 6, 1871; *O Liberal*, Recife, May 5, 1871.

49. Beaurepaire Rohan, "A Ilha," 30; Costa, *O caos ressurgirá da ordem*, 159–171.

50. Padre José Esteves Viana to the Presídio Commander, Fernando de Noronha, June 20, 1876 (recopied June 25, 1881), APEJE, livro FN-21, no f. nos; Costa, *O caos ressurgirá da ordem*, ch. 2.

51. Almeida, *Estado*, 11, 40–41; Bandeira Filho also referenced Lombroso and Spencer in "Informações," 25, 29.

52. Almeida, *Estado*, 40–41.

53. Beattie, "Cada," 224.

54. Hunt, *Inventing Human Rights*, 142.

55. Almeida, *Estado*, 40–41; Brazil, Ministerio da Justiça, *Relatorio . . . Dr. Francisco d'Assis Rosa e Silva*, 1889, 128–129.

56. Bandeira Filho, "Informações," 32–33.

57. Foremost among these criminologists was Nina Rodrigues, who expounded Lombrosian theory in his *As raças humanas e a responsabilidade penal no Brazil*.

58. Fleury, "Parecer," 7, 15.

59. Fleury, "Parecer," 7, 15.

60. Fleury, "Parecer," 8.

61. Bandeira Filho, "Informações," 34.

62. Bandeira Filho, "Informações," 32–34; Fleury, "Parecer," 8.

63. JBSM ao MCCC, FN, Sept. 20, 1876, APEJE, FN-17, f. 209–210.

64. Windler, "City of Children," 106–107; Fleury, "Parecer," 8; Bandeira Filho, "Informações," 34.

65. Bandeira Filho, "Informações," 32; AFC ao LCQB, FN, Oct. 17, 1885, APEJE, l. FN-24, no f. nos.

66. Brazil, Ministerio da Justiça, *Relatorio . . . Manoel Pinto de Souza Dantas*, 1882, 157; Brazil, Ministerio da Justiça, *Relatorio . . . Samuel Wallace MacDowell*, 1887, 160.

67. Bandeira Filho complains that commanders had no knowledge of penology; "Informações," 16.

68. Quartel de Commando do Presídio, FN, Aug. 25, 1866, APEJE, l. FN-12, no f. nos.

69. FJPL ao JCR, May 20, 1885, APEJE, l. FN-24, no f. nos; also, ACM ao HPL, FN, July 8, 1873, APEJE l. FN-16, f. 146; SARB ao FAPR, FN, July 12, 1870, APEJE, l. FN-14, f. 271.

70. JPQ ao IMAG, FN, n.d., APEJE, l. FN-28, f. 249.

71. FJPL ao JMF, FN, March 22, 1884, APEJE, l. FN-23, no f. nos; on mainland practices in relation to the honor of poor women, see Abreu Esteves, *Meninas Perdidas*; Caulfield, *In Defense of Honor*.

72. JIRR (José) ao IJSL, FN, APEJE, l. FN-25, Nov. 21, 1886, f. 256–258; for similar statements, FJPL ao SBP, FN, Jan. 22, 1885, APEJE, l. FN-24, no f. nos; JIRR (José) ao IJSL, FN, Sept. 21, 1886, APEJE, l. FN-25, f. 257.

73. JAFM ao JJOA, May 26, 1888, APEJE, l. FN-27, f. 131.

74. ABA ao AALF, FN, April 17, 1878, APEJE, l. FN-18, f. 116.

75. FJPL ao JRC, FN, Aug. 21, 1885, APEJE, l. FN-24, no f. nos.

76. JAFM ao PVA, FN, Aug. 21, 1887, APEJE, l. FN-26, f. 247.

77. Bandeira Filho, "Informações," 33.

78. Protesto de FJPL ao JRC, FN, Sept. 4, 1885, APEJE, FN-24, no f. nos; LPHV ao MAA, FN, 6 Nov. 1889, APEJE, l. FN-28, f. 466; Sentenciado pobre Vicente d'Assis Tavares ao LPHV, FN, Nov. 2, 1889, APEJE, l. FN-28, f. 467–468; Boyer notes similar claims made by colonial Mexican slaves in "Honor among Plebeians," esp. 162–163.

79. FJPL ao BVB, FN, July 13, 1868, APEJE, l. FN-13, f. 352.

80. SARB ao FAA, FN, Jan. 20, 1870, APEJE, l. FN-14, f. 209.

81. HJC ao HPL, FN, March 3, 1875, APEJE, l. FN-16, f. 361.

82. JAFM ao BSL, FN, June 15, 1889, APEJE, l. FN-28, f. 328.

83. ACM ao HPL, FN, July 7, 1873, APEJE, l. FN-16, f. 140.

84. JBSM ao MCCC, FN, Sept. 13, 1876, APEJE, l. FN-17, f. 209–210.

85. José Antonio de Oliveira ao JAFM, Feb. 17, 1889, APEJE, FN-28, f. 143; JAFM ao IMAG, FN, Feb. 17, 1889, APEJE, l. FN-28, f. 144.

86. Bandeira Filho, "Informações," 32.

87. Pessoa, *Cadernos de pesquisa*, 54.

88. JPQ ao IJSL, FN, May 23, 1889, APEJE, l. FN-28, f. 294.

6. "A STENCH IN THE NOSTRILS OF GOD"?

1. Branner, "The Convict Island," 38.

2. Beaurepaire Rohan, "A Ilha," 28.

3. Branner, "The Convict Island," 40.

4. "Acção dos banhos do mar nas molestias de pele," *Diário de Pernambuco*, Recife, Oct. 1, 1886; "Acção dos banhos do mar nas molestias de pele," *Diário de Pernambuco*, Oct. 18, 1886.

5. On this point I have been influenced by my colleague Lisa Fine's study on working-class leisure in Michigan's automotive industry, *The Story of Reo Joe*.

6. Semmes, *My Adventures Afloat*, 596–598.

7. Semmes, *My Adventures Afloat*, 596–609.

8. Said, *Orientalism*.

9. On southern attitudes toward fancy slave women in the domestic U.S. slave trade, see Baptist, " 'Cuffy.' "

10. Semmes, *My Adventures Afloat*, 599.

11. Semmes, *My Adventures Afloat*, 600.

12. Semmes, *My Adventures Afloat*, 600.

13. Semmes, *My Adventures Afloat*, 601; Stein, *Vassouras*, 164; Beattie, *The Tribute of Blood*, 164, 184.

14. Semmes, *My Adventures Afloat*, 602.

15. Semmes, *My Adventures Afloat*, 608–609.

16. Shingleton, *High Seas Confederate*, 74.

17. One measure of the CSS *Alabama*'s celebrity was that *O Alabama* became the name of a pro-slavery newspaper in Salvador, Bahia, in the 1860s.

18. Branner, "The Convict Island," 36.

19. ABA ao AB, FN, April 15, 1879, APEJE, l. FN-19, f. 155.

20. CJA ao HHML, FN, Feb. 14, 1850, APEJE, l. FN-4A, f. 51; "Os liberais," CJA ao HHML, FN, Feb. 14, 1850, f. 52–53.

21. CJA ao HHCL, FN, Jan. 11, 1850, APEJE, l. FN-4A, f. 7–8; CJA ao HHCL, FN, Jan. 31, 1850, f. 22.

22. CJA ao HHCL, FN, Feb. 14, 1850, APEJE, l. FN-4A, f. 55.

23. CJA ao HHCL, FN, March 4, 1850, APEJE, l. FN-4A, f. 71.

24. Beaurepaire Rohan, "A Ilha," 24.

25. CJA ao HHCL, FN, April 2, 1850, APEJE, l. FN-4A, f. 79–80.

26. Fonseca ao HHCL, Ilha das Ratas, March 28, 1850, APEJE, l. FN-4A, f. 80.

27. CJA ao HHCL, FN, April 5, 1850, APEJE, l. FN-4A, f. 85.

28. CJA ao HHCL, FN, May 9, 1850, APEJE, l. FN-4A, f. 109–112.

29. JMIJVPM ao JISR, APEJE, FN, July 9, 1850, FN-4B, f. 58–62.

30. JMIJVPM ao JISR, APEJE, FN, July 23, 1851, FN-4B, f. 69.

31. Silveira ao FJPL, FN, Feb. 22, 1882, APEJE, l. FN-22, f. 121–122; FJPL ao AEBC, FN, Feb. 22, 1882, APEJE, l. FN-22, f. 121.

32. AGL ao BAMT, FN, Dec. n.d., 1857, APEJE, l. FN-6, f. 584.

33. AGL ao BAMT, FN, Nov. 28, 1857, APEJE, l. FN-6, f. 585.

34. Branner, "The Convict Island," 37.

35. Ordem do Dia, JAMR, FN, Jan. 3, 1871, APEJE, FN-15, f. 65.

36. Telegram JIRR (João) to the governor of Pernambuco Antonio Francisco Correia de Araujo, FN, June 5, 1897; June 7, 1897; June 9, 1897, all in ANR, Presídio de Fernando de Noronha, Registro de telegramas do Director, 1892–1909, IIJ 7 10, Livro 248.

37. Bandeira Filho, "Informações," 24–25.

38. Padre João Manuel [Carvalho] referred to President Floriano Peixoto as "our 29, our Honra e Gloria, our pride" in *Reminiscências*, 264; Silva, *Diccionario bibliographico portugues*, 117.

39. Ordem do Dia, FN, May 7, 1882, APEJE, l. FN-22, f. 213.

40. Bandeira Filho, "Informações," 24–25.

41. Fleury, "Parecer," 7.

42. Relatorio, FN, Jan. 1, 1884, APEJE, l. FN-23, f. 14.

43. Branner, "The Convict Island," 38.

44. Melo, *Archipélago*, 68.

45. Sweet relates how crazes over Moorish treasure animated eighteenth-century Portuguese peasants in *Domingos Álveres*, 203–207.

46. Lea, "The Island," 434.

47. Genovese in *Roll Jordan Roll* famously compared slave laborers' conditions in the U.S. South to those of workers in industry, mining, and agriculture. Read, *The Hierarchies of Slavery*, is an innovative evaluation of the life chances of Brazilian slaves.

48. Diniz, "As artes de curar nos tempos da cólera," 355–386.

49. On midwifery and professional medicine in nineteenth-century Brazil, see Sampaio, *Nas trincheiras da cura*; Windler, "Madame Durocher's Performance."

50. CJA ao HHCL, FN, Feb. 12, 1850, APEJE, l. FN-4a, f. 47.

51. Freyre, *The Masters and the Slaves*, 71.

52. Beaurepaire Rohan, "A Ilha," 31.

53. Scott, *The Arts of Domination and Resistance*.

54. Bandeira Filho, "Informações," 27.

55. CJA ao JISR, FN, July 10, 1850, APEJE, l. FN-4A, f. 149.

56. Carvalho, "Agostinho José Pereira," 23–52.

57. *Diário de Pernambuco*, Recife, Sept. 11, 1885.

58. JAFM ao PVA, FN, Oct. 18, 1878, APEJE, l. FN-13, f. 299.

59. Mintz, *Sweetness and Power*; Topik, "Coffee Anyone?"

60. Beattie, *The Tribute of Blood*, 163; Barickman, *A Bahian Counterpoint*, 46.

61. JAFM ao JJOA, FN, May 24, 1888, APEJE, l. FN-27, f. 119; JAFM ao JJOA, FN, Sept. 22, 1888, APEJE, l. FN-27, f. 217; JAFM ao JJOA, FN, May 25, 1888, APEJE, l. FN-27, f. 123; JAFM ao JJOA, FN, Oct. 14, 1888, APEJE, l. FN-27, f. 224; JAFM ao JJOA, FN, Oct. 20, 1888, APEJE, l. FN-27, f. 235; JAFM ao JJOA, FN, Dec. 19, 1888, APEJE, l. FN-27, f. 274.

62. FJPL ao BVB, FN, July 27, 1868, APEJE, l. FN-13, f. 358; on cane cutters' wages, see Eisenberg, *The Sugar Industry*, 188–190.

63. Beaurepaire Rohan, "A Ilha," 26.

64. AGL a BAMT, FN, Nov. 13, 1857, APEJE, l. FN-6, f. 574.

65. Bandeira Filho, "Informações," 41.

66. Branner, "The Convict Island," 34–35.

67. JMIJVPM ao JISR, FN, Feb. 14, 1851, APEJE, l. FN-4b, f. 5.

68. JAMR ao DVCA, FN, Feb. 24, 1871, APEJE, l. FN-15, f. 48.

69. ACM ao JJOJ, FN, Feb. 20, 1872, APEJE, l. FN-15, f. 419.

70. ABA ao LCA, FN, March 11, 1880, APEJE, l. FN-20, f. 162; ABA ao LCA, FN, Oct. 2, 1880, APEJE, l. FN-27, f. 363.

71. FJPL ao BVB, FN, March 10, 1878, APEJE, FN-13, f. 260.

72. Bandeira Filho, "Informações," 38.

73. Relatorio, FN, Aug. 17, 1850, APEJE, l. FN-4A, f. 176.

74. Relatorio de FJPL, FN, Jan. 1, 1869, APEJE, l. FN-13, f. 1–17.

75. Beaurepaire Rohan, "A Ilha," 28–29.

76. Beaurepaire Rohan, "A Ilha," 28.

77. Almeida, "Dissertação abreviada sobre o horrível masmona," 23.

7. CRIME, CONFLICT, CORRUPTION

1. Branner, "The Convict Island," 37.

2. FJPL ao AEBC, FN, March 7, 1882, APEJE, l. FN-22, f. 109.

3. JMIJVP ao VO, FN, Aug. 18, 1851, APEJE, l. FN-4b, f. 103–104.

4. FFMV ao FAR, FN, March 28, 1853, APEJE, l. FN-5, f. 111.

5. This estimate is based on slave prices in Eisenberg, *The Sugar Industry*, 153.

6. Major Manoel Pereira d'Abreu ao ABA, FN, May 20, 1879, APEJE, l. FN-19, f. 228; Major Manoel Pereira d'Abreu ao ABA, FN, July 13, 1879, APEJE, l. FN-19, f. 260.

7. Major Manoel Pereira d'Abreu ao ABA, FN, Sept. 17, 1879, APEJE, l. FN-19, f. 318.

8. Freyre referenced the house and the street to analyze patriarchy in *The Mansions and the Shanties*, 26–56; anthropologist da Matta built on Freyre's ideas in *A casa e a rua*, 31–69, and *Carnavais, malandros, e hérois*, 35–66. Others have added to these insights; e.g., Graham, *House and Street*, 3–27; Carvalho, *Os bestializados*, 126–139; Scheper-Hughes, *Death without Weeping*, 76–92; Beattie, *The Tribute of Blood*, 8–10.

9. ABA ao AB, FN, Oct. 17, 1879, APEJE, l. FN-19, f. 342.

10. Manoel Accioly de Moura Gondim ao MGPL, FN, Dec. 24, 1885, APEJE, l. FN-24, no f. nos.

11. FJPL ao JFM, FN, March 8, 1884, APEJE, FN-23, no f. nos.

12. DTR ao LRB, FN, June 22, 1819, APEJE, FN-1, f. 50–51.

13. ACM ao MNMP, FN, Nov. 8, 1871, APEJE, l. FN-15, f. 270–273.

14. Brazil, Ministerio de Justiça, *Relatorio . . . Conselheiro Manoel Pinto de Souza Dantas*, 1882, 159.

15. FJPL ao JMF, FN, March 22, 1884, APEJE, l. FN-23, no f. nos.

16. ACM ao MNMP, FN, Nov. 16, 1871, APEJE, l. FN-15, f. 277.

17. FJPL ao JMF, FN, Aug. 15, 1884, APEJE, l. FN-23, no f. nos.

18. ACM ao HPL, FN, June 20, 1872, APEJE, l. FN-16, f. 135–139.
19. SJBP ao HPL, FN, May 12, 1874, APEJE, l. FN-16, f. 237.
20. ABA ao AB, FN, Dec. 31, 1878, APEJE, FN-18, f. 586–587.
21. Bandeira Filho, "Informações," 26.
22. ACM ao HPL, FN, Aug. 25, 1873, APEJE, l. FN-16, f. 153.
23. FJPL ao ASL, FN, April 2, 1885, APEJE, FN-24, no f. nos.
24. MGPL ao IJSL, FN, April 19,1886, APEJE, l. FN-25, f. 142.
25. Branner, "The Convict Island," 39.
26. Branner, "The Convict Island," 39.
27. AJM ao LRB, FN, March 16, 1821, APEJE, l. FN-1, f. 78–79.
28. AJM ao LRB, FN, March 16, 1821, APEJE, l. FN-1, f. 78–79.
29. JMIJVP ao VO, FN, Aug. 18, 1851, APEJE, l. FN-4b, f. 103–104.
30. JAFM ao Captain Ernesto Alves Pacheco, FN, July 19, 1888, APEJE, l. FN-27, f. 163–169; JIRR (José) ao JJOA, FN, July 20, 1888, APEJE, l. FN-27, f. 152; JAFM ao JJOA, FN, Aug. 11, 1888, APEJE, l. FN-27, f. 189.
31. ACM ao HPL, FN, April 28, 1873, APEJE, l. FN-16, f. 109.
32. "Ilha de Fernando de Noronha," O Liberal, Recife, Sept. 28, 1871.
33. Comissão de Syndicancia ao DVCA, FN, April 22, 1871, APEJE, FN-15, f. 91–92.
34. Bandeira Filho, "Informações," 10.
35. FJPL ao AEBC, FN, Jan. 15, 1882, APEJE, l. FN-22, f. 5–7.
36. Eisenberg, The Sugar Industry, 153.
37. Captain Justino Rodrigues da Silveira ao AEBC, FN, Feb. 17, 1882, APEJE, l. FN-22, f. 80.
38. FJPL ao AEBC, FN, Jan. 15, 1882, APEJE, l. FN-22, f. 3–5.
39. Galvão, Diccionario, 242.
40. Reis, "Batuque."
41. Captain Justino Rodrigues da Silveira ao FJPL, APEJE, FN, Feb. 22, 1882, APEJE, l. FN-22, f. 121–122; FJPL ao AEBC, FN, Feb. 22, 1882, APEJE, l. FN-22, f. 121.
42. Scott, The Arts of Domination and Resistance; da Matta, Carnavais, malandros e hérois, 67–106.
43. Diário de Pernambuco, Recife, Sept. 11, 1885.
44. MacCord, O Rosário de D. Antonio, esp. ch. 3; on knives, see Sweet, Domingos Álvares, 124; Vainfas and Mello e Souza, "Catolização e poder."
45. FJPL ao JMF, reservado, FN, April 3, 1884, APEJE, l. FN-23, no f. nos.
46. Brazil, Ministerio da Justiça, Relatorio . . . Conselheiro Affonso Augusto Moreira Penna, 1885, 174.
47. Relação nominal dos introductores de bebidas alccolicas apprehendidas pela commissão no desembarque do Vapor Mandahú chegado em 15 de Março de 1884, FN, April 21, 1884, APEJE, l. FN-23, no f. nos.
48. Justino Rodriques da Silveira ao AEBC, FN, Feb. 18, 1882, APEJE, l. FN-22, f. 98.
49. Branner, "The Convict Island," 34–35.
50. FJPL ao ASL, FN, Feb. 21, 1885, APEJE, l. FN-24, no f. nos.

51. SARB ao CB, FN, March 29, 1869, APEJE, l. FN-14, f. 69.

52. SARB ao CB, FN, April 27, 1869, APEJE, l. FN-14, f. 90; Ministerio dos Negocios da Guerra ao JLCP (copy), FN, Nov. 6, 1867, APEJE, l. FN-14, f. 92.

53. FJPL ao JRC, FN, Aug. 21, 1885, APEJE, l. FN-24, no f. nos.

54. José Joaquim de Aguiar ao Capitão Antonio Francisco da Costas, FN, June 18, 1885, APEJE, FN-24, no f. nos; Capitão Antonio Francisco da Costa ao FJPL, FN, June 20, 1885, APEJE, FN-24, no f. nos, Dr. Francisco Pereira da Motta ao FJPL, FN, Jan. 20, 1885, APEJE, FN-24, no f. nos.

55. *Diário de Pernambuco*, Recife, July 21, 1854.

56. SARB a STM, FN, Oct. 11, 1856, APEJE, l. FN-6, f. 441; Freitas, *Cabanos*, 160.

57. JAP ao JBCF, FN, Jan. 29, 1854, APEJE, l. FN-6, f. 26–33.

58. *Diário de Pernambuco*, Recife, July 21, 1854.

59. Scott, *The Arts of Domination and Resistance*.

60. *Diário de Pernambuco*, Recife, July 21, 1854.

61. Relação dos sentenciados que [illegible] presos [illegible] sedições de 21 de Jan. e 27 de Abril de 1854, JAP a JBCF, FN, Dec. 15, 1855, APEJE, l. FN-6, f. 355.

62. QCPFN, FN, Jan. 1, 1865, APEJE, l. FN-12, f. 1.

63. QCPFN, FN, Jan. 1, 1865, APEJE, l. FN-12, f. 1.

64. SJBP ao HPL, FN, Jan. 7, 1875, APEJE, l. FN-16, f. 343–344.

65. SJBP ao HPL, FN, Jan. 7, 1875, APEJE, l. FN-16, f. 343–344; SJBP ao HPL, FN, Feb. 6, 1875, APEJE, l. OE-20, f. 410–23.

66. *Revista Illustrada*, Rio, Jan. 13, 1877; JBSM ao MCCC, FN, Dec. 24, 1876, APEJE, l. FN-17, f. 278.

67. *Diário de Pernambuco*, Recife, Dec. 27, 1876.

68. *Diário de Pernambuco*, Recife, Dec. 30, 1876.

69. Bandeira Filho, "Informações," 35; Castro, *O espírito militar*.

70. Observador, Carta Anomyna [*sic*], April 6, 1877, ANR, IG-85, no f. nos.

71. AFC ao MGPL, FN, Dec. 22, 1885, APEJE, l. FN-24, Dec. 22, 1885, no f. nos.

72. *Diário de Pernambuco*, Recife, Aug. 26, 1885.

73. *Diário de Pernambuco*, Recife, Sept. 11, 1885.

74. *Diário de Pernambuco*, Recife, Aug. 26, 1885.

75. *Journal do Recife*, Aug. 26, 1885.

76. *Diário de Pernambuco*, Recife, Aug. 28, 1885.

77. FJPL ao JRC, FN, Sept. n.d., 1885, APEJE, l. FN-24, no f. nos.

78. Protesto do FJPL ao JCR, FN, Sept. 4, 1885, APEJE, l. FN-24, no f. nos.

79. Copia Syndicancia JFPL ao JRC, FN, Jul. 27, 1885, APEJE, l. FN-24, no f. nos.

80. Brazil, Ministério da Justiça, *Relatorio . . . Conselheiro Joaquim Delfino Ribeiro da Luz*, 1886, 13–14.

81. Brazil, Ministério da Justiça, *Relatorio . . . Conselheiro Manoel Pinto de Souza Dantas*, 1882, 158; Brazil, *Relatorio . . . Conselheiro Joaquim Delfino Ribeiro da Luz*, 1886, 15.

82. *Diário de Pernambuco*, Recife, Sept. 11, 1885.

83. AFC ao JFCP, FN, Nov. 20, 1885, APEJE, l. FN-43, no f. nos.

84. JAFM ao PVA, FN, Jan. 1, 1887, APEJE, l. FN-26, f. 5–6.

85. *Diário de Pernambuco*, Recife, Dec. 21, 1886.

86. JAFM ao PVA, FN, Dec. 12, 1886, APEJE, l. FN-25, f. 355.

87. Empregados, Sentenciados, e Guardas de Fernando de Noronha ao JAFM, FN, Dec. 20, 1886, APEJE, Fernando, l. FN-25, f. 373.

88. JAFM ao PVA, FN, Dec. 20, 1886, APEJE, l. FN-25, f. 370.

89. Brazil, Ministério da Justiça, *Relatório . . . pelo Conselheiro Samuel Wallace MacDowell*, 1887, 25–26.

90. Reis, *Rebelião escrava no Brasil*; Beattie, *The Tribute of Blood*, 177–203; Love, *The Revolt of the Whip*.

8. TREATMENT AND CATEGORIZATION

1. Machado, *Crime e escravidão*; Aufderheid, "Order and Violence"; McCann, "The Whip and the Watch," 36–37; Chalhoub, *Visões de liberdade*; Holloway, *Policing Rio de Janeiro*; Algranti, *O feitor ausente*, 193–198; Soares de Souza, "Os escravos e a pena de morte"; Brown, "'A Black Mark on Our Legislation'"; Karasch, *Slave Life*, ch. 5; Ferreira, *Senhores de poucos escravos*; Guimarães, *Violência entre parceiros de cativeiro*; Campos, "Crime e escravidão," 209–235; Ribeiro, *No meio das galinhas*.

2. The slave convict survey referred to throughout this chapter is Capitão Antonio Gracindo de Gusmão Lobo, "Relação nominal de escravos sentenciados," FN, 27 Oct. 1881, APEJE, l. FN-21, no f. nos.

3. Barickman, "Reading the 1835 Parish Censuses." Barickman follows paths blazed by Kuznesof, "Ethnic and Gender Influences on 'Spanish' Creole Society"; and Nazzari, "Vanishing Indians."

4. A penal expert noted two slave lynchings in Leopoldina, Minas Gerais, in 1876 and Itu, São Paulo, in 1879; Fleury, "Parecer," 15. The abolitionist José de Patrícinio noted that slave lynchings occurred in Itu, Rio Bonito, Resende, Rio do Peixe, Madalena, and Rio de Janeiro to prevent Pedro II from commuting their sentences; *Cidade do Rio de Janeiro*, April 29, 1889. Ricardo Alexandre Ferreira offers data on slave suspects denounced in Franca, São Paulo where in more than one hundred cases from 1830 to 1888 only 18 percent stood trial. Most cases never went to trial either because the defendant died or escaped, the master illegally sold the slave to a distant market, or the court absolved the defendant. In sixty-six cases, Ferreira found that 45.5 percent of slave defendants were never formally processed, 21.2 percent were named as defendants but never prosecuted, and in 25.5 percent of the cases, they were absolved. Only 7.6 percent were tried and condemned; *Senhores de poucos escravos*, 92–96. Low conviction rates were common to the Brazilian jury system; Flory, *Judge and Jury*. Brundage in *Under Sentence of Death*, 98, argues that slave lynchings were more common in the antebellum United States than supposed.

5. Brazil, *Constituição política do Império do Brasil*, art. 179, para. 19; Queiroz, *Escravidão negra em São Paulo*, 53–55. Machado found that in Taubaté, São Paulo, from 1850 to 1888, no jury sentenced slave convicts to hang; 16, to galés; and 82, to be flogged. In Campinas from 1830 to 1888, Machado found that juries sentenced

12 slaves to hang; 16 to galés; and 82 to be flogged; *Crime e escravidão*, 39–40, 53. In Franca, São Paulo, Ferreira found that of 20 slaves convicted from 1830 to 1888, 1 was executed; 3 had capital sentences commuted to galés perpetuas; 1 was sentenced to galés perpetuas; and 15 were flogged; *Senhores de poucos escravos*, 96. In Juiz de Fora, Silva Guimarães found from 1850 to 1888 that of 16 homicides where a slave killed another slave, 2 were sentenced to galés perpétuas; 12 to be flogged; and two sentences were unknown; *Violência*, 114.

6. Série Justiça, Fundo ND, Seção de Guarda Codes, Rio, 1857–1858, ANR, livro IVJ 7 2.

7. Fleury, "Parecer," 6–9.

8. For a description of prison labor on Rio's dikes, see Almeida, "Dissertação abreviada sobre o horrível masmona."

9. Fleury, "Parecer," 15.

10. The numbers given here are recent adjustments upward from the totals cited in Ribeiro's *No meio das galinhas*, 296–298, 314–315. These numbers are based on research subsequent to his book's publication. In an October 27, 2008, e-mail communication from Ribeiro, he confirmed, "O número de execuções que consigno em No Meio das Galinhas não é de modo algum o total de execuções no Brasil, no período entre 1833 e 1876, pois só fiz pesquisas sistemáticas nas fontes do Rio, de Minas [Gerais] e de São Paulo; Mas é sem dúvida a maioria."

11. Fleury, "Parecer," 15; on improper sentencing, see Bandeira Filho, "Informações," 21. Two scholars suggest that courts did not sentence free convicts to galés, but table 1 clearly shows that this was not the case; Brown, " 'A Black Mark on Our Legislation,' " 104; and Aufderheid, "Order and Violence," 307.

12. Ruschenberger, *Three Years*, 28; Ribeiro, *No meio das galinhas*, 58; Debret, *Viagem*, 1:265.

13. JB ao FPC, FN, Oct. 27, 1826, APEJE, l. FN-1, f. 134–135; Soares and Mello, "O resto perdeu-se?," 14–25.

14. In his diaries, Pedro II noted his opposition to the death penalty; Hélio Vianna, "Diário de 1862," *Anuário do Museu Imperial* 17 (1956): 19, 76; Diary entries for May 31, 1890, and June 15, 1890, in the AHMI, Coleção Pedro d'Orléans e Bragança, Catalogo B, Maço 35, Doc. 1,057. I thank Roderick J. Barman for sharing these sources. Ricardo Ferreira nicely summarizes the modifications to the June 10, 1835, law. Only in 1854 were slaves sentenced to death for killing their master, a member of the master's family, or their overseer allowed to petition for clemency. Ferreira, "O tronco na enxovia," 1:194–197.

15. Instituto Brasileiro de Geografia e Estatística [IBGE], *Estatísticas históricas*, 31–33.

16. A brief notice in an American newspaper notes Carpenter's participation in the imperial geographical survey and praises his knowledge of Portuguese and Rio de Janeiro; *The American*, Philadelphia, Jan. 24, 1884, 220; also see his incisive, if racist, musings about color in Brazil, "Race in Brazil," 82–86.

17. Carpenter, *Round about Rio*, 328–329.

18. *Journal do Comércio*, Rio, May 20, 1879; *Arauto de Minas*, São João d'el Rey, July 14, 1881; observations about slave lynchings originally cited in Ribeiro, *No meio das galinhas*, 285–286, 292, 303, 304, 308. Stein made similar observations about slave violence and how newspapers in the 1870s fed fears that slaves murdered to live a life of leisure in jail in *Vassouras*, 140–141; Fleury referred to slave lynchings as "acts of sedition and barbarism" in "Parecer," 15.

19. FJPL ao JMF, FN, April 20, 1884, APEJE, l. FN-23, no f. nos.

20. Ao rogo do supplicante Antonio Ferreira [por Liberalino Rodrigues Machado] ao Generalíssimo Chefe do Governo Provisório dos Estados Unidos do Brasil (hereafter, EUB), FN, May 20, 1890, APEJE, l. FN-29, f. 197.

21. Slave convict and ex-slave in this case study are one and the same. To limit confusion, however, I privilege the term "slave convict," but "ex-slave" appears in citations and some analysis. In 1875, a report indicated that four male and female slaves were resident on the island; Relação, Jan. 1, 1876, FN, APEJE, l. FN-17, f. 145–179.

22. [Agostinho Marques] Perdigão Malheiro, *A escravidão no Brasil*, 1:17–75, 95, 181–183; 2:123–124; the citation was translated into English in Conrad, *Children of God's Fire*, 237–245.

23. Bandeira Filho, "Informações," 28.

24. One inspector observed that records were often incomplete; Bandeira Filho, "Informações," 11, 13.

25. The slave João Bras is listed as the former slave of the Baronice de Itu in an 1889 petition; JAFM ao IMAG, FN, Jan. 5, 1889, APEJE, l. FN-28, f. 94.

26. Confusion over a minor's sentence is telling: "Bento Leite [que foi escravo] de João Nepumuceno de Mello em que alega estar sofrendo immericida pena, por ter sido julgado em Pesqueira e repercutou a pena de 20 anos de prisão attenta a sua menor idade, e no entanto o guia que o accompanhou consta de vir expiar a de galés perpétuas"; JAFM ao PVA, FN, Sept. 22, 1887, APEJE, l. FN-26, f. 278; Ribeiro, *No meio das galinhas*, 525–530.

27. One of them was "Sebastião, known as Kangaroo, ex-slave of Pedro Antonio de Sá Cavalcante," and the other two were free men. One of the free men, Vicente d'Assis Tavares, wrote a petition asking to be liberated from one of the island's few prison cells so that he could live with his new wife. He wrote, "Igualdade e fraternidade deve ser a bandeira existente entre os sentenciados." LPHV ao MAA, FN, Nov. 6, 1889, APEJE, l. FN-28, f. 466; Do sentenciado pobre Vicente d'Assis Tavares ao LPHV, FN, Nov. 2, 1889, APEJE, l. FN-28, f. 467–468.

28. Bandeira Filho, "Informações," 25.

29. This is why the director refers to 263 ex-slave convicts, but based on all entries, this book refers to 264.

30. The Sexagenarian Law freed slaves older than sixty-five immediately, but it required that slaves age sixty to sixty-four continue to provide service until they reached age sixty-five.

31. JPQ ao IMAG, FN, April 20, 1889, APEJE, l. FN-28, f. 261.

32. Livro de guias, 1830, ANR, Serie Justiça, FN, Código do Fundo ND, livro IIJ 2 7, Seção de Guarda Codes; Ribeiro, *No meio das galinhas*, 284.

33. Beattie, *The Tribute of Blood*, ch. 6.

34. Livro de guias, 1830, ANR, Serie Justiça, FN, Código do Fundo ND, livro IIJ 2 7, Seção de Guarda Codes; this estimate is quite conservative as Bandeira Filho noted that there were three hundred slave convicts on the island when he visited it in 1879; "Informações," 17.

35. Bandeira Filho, "Informações," 29, 41.

36. Similarly, a list of slaves who entered a Rio de Janeiro prison in 1857 and 1858 did not include a category for color; Série Justiça, Fundo ND, Seção de Guarda Codes, Rio, 1857–1858, ANR, livro IVJ 7 2.

37. Mattos, *Das cores do silêncio*, 96–103; Bandeira Filho, "Informações," 13.

38. Fleury cited in Morais, *Prisões*, 79–80; on vices and slavery, see Beattie, "'The Slave Silvestre's Disputed Sale.'"

39. Slenes, *Na Senzala uma flor*, 86, 148–180; Barickman, "A Bit of Land, Which They Call 'Roça'"; Motta, *Corpos escravos, vontades livres*," 209–225, 289–354; Florentino, *A Paz das senzalas*, 147–178; Castro Faria, *A colônia em movimento*, 312–322; Schwartz, *Sugar Plantations*, 382–394; Borges, *The Family in Bahia Brazil*, 1870–1945, 64; Dean, *Rio Claro*, 77–79.

40. Parecer, Rio de Janeiro, Nov. 6, 1854, Arquivo do Visconde de Uruguai, pasta Recurso ao Poder Moderador, Instituto Histórico Geografico Brasileiro, Rio de Janeiro; cited in Soares de Souza, "Os escravos e a pena de morte," 17; on slave marriage, see Perdigão Malheiro, *A escravidão no Brasil*, 1:59–61.

41. Barickman, "Reading the 1835 Parish Censuses," 318.

42. In imperial Brazil, the right to vote hinged on whether one was a head of household (unless one held a commissioned military officer's rank or an advanced degree). The law assumed that household dependents lacked the liberty to vote their conscience; Barickman, "Reading the 1835 Parish Censuses," 318–319.

43. FJPL ao SBP, FN, Dec. 13, 1884, APEJE, l. FN-23, no f. nos.

44. JGC ao JACS, "Relação nominal dos sentenciados, sentenciadas, e deportados que seguem a bordo do vapor Beberibe," FN, Nov. 19, 1890, APEJE, l. FN-29, f. 381–382.

45. Bandeira Filho, "Informações," 16.

46. Bandeira Filho complained that many of the convicts who had the benefit of a convict domestic were galés; "Informações," 19, 23, 24, 29; Fleury, "Parecer," 15.

47. Bandeira Filho, "Informações," 12, 28–29; Fleury, "Parecer," 8–9, 16. The governor's concern arose after abusive flogging of free convicts was highlighted in Pernambuco's opposition press. See "Ilha de Fernando," *O Liberal* (Recife), Sept. 28, 1871 (newspaper clipping found in APEJE, l. FN-15, f. 253); "Fernando Noronha: The Penal Settlement of Brazil," *Scribner's Monthly*, Feb. 1876, 538; a list of floggings for convicts and their infractions can be found in ACM ao MNMP, FN, Oct. 23, 1871, APEJE, l. FN-15, f. 253.

48. FJPL ao JASL, FN, Nov. 18, 1881, APEJE, l. FN-21, no f. nos.

49. FJPL ao JASL, FN, Nov. 11, 1881, APEJE, l. FN-21, no f. nos. An American journalist reported, "The only fettered man on the island was here a large boned, flabby, ungainly, scowling individual, evidently despised by his fellow prisoners for having murdered a man in his sleep"; "Fernando de Noronha," *Scribner's Monthly*, Feb. 1876, 538–539.

50. FJPL ao JASL, FN, Nov. 11, 1881, APEJE, l. FN-21, no f. nos.

51. "Relatório," FN, Jan. 1, 1884, APEJE, l. FN-23, f. 22–24.

52. "Relatório," FN, Jan. 1, 1884, APEJE, l. FN-23, f. 22–24; "Fernando Noronha," *Scribner's Monthly*, Feb. 1876, 538–539.

53. Conrad, *The Destruction of Brazilian Slavery*; Beattie, *The Tribute of Blood*, 95–98.

54. One report noted fifty-nine petitions from 1884 to 1888 from free and slave convicts; JAFM ao IJSL, "Mapa de recursos de graças," FN, Feb. 18, 1888, APEJE, l. FN-27, f. 36–40; on stamps, ABA ao AB, FN, June 26, 1878, APEJE, l. FN-18, f. 227.

55. JAFM ao JRC, FN, July 12, 1885, APEJE, l. FN-24, no f. nos; JAFM ao BSL, FN, June 15, 1889, APEJE, l. FN-28, f. 322.

56. JAFM ao JRC, FN, May 20, 1885, APEJE, l., FN-24, no f. nos; JAFM ao BSL, FN, June 15, 1889, APEJE, l. FN-28, f. 322. Another letter shows that the slave convict Marçal Correia was pardoned and returned to Recife on May 13, 1889; LPHV ao MAA, FN, Nov. 17, 1889, APEJE, l. FN-28, f. 479.

57. JAFM ao PVA, FN, May 20, 1887, APEJE, l. FN-26, f. 156. Similarly, Pedro pardoned the slave Cesário on April 23, 1886, as published in the *Diário Official* according to GPL ao IJSL, FN, May 13, 1886, APEJE, l. FN-25, f. 167; "Constando do Diário Official numero 94 de 5 de Abril ultimo que forão perdoados os sentencia-dos Manoel Francisco dos Santos conhecido por Gongó, Antonio Justino Riberio, e Francisco Angola os quaes nesta data faço embarcar"; JAFM ao JRC, May 20, 1885, APEJE, l. FN-24, no f. nos; also see pardon for João Marques, Copia do Guia do Sen-tenciado João Marques, escravo que foi dos Frades Benedictos de Olinda, FN, July 2, 1878, APEJE, l. FN-18, f. 255.

58. JRS ao Cidadão General Governador do Estado de Pernambuco (no name given), FN, Dec. 17, 1889, APEJE, l. FN 28, f. 496.

59. Ao rogo do Supplicante Francisco de Assis (Sobel Henriques de Miranda) ao Cidadao Chefe do Governo Provisorio dos EUB, FN, May 21, 1890, APEJE, l. FN-29, f. 268.

60. Manoel de Miranda ao Cidadão Generalissimo Chefe do Governo Provisório dos EUB, May 5, 1890, APEJE, l. FN-29, f. 189; Manoel de Miranda ao Cidadão Generalissimo Chefe do Governo Provisório dos EUB, FN, May 20, 1890, APEJE, l. FN-29, f. 188.

61. Cadete João da Costa Medeiros Sobrinho ao Cidadão General e Chefe do Governo Provisório dos EUB, FN, Jan. 8, 1890, APEJE, l. FN-29, f. 4.

62. Gilroy, *Black Atlantic*, 27–28.

63. Of 205 ex–slave convicts found in matriculation records, the emperor had pardoned some thirty before the Nov. 15, 1889, coup. Thirty-four other slave convicts

died on the island between 1887 and 1891; Livro da Matricula . . . 1865; Livro da Matricula . . . 1885. Correspondence shows that while some slaves returned to the continent in 1889, larger numbers began to return in 1890, and continued to return until 1892; see, e.g., JGC ao JACS, FN, Nov. 19, 1890, APEJE, l. FN-29, f. 386; "Relacao nominal dos sentenciados, sentenciadas, e deportados que seguem a bordo do vapor Beberibe," FN, Nov. 19, 1890, APEJE, l. FN-29, f. 381–382. Other slave convicts who had been sentenced more recently continued in the colony; Pessoa, *Cadernos de pesquisa*, 54.

64. Silva, *Prince of the People*, ch. 7.

65. Fleury, "Parecer," 20–21.

66. The number is based on Ribeiro's count of 199 confirmed slave executions, 135 slaves condemned to die whose executions could not be confirmed, and 523 whose sentences were commuted; *No meio das galinhas*, 314–315; personal communication with Ribeiro, Oct. 27, 2008.

67. Algranti, *O feitor ausente*, 36–37.

68. Ferreira, "O tronco na enxovia," 180.

69. Slaves' initiatives spurred further associational abolitionist activism on the mainland. As Castillo and Cowling demonstrate, the efforts of slaves to construct narratives to favor their petitions for freedom from emancipationist societies created a better general context for slaves to press for their liberation; "Funding Freedom." Also Cowling, *Conceiving Freedom*.

9. OF CAPTIVITY AND INCARCERATION

1. Beattie, "Conscription versus Penal Servitude."

2. Brazil, Ministério da Justiça, *Relatório . . . MacDowell*, 1887, 159.

3. The republic's separation of Church and state made it possible to implement a reform imperial politicians had only succeeded in debating: civil marriage. Civil marriage inspired backland residents to resist federal authority in the Canudos Rebellion of 1896–1897; Levine, *Vale of Tears*, 56–57, 64, 127, 144, 227, 278n95.

4. Pernambuco, *Falla . . . João Pedro Carvalho de Moraes . . .* , 1876, 26.

5. Bandeira Filho, "Informações," 12.

6. Love, *The Revolt of the Whip*; on the composition of the navy's enlisted men, see Jeha, "A galera heterogênea."

7. Caminha, *Bom Crioulo*, 78.

8. Beattie, "Adolfo"; Beattie, "Conflicting Penile Codes." Caminha's plot deconstructed novelist José de Alencar's novels that depicted Brazil's colonial origins through the heterosexual romances of indigenous and Portuguese nobility; Sommer, *Foundational Fictions*, ch. 5.

9. Love, *The Revolt of the Whip*, 88; Carew, *The Lower Deck of the Royal Navy 1900–1930*, 31; Hélio Leôncio Martins, "A revolta dos marinheiros–1910," in *História Naval Brasileira*, vol. 5, tomo 1 B (Rio de Janeiro: Ministério da Marinha, Serviço de Documentação da Marinha, 1997). Love cites both these sources.

10. Anonymous, "A Plea in Favor of Maintaining Flogging in the Navy," n.p., n.d., Navy Department Library website, http://www.history.navy.mil/online/flogging.htm (consulted Sept. 8, 2012).

11. Fleury, "Parecer," 16.

12. Fleury, "Parecer," 8.

13. ABA ao AALF, FN, Dec. 11, 1879, APEJE, l. FN-19, f. 411–412; ABA ao LCA, FN, Jan. 13, 1880, APEJE, l. FN-20, f. 2–7.

14. Bandeira Filho, "Informações," 29.

15. Branner, "The Convict Island," 37.

16. Branner, "The Convict Island," 37.

17. Fleury, "Parecer," 16.

18. Needell, "Politics, Parliament, and the Penalty of the Lash."

19. Schenk, *Work or Fight!*

20. Davis, *From Homicide to Slavery*, 17; an important exception is Ribeiro, *No meio das galinhas.*

21. Hood, *The Death Penalty*, 55; only fifty-six nations currently apply the death penalty for civilian, peacetime crimes. Another thirty-six countries have the law on the books but never employ it. Thirty-five U.S. states practice the death penalty; "Geography," *National Geographic* 218, no. 2 (Aug. 2009): 20.

22. Ribeiro, *No meio das galinhas*, 43–316; Beattie, " 'Born under the Cruel Rigor of Captivity,' " 47–55.

23. This diffuse opposition to cruel punishments comports well with Schwartz's interpretation of ideas of religious tolerance in *All Can Be Saved.*

24. Citation from the trial transcript, O Escravo Thomaz, Recife, 1869, Coleção Tribunal da Relação de Pernambuco, IAHGP, caixa 5, f. 81 (hereafter, O Escravo Thomaz, IAHGP).

25. Nabuco, *A escravidão.*

26. Two fellow scholars have analyzed Thomaz's trials; Castilho, "A Slave Murders, a System Critiqued"; and Galvão, "O preto senhor Thomaz."

27. Soares de Souza, "Os escravos e a pena de morte."

28. Nabuco, *A escravidão*, 45.

29. Anderson, *Imagined Communities.*

30. Nabuco, *A escravidão*, 41.

31. Carvalho, *Liberdade*, ch. 10.

32. Nabuco, *A escravidão*, 42.

33. Nabuco, *A escravidão*, 39–40.

34. Nabuco, *A escravidão*, 18–19.

35. Brown notes that British abolitionists described slavery as a "proof of collective vice" in *Moral Capital*, 153.

36. Cited in Paes Barretto, *A abolição e a federação no Brasil*, 11–12.

37. Beattie, "The Slave Silvestre's Disputed Sale."

38. See the police report in the transcript, O Escravo Thomaz, IAHGP, f. 3–5.

39. Nabuco translated and cited in Carolina Nabuco, *The Life of Joaquim Nabuco*, 20.

40. Nabuco, *A escravidão*, 41.

41. Nabuco, *A escravidão*, 39.

42. Nabuco, *The Life of Joaquim Nabuco*, 26.

43. Neder, "Sentimentos e idéias jurídicas no Brasil."

44. Caminha, *Bom Crioulo*; Beattie, "Conflicting Penile Codes."

45. Partrocínio, *Motta Coqueiro*, 36.

46. Ribeiro, *No meio das galinhas*, 302–305.

47. Azevedo, *Abolicionismo*; Conrad, *The Destruction of Brazilian Slavery*, 49; Parron, *A política da escravidão*, 51–72. On the moral defense of slavery in the United States, see Greenberg, *Honor and Slavery*, 87–114.

48. Brown, *Moral Capital*, 153.

49. Livingston, *A System of Penal Law for the State of Louisiana*, 116.

50. Davis, *From Homicide to Slavery*, 26–27; Neder, "Sentimentos e idéias jurídicas," 1:102.

51. Banner, *The Death Penalty*, 98; Beckman, "Three Penal Codes Compared," 166.

52. Social psychologists suggest that the legacy of slavery explains the death penalty's persistence in the South and argue that states with a higher percentage of slaves were more likely to execute criminals; Nisbett and Cohen, *Culture of Honor*, 71–72.

53. Ferrell, *The Abolitionist Movement*, 44; Tilly, *Popular Contention in Great Britain*, 85–86.

54. Barrows, *Penal Codes of France, Germany, Belgium and Japan*, 13.

55. Nabuco, *A escravidão*, 43–44.

56. Mercer, *When the Guillotine Fell*, 136–142; Franck, Nyman, and Schabas, *The Barbaric Punishment*, 51–52.

57. An American naval officer visiting Brazil in 1831 observed: "Taking away life is a punishment hardly known in Brazil"; Ruschenberger, *Three Years*, 28. The French artist Jean-Baptiste Debret wrote that in fifteen years of residence in Rio de Janeiro he had witnessed only two executions; *Viagem*, 1:261, 2:211; Ribeiro, *No meio das galinhas*, 19–20, 314–315.

58. Hood, *The Death Penalty*, 55–57; Caldeira, *City of Walls*, 346–348. Hood and Caldeira repeat a common misconception that the last legal execution took place in Brazil in 1855, when it took place in 1876.

59. Nabuco, *A escravidão*, 35.

60. Schwarz, *Slave Laws in Virginia*, 68.

61. Ribeiro, *No meio das galinhas*, 296–298, 314–315; Schwarz, *Slave Laws in Virginia*, 68; Brown, " 'A Black Mark on Our Legislation,' " 101–103; Soares de Souza, "Os escravos e a pena de morte."

62. Stroud, *A Sketch of the Laws Relating to Slavery*; Flanigan, "Criminal Procedure in Slave Trials in the Antebellum South."

63. Wahl, *The Bondsmen's Burden*, 259n157; Wyatt-Brown, *The Shaping of Southern Culture*, 152; Barclay, *A Practical View of the Present State of Slavery in the West Indies*; Gaspar, *Bondsmen and Rebels*, 192–202.

64. Frazier, *Runaway and Freed Missouri Slaves*, 87; Ingersoll, "Slave Codes and Judicial Practice in New Orleans, 1718–1807"; Duncan, *Contra el silencio*, 79. In a personal communication, Professor Jane Landers stated she had never seen a case in which Spanish courts compensated owners for executed slaves in the archives of Ecuador, Mexico, Cuba, Colombia, or the Dominican Republic. On Spanish Florida, see Landers, *Black Society in Spanish Florida*, 183–201. In the late eighteenth century, Spanish authorities resorted to capital punishment for heinous crimes but preferred to use convicts as penal labor; Pike, "Penal Servitude in the Spanish Empire."

65. Nabuco, *A escravidão*, 35–36.

66. Bethel and Carvalho, *Joaquim Nabuco*; Costa, *The Brazilian Empire*, ch. 9; Skidmore, *Black into White*.

67. Nabuco, *A escravidão*. See Nabuco's correspondence with leading abolitionists in Bethel and Carvalho, *Joaquim Nabuco*.

68. Nabuco, *A escravidão*, 2–3.

69. Davis, *From Homicide to Slavery*, 22; Greenberg, *Honor and Slavery*, 87–114.

70. Nabuco, *Abolitionism*, 94.

71. Schwarz, *Slave Laws in Virginia*, 70.

72. Blanchard, *Under the Flags of Freedom*.

73. Andrews, *Afro-Latin America*, ch. 1.

74. Salvatore, "Death and Liberalism"; Berquist, *Coffee and Conflict in Colombia*, 11–12; Díaz, "Vicenta Ochoa, Dead Many Times."

75. Hood, *The Death Penalty*, 55–57.

76. Baker, *Affairs of Party*, 185.

77. Azevedo notes in *O direito dos escravos* that law students in São Paulo worked to abrogate the death penalty.

78. Linebaugh, *The London Hanged*; Beattie, *Policing and Punishment in London*. Some U.S. states experimented with the "milder" punishment of castration for slaves convicted of rape; see Summerville, "Rape, Race, and Castration"; Coates, *Convicts and Orphans*; Bender, *Angola under the Portuguese*.

79. Morais Filho, *Festas e tradições populares do Brasil*, 355–366; Magalhães Jr., *Deodoro: A Espada contra o Império*, 1:115–116.

80. Ribeiro, *No meio das galinhas*, 301, 316.

81. Galliher et al., *America without the Death Penalty*, 21.

82. Bruce, "Billy Budd and Capital Punishment."

83. Scheick, *The Half Blood*, 36–37.

84. Child, "The Juryman: A Sketch," *Emancipator and Republican*, Jan. 12, 1850; cited in Isenberg, *Sex and Citizenship in Antebellum America*, 124.

85. Hunt, *Inventing Human Rights*, 39.

86. MacKey, "Edward Livingston," 160.

87. Andrews, *Blacks and Whites in São Paulo*, 146–156; Butler, *Freedoms Given, Freedoms Won*, 88–128; Helg, *Our Rightful Share*, 193–220.

88. Skidmore, *Black into White*; Ribeiro, *No meio das galinhas*, 303n8.

89. Hunt, *Inventing Human Rights*, 34.

90. Garland, *Punishment and Modern Society*, 3–4; Hood, *The Death Penalty*, 57.

91. Article 5, LVIIa, prohibits the death penalty in Brazil "except in cases where war has been declared"; Brazil, *Constituição da república federativa do Brasil*.

92. Zimring and Hawkins, *Capital Punishment and the American Agenda*, 144; Galliher et al., *America without the Death Penalty*, 190–191.

CONCLUSION

Epigraph: Lins do Rego, *Usina*, 17–18.

1. Nicoll, *Three Voyages of a Naturalist*, 13.

2. Lins do Rego, *Usina*, 63–71. On Freyre's decided influence over Lins do Rego, see Ellison, *Brazil's New Novel*, 45–82.

3. Freyre, *The Mansions and the Shanties*, 109.

4. To support this point, Freyre cites a Capuchin friar's 1842 missive to the governor that in Recife's shanties "men calmly engaged in the practice of trading wives, in a true sexual communism"; Freyre, *The Mansions and the Shanties*, 109.

5. Almeida, "Dissertação abreviada sobre o horrível masmona," 24.

6. Brazil, Ministerio de Justiça, *Relatorio . . . Conselheiro Manoel Pinto de Souza Dantas*, 1882, 104–105.

7. Pernambuco, *Falla . . . Conselheiro Sergio de Teixeira Macedo . . .*, 1857, 92.

8. Diacon, *Stringing Together a Nation*; Blake, *The Vigorous Core of Our Nationality*, 31–32.

9. Kraay, "Patriotic Mobilization in Brazil"; Beattie, *The Tribute of Blood*, ch. 2.

10. Lins do Rego, *Usina*, 21.

11. Hay, "Afterword: Law and Society in Comparative Perspective."

12. Garland, *Punishment and Modern Society*, 19.

13. Skidmore, *Black into White*; Costa, *The Brazilian Empire*, ch. 9.

14. Ayers, *Vengeance and Justice*; there were exceptions. Apparently French and Spanish legal traditions distinguished Louisiana and to a lesser degree Missouri from other states. Antebellum Louisiana courts commonly sentenced slaves to lengthy jail sentences and incarcerated them alongside free black and white convicts, something most other southern states avoided. In 1860, Louisiana's penitentiary held 96 slaves, 11 free colored men, and 236 whites; Phillips, *American Negro Slavery*, 391; Frazier, *Slavery and Crime in Missouri*; Schafer, "Slaves and Crime"; Oshinsky, *Worse Than Slavery*; Curtin, *Black Prisoners and Their World*.

15. Citation from Oshinsky, *Worse Than Slavery*, 153–154.

16. Guimarães Dias, *A questão sexual nas prisões*, 70.

17. "O Contato dos presos com o mundo exterior" O Brasil atrás das grades, Human Rights Watch website, 1997, http://199.173.149.140/portuguese/reports /presos/agrad.htm (accessed March 3, 2008).

18. Beattie, "Cada homem," 2:239–240.

19. Andrews, for example, argues that "only in Brazil did war not play a major role in slave liberation"; *Afro-Latin America*, 80.

20. A rare analysis of whiteness in Brazil can be found in Lewin, "Who Was 'O Grande Romano'?"; also Barman, "Listen for the Silences." See the cartoons of President Nilo Peçanha (1909–1910) that depict him as a *capoeira* in an unsubtle reference to his partial African ancestry; Lustosa, *Histórias de presidentes*, 56; Spitzer, *Lives In Between*; Grinberg, *O fiador dos brasileiros*.

21. Roediger, *The Wages of Whiteness*; Scott, *Degrees of Freedom*, 166–171. Stoler demonstrates similar comparisons could be extended to European colonial communities in Asia, Africa, and Latin America, where authorities expended energy and treasure to define and defend the lower bounds of national identity and "whiteness"; *Carnal Knowledge and Imperial Power*, 29–40.

22. Andrews, "Black and White Workers"; Stolke, "Trabalho e moralidade familiar."

23. "French Convict Marriages," in Chambers and Chambers, *Chambers's Journal of Popular Literature*, 486–487; Redfield, *Space in the Tropics*, 197.

24. West, *History of Tasmania*, 2:181–182; Pybus, *Black Founders*, 91–92.

25. Chekhov, *Sakhalin Island*, 85–97, 212, 239.

26. Sarti, "'All Masters Discourage the Marrying of Their Male Servants.'" For similar tensions over domestics and living arrangements in Brazil, see Graham, *House and Street*.

27. Vergara, *Copper Workers*, 37–38; Klubock, *Contested Communities*.

28. Mintz, *Caribbean Transformations*.

29. Graham, *Caetana Says No*, 32; Slenes, *Na senzala*.

30. Barickman, "Reading the 1835 Parish," 308.

31. Tannenbaum, *Slave and Citizen*. See the forum "What Can Frank Tannenbaum Still Teach Us about Slavery," in *Law and History Review*. The forum centers on an article by Fuente, "Slave-Law and Claims Making in Cuba"; Díaz, "Beyond Tannenbaum"; and Schmidt-Nowara, "Still Continents"; also see Ingersoll, "Slave Codes"; Grinberg, "Alforria," 1–21.

32. Scott, *The Arts of Domination and Resistance*.

PERIODICALS

American Naturalist, Chicago
Cidade do Rio de Janeiro, Rio de Janeiro
Cornell Alumni News, Ithaca, NY
Diário de Pernambuco, Recife
O Liberal, Recife
Lippencott's Magazine of Popular Literature and Science, Philadelphia
Pennsylvania Magazine of History and Biography, Philadelphia
Popular Science Monthly, New York
Provincia, Recife
Quarterly Review, London
Rio Branco, Recife
Scribner's Monthly, New York
O Tempo, Recife

DISSERTATIONS AND UNPUBLISHED PAPERS

Almeida, Cypriano José Barata de [attributed]. "Dissertação abreviada sobre o horrível masmona—pressiganga—existente no Rio de Janeiro." In IHGB, lata 48, doc. 12, May 26, 1829.

Aufderheid, Patricia Ann. "Order and Violence: Social Deviance and Social Control in Brazil, 1780–1840." PhD diss , University of Minnesota, 1976.

Barman, Roderick J. "Listen for the Silences: Race in the Official World of Imperial Brazil 1822–1872." Paper presented for the panel "Racial Silences in the Archive and the Historiography of Race in Postcolonial Latin America," American Historical Association Meeting, Chicago, January 7, 2012.

Câmara, Bruno Augusto Dornelas. "O 'retalho' do comércio: A política partidária, a comunidade portuguesa e a nacionalização do comércio a retalho, Pernambuco 1830–1870." PhD diss., Universidade Federal de Pernambuco, 2012.

Carvalho, Marcus Joaquim Maciel de. "Hegemony and Rebellion in Pernambuco, Brazil 1821–1835." PhD diss., University of Illinois, 1989.

Castilho, Celso Thomas. "Abolitionism Matters: The Politics of Anti-slavery Movements in Pernambuco 1869–1888." PhD diss., University of California, Berkeley, 2008.

Castilho, Celso Thomas. "A Slave Murders, a System Critiqued: Political and Anti-slavery Thought in Recife, ca. 1870." Brazilian Studies Association Conference, Nashville, Tennessee, October 14, 2006.

Czeblakow, Agnieska. "A Prison by Any Other Name: Incarceration in Seventeenth and Eighteenth-Century Audiencia de Quito." PhD diss., Emory University, 2011.

Hendricks, Howard Craig. "Education and the Maintenance of the Social Structure: The Faculdade de Direito do Recife and the Brazilian Northeast, 1870–1939." PhD diss., State University of New York at Stony Brook, 1977.

Jeha, Silvana Cassab. "A galera heterogênea: Naturalidade, trajetória e cultural dos recrutas e marinheiros da Armada Nacional e Imperial do Brasil 1822–1854." PhD diss., Pontífica Universidade do Rio de Janeiro, 2011.

Maia, Clarissa Nunes. "Policiados: Controle e disciplina das classes populares na cidade do Recife, 1865–1915." PhD diss., Universidade Federal de Pernambuco, 2001.

Mamigonian, Beatriz Gallotti. "To Be a Liberated African in Brazil: Labour and Citizenship in the Nineteenth Century." PhD diss., University of Waterloo, 2002.

Reyes, Victoria Livia Unzueta. "La Justicia Militar: Un estudio comparativo Mexico (1855–1901)—Italia (1859–1896)." PhD diss., Universita degli Studi di Torino, 2005.

Windler, Erica M. "City of Children: Boys, Girls, Family and State in Imperial Rio de Janeiro." PhD diss., University of Miami, Coral Gables, 2003.

PUBLICATIONS

Abbot, Elizabeth. *A History of Celibacy*. Cambridge, MA: Da Capo, 2001.

Abreu e Lima, José Inácio. "Apontamentos sobre a Ilha de Fernando de Noronha." *Revista do Instituto Archeologico e Geographico Pernambucano*, no. 38 (1890): 3–17.

Abreu Esteves, Martha de. *Meninas perdidas: Os populares e o cotidiano do amor no Rio de Janeiro da belle époque*. Rio: Paz e Terra, 1989.

Aguirre, Carlos. "Cimarronaje, bandolerismo y desintegración esclavista." In *Bandoleros, abigeos, y montoneros: Criminalidad y violencia en el Perú, siglos XVIII–XIX*, edited by Carlos Aguirre and Charles Walker. Lima: Instituto de Apoyo Agrario, 1990.

Aguirre, Carlos. *The Criminals of Lima and Their Worlds: The Prison Experience, 1850–1935*. Durham, NC: Duke University Press, 2005.

Aguirre, Carlos, and Charles Walker, eds. *Bandoleros, abigeos, y montoneros: Criminalidad y violencia en el Perú, siglos XVIII–XIX*. Lima: Instituto de Apoyo Agrario, 1990.

Alberto, Paulina. *Terms of Inclusion: Black Intellectuals in Twentieth-Century Brazil*. Stanford, CA: Stanford University Press, 2012.

Algranti, Leila Mezan. *O feitor ausente: Estudo sobre a escravidão urbana no Rio de Janeiro.* Petrópolis: Vozes, 1988.

Algranti, Leila Mezan. *Honradas e devotas: Mulheres da colônia.* Rio: José Olympio, 1993.

Almeida, Horacio de. *Brejo de Areia.* 2nd ed. João Pessoa: Paraíba, 1980.

Almeida, José Ricardo Pires de. *Homosexualismo (a libertinagem no Rio de Janeiro).* Rio: Laemmert, 1906.

Almeida, Manuel Antonio de. *Memórias de um sargento de milicias.* São Paulo: Círculo do Livro, n.d.

Almeida, Rufino Augusto de. *Estado actual das prisões da província de Pernambuco.* Recife: Typ. De M. Figeroa, 1874.

Almeida Camillo, Alexandre Augusto de. *O onanismo da mulher, sua influencia sobre o physico e a moral.* Rio: Portella, 1886.

Anderson, Benedict. *Imagined Communities: Reflections on the Origins and Spread of Nationalism.* Rev. ed. New York: Verso, 1991.

Andrade, Manuel Correia de. *A guerra dos cabanos.* Rio: 1965; Recife: Editora da UFPE, 2005.

Andrews, George Reid. *Afro-Latin America 1800–2000.* Oxford: Oxford University Press, 2004.

Andrews, George Reid. "Black and White Workers: São Paulo, Brazil, 1888–1928." *Hispanic American Historical Review* 68:3 (1988): 514–518.

Andrews, George Reid. *Blacks and Whites in São Paulo, Brazil, 1888–1988.* Madison: University of Wisconsin Press, 1991.

Anonimo. "Revoluções, ideia geral do Pernambuco em 1817." In *Revista do Instituto Archeologico e Geografico Pernambucano* 4:2, segundo semestre de 1883, no. 29. Recife: Tipografia Industrial, 1884.

Anonymous. "A Plea in Favor of Maintaining Flogging in the Navy." N.p., n.d. Navy Department Library website, http://www.history.navy.mil/online/flogging.htm, consulted Sept. 8, 2012.

Ayers, Edward L. *Vengeance and Justice: Crime and Punishment in the 19th Century American South.* New York: Oxford University Press, 1984.

Azevedo, Alcene. *O direito dos escravos: Lutas jurídicas e abolicionismo na província de São Paulo.* Campinas: Editora Unicamp, 2010.

Azevedo, Célia Maria Marinho de. *Abolicionismo: Estados Unidos e Brasil, uma história comparada, século XIX.* São Paulo: Annablume, 2003.

Bailey, John. *The Lost German Slave Girl.* New York: Atlantic Monthly Press, 2003.

Baker, Jean H. *Affairs of Party: The Political Culture of Northern Democrats.* New York: Fordham University Press, 1998.

Bandeira Filho, Antonio Herculano de Souza. "Informações sobre o presidio de Fernando de Noronha," annexo I, 3–114. In Brazil, Ministerio da Justiça, *Relatorio apresentado á asembléa geral legislativa . . . pelo ministerio e secretario de estado dos negocios de justiça Conselheiro de Estado Manoel Pinto de Souza Dantas.* Rio: Imprensa Nacional, 1880.

Banner, Stuart. *The Death Penalty: An American History*. Cambridge, MA: Harvard University Press, 2002.

Baptist, Edward E. "'Cuffy,' 'Fancy Maids,' and 'One-Eyed Men': Rape, Commodification, and the Domestic Slave Trade in the United States." *American Historical Review* 106:5 (Dec. 2001): 1619–1650.

Barclay, Alexander. *A Practical View of the Present State of Slavery in the West Indies*. London: Smith, Elder, 1827.

Barickman, B. J. *A Bahian Counterpoint: Sugar, Tobacco, Cassava, and Slavery in the Recôncavo, 1780–1860*. Stanford, CA: Stanford University Press, 1998.

Barickman, B. J. "A Bit of Land, Which They Call 'Roça': Slave Provision Grounds in the Bahian Recôncavo, 1780–1860." *Hispanic American Historical Review* 74:4 (Nov. 1994): 649–687.

Barickman, B. J. "Reading the 1835 Parish Censuses from Bahia: Citizenship, Kinship, Slavery, and Household in Early Nineteenth Century Brazil." *The Americas* 59:3 (2003): 287–323.

Barman, Roderick J. "The Brazilian Peasantry Reexamined: The Implications of the Quebra Quilo Revolt 1874–1875." *Hispanic American Historical Review* 57:3 (1977): 402–424.

Barman, Roderick J. *Brazil, the Forging of a Nation, 1798–1852*. Stanford, CA: Stanford University Press, 1988.

Barman, Roderick J. *Citizen Emperor: Pedro II and the Making of Modern Brazil 1825–1891*. Stanford, CA: Stanford University Press, 1999.

Barman, Roderick J. *Princess Isabel of Brazil: Gender and Power in the Nineteenth Century*. Wilmington, DE: SR Books, 1996.

Barrows, S. J. [U.S. Commissioner]. *Penal Codes of France, Germany, Belgium and Japan (Reports Prepared for the International Prison Commission)*. U.S. House of Representatives. Washington: Government Printing Office, 1901.

Beattie, J. M. *Policing and Punishment in London 1660–1750: Urban Crime and the Limits of Terror*. Oxford: Oxford University Press, 2001.

Beattie, Peter M. "Adolfo Ferreira Caminha: Navy Officer, Ardent Republican, and Naturalist Novelist." In *The Human Tradition in Modern Brazil*, edited by Peter M. Beattie, 89–106. Wilmington, DE: Scholarly Resources, 2004.

Beattie, Peter M. "'Born under the Cruel Rigor of Captivity, the Supplicant Left It Unexpectedly by Committing a Crime': Categorizing and Punishing Slave Convicts in Brazil, 1830–1897." *The Americas* 66:1 (July 2009): 11–55.

Beattie, Peter M "'Cada homem traz dentro de si sua tragédia sexual': Visitas conjugais, gênero e A Questão sexual nas prisões (1934) de Lemos Britto." Translated by Marcos Bretas. In *História das prisões no Brasil*, edited by Clarissa Nunes Maia, Flávio de Sá Neto, Marcos Costa, and Marcos Bretas, 2 vols., 2:215–248. Rio: Rocco, 2009.

Beattie, Peter M. "Conflicting Penile Codes: Modern Masculinity and Sodomy in the Brazilian Military 1860–1916." In *Sex and Sexuality in Latin America*, edited by Donna Guy and Daniel Bouldersten, 65–85. New York: New York University Press, 1997.

Beattie, Peter M. "Conscription versus Penal Servitude: Army Reform's Influence on the Brazilian State's Management of Social Control, 1870–1930." *Journal of Social History* 32:4 (June 1999): 339–371.

Beattie, Peter M. "The Slave Silvestre's Disputed Sale: Corporal Punishment, Mental Health, Sexuality, and 'Vices' in Recife, Brazil, 1869–1878." *Estudios Interdisciplinarios de America Latina y El Caribe* 16:1 (2005): 41–65.

Beattie, Peter M., ed. *The Human Tradition in Modern Brazil*. Wilmington, DE: Scholarly Resources, 2004.

Beattie, Peter M. "Measures of Manhood: Poor Free Men, Honor, and Slavery's Decline in Brazil, 1850–1889." In *Changing Men and Masculinities in Latin America*, edited by Matthew C. Gutmann, 233–255. Durham, NC: Duke University Press, 2003.

Beattie, Peter M. "'ReCapricorning' the Atlantic." Introduction to special issue of *Luso-Brazilian Review* 45:1 (June 2008): 1–5.

Beattie, Peter M. *The Tribute of Blood: Army, Honor, Race, and Nation in Brazil 1864–1945*. Durham, NC: Duke University Press, 2001.

Beaurepaire Rohan, Henrique Pedro Carlos de. "Considerações acerca da conquista, catechese e civilisação dos selvagens do Brasil." *Guanabara* (Rio), no. 2: 191–192.

Beaurepaire Rohan, Henrique Pedro Carlos de. "A Ilha de Fernando de Noronha: Considerada em relação ao estabelecimento de uma colonia agricola-penitenciaria." In *Relatorio apresentado á assembléa geral legislativa . . . pelo ministro e secretario de estado dos negocios da guerra Visconde de Camamú*, 1–45. Rio: Typ. Universal de Laemmert, 1865.

Beckman, Gail McKnight. "Three Penal Codes Compared." *American Journal of Legal History* 10:2 (April 1966): 148–173.

Bederman, Gail. *Manliness and Civilization: A Cultural History of Gender and Race in the United States, 1880–1917*. Chicago: University of Chicago Press, 1995.

Bender, Gerald J. *Angola under the Portuguese: The Myth and Reality*. Berkeley: University of California Press, 1978.

Berquist, Charles. *Coffee and Conflict in Colombia, 1886–1910*. Durham, NC: Duke University Press, 1986.

Bethel, Leslie. *The Abolition of the Brazilian Slave Trade: Britain, Brazil and the Slave Trade Question, 1807–1869*. Cambridge: Cambridge University Press, 1970.

Bethel, Leslie, and José Murilo de Carvalho, eds. *Joaquim Nabuco, British Abolitionists, and the End of Slavery in Brazil: Correspondence 1880–1905*. London: Institute for the Study of the Americas, University of London Press, School of Advanced Studies, 2009.

Bieber, Judy. "Slavery and Social Life: Attempts to Reduce Free People to Slavery in the Sertão Mineiro, Brazil, 1850–1871." *Journal of Social History* 26:3 (1994): 597–619.

Blackburn, Robin. *The Making of New World Slavery: From the Baroque to the Modern, 1492–1800*. London: Verso, 2010.

Blake, Stanley E. *The Vigorous Core of Our Nationality: Race and Regional Identity in Northeastern Brazil*. Pittsburgh: University of Pittsburgh Press, 2011.

Blanchard, Peter. *Under the Flags of Freedom: Slave Soldiers and the Wars of Independence in Spanish America*. Pittsburgh: University of Pittsburgh Press, 2008.

Borges, Dain Edward. *The Family in Bahia Brazil, 1870–1945*. Stanford, CA: Stanford University Press, 1992.

Borges Lins e Silva, Marieta. *Fernando de Noronha: Cinco séculos de história*. Recife: Celpe, 2007.

Boxer, Charles. *The Portuguese Seaborne Empire 1415–1825*. London: Hutchison, 1969.

Boyer, Richard. "Honor among Plebeians: *Mala Sangre* and Social Reputation." In *The Faces of Honor: Sex, Shame, and Violence in Colonial Latin America*, edited by Sonya Lipsett-Rivera and Lyman L. Johnson, 152–178. Albuquerque: University of New Mexico Press, 1998.

Branner, John C. "The Convict Island of Brazil—Fernando de Noronha." *Popular Science Monthly* 35 (1889): 33–39.

Branner, John C. "Notes on the Fauna of the Islands of Fernando de Noronha." *American Naturalist* 22:262 (Oct. 1888): 861–871.

Branner, John C. "Orville A. Derby." *Journal of Geology* 24:3 (April–May 1916): 209–214.

Brazil. *Codigo Criminal do Imperio do Brazil*. Rio: Typografia de Quirino e Irmão, 1861.

Brazil. *Codigo do processo criminal de primeira instancía do imperio do Brazil: Com a disposição provisoria a cerca da administração da justiça civil*. Rio: Seignot-Plancher, 1833.

Brazil. *Constituição da república federativa do Brasil*. 35th ed. Brasília: Biblioteca Digital da Câmara do Deputados, 2012. http://bd.camara.gov.br, accessed June 20, 2014.

Brazil. *Constituição política do Império do Brasil*. Rio: Typ. de Plancher, 1824.

Brazil. Ministerio da Guerra. *Relatorio apresentado á assemblea geral legislativa na terceira sessão da decima segunda legislatura pelo ministro e secretario dos negocios de guerra Visconde de Camamú*. Rio: Typ. Laemmert, 1865.

Brazil. Ministerio da Guerra. *Relatorio apresentado á assemblea geral legislativa na primeira sessão da decima sexta legislatura pelo ministro e secretario dos negocios de guerra Duque de Caxias*. Rio: Empreza de Figaro, 1877.

Brazil. Ministerio da Guerra. *Relatorio apresentado á assemblea geral legislativa na segunda sessão da decima oitava legislatura pelo ministro e secretario dos negocios de guerra Affonso Augusto Moreira Penna*. Rio: Typ. Nacional, 1882.

Brazil. Ministerio da Justiça. *Relatorio apresentado á Assembléa Geral Nacional na primeira sessão da decima septima legislatura pelo ministro do estado de justiça e negocios exteriores Conselheiro Lafayette Rodrigues Pereira*. Rio: Typ. Nacional, 1877.

Brazil. Ministerio da Justiça. *Relatorio apresentado á Assembléa Geral Nacional na segunda sessão da decima oitava legislatura pelo ministro do estado de justiça e negocios exteriores Conselheiro de Estado Manoel da Silva Mafra*. Rio: Typ. Nacional, 1882.

Brazil. Ministerio da Justiça. *Relatorio apresentado á Assembléa Geral Nacional na terceira sessão da decima septima legislatura pelo ministro do estado de justiça e* negocios exteriores Conselheiro de Estado Manoel Pinto de Souza Dantas. Rio: Typ. Nacional, 1882.

Brazil. Ministerio da Justiça. *Relatorio apresentado á Assembléa Geral Nacional na terceira sessão da decima oitava legislatura pelo ministro do estado de justiça e negocios exteriores Conselheiro João Ferreira de Moura.* Rio: Typ. Nacional, 1883.

Brazil. Ministerio da Justiça. *Relatorio apresentado á Assembléa Geral Nacional na primeira sessão da decima nona legislatura pelo ministro do estado de justiça e negocios exteriores Conselheiro Affonso Augusto Moreira Penna.* Rio: Typ. Nacional, 1885.

Brazil. Ministerio da Justiça. *Relatorio apresentado á Assembléa Geral Nacional na primeira sessão da vigessima legislatura pelo ministro do estado de justiça e negocios exteriores Conselheiro Joaquim Delfino Ribeiro da Luz.* Rio: Typ. Nacional, 1886.

Brazil. Ministerio da Justiça. *Relatorio apresentado á Assembléa Geral Nacional na segunda sessão da vigessima legislatura pelo ministro do estado de justiça e negocios exteriores Conselheiro Samuel Wallace MacDowell.* Rio: Typ. Nacional, 1887.

Brazil. Ministerio da Justiça. *Relatorio apresentado á Assembléa Geral Nacional na terceira sessão da vigessima legislatura pelo ministro do estado de justiça e negocios exteriores Antonio Ferreira Vianna.* Rio: Typ. Nacional, 1888.

Brazil. Ministerio da Justiça. *Relatorio apresentado á Assembléa Geral Nacional na quarta sessão da vigessima legislatura pelo ministro do estado de justiça e negocios exteriores Dr. Francisco d'Assis Rosa e Silva.* Rio: Typ. Nacional, 1889.

Brazil. Ministerio da Justiça. *Relatorio apresentado ao Presidente da Republica dos Estados Unidos do Brasil pelo ministro do estado de justiça e negocios exteriores General Dr. Manoel Ferras de Campos Salles.* Rio: Typ. Nacional, 1891.

Brazil, Ministerio da Justiça. *Relatorio apresentado ao Presidente da Republica dos Estados Unidos do Brasil pelo Dr. Almaro Cavalcante Ministro do Estado de Justiça e Negocios exteriores.* Rio: Imprensa Nacional, 1898.

Brooks, David. *Captives and Cousins: Slavery, Kinship, and Community in the Southwest Borderlands.* Chapel Hill: University of North Carolina Press, 2001.

Brown, Alexandra K. "'A Black Mark on Our Legislation': Slavery, Punishment, and the Politics of Death in Nineteenth-Century Brazil." In "State, Society, and Political Culture in Nineteenth Century Brazil," special issue, *Luso-Brazilian Review* 27:2 (Winter 2000): 95–121.

Brown, Christopher Leslie. *Moral Capital: Foundations of British Abolitionism.* Chapel Hill: University of North Carolina Press, 2006.

Bruce, Franklin H. "Billy Budd and Capital Punishment: A Tale of Three Centuries." *American Literature* 69:2 (1997): 337–359.

Brüggei, Silvia Maria Jardim. "Legitimidade, casamento, e relações ditas ilícitas em São João del Rei, 1730–1850." In *Anais do seminário sobre a economia mineira,* 9:37–46. Diamantina: Cedeplar / Face / UFMG, 2000.

Brundage, William Fitzhugh. *Under Sentence of Death: Lynching in the South.* Chapel Hill: University of North Carolina Press, 1997.

Burns, Bradford E. *A History of Brazil.* 3rd ed. New York: Columbia University Press, 1993.

Bush, Barbara. *Slave Women in Caribbean Society 1650–1838*. Bloomington: University of Indiana Press, 1990.

Butler, Kim. *Freedoms Given, Freedoms Won: Afro-Brazilians in Post-abolition São Paulo and Salvador*. New Brunswick, NJ: Rutgers University Press, 1998.

Caldeira, Teresa Pires. *City of Walls: Crime, Segregation and Citizenship in São Paulo*. Berkeley: University of California Press, 2000.

Camara, Paulo Perestrello da. *Collecção de proverbios, adagios, rifãos anexins sentenças moraes e idiotismos da lingua portugueza*. Rio: Eduardo e Henrique Laemmert, 1848.

Caminha, Adolfo. *Bom Crioulo: The Black Man and the Cabin Boy*. Translated by E. A. Lacey. San Francisco: Gay Sunshine, 1982 [1897].

Campos, Adriana Pereira. "Crime e escravidão: Uma interpretação alternativa." In *Nação e cidadania no império: Novos horizontes*, edited by José Murilo de Carvalho. Rio: Civilização Brasileira, 2006.

Canaday, Margot. *The Straight State: Sexuality and Citizenship in Twentieth-Century America*. Princeton, NJ: Princeton University Press, 2011.

Carew, Anthony. *The Lower Deck of the Royal Navy 1900–1930: The Invergordon Mutiny in Perspective*. Manchester, UK: University of Manchester Press, 1981.

Carpenter, Frank D. Y. "Race in Brazil." *Lippencott's Magazine of Popular Literature and Science* 27:1 (Jan. 1881): 82–86.

Carpenter, Frank D. Y. *Round about Rio*. Chicago: Jansen, McClurg, 1884.

Carvalho, Padre João Manuel. *Reminiscências sobre vultos e factos do Império e da República*. Amparo: Correio Amparence, 1894.

Carvalho, José Murilo de. *Os bestializados: O Rio de Janeiro e a República que não foi*. São Paulo: Companhia das Letras, 1987.

Carvalho, José Murilo de. *A construção da ordem: A elite politica imperial; Teatro de sombras: A politica imperial*. 3rd ed. Rio: Record, 2003.

Carvalho, Marcus Joaquim Maciel de. "Agostinho José Pereira: The Divine Teacher." In *The Human Tradition in Modern Brazil*, edited by Peter M. Beattie, 23–52. Wilmington, DE: Scholarly Resources, 2004.

Carvalho, Marcus Joaquim Maciel de. "The 'Commander of All the Forests' against the Jacobins of Brazil: The Cabanada, 1832–1835." In *Rethinking Histories of Resistance in Brazil and Mexico*, edited by John Gledhill, 81–99. Durham, NC: Duke University Press, 2012.

Carvalho, Marcus Joaquim Maciel de. "Os índios de Pernambuco no ciclo das insurreições liberais, 1817/1948, ideologias e resistência." *Revista de Sociedade Brasileira de Pesquisa Histórica* 11 (1997): 51–69.

Carvalho, Marcus Joaquim Maciel de. *Liberdade: Rotinas e rupturas de escravismo, Recife 1822–1850*. Recife: UFPE, 1998.

Carvalho, Marcus Joaquim Maciel de. "'Quem furta mais e esconde': O roubo de escravos em Pernambuco, 1832–1855." *Revista do Instituto Histórico e Geográfico Brasileiro* 150:363 (April/June 1989): 317–344.

Castilho, Celso, and Camillia Cowling. "Funding Freedom, Popularizing Politics: Abolitionism and Local Emancipation Funds in 1880s Brazil." *Luso-Brazilian Review* 47:1 (2010): 89–120.

Castro, Celso. *O espírito militar: Um estudo de antropologia social na Academia Militar de Agulhas Negras.* Rio: Jorge Zahar, 1990.

Castro, Celso. *Os militares e a república: Um estudo sobre cultura e acão política.* Rio: Jorge Zahar, 1995.

Castro, Jeanne Berrance de. *A milícia cidadã: A Guarda Nacional de 1831 a 1850.* São Paulo: Companhia Editora Nacional, 1977.

Castro Faria, Sheila de. *A Colônia em movimento: Fortuna e família no cotidiano colonial.* Rio: Nova Fronteira, 1998.

Castro Faria, Sheila de. "Família, escrava e legitimidade: Estratégias de preservação da autonomia." *Estudos Afro-Asiáticos* 23 (1992): 113–131.

Caulfield, Sueann. *In Defense of Honor: Sexual Morality, Modernity, and Nation in Early Twentieth-Century Brazil.* Durham, NC: Duke University Press, 2000.

Chalhoub, Sidney. *A força da escravidão: Ilegaldade e costume no Brasil oitocentista.* São Paulo: Companhia das Letras, 2012.

Chalhoub, Sidney. "The Politics of Disease Control: Yellow Fever and Race in Nineteenth Century Rio de Janeiro." *Journal of Latin American Studies* 25:8 (May 1993): 441–463.

Chalhoub, Sidney. *Trabalho, lar, e botequim: O cotidiano dos trabalhadores do Rio de Janeiro da belle époque.* Rio: Brasiliense, 1986.

Chalhoub, Sidney. *Visões da liberdade: Uma história das últimas décadas da escravidão na Corte.* São Paulo: Cia. das Letras, 1990.

Chalhoub, Sidney, Vera Regina Beltrão Marques, Gabriela dos Reis Sampaio, and Carlos Alberto Galvão Sobrinho, eds. *Artes e ofícios de curar no Brasil.* Campinas: Editora Unicamp, 2003.

Chambers, William, and Robert Chambers, eds. *Chambers's Journal of Popular Literature, Science, and Art.* London: W. and R. Chambers, 1883.

Chandler, Billy Jaynes. *The Bandit King Lampião of Brazil.* College Station: Texas A&M University Press, 1978.

Chasteen, John. *Heroes on Horseback: A Life and Times of the Last Gaucho Caudillos.* Albuquerque: University of New Mexico Press, 1995.

Chekhov, Anton. *Sakhalin Island.* Translated by Brian Reeve. London: One World Classics, 2007 [1895].

Clinton, Catherine, and Michele Gillespie, eds. *Sex and Race in the Early South.* New York. Oxford University Press, 1997.

Coates, Timothy J. *Convicts and Orphans: Forced and State-Sponsored Colonizers in the Portuguese Empire, 1550–1755.* Stanford, CA: Stanford University Press, 2001.

Conrad, Robert. *Children of God's Fire: A Documentary History of Black Slavery in Brazil.* University Park: Penn State University Press, 1994.

Conrad, Robert. *The Destruction of Brazilian Slavery 1850–1888.* Berkeley: University of California Press, 1972.

Cooke, Bill. "The Denial of Slavery in Management Studies." *Journal of Management Studies* 40:8 (Dec. 2003): 1895–1918.

Cope, Douglas. *The Limits of Racial Domination: Plebeian Society in Colonial Mexico 1660–1720*. Madison: University of Wisconsin Press, 1994.

Coser, Lewis A. *Greedy Institutions: Patterns of Undivided Commitment*. New York: The Free Press, 1974.

Costa, Emília Viotti da. *The Brazilian Empire: Myths and Histories*. Rev. ed. Chapel Hill: University of North Carolina Press, 2000.

Costa, Jurandir Freire. *Ordem médica e norma familiar*. 3rd ed. Rio: Graal, 1989.

Costa, Marcos. "Fernando e o mundo: O presídio de Fernando de Noronha no século XIX." In *História das prisões no Brasil*, edited by Clarissa Nunes Maia et al., 2 vols., 1:135–167. Rio: Rocco, 2009.

Costa, Marcos. *O caos ressurgirá da ordem: Fernando de Noronha e a reforma prisional no império*. São Paulo: IBCCRIM, 2009.

Cowling, Camillia. *Conceiving Freedom: Women of Color, Gender, and the Abolition of Slavery in Havana and Rio de Janeiro*. Chapel Hill: University of North Carolina Press, 2013.

Curtin, Mary Ellen. *Black Prisoners and Their World: Alabama, 1865–1900*. Charlottesville: University of Virginia Press, 2000.

da Cunha, Euclides. *Rebellion in the Backlands*. Translated by Samuel Putnam. Chicago: University of Chicago Press, 1944.

da Matta, Roberto. *Carnivais, malandros, e heróis: Para uma sociologia do dilema brasileira*. Rio: Jorge Zahar, 1979.

da Matta, Roberto. *A casa e a rua: Espaço, cidadania, mulher, e morte no Brasil*. Rio: Guanabara, 1987.

D'Andrada e Silva, José Bonifacio. *Memoir Addressed to the General Constituent and Legislative Assembly of the Empire of Brazil on Slavery*. Translated by William Walton. London: A. Redford and W. Robins, 1836.

Darnton, Robert. "The Forbidden Best-Sellers of Pre-Revolutionary France." In *The French Revolution: The Essential Readings*, edited by Ronald Schechter. New York: Blackwell, 2001.

Davis, David Brion. *From Homicide to Slavery: Studies in American Culture*. New York: Oxford University Press, 1988.

Dean, Warren. *Rio Claro: A Brazilian Plantation System 1820–1920*. Stanford, CA: Stanford University Press, 1976.

Debret, Jean-Baptiste. *Viagem pitoresca e histórica ao Brasil*. 2 vols. São Paulo: Livraria Martins, 1940.

Diacon, Todd. *Stringing Together a Nation: Cândido Mariano da Silva Rondon and the Construction of a Modern Brazil, 1906–1930*. Durham, NC: Duke University Press, 2004.

Díaz, Arlene J. "Vicenta Ochoa. Dead Many Times: Gender, Politics, and a Death Sentence in Early Republican Caracas." In *Gender, Sexuality, and Power in Latin*

America since Independence, edited by William E. French and Katherine Elaine Bliss, 31–51. Lanham, MD: Rowman and Littlefield, 2006.

Díaz, María Elena. "Beyond Tannenbaum." *Law and History Review* 22:2 (Summer 2004): 371–376.

Diffie, Bailey Wallys, and Edwin J. Perkins. *A History of Colonial Brazil, 1500–1792*. Malabar, FL: R. E. Krieger, 1987.

Diniz, Ariosvaldo da Silva. "As artes de curar nos tempos da cólera: Recife 1856." In *Artes e ofícios de curar no Brasil*, edited by Sidney Chalhoub et al., 355–386. Campinas: Editora Unicamp, 2003.

Dodsworth, Jorge João (2nd Barão de Javari). *Organizações e programas ministeriais: Regime parlamentar no Império*. 2nd ed. Rio: Arquivo Nacional, 1962 [1889].

Doratioto, Francisco. *Maldita guerra: Nova história da Guerra do Paraguai*. São Paulo: Cia. das Letras, 2002.

Duncan, Quince. *Contra el silencio: Afrodescendientes y racismo en el Caribe Continental Hispánico*. San José: EUNED, 2001.

Edmonds, Alexander. *Pretty Modern: Beauty, Sex, and Plastic Surgery in Brazil*. Durham, NC: Duke University Press, 2010.

Edwards, Ryan. "From the Depths of Patagonia: The Ushuaia Penal Colony and the Nature of 'The End of the World.'" *Hispanic American Historical Review* 94:2 (2014): 271–302.

Eisenberg, Peter. *The Sugar Industry in Pernambuco, 1840–1910*. Berkeley: University of California Press, 1974.

Ellison, Fred P. *Brazil's New Novel*. Berkeley: University of California Press, 1954.

Evans, Amos A. "Journal Kept on Board the United States Frigate 'Constitution' 1812." *Pennsylvania Magazine of History and Biography* (Historical Society of Pennsylvania, n.d.).

Feijó, Diogo Antônio. *Diogo Antônio Feijó*. Edited by Jorge Caldeira. São Paulo: Editora 34, 1999.

Ferreira, Ricardo Alexandre. *Senhores de poucos escravos: Cativeiro e crime num ambiente rural (1830–1888)*. São Paulo: Editora UNESP, 2005.

Ferreira, Ricardo Alexandre. "O tronco na enxovia: Escravos e livres nas prisões paulistas dos oitocentos." In *História da prisão no Brasil*, edited by Clarissa Nunes Maia et al., 2 vols., 1:179–215. Rio: Rocco, 2009.

Ferrell, Claudine. *The Abolitionist Movement*. Santa Barbara, CA: Greenwood, 2006.

Figueira de Melo, Jeronimo Martiano. *Crônica da Rebelião Praieira, 1848 e 1849*. Brasília: Senado Federal, 1978.

Fine, Lisa. *The Story of Reo Joe: Work, Kin, and Community in Autotown, USA*. Philadelphia: Temple University Press, 2004.

Flanigan, Daniel J. "Criminal Procedure in Slave Trials in the Antebellum South." *Journal of Southern History* 11:4 (November 1974): 537–564.

Fleury, Conselheiro André Augusto de Padua. "Parecer sobre o presidio de Fernando de Noronha." In *Relatorio . . . Conselheiro de Estado Manoel Pinto de*

Souza Dantas, Brazil, Ministerio da Justiça, annexo J, 1–31. Rio: Imprensa Nacional, 1880.

Florence, Afonso Bandeira. "Resistência escrava em São Paulo: A luta dos escravos da fábrica de ferro São João de Ipanema, 1828–1842." *Afro-Ásia* 18 (1996): 7–32.

Florentino, Manolo. *A Paz das senzalas: Famílias escravas e tráfico atlântico, Rio de Janeiro, c.1790–c.1850.* Rio: Civilização Brasileira, 1997.

Flory, Thomas. *Judge and Jury in Imperial Brazil, 1808–1871: Social Control and Political Stability in the New State.* Austin: University of Texas Press, 1981.

Foucault, Michel. *Discipline and Punish: The Birth of the Prison.* Translated by Alan Sheridan. New York: Pantheon Books, 1977.

Foucault, Michel. *The History of Sexuality.* Vol. 1. New York: Vintage, 1990 [1976].

Fraga Filho, Walter. *Encruzilhadas da liberdade: História de escravos e libertos na Bahia, 1870–1910.* Campinas: Editora Unicamp, 2006.

Fraga Filho, Walter. *Mendigos, moleques, e vadios na Bahia do Século XIX.* São Paulo: Editora Hucitec, 1996.

Franck, Hans Göran, Klas Nyman, and William Schabas. *The Barbaric Punishment: Abolishing the Death Penalty.* Leiden: Martinus Nijhoff, 2003.

Frank, Zephyr. *Dutra's World: Wealth and Family in Nineteenth-Century Rio de Janeiro.* Albuquerque: University of New Mexico Press, 2004.

Frazier, Harriet C. *Runaway and Freed Missouri Slaves and Those Who Helped Them, 1763–1865.* Jefferson, NC: McFarland, 2004.

Frazier, Harriet C. *Slavery and Crime in Missouri, 1773–1865.* Jefferson, NC: McFarland, 2001.

Freitas, Décio. *Cabanos: Os guerrilheiros do imperador.* 2nd ed. Rio: Graal, 1982 [1978].

French, William E., and Katherine Elaine Bliss, eds. *Gender, Sexuality, and Power in Latin America since Independence.* Lanham, MD: Rowman and Littlefield, 2006.

Frevert, Ute. *The Nation in Barracks: Modern Germany, Military Conscription, and Civil Society.* New York: Oxford University Press, 2004.

Freyre, Gilberto. *The Mansions and the Shanties.* Translated by Harriet de Onís. New York: Knopf, 1963 [1936].

Freyre, Gilberto. *The Masters and the Slaves: A Study in the Development of Brazilian Civilization.* Translated by Samuel Putnam. Berkeley: University of California Press, 1986 [1933].

Fuente, Ariel de la. "Slave-Law and Claims Making in Cuba: The Tannenbaum Debate Revisited." *Law and History Review* 22:2 (Summer 2004): 339–369.

Galliher, John F., et al. *America without the Death Penalty: States Leading the Way.* Lebanon, NH: Northeastern University Press, 2002.

Galvão, Sebastião de Vasconcelos. *Diccionario chorographico, historico, e estatistico de Pernambuco.* Rio: Perdigão, 1908.

Galvão, Tácito Luiz Cordeiro. "O preto senhor Thomaz." *Revista do Instituto Arqueológico, Histórico e Geográfico Pernambucano* 61 (July 2005): 1–24.

Garland, David. *Punishment and Modern Society: A Study in Social Theory.* Chicago: University of Chicago Press, 1990.

Gaspar, David Barry. *Bondsmen and Rebels: A Study of Master-Slave Relations in Antigua.* Baltimore: Johns Hopkins University Press, 1985.

Genovese, Eugene. *Roll Jordan Roll: The World the Slaves Made.* New York: Vintage Books, 1976 [1972].

Gilroy, Paul. *Black Atlantic: Modernity and Double Consciousness.* London: Verso, 1993.

Gledhill, John, ed. *Rethinking Histories of Resistance in Brazil and Mexico.* Durham, NC: Duke University Press, 2012.

Glenn, Myra C. *Against Corporal Punishment: Prisoners, Sailors, Women, and Children in Antebellum America.* Albany: State University of New York Press, 1984.

Goffman, Erving. *Asylums: Essays on the Social Situation of Mental Patients and Other Inmates.* Chicago: Aldine, 1961.

Goldstein, Donna. *Laughter Out of Place: Race, Class, Violence, and Sexuality in a Brazilian Shanty Town.* Berkeley: University of California Press, 2003.

Gomes da Cunha, Olivia. *Intenção e gesto: Pessoa, cor e a produção da (in)diferença no Rio de Janeiro, 1927–1942.* Rio: Arquivo Nacional, 2002.

Gomes da Cunha, Olívia Maria, and Flávio dos Santos Gomes, eds. *Quase cidadão: Histórias e antropologias da pós-emancipação no Brasil.* Rio: Editora Fundação Getúlio Vargas, 2007.

Graden, Dale T. "An Act 'Even of Public Security': Slave Resistance, Social Tensions, and the End of the International Slave Trade to Brazil 1835–1856." *Hispanic American Historical Review* 76:2 (May 1996): 249–282.

Graham, Richard. *Patronage and Politics in Nineteenth-Century Brazil.* Stanford, CA: Stanford University Press, 1990.

Graham, Sandra Lauderdale. *Caetana Says No: Women's Stories from a Brazilian Slave Frontier.* New York: Cambridge University Press, 2002.

Graham, Sandra Lauderdale. "Honor among Slaves." In *The Faces of Honor: Sex, Shame, and Violence in Colonial Latin America,* edited by Sonya Lipsett-Rivera and Lyman L. Johnson, 221–228. Albuquerque: University of New Mexico Press, 1998.

Graham, Sandra Lauderdale. *House and Street: The Domestic World of Servants and Masters in Nineteenth-Century Rio de Janeiro.* Cambridge: Cambridge University Press, 1988.

Green, Jack P., and Philip Morgan, eds. *Atlantic History: A Critical Appraisal.* New York: Oxford University Press, 2009.

Green, Jack P., and Philip Morgan. "Introduction: The Present State of Atlantic History." In *Atlantic History: A Critical Appraisal,* edited by Jack P. Green and Philip Morgan, 3–33. New York: Oxford University Press, 2009.

Greenberg, Kenneth S. *Honor and Slavery.* Princeton, NJ: Princeton University Press, 1996.

Grinberg, Keila. "Alforria, direito e direitos no Brasil e nos Estados Unidos." *Estudos Históricos* 27:1 (2001): 1–21.

Grinberg, Keila. *O fiador dos brasileiros: Cidadania, escravidão e direito civil no tempo de Antonio Pereira Rebouças.* Rio: Civilização Brasileira, 2002.

Guimarães, Antonio Sérgio. "Race, Colour, and Skin Colour in Brazil." *FMSH-PP*, no. 4 (July 2012): 1–10.

Guimarães, Elione Silva. *Violência entre parceiros de cativeiro: Juiz de Fora, segunda metade do século XIX*. São Paulo: Anna Blume, 2006.

Guimarães Dias, Astor. *A questão sexual nas prisões*. São Paulo: Saraiva, 1955.

Gutmann, Matthew C., ed. *Changing Men and Masculinities in Latin America*. Durham, NC: Duke University Press, 2003.

Hamnet, Brian R. "Process and Pattern: A Re-examination of Ibero-American Independence Movements 1808–1826." *Journal of Latin American Studies* 29:2 (May 1997): 279–328.

Harms, Robert. *The Diligent: A Voyage through the Worlds of the Slave Trade*. New York: Basic Books, 2002.

Hay, Douglas. "Afterword: Law and Society in Comparative Perspective." In *Crime and Punishment in Latin America: Law and Society since Late Colonial Times*, edited by Ricardo D. Salvatore, Carlos Aguirre, and Gilbert M. Joseph, 415–430. Durham, NC: Duke University Press, 2001.

Helg, Aline. *Our Rightful Share: The Afro-Cuban Struggle for Equality, 1886–1912*. Chapel Hill: University of North Carolina Press, 1995.

Hendricks, Howard Craig, and Robert M. Levine. "Pernambuco's Political Elite and the Recife Law School." *The Americas* 37:3 (1981): 291–313.

Heredia Sá, Miguel Antônio. "Algumas reflexões sobre a cópula, onanismo, e prostituição." Rio: Typ. Universal de Laemmert, 1845.

Holloway, Thomas. "O Calabouço e o Aljube do Rio de Janeiro no Século XIX." In *História das prisões no Brasil*, edited by Clarissa Nunes Maia et al., 2 vols., 1:253–281. Rio: Rocco, 2009.

Holloway, Thomas. "'A Healthy Terror': Police Repression of Capoeiras in Nineteenth Century Rio de Janeiro." *Hispanic American Historical Review* 69:4 (Nov. 1989): 637–676.

Holloway, Thomas. *Policing Rio de Janeiro: Repression and Resistance in a Nineteenth-Century City*. Stanford, CA: Stanford University Press, 1993.

Holston, James. *The Modernist City: An Anthropological Critique of Brasília*. Chicago: University of Chicago Press, 1989.

Hood, Roger. *The Death Penalty: A Worldwide Perspective*. New York: Oxford University Press, 2002.

Hughes, Robert. *Fatal Shore: The Epic of Australia's Founding*. New York: Knopf, 1986.

Hunt, Lynn. *Inventing Human Rights: A History*. New York: Norton, 2007.

Ignatieff, Michael. *A Just Measure of Pain: The Penitentiary in the Industrial Revolution 1750–1850*. New York: Pantheon, 1978.

Ingersoll, Thomas N. "Slave Codes and Judicial Practice in New Orleans, 1718–1807." *Law and History Review* 13:1 (Spring 1995): 23–62.

Instituto Brasileiro de Geografia e Estatística [IBGE]. *Estatísticas históricas do Brasil*. 2nd ed. Rio: IBGE, 1990.

Isenberg, Nancy. *Sex and Citizenship in Antebellum America*. Chapel Hill: University of North Carolina Press, 1998.

Izechsohn, Vitor. *Slavery and War in the Americas: Race, Citizenship, and State Building in the United States and Brazil, 1861–1870*. Charlottesville: University of Virginia Press, 2014.

"Journal of a Cruize Made to the Pacific Ocean by Captain David Porter in the United States Frigate Essex in the Years 1812, 1813, and 1814." *Quarterly Review* (London), no. 13 (April–July 1815).

Karasch, Mary C. *Slave Life in Rio de Janeiro 1808–1850*. Princeton, NJ: Princeton University Press, 1987.

Kirkendall, Andrew J. *Class Mates: Male Student Culture and the Making of a Political Class in Nineteenth-Century Brazil*. Lincoln: University of Nebraska Press, 2002.

Klubock, Thomas. *Contested Communities: Class, Gender, and Politics in Chile's El Teniente Copper Mine, 1904–1951*. Durham, NC: Duke University Press, 2001.

Koster, Henry. *Travels in Brazil in the Years 1809–1815*. 2 vols. Philadelphia: M. Carey and Son, 1817.

Kraay, Hendrik. "Patriotic Mobilization in Brazil: The Zuavos and Other Black Companies." In *I Die with My Country: Perspectives on the Paraguayan War, 1864–1870*, edited by Hendrik Kraay and Thomas L. Whigham, 61–80. Lincoln: University of Nebraska Press, 2004.

Kraay, Hendrik. "'The Shelter of the Uniform': The Brazilian Army and Runaway Slaves, 1800–1888." *Journal of Social History* 29:3 (March 1996): 637–657.

Kraay, Hendrik, and Thomas L. Whigham, eds. *I Die with My Country: Perspectives on the Paraguayan War 1864–1870*. Lincoln: University of Nebraska Press, 2004.

Kuznesof, Elizabeth Anne. "Ethnic and Gender Influences on 'Spanish' Creole Society in Colonial Spanish America." *Colonial Latin American Review* 4:1 (1995): 153–201.

Kuznesof, Elizabeth Anne. "Sexual Politics, Race, and Bastard-Bearing in Nineteenth-Century Brazil: A Question of Power or Culture?" *Journal of Family History* 16:3 (1991): 241–260.

Kuznesof, Elizabeth Anne. "Who Were the Families of 'Natural' Born Children in Nineteenth Century Rio de Janeiro Brazil: A Comparison of Baptismal and Census Records." *History of the Family* 2:2 (1997): 171–182.

Landers, Jane. *Black Society in Spanish Florida*. Urbana-Champagne: University of Illinois Press, 1999.

Lea, Rev. T. S. "The Island of Fernando do [*sic*] Noronha 1887." In *Proceedings of the Royal Geographic Society*, vol. X. London: Edward Stanford, 1888.

Lemos Britto, José Gabriel de. *A Questão sexual nas prisões*. Rio: J. Ribeiro dos Santos e Cia., 1934.

Levine, Robert M. *Pernambuco in the Brazilian Federation, 1889–1937*. Stanford, CA: Stanford University Press, 1978.

Levine, Robert M. *Vale of Tears: Revisiting the Canudos Massacre in Northeastern Brazil, 1893–1897*. Berkeley: University of California Press, 1992.

Lewin, Linda. "The Oligarchical Limitations of Social Banditry in Brazil: The Case of the 'Good' Thief Antonio Silvino." *Past and Present* 82 (Feb. 1979): 116–146.

Lewin, Linda. *Politics and Parentela: A Case Study of Oligarchy in Brazil's Old Republic.* Princeton, NJ: Princeton University Press, 1987.

Lewin, Linda. *Surprise Heirs I: Illegitimacy, Patrimonial Rights, and Legal Nationalism in Luso-Brazilian Inheritance, 1750–1821.* Stanford, CA: Stanford University Press, 2003.

Lewin, Linda. *Surprise Heirs II: Illegitimacy, Inheritance Rights, and Public Power in the Formation of Imperial Brazil, 1822–1889.* Stanford, CA: Stanford University Press, 2003.

Lewin, Linda. "Who Was 'O Grande Romano'? Geneological Purity, the Indian 'Past' and Whiteness in Brazil's Northeastern Backlands." *Journal of Latin American Lore* 19:1–2 (Summer/Winter 1996): 129–179.

Libby, Douglas Cole, and Zephyr Frank. "Voltando aos registros paroquiais in Minas colonial: Etnicidade em São José do Rio das Mortes 1780–1810." *Revista Brasileira da História* 29:58 (Dec. 2009): 383–415.

Lindoso, Dirceu. *A utopia armada: Rebeliões de pobres nas matas do Tombo Real.* Rio: Paz e Terra, 1983.

Linebaugh, Peter. *The London Hanged: Crime and Civil Society in the Eighteenth Century.* New York: Verso, 2003.

Linebaugh, Peter, and Marcus Rediker. *The Many-Headed Hydra: Sailors, Slaves, Commoners, and the Hidden History of the Revolutionary Atlantic.* Boston: Beacon, 2001.

Lins do Rego, José. *Usina.* 4th ed. Rio: José Olympio, 1956 [1936].

Livingston, Edward. *A System of Penal Law for the State of Louisiana.* Philadelphia: James Kay, Jun. and Company, 1833.

Lombroso, Cesare. *Criminal Man.* Translated by Mary Gibson and Nicole Hahn Rafter. Durham, NC: Duke University Press, 2006.

Lopes, Nei. *Enciclopédia brasileira da Diáspora Africana.* São Paulo: Selo Negro, 2004.

Love, Joseph. *The Revolt of the Whip.* Stanford, CA: Stanford University Press, 2012.

Loveman, Mara. "Blinded Like a State: The Revolt against Civil Registration in Nineteenth-Century Brazil." *Comparative Studies in Society and History* 49:1 (2007): 5–39.

Loveman, Mara. "The Race to Progress: Census Taking and Nation Making in Brazil, 1870–1920." *Hispanic American Historical Review* 89:3 (Aug. 2009): 435–470.

Lüsebrink, Hans Júrgen, and Rolf Reichardt. *The Bastille: History of a Symbol of Despotism and Freedom.* Translated by Nobert Shürer. Durham, NC: Duke University Press, 1997 [1990].

Lustosa, Isabel. *Histórias de presidentes: A República no Catete.* Petrópolis: Vozes, 1989.

MacCord, Marcelo. *Artífices da cidadania: Mutualismo, educação e trabalho no Recife oitocentista.* Campinas: Editora Unicamp, 2012.

MacCord, Marcelo. "Uma família de artífices 'de cor': Os Ferreira Barros e sua mobilidade social no Recife Oitocentista." *Luso-Brazilian Review* 47:2 (1910): 26–48.

MacCord, Marcelo. *O Rosário de D. Antônio: Irmandades negras, alianças e conflitos na história social do Recife, 1848–1872*. Recife: FAPESP / Editora Universitária da UFPE, 2005.

Machado, Maria Helena P. T. *Crime e escravidão: Trabalho, luta, e resistência nas lavouras paulistas, 1830–1888*. São Paulo: Brasiliense, 1987.

Machado de Assis, Joaquim Maria. *The Posthumous Memoirs of Brás Cubas*. Translated by Gregory Rabassa. Oxford: Oxford University Press, 1997.

Maciel da Silva, Alfredo Pretextato. *Os generaes do exército brasileiro de 1822 a 1889*. Rio: M. Orosco e Cia, 1906.

MacKey, Philip English. "Edward Livingston and the Origins of the Movement to Abolish Capital Punishment in America." *Louisiana History* 16:2 (Spring 1975): 146–166.

Magalhães, Raimundo, Jr. *Deodoro: A Espada contra o Império*. 2 vols. São Paulo: Cia. Nacional, 1957.

Maia, Clarissa Nunes. "A Casa da Detenção do Recife: Controle e conflitos (1855–1915)." In *História da prisão no Brasil*, edited by Clarissa Nunes Maia et al., 2 vols., 2:111–153. Rio: Rocco, 2009.

Maia, Clarissa Nunes, Flávio de Sá Neto, Marcos Costa, and Marcos Luiz Bretas, eds. *História da prisão no Brasil*. 2 vols. Rio: Rocco, 2009.

Marson, Izabel Andrade. *O Império de progresso: A revolução praieira em Pernambuco (1842–1855)*. São Paulo: Editora Brasiliense, 1987.

Martinez-Alier, Verena. *Marriage, Class and Colour in Nineteenth Century Cuba: A Study of Racial Attitudes and Sexual Values in a Slave Society*. 2nd ed. Cambridge: Cambridge University Press, 1974.

Mattos, Hebe Maria. *Das cores do silêncio: Os significados de liberdade no sudeste escravista—Brasil século XIX*. 2nd ed. Rio: Nova Fronteira, 1995.

Maxwell, Kenneth. *Conflicts and Conspiracies: Brazil and Portugal, 1750–1808*. Cambridge: Cambridge University Press, 1973.

McCann, Bryan Daniel. "The Whip and the Watch: Overseers in the Paraíba Valley, Brazil." *Slavery and Abolition* 18:2 (Aug. 1997): 36–37.

Meade, Everard. "From Sex Strangler to Model Citizen: The Trial and Execution of Felipe Ángeles." *Mexican Studies/Estudios Mexicanos* 26:10 (Summer 2010): 119–149.

Mello, Barão Homem de. *Biografia do Visconde de Beaurepaire Rohan*. Rio: Typografia Leuzinger, 1889.

Mello, Evaldo de Cabral. *Olinda restaurada: Guerra e açucar no nordeste 1630–1654*. São Paulo: Editora 34, 2007 [1975].

Melo, Mario Carneiro do Rego. *Arquipélago de Fernando de Noronha: Geographia physica e política*. Recife: Imp. Industrial, 1916.

Mercer, Jeremy. *When the Guillotine Fell: The Bloody Beginning and Horrifying End to France's River of Blood, 1791–1977*. New York: Palgrave Macmillan, 2008.

Metcalf, Alida. *Go Betweens and the Colonization of Brazil 1500–1600*. Austin: University of Texas Press, 2005.

Meznar, Joan E. "Carlota Lucia de Brito: Women, Power, and Politics in Northeastern Brazil." In *The Human Tradition in Modern Latin America*, edited by William H. Beezley and Judith Ewell, 41–52. Wilmington, DE: Scholarly Resources, 1997.

Meznar, Joan E. "The Ranks of the Poor: Military Service and Social Differentiation in Northeast Brazil, 1835–1875." *Hispanic American Historical Review* 72:3 (1992): 335–351.

Minas Gerais. *Falla dirigida á Assembléa Legislativa Provincial de Minas Geraes na sessão ordinaria do anno de 1846, pelo presidente da provincia, Quintiliano José da Silva*. Ouro Preto: Typ. Imparcial de B.X. Pinto de Sousa, 1846.

Mintz, Sidney. *Caribbean Transformations*. Chicago: Aldine, 1974.

Mintz, Sidney. *Sweetness and Power: The Place of Sugar in Modern History*. New York: Penguin, 1985.

Moraes, Evaristo de. *Prisões e instituições penitentiarias no Brasil*. Rio: Liv. Ed. Conselheiro C. de Oliveira, 1923.

Morais Filho, A. J. de Mello. *Festas e tradições populares do Brasil*. Rev. ed. Rio: H. Garnier, 1901 [1888].

Mosher, Jeffrey C. *Political Struggle, Ideology, and State-Building: Pernambuco and the Construction of Brazil, 1817–1850*. Lincoln: University of Nebraska Press, 2008.

Motta, José Flávio. *Corpos escravos, vontades livres: Posse de cativos e família escrava em Bananal*. São Paulo: Editora Anna Blume, 1999.

Motta, Leonardo. *Violeiros do norte: Poesia e linguagem do sertão nordestino*. São Paulo: Monteiro Lobato, 1925.

Nabuco, Carolina. *The Life of Joaquim Nabuco*. Translated by Ronald Hilton. Stanford, CA: Stanford University Press, 1950.

Nabuco, Joaquim. *Abolitionism: The Brazilian Antislavery Struggle*. Translated by Robert Conrad. Urbana: University of Illinois Press, 1977 [1883].

Nabuco, Joaquim. *A escravidão*. Rio: Nova Fronteira, 1999 [1869].

Nabuco, Joaquim. *Um estadista do Império: Nabuco de Araujo: Sua vida, suas opiniões, sua época*. 3 vols. Rio: Garnier, 1899–1900.

Naro, Nancy Priscilla. "Antislavery and Abolitionism: Thinkers and Doers in Imperial Brazil." In *Blacks, Coloureds, and National Identity in Nineteenth-Century Latin America*, edited by Nancy Priscilla Naro, 143–162. London: Institute of Latin America, 2003.

Naro, Nancy Priscilla, ed. *Blacks, Coloureds, and National Identity in Nineteenth-Century Latin America*. London: Institute of Latin America, 2003.

Nascimento, Álvaro Pereira do. *Cidadania, cor e disciplina na Revolta dos Marinheiros de 1910*. Rio: FAPERJ, 2008.

Nazzari, Muriel. "Vanishing Indians: The Social Construction of Race in Colonial Sao Paulo." *The Americas* 57:4 (April 2001): 497–524.

Neder, Gizlene. "Sentimentos e idéias jurídicas no Brasil: Pena de morte e degredo em dois tempos." In *História das prisões no Brasil*, edited by Clarissa Nunes Maia et al., 2 vols., 1:79–108. Rio: Rocco, 2009.

Neder, Gizlene, Nancy Naro, and José Luiz Werneck da Silva. *A polícia na Corte e no Distrito Federal 1831–1930*. Rio: Pontífica Universidade Católica do Rio de Janeiro, 1981.

Needell, Jeffrey. "The Abolition of the Brazilian Slave Trade in 1850: Historiography, Slave Agency and Statesmanship." *Journal of Latin American Studies* 33:4 (Nov. 2001): 681–711.

Needell, Jeffrey. *The Party of Order: The Conservatives, the State, and Slavery in the Brazilian Monarchy, 1831–1871*. Stanford, CA: Stanford University Press, 2006.

Needell, Jeffrey. "Politics, Parliament, and the Penalty of the Lash: The Significance of the End of Flogging in 1886." *Almanack Guarulhos* 4, segundo semestre de 2012: 91–100.

Nicoll, M. J. *Three Voyages of a Naturalist*. London: Witherby and Co., 1908.

Nina Rodrigues, Raimundo. *As raças humanas e a responsibilidade penal no Brasil*. Rio: Guanabara, Waissman Koogan, 1894.

Nisbett, Richard E., and Dov Cohen. *Culture of Honor: The Psychology of Violence in the South*. Boulder, CO: Westview, 1996.

Norton, Mary Beth. *Foundational Mothers and Fathers: Gendered Power and the Forming of American Society*. New York: Vintage Books, 1996.

Orem, Gerard. "'The Administration of Discipline by the English Is Very Rigid': British Military Law and the Death Penalty (1868–1918)." *Crime, History, and Societies* 5:1 (2001): 93–110.

Oshinsky, David M. *Worse Than Slavery: Parchman Farm and the Ordeal of Jim Crow Justice*. New York: The Free Press, 1996.

Paes Barretto, Fernando de Castro. *A abolição e a federação no Brasil*. Paris: Giard & E. Brière, 1906.

Pang, Eul-Soo, and Ron L. Seckinger. "The Mandarins of Imperial Brazil." *Comparative Studies in Society and History* 14 (March 1972): 215–244.

Parron, Tâmis. *A política da escravidão no Império brasileiro 1826–1865*. Rio: Civilização Brasileira, 2011.

Partrocínio, José do. *Motta Coqueiro, ou a pena de morte*. Rio: Francisco Alves, 1977 [1877].

Perdigão Malheiro, [Agostinho Marques]. *A escravidão no Brasil: Ensaio histórico, jurídico, social*. 2 vols. 3rd ed. Petropolis: Vozes, 1976 [1867–1869].

Peregalli, Henrique. *Recrutamento Militar no Brasil Colonial*. Campinas: Editora Unicamp, 1986.

Pereira da Costa, Francisco Augusto. *Fernando de Noronha: Noticia historica, geographica, e economica*. Recife: Typographia Manuel Figueiroa de Faria e Filhos, 1887.

Pereira de Jesus, Reinaldo. *Visões da monarquia: Escravos, operários, e abolicionismo na Corte*. Belo Horizonte: Argumentum, 2009.

Pernambuco. *Falla apresentado á assembléa legislativa provincial de Pernambuco apresentou no dia da abertura da sessão ordinario O Exm. Sr. Conselheiro Sergio de Teixeira Macedo*. Recife: Typographia M. F. de Faria, 1857.

Pernambuco. *Falla recitada na abertura da Assemblêa Legislativa Provincial de Pernambuco pelo excellentissimo presidente da provincia, conselheiro Diogo Velho Cavalcanti de Albuquerque no dia 1.o de março de 1871.* Recife: Typ. de M.F. de F. & Filhos, 1871.

Pernambuco. *Falla com que o excellentissimo senhor desembargador Henrique Pereira de Lucena abrio a Assemblêa Legislativa Provincial de Pernambuco em o 1.o de março de 1875.* Recife: Typ. de M. Figueiroa de F. & Filhos, 1875.

Pernambuco. *Falla com que o exm. sr. commendador João Pedro Carvalho de Moraes abrio a sessão da Assembléa Legislativa Provincial em o 1.o de março de 1876.* Pernambuco: Typ. de M. Figueiroa de Faria & Filhos, 1876.

Pernambuco. *Falla com que o exm. sr. dr. Franklin Americo de Menezes Doria abriu a sessão da Assembléa Legislativa Provincial de Pernambuco em 1 de março de 1881.* Recife, Typ. de Manoel Figueiroa de Faria & Filhos, 1881.

Pernambuco. *Mensagem apresentado ao Congresso Legislativo do estado em 6 de Março de 1897 pelo Governador de Pernambuco Dr. Joaquim Correa de Araujo.* Recife: Typ. de Manoel Figueroa de Faria & Filhos, 1899.

Pernambuco. *Mensagem apresentado ao Congresso Legislativo do Estado em 6 de Março de 1900 pelo Exm. Sr. Desembargador Sigismundo Antonio Gonçalves Vice-presidente do Senado no Exercicio do Cargo do Governador do Estado.* Recife: Typ. de Manoel Figeroa de Faria & Filhos, 1900.

Pessoa, Gláucia Tomaz de Aquino. *Cadernos de pesquisa: Fernando de Noronha, uma ilha-presídio nos trópicos.* Rio: Arquivo Nacional, 1994.

Phillips, Ulrich Bonnell. *American Negro Slavery: A Survey of the Supply, Employment, and Control of Negro Labor as Determined by the Plantation Regime.* Baton Rouge: Louisiana State University Press, 1966 [1918].

Piccato, Pablo. "'Such a Strong Need': Sexuality and Violence in Belem Prison." In *Gender, Sexuality, and Power in Latin America since Independence*, edited by William E. French and Katherine Elaine Bliss, 87–108. Lanham, MD: Rowman and Littlefield, 2007.

Pike, Ruth. "Penal Servitude in the Spanish Empire: Presidio Labor in the Eighteenth Century." *Hispanic American Historical Review* 58:1 (Feb. 1978): 21–40.

Pinheiro, Domingos Firmino. *O androphilismo.* Bahia: Imp. Econômica, 1898.

Pybus, Cassandra. *Black Founders: The Unknown Story of Australia's First Black Settlers.* Sydney: University of New South Wales Press, 2006.

Queiroz, Suely Robles Reis de. *Escravidão negra em São Paulo: Um estudo das tensões provocadas pelo escravismo no século XIX.* Rio: José Olympio, 1977.

Queiroz Duarte, Paulo de. *Os voluntários da pátria na Guerra do Paraguai: O comando de Osório.* 5 vols. Rio: Biblioteca do Exercito, 1981.

Ramos, Donald. "From Minho to Minas: The Portuguese Roots of the Mineiro Family." *Hispanic American Historical Review* 73:4 (Nov. 1993): 639–662.

Ramos, Donald. "União consensual e a família no século XIX: Minas Gerais, Brasil." *Estudo Econômicos* 20:3 (1990): 381–405.

Raulino, E. *Sentenciado 304 (Leitura para as prisões)*. Bahia: Typ. Salesiana, 1902.

Read, Ian. *The Hierarchies of Slavery in Santos, Brazil 1822–1888*. Stanford, CA: Stanford University Press, 2012.

Rebouças, André. *Agricultura nacional*. Rio: Lamoureux, 1883 [1875].

Redfield, Peter. *Space in the Tropics: From Convicts to Rockets in French Guiana*. Berkeley: University of California Press, 2000.

Reis, João José. "Batuque: African Drumming and Dance between Repression and Concession, Bahia 1808–1855." *Bulletin of Latin American Research* 24:2 (2005): 201–214.

Reis, João José. *Death Is a Festival: Funeral Rites and Rebellion in Nineteenth-Century Brazil*. Translated by H. Sabrina Gledhill. Chapel Hill: University of North Carolina Press, 2003.

Reis, João José. *Rebelião escrava no Brasil: A história do levante dos Malês (1835)*. São Paulo: Companhia das Letras, 2003.

Ribeiro, Gladys Sabina. *A liberdade em construção: Identidade nacional e conflitos antilusitanos no Primeiro Reinado*. Rio: Relume Dumará / FAPERJ, 2002.

Ribeiro, João Luiz. *No meio das galinhas as baratas não tem razão: A Lei de 10 de Junho de 1835, os escravos e a pena de morte no império brasiliero*. Rio: Renovar, 2005.

Richardson, Kim. *Quebra-Quilos and Peasant Resistance: Peasants, Religion, and Politics in Nineteenth-Century Brazil*. Lanham, MD: University Press of America, 2011.

Rodrigues, Jaime. "De escravos á operários: A trajetória dos africanos livres empregados na primeira siderúrgica brasileira revela a importância dos trabalhadores negros nos primórdios da industrialização do país." *História Viva* 82 (Aug. 1910). http://www2.uol.com.br/historiaviva/reportagens/de_escravos_a_operarios_imprimir.html.

Rodrigues, José Honório, et al., eds. *O parlamento e a evolução nacional*. 5 vols. Brasília: Senado Federal, 1972.

Rodrigues, Raimundo Nina. *As raças humanas e a responsibilidade penal no Brasil*. Rio: Guanabara, Waissman Koogan, 1894.

Roediger, David R. *The Wages of Whiteness: Race and the Making of the American Working Class*. New York: Verso, 1991.

Ruschenberger, W. S. W. *Three Years in the Pacific Including Notices of Brazil, Chile, Bolivia, and Peru*. Philadelphia: Carey, Lea, and Blanchard, 1834.

Said, Edward. *Orientalism*. New York: Vintage Books, 1979.

Salla, Fernando, and Sérgio Adorno. "Criminalidade organizada nas prisões e os ataques do PCC." *Estudos Avançados* 21:61 (Sept.–Dec. 2007): 7–29.

Salla, Fernando, and Sérgio Adorno. *As prisões em São Paulo: 1822–1940*. São Paulo: Annablume / Fapesp, 1999.

Salvatore, Ricardo D. "Death and Liberalism: Capital Punishment after the Fall of Rosas." In *Crime and Punishment in Latin America: Law and Society since Late*

Colonial Times, edited by Ricardo D. Salvatore, Carlos Aguirre, and Gilbert M. Joseph, 342–358. Durham, NC: Duke University Press, 2001.

Salvatore, Ricardo D., Carlos Aguirre, and Gilbert M. Joseph, eds. *Crime and Punishment in Latin America: Law and Society since Late Colonial Times*. Durham, NC: Duke University Press, 2001.

Sampaio, Gabriela dos Reis. *Nas trincheiras da cura: As diferentes medicinas no Rio de Janeiro imperial*. Campinas: Editora Unicamp, 2002.

Santos, Martha. *Cleansing Honor with Blood: Masculinity, Violence, and Power in the Backlands of Northeast Brazil, 1845–1889*. Stanford, CA: Stanford University Press, 2011.

Sarti, Raffaella. "'All Masters Discourage the Marrying of Their Male Servants and Admit Not by Any Means the Marriage of the Female': Domestic Service and Celibacy in Western Europe from the Sixteenth to the Nineteenth Century." *European Historical Quarterly* 38:3 (2008): 417–449.

Schafer, Judith Kelleher. "Slaves and Crime: New Orleans 1846–62." In *Local Matters: Race, Crime, and Justice in the Nineteenth-Century South*, edited by Christopher Waldrep and Donald G. Niemann, 53–91. Athens: University of Georgia Press, 2001.

Scheick, William J. *The Half Blood: A Cultural Symbol in Nineteenth-Century American Fiction*. Lexington: University Press of Kentucky, 1979.

Schenk, Gerald E. *"Work or Fight!": Race, Gender, and the Draft in World War One*. New York: Palgrave Macmillan, 2005.

Scheper-Hughes, Nancy. *Death without Weeping: The Violence of Everyday Life in Brazil*. Berkeley: University of California Press, 1992.

Schmidt-Nowara, Christopher. "Still Continents (and an Island) with Two Histories?" *Law and History Review* 22:2 (Summer 2004): 377–382.

Schulz, John. *O Exército na Política: Origens da Intervenção Militar 1850–1894*. São Paulo: Edusp, 1994.

Schwarcz, Leila. *As barbas do imperador: Dom Pedro II um monarca nos trópicos*. São Paulo: Cia. das Letras, 1998.

Schwarcz, Leila. *Retrato em preto e branco: Jornais, escravos, e cidadãos em São Paulo no final do século XIX*. São Paulo: Companhia das Letras, 1987.

Schwartz, Stuart B. *All Can Be Saved: Religious Tolerance and Salvation in the Iberian Atlantic World*. New Haven, CT: Yale University Press, 2008.

Schwartz, Stuart B. *Sovereignty and Society in Colonial Brazil: The High Court of Bahia and Its Judges, 1609–1751*. Berkeley: University of California Press, 1973.

Schwartz, Stuart B. *Sugar Plantations in the Formation of Brazilian Society, 1550–1835*. New York: Cambridge University Press, 1985.

Schwarz, Philip J. *Slave Laws in Virginia*. Athens: University of Georgia Press, 1996.

Scott, James. *The Arts of Domination and Resistance: Hidden Transcripts*. New Haven, CT: Yale University Press, 1985.

Scott, James. *Seeing Like a State: How Certain Schemes to Improve the Human Condition Have Failed*. New Haven, CT: Yale University Press, 1998.

Scott, Joan. "Gender: A Useful Category of Analysis." *American Historical Review* 95:5 (Dec. 1986): 1053–1075.

Scott, Rebecca J. *Degrees of Freedom: Louisiana and Cuba after Slavery.* Cambridge, MA: Belknap, 2005.

Semmes, Admiral Raphael. *My Adventures Afloat: A Personal Memoir of My Cruises and Services in "The Sumter" and "The Alabama."* London: Richard Bentley, 1869.

Serbin, Kenneth P. *Needs of the Heart: A Social and Cultural History of Brazil's Clergy and Seminaries.* Notre Dame, IN: University of Notre Dame Press, 2006.

Shingleton, Royce. *High Seas Confederate: The Life and Times of John Newland Maffit.* Columbia: University of South Carolina Press, 1994.

Silva, Eduardo. *Prince of the People: The Life and Times of a Brazilian Free Man of Color.* New York: Verso, 1993.

Silva, Innocencio Francisco da. *Diccionario bibliographico portugues.* Lisbon: Imprensa Nacional, 1890.

Silva, Maciel Henrique. "Delindra Maria de Pinho: Uma preta forra de honra no Recife da primeira metade do século XIX." *Afro-Asia,* no. 32 (2005): 219–240.

Skidmore, Thomas. *Black into White: Race and Nationality in Brazilian Thought.* 2nd ed. Durham, NC: Duke University Press, 1992.

Skidmore, Thomas. *Brazil: Five Centuries of Change.* New York: Oxford University Press, 1999.

Slenes, Robert W. *Na senzala uma flor: Esperanças e recordações da família escrava— Brasil, sudeste século XIX.* Rio: Nova Fronteira, 1999.

Soares, Eugênio Líbano. *A negregada instituição: Os capoeiras no Rio de Janeiro.* Rio de Janeiro: Divisão de Editoração da Secretaria Municipal de Cultura, 1994.

Soares, Mariza de Carvalho, and Priscilla Leal Mello. "O resto perdeu-se? O caso dos muçulmanos de Alagoas." In *Fulé Fulé: Visibilidades negras,* edited by Bruno Cesar Cavalcante, Clara Suassuna, and Raquel Rocha de Almeida Barros, 14–25. Maceió: Núcleo de Estudos Afro-Brasileiros / EDUFAL, 2006.

Soares de Souza, José António. "Os escravos e a pena de morte." *Revista do Instituto Histórico e Geográfico Brasileiro,* no. 313 (1976): 5–19.

Sodré, Nelson Werneck. *História da imprensa no Brasil.* 4th ed. Rio: Mauad, 1999.

Sommer, Doris. *Foundational Fictions: The National Romances of Latin America.* Berkeley: University of California Press, 1991.

Songini, Marc. *The Lost Fleet: A Yankee Whaler's Struggle against the Confederate Navy and Arctic Disaster.* New York: St. Martin's, 2007.

Souza, Jorge Prata de. *Escravidão ou morte: Os escravos brasileiros na Guerra do Paraguai.* Rio: ADESA, 1996.

Spitzer, Leo. *Lives In Between: The Experience of Marginality in a Century of Assimilation.* New York: Hill and Wang, 1999.

Stein, Stanley. *Vassouras: A Brazilian Coffee County, 1850–1900.* Rev. ed. Princeton, NJ: Princeton University Press, 1985 [1958].

Stoler, Ann Laura. *Carnal Knowledge and Imperial Power: Race and the Intimate in Colonial Rule.* Berkeley: University of California Press, 2002.

Stolke, Verena. "Trabalho e moralidade familiar." In *Quase cidadão: Histórias e antropologias da pós-emancipação no Brasil*, edited by Olívia Maria Gomes da Cunha and Flávio dos Santos Gomes, 171–215. Rio: Fundação Getulio Vargas, 2007.

Stroud, George M. *A Sketch of the Laws Relating to Slavery in the Several States of the United States of America*. Philadelphia: Kimber and Sharpless, 1827.

Summerville, Diane Miller. "Rape, Race, and Castration in the Colonial and Early South." In *Sex and Race in the Early South*, edited by Catherine Clinton and Michele Gillespie, 74–89. New York: Oxford University Press, 1997.

Sweet, James H. *Domingos Álvares, African Healing, and the Intellectual History of the Atlantic World*. Chapel Hill: University of North Carolina Press, 2011.

Szuchman, Mark D., ed. *The Middle Period in Latin America*. Boulder, CO: Lynne Rienner, 1989.

Tannenbaum, Frank. *Slave and Citizen: The Negro in the Americas*. Boston: Beacon, 1992 [1946].

Taylor, Alan. *The Civil War of 1812: American Citizens, British Subjects, Irish Rebels, and Indian Allies*. New York: Random House, 2010.

Taylor, William B. "Bandit Gangs in Late Colonial Times: Rural Jalisco Mexico 1794–1821." *Biblioteca Americana* 1 (Nov. 1982): 46.

Tilly, Charles. *Popular Contention in Great Britain, 1758–1834*. Cambridge, MA: Harvard University Press, 1995.

Topik, Steven C. "Coffee Anyone? Recent Research on Latin American Coffee Societies." *Hispanic American Historical Review* 80:2 (2000): 225–266.

Topik, Steven. *Coffee: A World History*. Princeton, NJ: Princeton University Press, 2011.

Twine, France Winddance. *Racism in a Racial Democracy: The Maintenance of White Supremacy in Brazil*. New Brunswick, NJ: Rutgers University Press, 1998.

Um Contemporaneo. *Exposição dos serviços prestados pelo coronel José de Barros Falcão de Lacerda, em differentes provincias do imperio, desde 1788 até 1848 com especialidade nos annos de 1817, 1821, 1822, 1823 e 1824*. Recife: Typografia M. F. de Faria, 1849.

Vainfas, Ronaldo, and Marina de Mello e Souza. "Catolização e poder no tempo do tráfico: O reino do Congo da conversão coroada ao movimento antoniano, séculos XV–XVIII." *Tempo* 3 (Dec. 1998): 95–118.

Vanderwood, Paul. *Disorder and Progress: Bandits, Police, and Mexican Development*. Rev. ed. Lanham, MD: SR Books, 1992 [1981].

Van Young, Eric. *The Other Rebellion: Popular Violence, Ideology, and the Mexican Struggle for Independence, 1810–1821*. Stanford, CA: Stanford University Press, 2001.

Vergara, Angela. *Copper Workers, International Business, and Domestic Politics in Cold War Chile*. University Park: Pennsylvania State University Press, 2008.

Viotti da Costa, Emilia. *The Brazilian Empire: Myths and Histories*. Chapel Hill: University of North Carolina Press, 2000.

Voss, Stuart F. *Latin America in the Middle Period 1750–1929*. Wilmington, DE: Scholarly Resources, 2002.

Wahl, Jenny Bourne. *The Bondsmen's Burden: An Economic Analysis of the Common Law of Southern Slavery.* New York: Cambridge University Press, 1998.

Waldrep, Christopher, and Donald G. Niemann, eds. *Local Matters: Race, Crime, and Justice in the Nineteenth-Century South.* Athens: University of Georgia Press, 2001.

Warrin, Donald. *So This Day Ends: The Portuguese in American Whaling 1767–1927.* North Dartmouth: University of Massachusetts Dartmouth Center for Portuguese Studies and Culture, 2010.

West, John. *History of Tasmania.* 2 vols. Launceston: Henry Dowling, 1852.

Whigham, Thomas. *The Paraguayan War, Causes and Early Conduct.* Lincoln: University of Nebraska Press, 2002.

White, Richard. *The Middle Ground: Indians, Empires, and Republics in the Great Lakes Region, 1650–1815.* Cambridge: Cambridge University Press, 1991.

Windler, Erica M. "Madame Durocher's Performance: Cross-Dressing, Midwifery, and Authority in Nineteenth-Century Rio de Janeiro, Brazil." In *Gender, Sexuality, and Power in Latin America since Independence,* edited by William E. French and Katherine Elaine Bliss, 52–70. Lanham, MD: Rowman and Littlefield, 2007.

Wines, Enoch Cobb. *The State of Prisons and Child-Saving Institutions in the Civilized World.* Cambridge, UK: John Wilson and Son, 1880.

Wyatt-Brown, Bertram. *The Shaping of Southern Culture: Honor, Grace, and War 1760s–1880s.* Chapel Hill: University of North Carolina Press, 2001.

Zimring, Franklin E., and Gordon Hawkins. *Capital Punishment and the American Agenda.* New York: Cambridge University Press, 1986.

Zinoman, Peter. *The Colonial Bastille: A History of Imprisonment in Vietnam, 1862–1940.* Berkeley: University of California Press, 2001.

army officers (*continued*)
and, 92; contraband on Fernando de Noronha and, 65–66; convict marriage and, 110, 113; desire to command Fernando de Noronha, 157; distribution of cane brandy by, 128; Duke of Caxias as, 33; factions among, 162, 169, 194; Fernando de Noronha's architecture and, 24; Fernando de Noronha's records and, 76–77; hybrid disciplinary practices, 7, 49; managing convicts, soldiers, and slaves, 5, 107, 238; Remédios city plan and, 48; republicanism and, 45, 198; social origins of, 38; social pollutions and, 169, 273n49; struggle to motivate convict workers, 13
arranchar, 48–49, 74, 108–109
Assis Tavares, Vicente d', 53, 120, 170–173, 291n27

Beaurepaire Rohan, Pedro Carlos de: alcohol policy of, 64; batch-living policy of, 49, 58, 61, 74, 87, 111, 232; career, 107, 141; convict customs as described by, 124; on convict sentences and trustworthiness, 132; a convict's right to live in penal exile with wife and dependents according to, 99, 108, 114, 116, 118; employee corruption and policies of, 145–146; Indians and Brazilian civilization according to, 108, 141, 231; inspection of Fernando de Noronha by, 19, 91; penal colony commerce policies of, 97, 143; penal colony regulations of, 37, 49, 54, 61, 64, 68, 76, 87, 97, 99, 104, 107–109, 114, 117, 119, 128, 130, 140, 146, 154, 157, 163, 165, 203, 232, 235, 270n84; penal colony slaves according to, 98; same-sex sexuality according to, 108, 113
Bell, William, 72–73, 78, 83, 154
Bentham, Jeremy, 5, 10, 19, 43
beri beri, 14, 54, 186
Bloem, João, 94–96, 99, 107, 179
Borges da Fonseca, Antônio, 31, 34, 63, 130–133, 155, 165
Brito, Carlota Lucia de, 100

Cabanagem Revolt (1835–1840), 90, 92, 131
Cabanos Revolt (1832–1835), 31–34, 90, 141, 165
calungas, 160
Cambinda Velha, 134, 142, 158–160, 173
Caminha, Adolfo Ferreira, 202–203, 212, 294n8
capital punishment, 3–4, 8, 46, 66, 85, 167, 178–181, 183, 188, 196, 199–200, 204, 207–226, 235, 240, 250, 258, 290n14, 297n64
capoeira, 7, 46, 148, 299n20
Capuchin religious order, 35, 141, 148, 231, 298n4
Carnival, 134–135, 142, 158–160, 224
Carpenter, Frank de Yeaux, 1, 136, 180, 240
Carvalho, Marcus Joaquim Maciel de, 141, 209
category drift: classifications of, 76; decline of slavery and, 234; definition of, 6; intergenerational, 121; intractable poor's fear of, 23, 35; marriage and, 236; military recruitment and, 40, 79, 131; penal colony commanders and, 92; police and, 54; regional rebellion and, 27, 32; of a serial killer, 96; total institutions and, 10; and War of the Triple Alliance, 37
Catholic Church: Brazil's monarchy and, 45; civil marriage and, 40, 294n3; convict attendance at Mass and, 140; convict marriage and, 120, 189; Enlightenment attacks on, 104; government edicts and, 39; the jealous institution and, 10; marriage and, 103; Pernambucan Republican Revolution (1817) and, 27; Remédios's, 18, 97; separation from the state and, 46, 270n77, 294n3
Caxias, Duke of (Luíz Alves de Lima e Silva), 33, 38, 162, 231
celibacy: Capuchin missionaries, Brazilian Indians, and, 108; clerical, 10, 107; gender segregation and, 104; immorality of, 108; men and, 107
Chibata Revolt (1910), 203
chibatas, 202–203
civil condition: color and, 177, 230, 235; connections among categories of, 5–6;

convict matriculation books and, 78–79, 246; convict sentences and, 85, 251; democracy of, 198; evolving perceptions of, 2; inequality and, 209; integration and, 154, 229, 235; marriage and, 236; segregation and, 8, 43, 230; sexuality and, 107; social divisions and, 176

color: of army soldiers, 37, 95; Brazilian preference for term over "race," 82, 277n31; Brazilian tolerance for people of, 218, 230; category drift and, 234; civil condition and, 107, 112, 154, 177, 235–236; class and, 100, 107, 133; colonial militias and, 31; convict marital status and, 112, 191; convict sentences and, 85; convicts of, 248; convict solidarity and, 176; convict work assignments and, 52; education and, 81–82, 130, 133; elections and, 223; equality and, 52; esteem of manual labor and, 264n13; evolving perceptions of, 2, 7; the franchise and, 223; free men and women of, 6; gender and, 154; identity and, 188; integration and, 8, 13, 125, 132, 198, 229–230; intractable poor and, 49; kinship and, 239; literacy and, 249; "longed-for homogenization" and, 231; *lusophobia* and, 30; manners and, 81–82; miscegenation and, 224; nationality and, 209; Pernambucan Republican Revolution (1817) and, 28; physical features and, 81–82, 277n32; popular support for abolition and, 222; prejudice and, 53, 154, 185, 217; segregation and, 8, 37, 43, 230, 236, 240; of Pyrrho, Sebastião José Basílio (penal colony commander), 126; Semmes, Admiral Raphael, and, 126; sexuality and, 233, 240; slave convict survey and, 188, 191; slaves and, 52, 182, 209, 230, 292n36; status and, 49, 125, 190, 277n33, "weakness of complexion" and, 51–52; whiteness and, 51–52, 235; whitening and, 224. *See also* race

Confederation of the Equator (1824), 30, 92

convict chain gangs, 29–30, 146, 179, 215–216, 233, 268n31

death penalty. *See* capital punishment

Debret, Jean-Baptiste, 109, 215–216, 268n31, 296n57

desarranchar, 49, 108–109. See also *arranchar*

Diário de Pernambuco (Recife), 44, 103, 113–114, 159, 165, 170

Dias, Henrique, 27

dishonor: convicts and, 118, 127, 146; incarceration's impact on convict wives and, 115; male and female loners and, 115; military impressment and, 36; slaves and, 5; white American convicts' segregation and, 236. *See also* honor

ex-slaves, 37, 59, 142, 182, 187–197, 236, 291n21, 291n27. *See also* slave convicts

Feijó, Diogo Antônio, 105

Fernando de Noronha: abolition and, 45, 180, 197–200; accommodation on, 49, 110, 238; administration of, 28, 58, 116–117, 170, 191, 194, 227; army garrison of, 5, 62, 95, 269n62; Atlantic history and, 11; bandits on, 43, 226; category drift and, 6, 34; clash between old and new regime on, 5; clothing and, 143–144; commerce and, 7, 13, 48–50, 59–66, 74, 95–99, 111, 144–149, 155, 163, 169, 174–176; convict impunity on, 4, 180–181, 199, 204–205, 218, 226; convict sergeants on, 65–68, 88–90; criminal deterrence and, 31; cultural interpretations of, 2; depictions of, 1, 3, 18–23, 52, 76, 124, 228; drought and, 21, 40, 42, 55, 58, 142; free Africans on, 33; gender and, 8–10, 103–104, 114–116, 252; health care of, 139–140; imperial penal justice and, 47, 177, 239–240; Indians and, 267n15; integration and, 177, 230, 235; judiciary and, 29; labor on, 7, 11, 84, 228–229, 279n75; landing on, 16; leisure on, 125, 129–139; map of, 2, 15; marriage and, 9, 104–123, 197, 234, 239, 252; matriculation records of, 76, 79–82, 190, 276n3; missions of, 238; mutinies on, 168–169, 174–176; Pernambuco's House

House of Detention (Recife, Pernambuco), 14, 37, 43–46, 54, 78–79, 117, 120, 271n96. *See also* penitentiary

Indians: "Arrow Tip" and, 222; Capuchin missionary work with, 108, 141; celibacy and, 108; civil condition of, 5, 79, 251; civilization and, 108; convict nickname, 77; convicts who were, 71; Fernando de Noronha, 24, 267n15; frontier and, 108; integration of, 104–105, 108, 141, 231; intractable poor and, 5–6; marriage of women to Portuguese men, 105; percentage of Brazil's population who were, 28; racial homogenization and, 231; slaves and, 24; soldiers and, 19, 25, 32; wartime mobilization and, 234. *See also* indigenous population
indigenous population: the *aldeia* and, 19; ancestry of Brazilians and, 126; appearance of, 188; army enlisted men who were part of, 37; Census of 1872 and Brazil's, 34; convicts who were from, 82, 248–249; integration and, 230–231; militias of, 24; romance novels and, 294; traditions in *maracatu* and, 134; whitening and, 224. *See also* Indians
Instituto Arqueológico, Histórico e Geográfico Pernambucano, 94
integration: Brazilian preference for, 177, 235; Brazil's prisons and, 230–231; convicts and, 13, 132, 229; gender and, 176, 232; Indians and, 231; modern penology and, 49; prejudice and, 125; state institutions and, 8; U.S. prisons and, 232; whiteness and, 235–236
intractable poor: category drift and, 92, 121; clothing and, 144; definition of, 5–6; integration and, 8, 231; interconnection among categories of, 19, 23, 33, 76, 141, 147, 235; marriage and, 103–104, 109, 118, 234, 236–240; slavery and, 146; strategic diaspora of, 11; total institutions and, 9; treatment of, 199–206. *See also* army enlisted men; free Africans; Indians; navy enlisted men; slaves

jails: bars for, 88; bond (*fiança*) and, 78; category drift and, 6; cells in the *aldeia*'s, 19, 66, 69–70, 110–111, 120, 152–153, 171; convict sedition, 167–168, 171, 175; convicts employed to supervise the *aldeia*'s, 244; courts and, 42; depiction of municipal, 271n98; escapes from, 242; false marriage promises and, 119; Fernando de Noronha's storeowners and, 136; husbands and, 113–115, 233; idleness of prisoners in, 84, 291n18; integration in, 230, 298n14; lack of personnel to guard municipal, 41; Pernambucan police in, 35; political parties and, 43; poor conditions in, 44; preaching to slaves and, 141; prisoner revolts in Recife's, 267n23; provincial, and transportation to Fernando de Noronha, 14, 187, 199; security of municipal, 44; slave convicts and, 193, 291n18; slave quarters (*senzalas*) compared to, 265n20; wartime mobilization and, 6. *See also* penal colonies; penitentiary; prisoners; prisons
jealous institution, the: definition of, 10; male sexuality and, 26; military impressment and, 36; morality and, 114, 116; productivity and, 104, 120, 232–233, 236; rights under, 132; slaves and, 213, 238
Jesuit religious order, 39, 105
judiciary, 29, 32, 42, 104
jury, 54, 58, 66, 86, 96, 100, 181, 195, 197, 211, 213, 217, 223, 289nn4–5; *fianças* and a special, 78
justice of the peace, 29, 32, 103

Koster, Henry, 25, 29, 97, 269n62

liberto. See freedman
Lins do Rego, José, 227–229, 232
lusophobia (fear of the Portuguese), 30, 56

Madeira, Sergeant Quirino Joaquim, 55–60, 65, 68, 73, 89, 151, 157
major da praça (title of the garrison commander on Fernando de Noronha): and commerce, 60, 152, 158, 160, 273n46, 274n65; duties of, 94, 137; salary of, 243;

police (*continued*)
undermanned ranks of, 35, 269n56; violent crime and, 84; wartime mobilization and, 38; web of institutions fundamental to state building and, 200
Porto Rico (convict "nation"), 134, 158–160
praça de índio, 19, 25, 267n15
Praieira Revolt (1848–1849), 31, 34, 63, 90, 93, 100, 131, 165–167
Preta Izabel (slave), 12–13, 22, 48
preta velha, 160, 173
prisoners: agency of, 57; the *aldeia* and, 19, 73; American, 83; army soldiers and, 168–169, 174; batch living in, 237; civil condition of, 112, 251; color of, 82, 112, 292n36; commander's residence and, 130; conjugal visits to, 234; disciplinary classes of, 86; disembarkation of, 76; escapes of, 44, 85, 151–152, 208; executions of, 222; families of, 115; fetters and, 14, 71–73, 194, 293n49; flogging of, 192, 204; gender segregation of, 44; good disciplinary record of slave convict, 186; good fathers of family who were, 120; *guias* of, 76; highest paid, 140; idleness of, 85, 110; invalid, 20; labor of, 113–114, 271n96, 290n8; letters of, 138; marital status of, 112; marital violence of, 120; nudity of, 144; overcrowding of, 45, 79; physical and moral health of, 115; plebeian, 90; political, 66, 78, 90, 98, 130–133, 146, 155, 165, 167, 240; poor condition of, 30; privileged, 55, 90, 130; provincial origins of slave, 184; rebellion of, 79, 65–68, 234, 267n23; records, 276n3; requests to marry by, 120; scribes and, 81; segregation by age, gender, and severity of crime of, 49, 88; segregation of slave, 192–193; sentence tenure and trustworthiness of, 132–133; slaves of, 98, 182; slaves compared to, 146; suffering of, 1; tattoos of, 82; torture of, 172; transportation to Fernando de Noronha of, 14, 187; wartime, 11; women, 78; women and male, 115; the "world" and, 75; Yankee, 128–129

prisons: administration of, 92; age and work in, 186; the *aldeia* as, 73, 87, 110; army officers and, 191; capacity of, 45, 110, 118, 199, 201, 230; clothes in mainland, 144; convict chain gangs and, 29; convict slaves in, 177–199, 292n36; corruption in, 74; crime in, 188; curfew in, 137; debtor's, 115; depictions of Fernando de Noronha as, 1; escapes from, 241, 249; families and, 115–116; Fernando de Noronha and Recife's, 79; Fernando de Noronha's closure as national, 46, 201; Fernando de Noronha's overpopulation as, 21; flogging in, 43, 177–178, 204, 210; flogging versus a sentence requiring, 177–178; Foucauldian studies of, 10–11; guards of, 37, 44; *guias* and, 77, 183; homicide in, 53; integration of, 198; International Convention on Prisons and Child Saving Institutions (1872), 58; labor in, 6, 85, 88, 178–179, 229; life sentences in, 3, 100; links between elections, policing, military impressment, and, 47, 92–93; literacy and, 20; naming practices in, 182; overcrowding in, 42, 145, 187; penal colonies and, 48, 74, 231; punishment on Fernando de Noronha for crimes and misbehavior in, 70, 120; racial prejudice in, 53; Rat Island as, 133; reform of, 44, 111, 116; science of, 117, 191; security of, 43; seditious plots in, 131, 167; segregation in, 4, 43, 230; segregation from society in, 8; sentence of *galés* and, 3; sentences requiring, 250; sentences requiring work in, 31, 263n4; ship-hulk, 146, 230; size of nonwhite population and limited capacity of, 43; slave, 212, 230; slaves and, 2–3; social control in, 74; social leveling and, 230, 291n27; state building and, 200; survey of mainland, 83; theater in, 137; time served as a slave and that served in, 196; total institutions and, 9, 104; treatment of slave and free in, 198; unplanned-for "dark twins" of, 48; uprisings in, 74; warehousing of, 43; women and, 119. *See also* jails; penal colonies; prisoners

Pyrrho, Major Sebastião José Basílio, 62, 94, 125–129, 167–168

Quebra Quilos (Kilo Breaking) Revolt (1874–1875), 39–40, 86, 103

race: army officers and, 99, 126; army soldiers and, 37; Brazilian Indians and, 231; Brazilian law and, 209; Brazilian preference for term "color" over, 82, 277n31; Brazil's international image and, 200; citizenship and, 200; Fernando de Noronha's garrison troops, 95; Frank de Yeaux Carpenter and, 290n16; mixture of, 200, 221–224, 235; relations between, 217–218, 225; segregation and, 200; sexuality and, 233; slave convicts and, 193, 231; "of Sodom," 169; white Americans and, 217; whitening and, 224. See also color

reinóis, 30–31

Religious Question (1872–1875), 39, 45, 103

Remédios, Fernando de Noronha: cemetery of, 75; city square of, 25; clergy in, 140–141; curfew in, 164; description of, 15–22; distribution of convict rations in, 59; exile from, 55, 69–70, 155; Justice Ministry's ideas for reforming, 111; Pernambucana Steamship Company's crews in, 64; planned city of, 13, 48; map showing location of, 15; rebellion in, 168, 175; secrets of, 148; security in, 154; segregation of slave convicts outside of, 195; theater of, 136; warehouse of, 152. See also Fort Remédios

Ribeiro, João Luiz, 178, 216

sailors. See navy enlisted men

samba, 36, 160, 173

segregation: Afro-Brazilian institutions and, 224; age and, 43; batch living and, 104; civil condition and, 8; color and, 8, 240; costs and, 235; gender and, 26–27, 43, 104–106; Indians and, 105; Jesuits and, 231; modern prisons and, 8; race mixture and, 200; racial, 221, 233; severity of crime and prisoner, 43;

sexuality and, 103–105; slave convicts and, 193; U.S. prisons and, 236. See also integration

Semmes, Admiral Raphael, 17, 21, 94, 97, 125–129

sem ofício, 79–81, 186, 247

senzalas, 236, 278n44; compared to jails, 265n20

Sexagenarian Law (1885), 45, 186, 291n30

sexuality: batch living and, 104, 106, 108; Brazilian assumptions about male, 10, 25, 103–107, 113–114; color and, 224, 233, 240; companionate relationships and, 228; contemporary policies of conjugal prison visits and, 234; convict wives and, 253; crime on Fernando de Noronha and, 118; cultural attitudes toward miscegenation and, 109; cultural attitudes toward slave marriage and, 109; family and, 240; Fernando de Noronha's employees and, 117, 170; gender and, 8, 23, 77, 100, 240; gender integration and, 88, 104, 118, 176; health and, 116, 139–140; heterosexual citizenship and, 11; heterosexual conjugality to stem same-sex, 10, 26, 114, 121–122; heterosexual conjugality, worker productivity, and, 10, 113–114; heterosexual conjugal living and, 4, 108, 203; heterosexual consensual conjugality (amaziado) and, 105, 111–112, 176, 190, 239; heterosexual penal conjugality and, 9; heterosexual relationships and, 4, 7–8, 10, 107; interracial, 203–204, 224, 231, 235, 294n8; the jealous institution and, 10, 36, 104; male celibacy and, 104–105; marriage and, 13, 26, 100, 103, 232; penal reform and, 7; populating the nation and, 103; prohibition of women on Fernando de Noronha and, 26; prostitution and, 108; same-sex relationships and, 10, 26, 75, 77, 104–105, 108, 118, 121–122, 190, 203, 228–229; soldiers and, 108; transgressions and, 228; Victorian views of, 106; women and, 118; "women of the world" and, 90–91 slave convicts: African-born, 182; barracks of, 18; barter and, 12; Brazilian-born, 182; Brazilian state's confiscation of, 179, 216; chain gangs of, 216; civil condition and, 79; color of, 82, 188, 293n36; commanders and, 13; commutations of, 180; convict plot revealed by, 167; cooperation with free convicts by, 151–152; crime and, 149–151, 157, 163, 180–187; domestic, 156, 197–198; executions of, 216, 294n66; Fernando de Noronha and, 31, 45, 180, 292n34; fetters and, 179, 193–194; flogging of, 206, 235; *guia* of, 77; hangmen who were, 30, 212–213, 222; homicide and, 70, 170, 178, 182–184, 209; impunity of, 1, 180–181; integration of, 49, 51, 137, 185–186, 229–232, 298n14; invalid, 192; labor of, 191; leisure of, 117, 153, 185; minor, 185; names of, 78, 182; pardons for, 293n57; petitions from, 182–183, 190, 193, 195–199, 211, 226, 293n54, 293n57, 294n69; praise of, 179; provincial origins of, 184, 187, 256; provision grounds of, 12; segregation of, 192–194; *sem ofício* and, 185; sentences of, 85, 177–179, 251, 255, 289–290n5, 290n14, 297n78; survey of, 177, 181–190, 256, 276n3, 289n2; theater and, 136; time spent in provincial jails before arriving at Fernando de Noronha by, 187; treatment of, 8, 177, 191, 206; vices and, 210; women, 12, 185–186; work companies and, 51, 69, 80, 185, 231. *See also* slaveowners; slavery; slaves

slaveowners, 4, 28, 107–109, 121, 183, 195, 206, 213, 233, 238

slavery: abolition of, 39, 45, 195, 200, 202, 206–226, 232–240, 258; after 1850, 5, 7, 107, 221; Brazilian law and, 209–210, 216–226, 233–240, 291n30; Brazilian shame over, 213–220; Brazil's international image and, 208–213, 235; capital punishment and, 207–225, 296n52, 297n64; category drift and, 234; citizenship and, 209; convict lives compared to, 216; crime and, 211–212;

economic development and, 213; fears of re-enslavement and, 35, 40; flogging and, 206–220; gradual amelioration of, 201; human rights and, 33, 208–213; intractable poor and, 200–201; manhood and, 183; moral corruption and, 189; Portugal's Brazilian colony and, 24; priests and, 106–107; racial prejudice and, 201, 225; segregation and, 219, 223–224, 229; *sem ofício* and, 80–81; total institutions and, 9, 103–104; vices and, 213, 295n35; wartime mobilization and, 219, 234–235, 299n19; the whip and, 206; work and, 206, 236

slaves: African-born, 122; Brazilian law and, 3, 5, 198, 210; capital punishment and, 32, 46, 178, 183, 185, 213–214; category drift and, 6; clothing of, 144; *congadas* of, 134; convicts on Fernando de Noronha accompanied by, 98, 254; crime and, 6, 121, 177, 182–183, 189, 191, 216, 226, 249, 289–290n4; desire for freedom among, 147; escape from captivity by, 219, 235; executions of, 179, 216–217; faith healers (*curandeiros*) who were, 139; family and, 189–190, 213–216, 234–239; flogging of, 3, 72–73, 201–212, 271n96; former, 227, 229; free Africans and, 33; free labor and, 4; gender and, 104; Gilberto Freyre's depiction of masters and, 229; *guia* for, 76; honor and, 5, 106–107, 146, 195, 209, 215, 283n78; illicit commerce and, 62; Indians and, 24; industrial work discipline and, 94, 279n75, 281n21, 285n47; intractable poor and, 5, 104, 146, 226; kinship and, 239; leisure of, 159; *lusophobia* and, 27; lynchings of, 263n2, 289n4, 291n18; manumission of, 38; marriage of, 103, 112–113, 189, 234–239, 292n40; military impressment of, 36–37, 202; *pátrio poder* and, 189; peasantry and, 238; petitions of, 195–199, 211, 293n54, 294n69; population and percentage of in Brazil, 28, 33–34; poverty and, 5; prejudice against, 154; prices of, 60, 65, 149, 158, 243, 273n41,

286n5; prisons and, 2–3, 229, 271n96; provision grounds and, 49; rations of, 142; regional rebellions and, 28; religion and, 141; revolts and, 33, 176, 179, 269n15; roll call of, 8; serfs and, 237, 264n15; status of, 7, 36, 53, 190, 234–235, 246; same-sex sexuality and, 122; shoes and, 143; upbringing of, 203; vessels and, 33; vices and, 106; wartime mobilization of, 37–38, 219–221, 264n15; women, 273n41, 284n9. *See also* slave convicts; slaveowners; slavery

slave trade: Brazilian internal, 184; Indians and the, 24; transatlantic, 3, 30–33, 221, 268–269n49. *See also* slavery; slaves

soldiers. *See* army enlisted men

Thomaz (slave), 208–212, 215, 224

Varnhagen, Francisco Adolfo de, 108

Wanderley, Manuel da Rocha, 150, 161, 171
War of the Triple Alliance (1864–1870), 6, 37, 187, 201, 221, 234–235, 269n66
War of the Wasps (1852), 31, 35, 92, 202
whiteness, 4, 37, 52, 82, 235–236, 299n20
whitening, 224, 231, 235